RECOVERING THE
REFORMED
CONFESSION

RECOVERING THE
REFORMED
CONFESSION

Our Theology, Piety, and Practice

R. SCOTT CLARK

P.O. BOX 817 • PHILLIPSBURG • NEW JERSEY 08865-0817

Unless otherwise indicated, all Scripture quotations are the author's translation. Italics within Scripture quotations indicate emphasis added.

Scroll ornament © Dave Smith, istockphoto.com

Printed in Canada

Library of Congress Cataloging-in-Publication Data

Clark, R. Scott.
  Recovering the Reformed confession : our theology, piety, and practice / R. Scott Clark.
    p. cm.
  Includes bibliographical references and index.
  ISBN 978-1-59638-110-0 (pbk.)
  1. Reformed Church—Doctrines. 2. Church renewal—Reformed Church. I. Title.
  BX9422.3.C53 2008
  230'.42—dc22
                         2008032411

To Bob,
a confessional churchman,

and

to Darryl,
who says what I would think
if I had thought of it

Contents

Acknowledgments

I began this book during a sabbatical granted graciously by the board of Westminster Seminary California in the fall semester of the academic year 2002–3 and completed the second draft during a sabbatical in the fall semester of the academic year 2006–7. I am grateful to my colleagues for their assistance, and particularly to Mike Horton for carrying additional weight on his already overburdened shoulders.

I am grateful to the company of those who have read and commented on all or part of the typescript: Gabe Nave, Mike Horton, Casey Carmichael, Danny Hyde, Toby Kurth, Kim Riddlebarger, Dave VanDrunen, Shane Lems, John Fesko, and those students in the Reformed Confessions course who have read and improved this book.

Thanks to Marvin Padgett, his staff, Ray Wiersma, and Bryce Craig for getting this volume through the press.

Finally, special thanks are due to Barbara, Katie, Emily, and Angus who need not read this book since they have already heard it worked out over lunches and dinners.

Abbreviations

6/24	Six-day, twenty-four-hour (creation)
BC	Belgic Confession
BCO	Book of Church Order
BCP	Book of Common Prayer
BHS	*Biblia Hebraica Stuttgartensia.* Edited by A. Alt, O. Eissfeldt, P. Kahle. 5th ed. Stuttgart: Deutsche Bibelgesellschaft, 1997.
CD	Canons of Dort
CO	John Calvin. *Opera Quae Supersunt Omnia.* Edited by A. E. Cunitz et al. 59 vols. *Corpus Reformatorum.* Brunswick: C. A. Schwetschke and Sons, 1863–1900.
CR	*Corpus Reformatorum.* Edited by C. G. Bretschneider. 101 vols. Halle, 1834–1959.
CRC	Christian Reformed Church
CRCNA	Christian Reformed Churches in North America
Creeds	*The Creeds of Christendom.* Edited by Phillip Schaff. 3 vols. Grand Rapids: Baker, reprint 1983.
CTJ	*Calvin Theological Journal*
DPW	*A Directory for Publique Prayer, Reading the Holy Scriptures. Singing of Psalmes, Preaching of the Word, Administration of the Sacraments, and Other Parts of the Publique Worship of God, Ordinary and Extraordinary.* London, 1645.

EPC	Evangelical Presbyterian Church
ESV	English Standard Version
HC	Heidelberg Catechism
Institutes	John Calvin. *Institutes of the Christian Religion.* Translated by Ford Lewis Battles. 2 vols. Library of Christian Classics 20–21. Philadelphia: Westminster, 1960.
JETS	*Journal of the Evangelical Theological Society*
KJV	King James Version
LW	Martin Luther. *Luther's Works.* Edited by J. Pelikan. 55 vols. St. Louis: Concordia, 1958–.
LXX	Septuagint
MT	Masoretic Text
NAPARC	North American Presbyterian and Reformed Council
Niemeyer	H. A. Niemeyer. *Collectio Confessionum in Ecclesiis Reformatis Publicatarum.* Leipzig: Julius Klinkhardt, 1840.
NIV	New International Version
OED	*Oxford English Dictionary.* Edited by J. A. Simpson and Edmund Weiner. Oxford: Oxford University Press, 1989.
OPC	Orthodox Presbyterian Church
OS	John Calvin. *Joannis Calvini Opera Selecta.* Edited by Petrus Barth and W. Niesel. 5 vols. 3rd ed. Munich: Christian Kaiser, 1963–74.
PCA	Presbyterian Church in America
PCUSA	Presbyterian Church USA
PRRD	Richard A. Muller. *Post-Reformation Reformed Dogmatics: The Rise and Development of Reformed Orthodoxy,*

	ca. 1520 to ca. 1725. 2d ed. 4 vols. Grand Rapids: Baker Academic, 2003.
RCA	Reformed Church in America
RCH	*Reformed Confessions Harmonized with an Annotated Bibliography of Reformed Doctrinal Works.* Edited by Joel R. Beeke and Sinclair B. Ferguson. Grand Rapids: Baker, 1999.
RCUS	Reformed Church in the United States
RPCNA	Reformed Presbyterian Church of North America
RPW	Regulative Principle of Worship
ST	Thomas Aquinas. *Summa Theologiae.* Edited by Thomas Gilby. 61 vols. London and New York: Blackfriars and McGraw-Hill, 1964–80.
UCC	United Church of Christ
URCNA	United Reformed Churches in North America
WA	Martin Luther. *Luthers Werke Kritische Gesamtausgabe.* Edited by J. K. F. Knaake and G. Kawerau et al. Weimar: H. H. Böhlau, 1883–.
WCF	Westminster Confession of Faith
WLC	Westminster Larger Catechism
Works	*The Works of Jonathan Edwards.* Edited by Perry Miller et al. New Haven: Yale University Press, 1957.
WSC	Westminster Shorter Catechism
WTJ	*Westminster Theological Journal*

This doctrine the Synod judges to be drawn from the Word of God, and to be agreeable to the confession of the Reformed Churches.

... Wherefore, this Synod of Dort, in the name of the Lord, conjures as many as piously call upon the name of our Savior Jesus Christ to judge of the faith of the Reformed Churches, not from the calumnies which on every side are heaped upon it, nor from the private expressions of a few among ancient and modern teachers, often dishonestly quoted, or corrupted and wrested to a meaning quite foreign to their intention; but from the public confessions of the Churches themselves, and from this declaration of the orthodox doctrine, confirmed by the unanimous consent of all and each of the members of the whole Synod.

—Conclusion to the Canons of Dort

Fear of scholasticism is the mark of a false prophet.

—Karl Barth

CHAPTER
I

Whatever Became of Reformed Theology, Piety, and Practice?

This book is intended for those who identify with the Reformed branch of the Reformation. Readers from other traditions, however, may find it useful for clarifying their own identity, or perhaps they will decide that they like our confession and wish to join us. This book is not for those who think that all is well in the Reformed and Presbyterian churches in North America, because it is designed to provoke discontent and change, specifically reformation according to God's Word as confessed by the Reformed churches. If, however, you have an ill-defined sense that something is wrong with our churches but have trouble identifying what it is, this book is for you.

The Reformed and Presbyterian churches in North America belong to three great categories, the *mainline*, the *borderline*, and the *sideline*. The mainline Reformed (e.g., the Presbyterian Church USA, the Reformed Church in America, the United Church of Christ) shuttled significant elements of the historic Reformed confession (theology, piety, and practice) through the twentieth century.[1] The borderline denominations, for

---

1. The mainline denominations are represented in organizations such as the National Council of Churches and the World Alliance of Reformed Churches. On the rise of modernism and its consequences for the Presbyterian and Reformed mainline see Bradley J. Longfield, *The Presbyterian Controversy: Fundamentalists, Modernists and Moderates* (New York: Oxford University Press, 1991); D. G. Hart, *Defending the Faith: J. Gresham Machen and the Crisis of*

example, the Christian Reformed Churches in North America (CRCNA) and the Evangelical Presbyterian Church (EPC) are in transition but they are moving in opposite directions.[2] While the CRCNA seems to be moving (via broad evangelicalism) toward the mainline,[3] the EPC, founded by those leaving the mainline, appears to be moving in the opposite direction. The North American Presbyterian and Reformed Council (NAPARC) represents the sideline denominations.[4] This volume is relevant to all three segments of the Reformed churches but is aimed particularly at pastors, elders, and theology students in the borderline and sideline denominations. To those in the borderline who are moving away from the Reformed confessions, I hope to give some reason for reconsidering that journey. To those who are in the process of embracing the confessional vision of theology, piety, and practice, I hope to give reasons for carrying on. To those in the sideline, from where this book is written, I am issuing a warning that we are not as different from the mainline and borderline churches as we sometimes like to imagine.

Conservative Protestantism in Modern America (Grand Rapids: Baker, 1995); idem, *The Lost Soul of American Protestantism* (Lanham, MD: Rowman and Littlefield, 2002); Lefferts A. Loetscher, *The Broadening Church: A Study of Theological Issues in the Presbyterian Church since 1869* (Philadelphia: University of Pennsylvania Press, 1954). Like the PCUSA, the RCA is a member of both the National Council and World Council of Churches.

2. One counterargument to this taxonomy is the fact that the CRCNA, EPC, the PCUSA, and the UCC are all members of the mainline World Alliance of Reformed Churches (WARC). See http://www.warc.ch/list/church_list.html (accessed 1 September 2007).

3. There is strong evidence for the claim that the CRCNA is a borderline denomination. Despite strong opposition, Classis Kalamazoo (1995) set aside elements of the church order to permit the ordination of females to pastoral office. Since that time the denomination has lost tens of thousands of members so that there were celebrations when decline leveled off. In recognition of the trajectory of the CRCNA, the North American Presbyterian and Reformed Council, composed of confessional denominations, excluded the CRCNA in 2002. Classis Grand Rapids East (2006) agreed to bracket sections of the Heidelberg Catechism (HC) Q. 80 as inaccurate and unecumenical. News reports from Synods 2006 and 2007 read like reports from any mainline Presbyterian General Assembly from the 1960s. On the gradual "Americanization" of the CRCNA see James D. Bratt, *Dutch Calvinism in Modern America: A History of a Conservative Subculture* (Grand Rapids: Eerdmans, 1984).

4. North American Presbyterian and Reformed Council, "Constitution of the North American Presbyterian and Reformed Council" (as amended by the Third and Twenty-Second Meetings of the Council, 28–29 October 1977), http://traver.org/naparc2/cb.htm (accessed 26 March 2007).

Themes, Vocabulary, and Structure

This is a book about recovery, by which I mean to say that we have lost something that we can and must apprehend again: what we confess, that is, our theology, piety, and practice. I shall use the word "Reformed" mainly to denote the theology, piety, and practice of the Reformed and Presbyterian churches, not as a proper name of any particular denomination or federation. One of the major questions to be pursued is the relation between the word "Reformed" and the thing itself. Is the word "Reformed" merely a convention, a way of speaking, or does it have an objective referent? I contend that the word denotes a confession, a theology, piety, and practice that are well known and well defined and summarized in ecclesiastically sanctioned and binding documents.

By "confession," I mean narrowly the sixteenth- and seventeenth-century Reformed confessions, which we might call the six forms of unity (i.e., Belgic Confession [BC], HC, Canons of Dort [CD], Westminster Confession of Faith [WCF], Westminster Larger Catechism [WLC], and Westminster Shorter Catechism [WSC]). So the first sense of the word is "ecclesiastical dogma." Second, and more broadly, however, I mean the understanding of those confessions as articulated by the classical sixteenth- and seventeenth-century Reformed theologians and by those who continued that tradition, the outlines of which are evident to anyone who reads Calvin, Ursinus, Wollebius, Owen, Turretin, Witsius, Hodge, Bavinck, and Berkhof. Third, by "confession" I mean the theology, piety, and practice agreed upon by our churches, held in common by them, which bind us together, by which we have covenanted to live and worship together. So that, as used in this work, "confession" is a rich, multilayered term that has both fixed and developing aspects (*ecclesia reformata, semper reformanda*). In good Reformed fashion, this book has two grammatical moods: imperative and indicative.[5] First, we shall consider, as it were, the law. Second, we shall consider the good news, as it were, about being Reformed and some paths to recovery.

---

5. For more on law and gospel as Reformed categories see R. Scott Clark, "Letter and Spirit: Law and Gospel in Reformed Preaching," in *Covenant, Justification, and Pastoral Ministry: Essays by the Faculty of Westminster Seminary California*, ed. R. Scott Clark (Phillipsburg, NJ: P&R, 2006), 331–63.

Much of what passes as Reformed among our churches is not. Its sources, spirit, and methods are alien to Reformed theology, piety, and practice. There are significant segments within the Reformed communion that define "Reformed" in ways that our forefathers would not understand. For example, some define the Reformed identity according to one's view of the length of the creation days. Others define it according to one's view of the postcanonical application of Mosaic civil laws, and still others speak as if the Reformed confessions were ambiguous about covenant theology and the doctrine of justification. Practically, we have become fragmented. In our age, it seems that every definition of "Reformed" is regarded as valid and none is definitive. Consider the effect of such fragmentation when looking for a Reformed congregation. One shall have to choose between the "contemporary," "emerging," "traditional," "theonomic," "federal-vision," "psalm-singing," "neo-puritan," and "confessional" congregations to name but a few possibilities. In nearly every case, the adjective "confessional" is not sufficient to describe accurately the theology, piety, and practice of a given congregation. It is not that there are no ordinary Reformed churches about which one could say "confessional" without qualification, but such do seem to be in the minority. Rather than being the single common denominator among Reformed congregations, "confessional" has become simply one adjective among many. How can that be? Have not all Reformed ministers and elders subscribed a Reformed confession before God and his church, swearing to uphold, teach, and defend the same? If so, are we not all morally obligated to be confessional; if we are not, how did this happen?

It is the argument of this book that the Reformed confession is the only reasonable basis for a stable definition of the Reformed theology, piety, and practice. As a class of churches that profess allegiance to the Reformed theology, piety, and practice as revealed in God's Word and summarized in the Reformed confessions, we have drifted from our moorings. Some of us have become confused about what it is to be Reformed, while others of us have lost confidence altogether that Reformed theology, piety, and practice are even correct.

The Quest for a Redefinition of Reformed

In 1844, upon being made professor in the seminary of the Reformed Churches in the United States, Phillip Schaff gave his inaugural address that was translated by his colleague John Williamson Nevin and published the next year as *The Principle of Protestantism*.[6] He argued that American religion was infected with two diseases:[7] "Rationalism and sectarism then are the most dangerous enemies of our church at the present time. They are both but different sides of the one and the same principle—a one-sided false subjectivity, sundered from the authority of the objective. Rationalism is theoretic sectarism; sectarism is practical rationalism."[8] In the century and a half since Schaff issued this warning these two diseases have continued to afflict the Reformed churches.

What Schaff called rationalism we will call the Quest for Illegitimate Religious Certainty or QIRC, that is, the quest to know what God knows, the way he knows it. This quest often manifests itself in the attempt to find certainty on issues that are not of the *esse* (being) or even of the *bene esse* (well-being) of the Reformed confession. For those on this quest, what matters more than finding the truth or getting it right is *being* right. According to QIRC, there is no distinction between essential and nonessential doctrines or practices, since QIRC renders them all equally important. What Schaff called "sectarism" may also be described as the Quest for Illegitimate Religious Experience or QIRE. This is the pursuit of the immediate experience of God without the means of grace (i.e., the preaching of the gospel and the sacraments). It is the attempt to experience him in a way that he has not ordained, and more specifically, to experience him in a way that we do not confess. The first half of this work sketches the nature of the QIRC and QIRE, offers examples of both in the Reformed churches, and finally offers criticisms of both.

Tradition, *Sola Scriptura*, and *Semper Reformanda*

As the baby-boomer generation came of age in the 1960s and 1970s, it led a broad cultural and religious reaction to traditionalism in various

6. Phillip Schaff, *The Principle of Protestantism*, ed. Bard Thompson and George H. Bricker, trans. John W. Nevin, Lancaster Series on the Mercersburg Theology (Philadelphia: United Church Press, 1964).

7. Ibid., 129–55.

8. Ibid., 155.

spheres. This is the era that brought us Woodstock and post–Vatican II guitar masses. The evangelical version of the guitar mass is the Scripture chorus. Today, however, some of the children and grandchildren of the boomers are conducting their own social and liturgical revolution: they are looking to the past. Journalist Colleen Carroll documents a significant movement by young adults (born 1965–83) toward traditional worship and piety.[9] She notes that, in recent years, in the midst of a growing pluralism, having tried everything that secularism has to offer, many so-called Gen-Xers have already had their midlife crisis. They have seen that the writer of Ecclesiastes was fundamentally correct, that "all is vanity" (Eccl. 1:1–11). Repenting of the fast lane, they are turning to various forms of religious traditionalism (Roman and Protestant). Though some are following the boomer pattern of contemporary worship services, a remarkable number of postboomers are demanding preaching and worship that are substantial, confessional, and mysterious.[10] Renewed interest in the past is also manifesting itself in the emerging and emergent church movements and especially in their eclectic use of the past. According to Randall Balmer and Lauren Winner, the trend toward contemporary worship has competition.

> Many Protestant congregations, even those with decidedly low-church pedigrees, are also appropriating liturgy in their worship. In so doing, they not only connect with historic creeds and traditions, they attract a new generation of churchgoers, many of whom have grown weary of the contemporary worship styles that dominate the baby-boomer megachurches.[11]

9. Colleen Carroll, *The New Faithful: Why Young Adults Are Embracing Christian Orthodoxy* (Chicago: Loyola, 2002). See also Robert E. Webber, *The Younger Evangelicals: Facing the Challenges of the New World* (Grand Rapids: Baker, 2002), 77–80. Christian Smith, however, paints a less optimistic picture of the spiritual state of American teenagers. See Christian Smith and Melinda Lundquist Denton, *Soul Searching: The Religious and Spiritual Lives of American Teenagers* (Oxford: Oxford University Press, 2005). Though American teenagers are interested in spiritual things, they are inarticulate about the faith largely because their congregations have refused to teach them anything of substance.

10. One finds a similar approach in Marva J. Dawn, *Reaching Out without Dumbing Down: A Theology of Worship for the Turn-of-the-Century Culture* (Grand Rapids: Eerdmans, 1995).

11. Randall Balmer and Lauren F. Winner, *Protestantism in America* (New York: Columbia University Press, 2002), 202.

Balmer and Winner attribute this movement among evangelicals to a lessened suspicion of their Roman Catholic neighbors.

For confessional Reformed folk (a category missing from their analysis), however, the use of read prayers and Genevan robes is less the latest novelty and more a return to form.[12] Perhaps then it is a propitious time for Reformed folk to reconsider their past as well, since we also have something of considerable worth to offer to those looking for an alternative to the reigning evangelical paradigms. Our theology, piety, and practice were confessed before us and transmitted to us by others. It is, therefore, a tradition that we have received. Tradition is not simply an extracanonical idea, however, but a biblical concept. In the New Testament "tradition" (*paradosis*) occurs thirteen times. Sometimes it is used negatively, as in Matthew 15:2–6, where Jesus rebukes the Pharisees and the teachers of the law for placing "the traditions of the elders" above the authority of God's law, thereby effectively circumventing the intent of the law.[13] Paul likewise referred disparagingly to the "traditions" of his "fathers" in a similar way (Gal. 1:14). He also correlated the "traditions of men" to "vain and deceptive philosophy" and the "basic principles of this world," and these he juxtaposed to Christ and his gospel (Col. 2:8). In each of these cases, he uses "tradition" to describe a moralistic, self-justifying approach to God in distinction from the Christ-centered gospel of justification and salvation by grace alone, through faith alone, in Christ alone.

In other places, however, "tradition" is used favorably in the New Testament. The apostle Paul congratulated the Corinthian church for getting at least one thing right: they remembered Paul "in everything" and held to the "traditions" just as he had passed them on to the church (1 Cor. 11:2). In 2 Thessalonians 2:14–15 the apostle even used "tradition" as a synonym for the good news. Scripture says that God efficaciously called the Thessalonian Christians to faith "through our gospel." It is to this same gospel that Paul refers when he tells them to "stand firm and hold to the traditions we passed on to you" (2 Thess. 2:15). Tradition also refers to Paul's moral

---

12. On the omission of confessional Protestants as an analytical category, see Hart, *The Lost Soul of American Protestantism*, xv–xxxiv. Perhaps, because the study of American Protestantism has omitted confessionalism as a historical category, we who should be confessionalists find it difficult to think of ourselves as such since the category is not yet widely used.

13. See F. F. Bruce, *Tradition, Old and New* (Exeter: Paternoster, 1970), 19–28.

teaching. In the same epistle he says, "We command you, brothers, to keep away from every brother who is idle and does not live according to the tradition you received from us" (2 Thess. 3:6). In this case, the tradition is simple and clear: "For even when we were with you, we gave you this rule: 'If a man will not work, he shall not eat'" (2 Thess. 3:10). In either case, it is clear that Paul was not averse to describing his teaching, whether law or gospel, as a "tradition," that is, a body of theological or moral instruction that was to be received and considered authoritative and binding. Certainly, for confessional Protestants, there is a sharp distinction to be made between the apostolic tradition and subsequent, postcanonical Christian tradition. Nevertheless, it would seem difficult to reject tradition as unbiblical or even unhelpful, since we get the very notion from Scripture itself.

According to Heiko Oberman, there were two competing understandings of the relations between tradition and Scripture in the premodern church.[14] He described the first approach, the "single exegetical tradition of interpreted Scripture," as "Tradition I." The "two-sources theory which allows for extra-biblical oral tradition" he called "Tradition II."[15] He argued that the Council of Trent represented Tradition II, and the Reformers represented Tradition I.[16] According to Oberman, Luther was no individualist, because "his interpretation of the *sola Scriptura* principle does *not exclude, but includes* a high regard for Tradition I."[17] In the Reformation, the confessional Protestants adopted a careful approach to tradition. As Oberman noted, this view was not exclusive to Luther but was also expressed in the Second Helvetic Confession (1561): "Wherefore whenever this Word of God is now preached in the church by preachers called legitimately, we believe the same Word of God is proclaimed, and received by the faithful" (1.4).[18]

14. Heiko A. Oberman, "Quo Vadis, Petre? Tradition from Irenaeus to *Humani Generis*," in *The Dawn of the Reformation: Essays in Late Medieval and Early Reformation Thought* (Edinburgh: T&T Clark, 1992).

15. Ibid., 280. John E. Thiel says that the Roman belief is that "scripture and tradition make up a single deposit of divine revelation" so that "scripture's interpretive richness extends" to the tradition. John E. Thiel, *Senses of Tradition: Continuity and Development in Catholic Faith* (Oxford: Oxford University Press, 2000), 10.

16. Oberman, "Quo Vadis, Petre?" 283.

17. Ibid., 285.

18. "Proinde cum hodie hoc Dei verbum per pradicatores legitime vocatos annunciatur in Ecclesia, credimus ipsum verbum accunciari et a fidelibus recipi." Heinrich Bullinger, "Confessio et Expositio Brevis et Simplex Sincerae Religionis Christianae etc.," in *Creeds*, 3:237.

Oberman found the same position in the Reformed orthodox theologian Johannes Wollebius (1586–1629), who taught that

> this testimony is twofold, the principal and the ministerial. The principal is the strong testimony of the Holy Spirit in Scripture itself, and within the heart and mind of the believer being illuminated by the Spirit speaking to and persuading the believer of the divinity of Scripture. The ministerial testimony is the testimony of the church.[19]

In contrast to Tradition II, in which Scripture is controlled by a parallel source of authority in a developing tradition, the classical Reformed approach controlled tradition with the Scriptures but did not reject tradition as such. The Reformed tradition is what Wollebius called the "ministerial testimony" to the Scriptures.[20] The WCF expresses Tradition I when it says, "All synods or councils, since the apostles' times, whether general or particular, may err; and many have erred; therefore they are not to be made the rule of faith, or practice, but to be used as a help in both" (31.4).[21] It is not, however, as if the WCF grants to human assemblies no authority whatever, because every group calling itself "biblical" (e.g., the Socinians) and all the revisionists within the Reformed churches quote WCF 1.10.[22] It is well to remember that WCF 31.2 also says, "It belongeth to synods and councils, ministerially to determine controversies of faith, and cases of conscience; to set down rules and directions for the better ordering of the public worship of God." Further, such decisions are to be received with "reverence and submission." What makes us Reformed is how

---

Oberman cited only a portion of this text, because he followed Heppe's elliptical quotation. The fuller text is an even stronger statement of the view.

19. Oberman, "Quo Vadis, Petre?" 286 n. 63. Johannes Wollebius, *Christianae Theologiae Compendium*, ed. E. Bizer (Neukirchen: Kreis Moers, 1935), 2. "Testimonium hoc duplex est, principale et ministeriale. Principale est testimonius Spiritus Sancti fortis in ipsa Scriptura, intus vero in corde ac mente hominis fidelis ab ipso illuminati loquentis eique Scripturae divinitatem persuadentis. Ministeriale vero testimonium est testimonium ecclesiae."

20. Oberman, "Quo Vadis, Petre?" 288–89.

21. *Creeds*, 3:670.

22. "The supreme judge by which all controversies of religion are to be determined, and all decrees of councils, opinions of ancient writers, doctrines of men, and private spirits, are to be examined, and in whose sentence we are to rest, can be no other but the Holy Spirit speaking in the Scripture."

understand Scripture, and this understanding is summarized in our fession. If we thought that our confession was not biblical, we would not use it, and if anyone can show that our confession is unbiblical, the church ought to revise it to bring it into conformity with Scripture.

The confessional Reformed approach to tradition (Tradition I), however, neither canonizes the past nor ignores it nor suspects it as an enemy, but rather treats it with the respect deserved by fellow brothers and sisters in Christ. This is the approach that J. Gresham Machen (1881–1937) adopted. He rejected the idea that the Reformed confessions are an obstacle to doctrinal progress, unless that progress is conceived, in Schleiermachian terms, as an expression of the religious experience of a particular period. "Real doctrinal advance" does not mean substantial revision of classic or confessional Reformed theology. Instead, it means "greater precision and fullness of doctrinal statement," and that statement is the setting forth of the truth of Scripture.[23]

John Murray (1898–1975) also defended the necessity and usefulness of tradition.[24] "There is," he argued, "a catholic, protestant and a reformed tradition." To try to "extricate" ourselves from it would be "presumptuous and even absurd."[25] In practice this tradition means that there is a "certain atmosphere . . . animated by a certain spirit" which "embraces a certain viewpoint" and "is characterized by a certain type of life and practice" and even "maintains certain types of institutions." The difference between the confessional Reformed and Rome is not that we deny tradition, but that we do not venerate our Reformed tradition "with a feeling of piety and reverence equal to that with which Scripture is received and venerated."[26] Tradition, properly understood, is subject to the authority and test of Scripture and as such has no intrinsic authority. Its authority is derived from Scripture. The Reformed tradition as expressed in the confessions "is the bond of fellowship, a bulwark against the incursion of errors, a testimony to the faith once delivered unto the saints and an instrument

23. J. Gresham Machen, "The Creeds and Doctrinal Advance," *Presbyterian Guardian* 7 (1940): 35.

24. John Murray, "Tradition Romish and Protestant," in *Collected Writings of John Murray* (Edinburgh: Banner of Truth Trust, 1976–82), 4:264–73.

25. Ibid., 269.

26. Ibid., 270.

for the preservation of both purity and peace."[27] For Murray, the derived authority of tradition was not insignificant. It meant, for example, that one who has subscribed the Reformed confessions is bound to uphold them. If he can no longer do so, *sola scriptura* does not authorize him to argue against the confessions from *within* the church. Rather, "his resort in such a case must be to renounce subscription and with such renunciation the privileges incident to it. Then he may proceed to expose the falsity of the creedal position in the light of Scripture. In a true sense, therefore, the creed, even in a reformed church has regulative authority."[28] Murray was nothing if not a biblical theologian. So it is striking and instructive to note the degree to which he was willing to endorse and elaborate the historic Reformed approach to relating Scripture and tradition.

Perhaps another way of restating Murray's full-bodied idea of tradition is to compare it to marriage. Reformed folk have chosen, in the light of Scripture and in conversation with the historic church, to identify with a particular tradition, a community of like-minded persons that adheres to a particular way of reading Scripture and to certain conclusions that follow from that reading. When two Christians marry, they do not imagine that the other is perfect in every way. This will have practical consequences. They make use of the means of grace and aim for greater sanctity, but the sins and blemishes of one's spouse are not normally grounds for divorce or reasons for never marrying.[29]

Stephen R. Holmes argues that Christians are best served by reading Scripture *with* our tradition. He observes, "Serious Christian theology has almost always interaction with the earlier tradition."[30] More profoundly, Holmes notes, to "attempt to do theology without noticing the tradition, then, is to deny, or at least to attempt to escape from, our historical

27. Ibid., 271–72.

28. Ibid., 272.

29. Though we define tradition differently, nevertheless I agree with Joseph Cardinal Ratzinger (now Pope Benedict XVI) when he speaks of tradition as part of a "transtemporal relationship" and argues that the transmission and reception of tradition is what makes us human. The modern suspicion of tradition represents "an unwarranted assumption of *auctoritas.*" Joseph Cardinal Ratzinger, *Principles of Catholic Theology: Building Stones for a Foundation,* trans. Mary Francis McCarthy (San Francisco: St. Ignatius, 1987), 87, 90.

30. Stephen R. Holmes, *Listening to the Past: The Place of Tradition in Theology* (Grand Rapids: Baker Academic, 2002), 2.

locatedness."[31] D. G. Hart observes a similar discomfort among some conservative Reformed folk with "the human." He argues that the "awkwardness with church history in Reformed and Presbyterian circles is a partial indication of the drastic remedy our theological tradition has prescribed in an effort to avoid the dilemmas posed by the human."[32] Such avoidance of the human and the historical, as intuitive and attractive as it might be to Americans, would be not only ironic for Reformed folk, but downright contrary to our theology. It was the Anabaptists, not the Reformed, who sought to do theology without reference to the past.[33] We begin with the distinction between the Creator and creature. Only God is, as it were, not "situated." He is immense and simple. We are neither. We are complex (body and soul), local (*pace* our Lutheran cousins), and finite (*finitum non capax infiniti*). As such, to some degree we are products of the past, and therefore to refuse to account seriously for the past in our theology, piety, and practice is not only bad theology but is also dishonest.

As we begin to take steps toward recovering our own tradition, we have several examples to consider. Indeed, there is a renaissance of sorts occurring as folk from various traditions begin to reappropriate their own pasts as a way of equipping themselves to meet the future. This retrospective move grows out of dissatisfaction with late modernity.[34] Thomas Oden says,

> The agenda for theology at the end of the twentieth century, following the steady deterioration of a hundred years and the disaster of the last few decades, is to begin to prepare the postmodern Christian community for its third millennium by returning again to the careful study and respectful following of the central tradition of classical Christian exegesis.[35]

31. Ibid., 6.

32. D. G. Hart, "The Divine and the Human in the Seminary Curriculum," *WTJ* 65 (2003): 41.

33. Holmes, *Listening to the Past*, 15 nn. 40–42.

34. On this category see Zygmunt Bauman, "Postmodern Religion," in *Religion, Modernity and Postmodernity*, ed. Paul Heelas et al. (Oxford: Blackwell, 1998); idem, *Liquid Modernity* (Cambridge: Polity, 2000).

35. Thomas C. Oden, *After Modernity What? Agenda for Theology* (Grand Rapids: Zondervan, 1990), 34. See also Kenneth Tanner and Christopher A. Hall, eds., *Ancient*

Oden wants to recover what he calls classical Christianity, or the "ancient ecumenical orthodoxy," or "paleo-orthodoxy," that is, the history of exegesis and theology in the first millennium of the church.[36] To this end, he is sponsoring the publication, in English translation, of a multivolume patristic (and early medieval) biblical commentary.[37]

David Steinmetz has also turned his back on the modernist-critical approach to Scripture in favor of more traditional approaches. In his brilliant essay "The Superiority of Pre-Critical Exegesis," he argues that the historical-critical method as practiced for the last two hundred years has failed to win over the religious community not because of that community's sloth, ignorance, or conservatism, but because the historical-critical method does not work. "Until the historical-critical method becomes critical of its own theoretical foundations and develops a hermeneutical theory adequate to the nature of the text which it is interpreting, it will remain restricted . . . to the guild and the academy."[38] In this essay he contrasts the historical-critical method with medieval hermeneutics, but he might well have contrasted it with the way the sixteenth- and seventeenth-century Reformed theologians also read the Bible.

Richard Muller and John Thompson accept the invitation to recover and appropriate the premodern exegetical tradition. As they note, the term "precritical" was coined by modernists who used it derisively as a synonym for uncritical.[39] Nothing could be further from the truth. The precritical exegetes had a different method, different standards of evaluation, and a different stance toward the Bible. In describing the difference between the critical and premodern handling of Isaiah 7:14, Muller and Thompson note that what often separates critical from precritical biblical exegesis is

---

and Postmodern Christianity (Downers Grove, IL: InterVarsity, 2002). See also Thomas C. Oden, *The Rebirth of Orthodoxy: Signs of New Life in Christianity* (San Francisco: Harper San Francisco, 2003).

36. Oden, *After Modernity*, 36–37.

37. Thomas C. Oden et al., eds., *Ancient Christian Commentary on Scripture* (Downers Grove, IL: InterVarsity, 1998–).

38. David C. Steinmetz, "The Superiority of Pre-Critical Exegesis," *Theology Today* 37 (1980): 38.

39. Richard A. Muller and John L. Thompson, "The Significance of Precritical Exegesis: Retrospect and Prospect," in *Biblical Interpretation in the Era of the Reformation: Essays Presented to David C. Steinmetz in Honor of His Sixtieth Birthday*, ed. Richard A. Muller and John L. Thompson (Grand Rapids: Eerdmans, 1996), 335.

not disagreement over "critical method, but over critical presuppositions, indeed over the matter of the community of interpretation and what comprises its ethos. For the 'precritical' exegetes, a truly critical understanding must include a scrutiny of the text in the light of the broader scope of Isaiah's prophecy and of the relationship of the Old Testament to the New."[40] Unlike many modern Bible readers, "Christian exegetes traditionally have assumed that a divine purpose and divine authorship unite the text of the entire canon."[41] Precritical exegesis offers great help in recovering the notion that Bible interpretation is a "churchly exercise that must take place in such a way that particular texts are understood … in their immediate context and in their canonical relationships."[42]

Most recently John Thompson has advanced the project of reading Scripture with the church by considering a series of difficult biblical texts (e.g., the stories of Hagar, Jephthah's daughter, and Gomer) as they have been interpreted and applied by a series of premodern interpreters from the patristic period through the Reformation.[43] There are other examples of reappropriation of the past. For example, among some European Roman Catholics (e.g., Henri de Lubac) the reappropriation of patristic and medieval sources has come to be known as *ressourcement*.[44] Among (mainly) Anglicans, radical orthodoxy is a project devoted, in part, to recovering the broader Christian tradition. Led by John Millbank, Catherine Pickstock, and Graham Ward, Anglicans all, radical orthodoxy rejects both modernist mediating theology (the Ritschlian "kernel and husk" approach) and postmodern pluralism, arguing for a return to a Platonist vision of Augustinian Christianity.[45] Among evangelicals we have already observed Stephen Holmes's program for appropriation of the tradition, and there are others.

40. Ibid., 339.
41. Ibid., 340.
42. Ibid., 345.
43. John L. Thompson, *Reading the Bible with the Dead: What You Can Learn from the History of Exegesis That You Can't Learn from Exegesis Alone* (Grand Rapids: Eerdmans, 2007).
44. For example see Henri de Lubac, *Medieval Exegesis*, vol. 1: *The Four Senses of Scripture*, trans. Mark Sebanc (Grand Rapids: Eerdmans, 1998).
45. See John Millbank, Catherine Pickstock, and Graham Ward, eds., *Radical Orthodoxy: A New Theology* (New York: Routledge, 1999). R. R. Reno has criticized the movement as being mortally wounded by its neo-Platonism and its modernist and idealist approach to the tradition. See R. R. Reno, "The Radical Orthodoxy Project," *First Things* (February 2000).

D. H. Williams is mediating the idea of a broader catholic tradition and appreciation for patristic theology to the free church tradition.[46] Richard Lints calls evangelicals to take their discrete various traditions seriously.[47] He contends that the neoevangelical dream of a generic panevangelical theology is dead and gives us permission to be unapologetically, confessionally Reformed and to reengage our own tradition.

According to Richard Muller, what we find when we begin to read the confessional Reformed theologians from the period of orthodoxy (c. 1565–1700) is that they were "true to the Scriptural mandate of the Reformation. They consistently refused to place confession above Scripture and constantly affirmed their confessions as expressions of the truth taught in Scripture."[48] So, this call to reappropriate the confessional Reformed tradition is, in one sense, a call to look back, but only temporarily. There is nothing wrong with looking back long enough to gain sufficient wisdom and perspective to move forward.

Like Oden and radical orthodoxy, confessional Reformed folk have always had a deep appreciation for the fathers and the medieval theologians. Indeed, the early categories of modern patrology were established, in part, by Protestant scholars such as Johannes Oecolampadius (1482–1531) and Philipp Melanchthon (1497–1560), who searched the fathers for alternatives to the Roman doctrine of transubstantiation.[49] According to Irena Backus, Martin Bucer made considerable and thoughtful use of the fathers and the medieval tradition.[50] Calvin was a serious, if sometimes ambivalent, student of the fathers and medievals. Though there is little evidence that Calvin knew Thomas Aquinas's theology directly, there is evidence that he knew the primary textbook of medieval theology, the

---

46. D. H. Williams, *Evangelicals and Tradition: The Formative Influence of the Early Church* (Grand Rapids: Baker Academic, 2005).

47. Richard Lints, *The Fabric of Theology* (Grand Rapids: Eerdmans, 1993), 96.

48. Richard A. Muller, *Scholasticism and Orthodoxy in the Reformed Tradition: An Attempt at Definition* (Grand Rapids: Calvin Theological Seminary, 1995), 20.

49. See Pierre Fraenkel, *Testimonia Patrum: The Function of the Patristic Argument in the Theology of Philip Melanchthon* (Geneva: E. Droz, 1961). See also E. P. Meijering, *Melanchthon and Patristic Thought: The Doctrines of Christ, Grace, the Trinity and the Creation* (Leiden: Brill, 1983).

50. Irena Backus, "Ulrich Zwingli, Martin Bucer and the Church Fathers," in *The Reception of the Church Fathers in the West: From the Carolingians to the Maurists*, ed. Irena Backus (New York: E. J. Brill, 1997), 2:644–66.

Sentences of Peter Lombard (1155–58), and that he was particularly well read in Bernard of Clairvaux.[51]

The orthodox Reformed theologians from the late sixteenth century and through the seventeenth century had even greater access and recourse to the patristic and medieval theologians than most of the first and second generation Reformers.[52] The Reformed orthodox demonstrated a remarkable catholicity of spirit and knowledge and drew upon the entire Christian tradition to formulate their theology.[53] If we are to follow the classic Reformed pattern, we too must become scholars of the fathers and even of the medieval theologians, who established much of the Christian theological vocabulary and the intellectual categories in which both the Reformers and the post-Reformation theologians did their work.

For our purposes, it is important to realize that we have an even stronger historical and theological connection to the orthodox theologians of the sixteenth and seventeenth centuries, than we have to the patristic and medieval theologians, since it was the Reformed orthodox in the sixteenth and seventeenth centuries who formed our theology, piety, and practice. For all our genuine admiration of the intellectual and theological achievement of Anselm (without whom we might still be teaching the ransom theory of the atonement),[54] Thomas Aquinas, and Lombard (from whom we have received so much of our vocabulary), and particularly the late medieval neo-Augustinians (e.g., Thomas Bradwardine, Gregory of Rimini, Johann von Staupitz, and John Wycliffe), with whom we have much in common,[55] there is a gulf fixed between us and them: not Lessing's "ugly ditch" but

51. See A. N. S. Lane, *John Calvin: Student of the Fathers* (Grand Rapids: Baker, 1999). See also Johannes Van Oort, "John Calvin and the Church Fathers," in *The Reception of the Church Fathers in the West*, ed. Backus, 2:661–700.

52. Irena Backus shows that the older use of patristic sources did not disappear immediately. See "The Fathers and Calvinist Orthodoxy: Patristic Scholarship," in *The Reception of the Church Fathers in the West*, 2:839–65. See also E. P. Meijering, "The Fathers and Calvinist Orthodoxy: Systematic Theology," in *The Reception of the Church Fathers in the West*, 2:867–87.

53. Contra Stanley J. Grenz and John R. Franke, *Beyond Foundationalism: Shaping Theology in the Postmodern Context* (Louisville: Westminster John Knox, 2001), 105.

54. R. Scott Clark, "Atonement: Medieval Times and Reformation Era," in *Encyclopedia of the Bible and Its Reception*, ed. Hans-Josef Klauck et al. (Berlin: Walter de Gruyter, 2008).

55. See Heiko A. Oberman, *Forerunners of the Reformation: The Shape of Late Medieval Thought* (London: Lutterworth, 1967).

the Reformation. We live on this side of the Reformation, and though we embrace many of the same doctrines as our medieval forebears, we also embrace the conviction that sinners are justified only on the ground of the righteousness of Christ imputed to us and received through faith alone, a theological insight learned from Luther, Calvin, and Reformed orthodoxy, not from the fathers or the medieval theologians.

Narcissus Reformed

The purpose of the fable of Narcissus is to warn of the danger of self-absorption and to warn against mistaking subjective experience for objective reality. Like Narcissus many in the Reformed churches have spurned the objective reality of the Reformed confession in favor of their own reflection. Writing in the late 1970s, in his savage critique of late modern life, Christopher Lasch described the modern man as the "new narcissist,"[56] who has no interest in the future because he has no interest in or connection to the past. According to Lasch, because of the subjective, therapeutic religion of the age, modern man is losing his sense of historical continuity, that is, his ability to identify with those who went before him. Philip Rieff has reached a similar conclusion and describes the modern personality as "psychological man." Tom Wolfe describes late modern narcissism, including evangelicalism, as "The Me Generation and the Third Great Awakening."[57]

In an analogous way, students, parishioners, pastors, and elders are sometimes quite surprised to find that views and practices that they hold dear, which they assume to be Reformed and perhaps even essential to being genuinely Reformed, have actually very little to do with being

56. Christopher Lasch, *The Culture of Narcissism: American Life in an Age of Diminishing Expectations* (New York: W. W. Norton, 1978), xvi. Thomas De Zengotita has updated this criticism. See Thomas De Zengotita, *Mediated: How the Media Shapes Your World and the Way You Live in It* (New York: Bloomsbury, 2005).

57. Lasch, *Culture of Narcissism*, xvii, 5. Lasch was part of a stream of analysis of modernity including Philip Rieff, Tom Wolfe, and most recently Thomas De Zengotita. See Philip Rieff, *The Triumph of the Therapeutic: Uses of Faith after Freud*, fortieth anniversary edition (Wilmington, DE: ISI Books, 2006); Tom Wolfe, *Mauve Gloves and Madmen, Clutter and Vine, and Other Stories, Sketches, and Essays* (New York: Farrar, Straus and Giroux, 1976), 126–67; De Zengotita, *Mediated*.

Reformed as understood by the confessional tradition. It seems to be widely assumed today that whatever one understands Scripture to teach or imply must ipso facto be Reformed. The reasoning seems to be thus: I am Reformed, I think *p*, and therefore *p* must be Reformed. Of course, stating it like this shows immediately the folly of such logic. One may be thoroughly Reformed theologically and a member in good standing in a Reformed church and hold views at variance with our confession about any number of things.

How have we arrived at such a place where it is possible for Reformed folk to be narcissists about theology, piety, and practice? Is it possible that we are tempted to think that, having determined to bring every square inch under the lordship of Christ, we are now in no need of correction?[58] As we will see in the following chapters, it seems that just as we began to speak about bringing everything under Christ's dominion, we were really in the process of bringing less of Reformed theology, piety, and practice under Christ's dominion. Some in the Reformed community have come to believe that everything they do is premised on some Reformed principle and is, for that reason, beyond criticism. Isolated historically from the classical Reformed tradition, operating on the basis of timeless principles derived from Scripture, ostensibly bringing every thought captive to Christ, and at war with modernity over evolution, morality, and civil polity through the course of the twentieth century, many erstwhile Reformed folk unintentionally and unwittingly became narcissists, not necessarily in their lifestyle but in theology, piety, and practice.

Despite the enormous amount of labor that has been expended by Reformed schools and churches to oppose modernism, to insulate children from the ravages of unbelieving thought, and our commitment to Reformed principles notwithstanding, we are much more influenced by

58. I am indebted to Bob Godfrey for this point. There seems to be resurgence in interest in Abraham Kuyper's transformationalist approach to relating Christ and culture. See Peter S. Heslam, *Creating a Christian Worldview: Abraham Kuyper's Lectures on Calvinism* (Grand Rapids: Eerdmans, 1998); James D. Bratt, *Abraham Kuyper: A Centennial Reader* (Grand Rapids: Eerdmans, 1998); Vincent D. Bacote, *The Spirit in Public Theology: Appropriating the Legacy of Abraham Kuyper* (Grand Rapids: Baker, 2005). The transformationalist agenda seems to reach into every nook and cranny of life. See, e.g., Richard Mouw's claim that we must even redeem recreation, in *Politics and the Biblical Drama* (Grand Rapids: Eerdmans, 1976), 64.

modernity than we realize. As D. G. Hart has noted, by refusing to use the Reformed confessions as the norm by which questions of biblical interpretation and theological formulation were addressed, "conservatives were reduced to the same status as liberals, with each side claiming its views were biblical."[59] Just as the Enlightenment proclaimed a new era in human progress, analogously, with the arrival of Kuyper and Van Til, perhaps we told ourselves that we had arrived at a new epoch in Reformed theology. The effect of such thinking has been to create a divorce between our tradition and us. Some of the claims made about Van Til's uniqueness or importance have probably fueled such exaggerated self-perceptions. For example, John Frame calls Cornelius Van Til "perhaps the most important Christian thinker since Calvin."[60]

And so many Reformed folk unintentionally and unwittingly have become narcissists in the way they read the Bible and do theology. This way of reading Scripture has been well described as "biblicism." The earliest use of the word "biblicism" in English occurred in 1827 in a work by Sophei Finngan in criticism of "biblicism."[61] In 1874 J. J. van Osterzee defined it as "idolatry of the letter."[62] In theological literature, "biblicism" has most often been used derisively to describe approaches that ignore general revelation in the interpretation of Scripture. This obscurantism takes different forms. In some cases, the wrong text is used to prove a doctrine. In other cases, a biblical text is interpreted to teach physics or astronomy (e.g., geocentrism), or the Scriptures are read in isolation from the Christian tradition.[63]

Though the term "biblicism" is relatively modern, the stance toward ecclesiastical authority it signifies is not new. In the years leading up to

59. Hart, *The Lost Soul of American Protestantism*, 105.

60. John Frame, *Cornelius Van Til: An Analysis of His Thought* (Phillipsburg, NJ: P&R, 1995), 44.

61. Sophei Finngan, *The Mania of Seduction Unmasked, or a Scriptural View of the Rise, Progress and Decline of Biblicism* (Cork, Ireland: T. Geary, 1827).

62. "Biblicism" in *OED*.

63. John Frame offers a helpful summary of the various senses of the term. See John Frame, "In Defense of Something Close to Biblicism: Reflections on Sola Scriptura and History in Theological Method," *WTJ* 59 (1997): 269–91. See also H. Franz, "Biblicism," in *The Encyclopedia of Christianity*, ed. E. H. Palmer (Marshallton, DE: National Fund for Christian Education, 1964–72).

the Synod of Dort, the same spirit that prompted the Arminian conflict also manifested itself in the rejection of the authority of the HC. Hermanus Herbertsz, a pastor in Dordrecht and Gouda, refused to preach the catechism. From 1582 to 1607 Pastor Herbertsz repeatedly promised and then refused to use the HC as directed by various assemblies in the Dutch Reformed churches. As Donald Sinnema observes, Herbertsz's objections were not to the doctrine of the catechism but to its *authority*. He charged the Reformed churches with placing the catechism above God's Word. He said,

> You not only consider [the Catechism] equal to Holy Scripture ... but place it above; this I can prove by the following reasons: first, you have divided into fifty-two Sundays, and every Sunday read and explain a part of it from the pulpit as if it were God's Word ... ; second, you also place it so much above Holy Scripture that you make Holy Scripture a servant by which one must explain and interpret [the Catechism].[64]

Sinnema observes that this charge also became popular with the Remonstrants.[65] Herbertsz rejected the ecclesiastically agreed and sanctioned interpretation of Scripture in favor of his understanding of Scripture. It is not as if there were no mechanism in Reformed church government to reform the church's confession and bring it into line with Scripture. What Herbertsz portrayed as an act of piety was really an expression of autonomy and individual authority.

In his criticism of Klaas Schilder (1890–1952) and his followers in the Liberated (*Vrijgemaakt*) Reformed Church in the Netherlands, Valentine Hepp (1879–1950) accused Schilder of biblicism, the chief mark of which, as William Masselink summarized, is that the Schilderites consistently "pass by the confessions," so that, "by using terminology in conflict with the confessions, they are ushering in Biblicism."[66] Following Hepp, Masselink

64. Hermanus Herbertsz, *Naeder Verklaringhe over 32 Articulen* (1592) printed in *Documenta Reformatoria* (Kampen: Kok, 1960), 1:274, cited in Donald W. Sinnema, "The Second Service in the Early Dutch Reformed Tradition," *CTJ* 32 (1997): 315.

65. Sinnema, "Second Service," 315.

66. William Masselink, *General Revelation and Common Grace: A Defence of the Historic Reformed Faith over against the Theology and Philosophy of the So-Called "Reconstructionist Movement"* (Grand Rapids: Eerdmans, 1953), 24.

identified three types of biblicism: first, that which rejects all confessions as human productions; second, that which defends the propriety of confessions, but relativizes them so as to make them need constant revision; third, that which professes respect for the confessions but ignores or misinterprets them.[67] As a result of the third type of biblicism particularly, Masselink (and Hepp) argued that the great danger of the new Reformed biblicism is that it tends to be unhistorical, not accounting for the work of Calvin and the classic Reformed theologians. As a consequence, Hepp warned, we run the risk of Calvinism without Calvin.[68]

The nineteenth-century German-pietist biblical theology movement was a type of biblicism, an attempt to recover biblical vocabulary and thought categories in reaction to the arid and destructive higher-critical movement.[69] This movement tended to reject systematic theology as a discipline. In response, the Princeton theologians Geerhardus Vos and B. B. Warfield agreed that there is nothing intrinsic to biblical or exegetical theology that requires it to be at odds with dogmatic or systematic theology.[70] John Murray, a student of both Vos and Warfield, defended the same view at Westminster Seminary in the middle of the twentieth century.[71]

Through the twentieth century, certain elements of North American fundamentalism and neoorthodoxy have set systematic theology over against biblical theology, and this antisystematic use of Scripture is also described as biblicism. James Callahan proposes to unite the two approaches in a biblicism "rejuvenated" through dialogue with the so-called Yale School or postliberalism.[72] Without denying the benefits offered by the Yale School, chiefly the call to live with the Bible's conceptual world,

67. Ibid.

68. Ibid., 25.

69. See Geerhardus Vos, "The Idea of Biblical Theology," in *Redemptive History and Biblical Interpretation*, ed. Richard B. Gaffin Jr. (Phillipsburg, NJ: Presbyterian and Reformed, 1980).

70. Idem, *Dogmatiek*, 5 vols. in 3 (Grand Rapids: Theological School of the Christian Reformed Churches in North America, 1910), 65. See also B. B. Warfield, *Studies in Theology* (New York: Oxford University Press, 1932), 65.

71. John Murray, "Systematic Theology," in *Collected Writings of John Murray*, 1:9.

72. James Callahan, "The Bible Says: Evangelical and Postliberal Biblicism," *Theology Today* 53 (1997): 463.

the basic difficulty of uniting the postliberal reading of Scripture with what Callahan describes as "precritical" or "premodern" theology is that a confessional Reformed reading of Scripture presupposes that there are genuine extramental referents to the scriptural narratives. Postliberalism, however, while interested in reading Scripture within canonical limits, does not require or presuppose the same referents. For this reason, Michael Horton has suggested that postliberalism is "not postliberal enough."[73]

Though acknowledging the difficulties in reclaiming biblicism, John Frame has also proposed to rehabilitate biblicism for use by Reformed Christians.[74] He wants to resolve the problem, in part, by affirming that there are extrabiblical *data* for which the Christian must account in reading Scripture, but also by denying that there is any such thing as extrabiblical *knowledge*.[75] Therefore all knowledge is, by definition, biblical knowledge. His second step to rehabilitating biblicism is to affirm only slightly milder versions of the four versions of biblicism he earlier denied. For example, he argues that a genuine practice of *sola scriptura* will sometimes be confused with biblicism.[76]

There are three criticisms of this quasi-biblicist revision of *sola scriptura*, the first historical, the second theological, and the third confessional. Frame's claim that the genuine practice of *sola scriptura* will sometimes be confused with biblicism is unfounded historically. D. H. Williams is correct when he says that the sixteenth-century Protestant doctrine of *sola scriptura* was "not intended to be *scriptura nuda*."[77] That, according to the Reformers, Scripture functions as the norm of faith and practice did not mean that Scripture was the sole resource of the Christian faith.[78] It would be more accurate for Frame to say that the American evangelical appropriation of *sola scriptura* may look biblicist, because it often is.[79]

73. Michael S. Horton, *Covenant and Eschatology: The Divine Drama* (Louisville: Westminster John Knox, 2002), 96.

74. Frame, "In Defense of Something Close to Biblicism," 272.

75. Ibid., 273.

76. Ibid., 275.

77. Williams, *Evangelicals and Tradition*, 97.

78. Ibid.

79. Ibid., 99–102. As valuable as his work is, Williams's account of the development of the doctrine of justification is flawed (126–42) and owes more to secondary surveys of Luther's doctrine and the current evangelical ecumenical imperative than it does to a close reading of

As we have seen, Frame's characterization of *sola scriptura* does not accord with Oberman's account of the Reformation view of the relations between Scripture and tradition. Luther did rebel against a millennium of theology and against an enormously powerful ecclesiastical-civil complex. Nevertheless, he consistently claimed that he was recovering the best doctrine of the early church and even that of some of the better medieval theologians (e.g., Bernard). In preparation for the council that would eventually become the Council of Trent, Luther published in 1539 *On the Councils and the Church*.[80] There he mocked the papacy and magisterium as "masters" of the law, works, and sanctity but not Scripture. Even in the midst of satire, he was careful to note that he did not pretend to read Scripture by himself or as if no one had read it before him:

> For I know that none of them attempted to read a book of Holy Scripture in school, or to use the writings of the fathers as an aid, as I did. Let them take a book of Holy Scripture and seek out the glosses of the fathers; then they will share the experience I had when I worked on the letter to the Hebrews with St. Chrysostom's glosses, the letter to Titus and the letter to the Galatians with the help of St. Jerome, Genesis with the help of St. Ambrose and St. Augustine, the Psalter with all the writers available, and so on. I have read more than they think, and have worked my way through all the books; this makes them appear impudent indeed who imagine that I did not read the fathers and who want to recommend them to me as something precious, the very thing that I was forced to devaluate twenty years ago when I read the Scriptures.[81]

This passage is telling about his mature view of extrabiblical authority. Luther read Scripture *with* the fathers, but he was not enslaved to them. He understood that councils and the fathers often contradicted

---

primary Reformation sources. For an account of Luther's doctrine see R. Scott Clark, "*Iustitia Imputata*: Alien or Proper to Luther's Doctrine of Justification?" *Concordia Theological Quarterly* 70 (2006): 269–310; idem, "The Benefits of Christ: Justification in Protestant Theology before the Westminster Assembly," in *The Faith Once Delivered: Celebrating the Legacy of Reformed Systematic Theology and the Westminster Assembly (Essays in Honor of Dr. Wayne Spear)*, ed. Anthony T. Selvaggio (Phillipsburg, NJ: P&R, 2007).

80. *LW*, vol. 41.
81. *LW*, 41:19.

one another.[82] This passage is especially fascinating because the period to which he refers was that in which he was reaching his mature Protestant views on the doctrine of justification.[83] In other words, Luther did not reach his doctrine of justification by simply reading Scripture. Rather, he reached it by reading Scripture in dialogue with the Christian tradition. His reading of Scripture was definitive but not isolated.

Second, by way of theological criticism, by denying extrabiblical knowledge and making all knowledge "biblical," Frame, as David Wells points out, has neglected an important distinction in Reformed theology, between the "external beginning of knowledge" (*principium cognoscendi externum*) or general revelation and the "internal beginning of knowledge" (*principium cognoscendi internum*), or biblical revelation.[84] It is true that whatever a human being knows is conditioned by the existence of divine revelation. As creatures made in God's image, all humans live in a universe created by divine speech ("And God said . . ."), and even the most creative person is only reorganizing facts and truths that are the result of general revelation. Not everyone or everything, however, is revealed *in Scripture*. Special revelation speaks *to* football games, but not *of* them. Scripture speaks primarily, though not exclusively, about God's moral will for his image-bearers and about his saving acts and revelation in Christ, that is, law and gospel. By folding together general and special revelation, Frame has plunged us back into the very sort of biblicism that he ostensibly seeks to avoid.

As Richard Muller indicates in his response to Frame's criticisms, *sola scriptura* is the "doctrinal watchword in all matters of faith and life." The Reformed confession has always distinguished between the way Scripture speaks to Christian doctrine and living and the way it speaks to the rest of life.[85] As Muller notes, the net effect of Frame's exaggeration of the sufficiency of Scripture is not to elevate the authority of Scripture itself but to elevate Frame's *application* of it. A "broadly defined appeal to *sola*

82. *LW*, 41:20. See also 24. For more on this see Manfried Schulze, "Martin Luther and the Church Fathers," in *The Reception of the Church Fathers in the West*, 2:573–626.

83. On this see Clark, *"Iustitia Aliena."*

84. David F. Wells, "On Being Framed," *WTJ* 59 (1997): 294.

85. Richard A. Muller, "Historiography in the Service of Theology and Worship: Toward Dialogue with John Frame," *WTJ* 59 (1997): 302.

Scriptura or to methodological principles of Scripture" provides no help since, unless Scripture is read within a "confessional context," it can be "bent in all directions."[86]

Not every appeal to Scripture is Reformed or reforming. Any appeal to Scripture that fundamentally overturns what it is to be Reformed cannot itself be a Reformed appeal to Scripture. Frame's definition of theology is that it is the "application of the Word of God by persons to all areas of life."[87] Rather than beginning with God and his revelation as the objective norm relative to us and our experience, this definition begins with our experience and us because it is we who do the applying of Scripture. As a result, despite his disavowals of the bad forms of biblicism, Frame nevertheless affirms as models of creative biblicism, among other movements, theonomy and the revision of the doctrine of justification proposed by Norman Shepherd.[88]

As a confessional matter, Frame's proposal threatens to confuse the biblical and confessional notion of the unique, sole authority of Scripture with American evangelical individualism. It seems to give support to the Roman Catholic critique of Protestantism, that we really do subject the Christian religion to the whims of millions of private judgments. Yet, nothing could have been further from the minds of those who wrote our confessions. The WCF says, "The supreme judge by which all controversies of religion are to be determined, and all decrees of councils, opinions of ancient writers, doctrines of men, and private spirits, are to be examined, and in whose sentence we are to rest, can be no other but the Holy Spirit speaking in the Scripture" (1.10).[89] We confess that the Christian religion is a public religion that is measured by a publicly accessible, divinely revealed text. Notice that the Confession expressly mentions "opinions of ancient writers, doctrines of men, and private spirits" among those things to be tested by Scripture. In other words, the divines understood (and we confess with them) *sola scriptura* not to teach that the Bible means what one says it does, but

---

86. Ibid., 308.

87. John M. Frame, *The Doctrine of the Knowledge of God* (Phillipsburg, NJ: Presbyterian and Reformed, 1987), 81.

88. Frame, "In Defense of Something Close to Biblicism," 278.

89. *Creeds*, 3:605–6.

that the Scriptures, being God's Word, form the church, and the church in subjection to the Scriptures is able to interpret them well enough to decide controversies.

The Reformed have always understood that saying that Scripture alone is the final judge in all religious questions does not settle every interpretation of every text. We confess,

> All things in Scripture are not alike plain in themselves, nor alike clear unto all: yet those things which are necessary to be known, believed, and observed for salvation, are so clearly propounded, and opened in some place of Scripture or other, that not only the learned, but the unlearned, in a due use of the ordinary means, may attain unto a sufficient understanding of them. (WCF 1.7)[90]

Our confession strikes an admirable balance. On the one hand, there are difficult places in Scripture (e.g., the circumcision of Moses' son by Zipporah, Ex. 4:24–26). Nevertheless, on the other hand, in contrast to late modern subjectivism, what must be known can be known, so that even the "unlearned" by a "due use of the ordinary means" (the preaching of the Word and the administration of the sacraments) "may attain unto a sufficient" grasp of the teaching of Scripture.

The BC addresses the question of the relations between private and public, corporate and individual authority:

> Neither may we consider any writings of men, however holy these men may have been, of equal value with those divine Scriptures, nor ought we to consider custom, or the great multitude, or antiquity, or succession of times and persons, or councils or decrees or statutes, as of equal value with the truth of God, since the truth is above all; for all men are of themselves liars, and more vain than vanity itself. Therefore we reject with all our hearts whatever does not agree with this infallible rule, as the apostles have taught us, saying, Test the spirits, whether they are of God. Likewise: any one who comes to you and brings not this teaching, receive him not into your house. (Art. 7)[91]

90. Ibid., 3:603.
91. Ibid., 3:388–89.

The BC does not reject human interpretations of Scripture as valueless (that was an Anabaptist view), but neither does it confuse them with Scripture. The confession does not ignore the visible church, but neither does it make the Scriptures a creature of the church. The Scriptures have the unique office of not only being interpreted but of interpreting the interpreter.

Our Uneasy Relation to Our Own Past

Not all Reformed folk feel at ease with the Reformed tradition. This discomfort exists on two levels, practically and theoretically. On the practical level most Americans feel little real connection to the Christian past. To the degree that they realize that there is such a thing, they do not see that it has any relevance to them. This natural reluctance is the first thing that must be overcome.

The second level of dis-ease with the past is theoretical. To Ober-man's categories of Tradition I and Tradition II, Alister McGrath adds a third, which describes the radical (e.g., Anabaptist) approach to tradition, which he designates Tradition 0. This is a fundamentally individualistic approach to Scripture and tradition which "placed private judgment of the individual above the corporate judgment of the Christian church concerning the interpretation of Scripture. It was a recipe for anarchy."[92] It is this third approach to tradition that most American evangelicals have followed, mistaking it regularly for the Protestant doctrine of *sola scriptura*. It was this (T-0) approach that the notorious revivalist Charles Finney (1792–1875) advocated:

Every uninspired attempt to frame for the church an authoritative standard of opinion which shall be regarded as the unquestionable exposition of the word of God, is not only impious in itself, but also a tacit assumption of the fundamental dogma of the Papacy. The Assembly of Divines did more than to assume the necessity of a Pope to give law to the opinions of men; they assumed to create an immortal

92. Alister E. McGrath, *Reformation Thought: An Introduction*, 2d ed. (Oxford: Blackwell, 1993), 144–45.

one, or rather to embalm their own creed, and preserve it as the Pope of all generations. [93]

For Finney, the very act of creating an ecclesiastical statement of faith was a worse presumption than a papal bull, since popes die, but the Westminster Confession will not, at least not soon enough for Finney. He continued, however, by raising an even more profound question about the relevance of the Confession in the modern period: "That an instrument framed by that assembly should in the nineteenth century be recognized as the standard of the church, or of an intelligent branch of it, is not only amazing, but I must say that it is most ridiculous."[94] Finney assumed that all reasonable modern people would share his assumption, that we are mature, enlightened, and have progressed beyond the backward views of seventeenth-century Reformed orthodoxy.

Unfortunately, there are Reformed folk who, even if implicitly, share attitudes not altogether dissimilar from Finney's attitudes toward the past and the present. In Reformed circles, these attitudes are manifest in discomfort with the Reformed past, particularly with the period of Reformed orthodoxy. This form of self-loathing is particularly striking because it is often aimed at the period, theologians, and even confessions that gave us our theology, piety, and practice.

There is a second part to the theoretical problem. It is the nominalist spirit of our age that suggests that it is misleading to speak of *the* Reformed confession, or *the* Reformed theology, piety, and practice. Are there not in fact several traditions that call themselves Reformed? A proper answer to this question could and perhaps should take up another book. Briefly, however, as I read the history of Reformed theology, there has always been a genuine and substantial unity amidst the diversity and that unity is expressed in the Reformed confessions and in the mainstream of Reformed theology, piety, and practice.[95] Between 1523 and 1675, no fewer than twenty-five major confessions or catechisms appeared. In addition to these, there were too many regional, local, and minor confessions to

93. Dennis Carroll, ed., *Charles Finney's Systematic Theology*, new expanded ed. (Minneapolis: Bethany House, 1994), 3.
94. Ibid.
95. See Holmes, *Listening to the Past*, 82–85.

mention here.[96] Even if we consider only these twenty-five documents, nevertheless, in the space of 152 years, the Reformed churches published, on average, a major confession every six years. If we add just a few of the minor confessions, the frequency with which the Reformed churches published confessions becomes even greater. What is most important is that, despite the regional diversity and minor variations in expression, the doctrine was substantially the same in all the major documents. With respect to Reformed theology, consider the example of covenant theology. It is sometimes suggested that there were multiple Reformed approaches to covenant theology. Recent research, however, suggests that there was a typical covenant theology that developed in the sixteenth and seventeenth centuries.[97]

Another reason why contemporary Reformed folk may be ill at ease with their tradition is that, in the nineteenth and twentieth centuries, many accepted the premise that Calvin's theology is the norm for Reformed theology and the conclusion that his Reformed orthodox successors were not really faithful to him. Since Calvin's death, at least four camps have claimed to be the true heir of his theology: the Arminians, the Amyraldians, the orthodox Calvinists, and more recently the neoorthodox or Barthians. The approach that set Calvin against Reformed orthodoxy more or less dominated Calvin studies and consequently the understanding of Reformed orthodoxy from the middle of the nineteenth century through the late twentieth century.[98]

By now it is well known, or at least should be, that Alexander Schweizer (1808–88) argued that there was in Lutheranism and in Reformed theology

96. Unfortunately, many of these documents remain unavailable in English and can only be found in collections such as H. A. Niemeyer, *Collectio Confessionum in Ecclesiis Reformatis Publicatarum* (Leipzig: Julius Klinkhardt, 1840).

97. See R. Scott Clark, ed., *Covenant, Justification and Pastoral Ministry: Essays by the Faculty of Westminster Seminary California* (Phillipsburg, NJ: P&R, 2006), chapters 1, 6, 8, 12.

98. On this debate see Carl R. Trueman and R. Scott Clark, *Protestant Scholasticism: Essays in Reassessment* (Carlisle, UK: Paternoster, 1999). See also Richard A. Muller, *The Unaccommodated Calvin*, Oxford Studies in Historical Theology (New York: Oxford University Press, 2000); idem, *After Calvin: Studies in the Development of a Theological Tradition*, Oxford Studies in Historical Theology (Oxford: Oxford University Press, 2003); idem, *PRRD*; W. J. Van Asselt and Eef Dekker, *Reformation and Scholasticism: An Ecumenical Enterprise* (Grand Rapids: Baker, 2001).

a series of "central dogmas."[99] The Lutheran central dogma was said to be justification by grace alone through faith alone, and the Reformed central dogma was said to be predestination. He argued that the Reformed orthodox deduced a speculative theology from their doctrine of the divine decree.[100] Schweizer's account of Reformed theology was not organized according to the logic of the sixteenth- and seventeenth-century systems "but according to the requirements of his own Schleiermachian theological system."[101]

Writing about the same time, Heinrich Heppe (1820–79) argued that there were multiple and competing strains within Reformed theology.[102] One strain was said to be the Calvinist-predestinarian strain that prompted a covenantal, Melanchthonian reaction in the Palatinate "standing halfway between the Lutherans and the Calvinists."[103] Heppe's presentation of Reformed theology is particularly important because it was Karl Barth's primary source for his knowledge of Reformed orthodoxy, and Barth's influence has been massive, even in confessional Reformed circles. Further, Heppe's summary of Reformed orthodoxy was translated into English in the middle of the twentieth century and has been used widely by students of Protestant scholasticism.[104] Not having read the sources in context, they fail to recognize that his presentation is "marred by a series of profound problems."[105] Muller says that "Heppe arranges his dogmatics in such a way as to place the doctrine of predestination prior to creation, in relation to the doctrine of God. This was a pattern followed by a large number of seventeenth-century systems, but not by all of the Protestant scholastics—certainly not by all of those cited by Heppe."[106]

99. Alexander Schweizer, *Die Glaubenslehre der evangelisch-reformierten Kirche*, 2 vols. (Zürich: Orell, Füssli und Co., 1844–47); idem, *Die Protestantischen Centraldogmen in ihrer Entwicklung innerhalb der reformierten Kirche*, 2 vols. (Zürich: Orell, Füssli und Co., 1854–56).

100. Muller, *PRRD*, 1:124.

101. Ibid., 1:131.

102. Heinrich Heppe, *Geschichte des deutschen Protestantismus in den Jahren 1555–1581*, 4 vols. (Marburg: N. G. Elwert, 1852–59).

103. Muller, *PRRD*, 1:130.

104. Heinrich Heppe, *Die Dogmatik der evangelisch-reformierten Kirche* (Elberfeld: K. R. Friderichs, 1861); idem, *Reformed Dogmatics Set Out and Illustrated from the Sources*, ed. Ernst Bizer, trans. G. T. Thomson (London: George Allen and Unwin LTD, 1950).

105. Muller, *PRRD*, 1:130.

106. Ibid.

It is well known, however, that in the nineteenth and twentieth centuries, those who generally identified with sixteenth- and seventeenth-century Reformed orthodoxy also harbored at least some doubts about their orthodox forebears. One recent study of Joseph Addison Alexander (1809–60) suggests that he was not opposed to setting Calvin against the Calvinists, at least to a small degree.[107] Thus, when, in the early twentieth century, Charles Augustus Briggs (1841–1913) attempted to set Calvin against the Calvinists, he was not speaking only for liberals. He argued that the medieval theologians "combined the study of the Creeds and the Fathers with the Scriptures under the head of 'Positive Theology,' and so distinguished the Theology based on the authority of Christ and His Church, from the Scholastic Theology as systematized by the Scholastic theologians in the use of the Aristotelian philosophy."[108] The Reformers, he said,

> discarded the Scholastic Theology, and reverted to the Positive Theology, in which they recognized the Scriptures as the only divine authority, but the Creeds of the ancient Church as valid summaries of the doctrines of Scripture. . . . So Calvin sought his material in the Bible; but his structural principle was not the Aristotelian philosophy, but the order of the Apostles' Creed, which he follows strictly, only making a fourfold division instead of the traditional twelvefold.[109]

Of the Reformed orthodox Briggs said: "The successors of the Reformers in the seventeenth century reintroduced the Aristotelian philosophy as the constructive principle in their systems of Theology; and so gave a newer Scholastic Theology in which they merged the older Positive Theology. And so the distinction between Positive and Scholastic

107. Andrew J. Whealy, "A Reformed Biblicist, and Always Reforming Church Historian: An Appraisal of the Scriptural and Historical Hermeneutic of Joseph Addison Alexander, 1833–1860" (master of arts thesis, Westminster Seminary California, 2005), 89–100. See also Lefferts A. Loetscher, *Facing the Enlightenment and Pietism: Archibald Alexander and the Founding of Princeton Theological Seminary*, Contributions to the Study of Religion 8 (Westport, CT: Greenwood, 1983), 207, which suggests that Alexander might have been reacting to Johann Friedrich Stapfer, whom he read and who Muller says married Reformed orthodoxy with "rational supernaturalistic philosophy" with, however, little effect on the product (*PRRD*, 1:83).

108. Charles Augustus Briggs, *Theological Symbolics* (Edinburgh: T&T Clark, 1914), 6.

109. Ibid., 7.

Theology passed out of view."[110] By the time Karl Barth made similar claims in the early twentieth century, he was following a well-worn path and making sounds that resonated with those in and out of confessional Reformed circles.[111]

Nevertheless, it is a little surprising to witness a certain ambivalence toward the Reformed past within a citadel of Reformed orthodoxy such as the old Westminster Seminary faculty. For example, Cornelius Van Til's rhetoric about and approach to the past may have prepared his students to sympathize with the Calvin versus the Calvinists argument when writers such as Basil Hall and R. T. Kendall resuscitated it.[112] In Van Til's vocabulary, "scholastic" is nearly always a pejorative, most often referring to medieval theology, specifically Thomas Aquinas for whom Van Til had little patience.[113] He rarely interacted seriously, however, with his own theological tradition, at least as it existed between Calvin and Charles Hodge, a tradition which, despite his own rhetoric, he essentially accepted.[114] Sometimes, however, he even dismissed that tradition as

110. Ibid.

111. For a survey of the older literature and the outdated characterizations of Protestant scholasticism see Carl R. Trueman and R. Scott Clark, eds., *Protestant Scholasticism: Essays in Reassessment* (Carlisle, UK: Paternoster, 1999), xi–xix. See also W. J. van Asselt and Eef Dekker, eds., *Reformation and Scholasticism: An Ecumenical Enterprise* (Grand Rapids: Baker, 2001), 11–43; Willem J. van Asselt, "Protestant Scholasticism: Some Methodological Considerations in the Study of Its Development," *Nederlands Archief voor Kerkengescheidnis* 81 (2001): 265–74.

112. Basil Hall, "Calvin against the Calvinists," in *John Calvin*, ed. Gervase Duffield (Grand Rapids: Eerdmans, 1966); R. T. Kendall, *Calvin and English Calvinism to 1649* (Oxford: Oxford University Press, 1979). John Frame was quite critical of Brian Armstrong's version of the "Calvin versus the Calvinists" argument, but primarily on philosophical rather than historical grounds. See his review of Brian G. Armstrong, *Calvinism and the Amyraut Heresy: Protestant Scholasticism and Humanism in Seventeenth-Century France* (Madison: University of Wisconsin Press, 1969), in *WTJ* 34 (1972) and reprinted in John Frame, *The Doctrine of God: A Theology of Lordship* (Phillipsburg, NJ: P&R, 2002), 801–6). See also Richard Muller, *Christ and the Decree: Christology and Predestination in Reformed Theology from Calvin to Perkins* (Durham, NC: Labyrinth, 1986).

113. E.g., Cornelius Van Til, *The Defense of the Faith* (Philadelphia: Presbyterian and Reformed, 1955), 168–98.

114. For example, in Van Til, *A Christian Theory of Knowledge* (Nutley, NJ: Presbyterian and Reformed, 1969), one finds no reference to any of the orthodox Reformed theologians. In a chapter of idem, *Christianity and Barthianism* (Phillipsburg, NJ: P&R, reprint, 1977), 67–89, he surveys Barth's critique of Reformed orthodoxy, but in his rebuttal, later in the volume, he moves from medieval to modern theology, omitting any discussion of Reformed

having been corrupted with Aristotelian ideas. For example, in describing Valentine Hepp's history of theology, Van Til said, "the epistemology of Voetius and many Reformed theologians was very similar to that of Thomas. They were unable to extricate themselves from the influence of modern philosophy which began with the assumption of the autonomy of the human spirit."[115] There is no evidence in the discussion that follows, however, that Van Til disagreed with Hepp's analysis of the seventeenth-century Reformed theologians. Further, there is precious little evidence that Van Til's claim about Voetius was true.[116]

His negative assessment of Voetius was particularly ironic, since Voetius opposed Descartes' autonomous turn with the same degree of vehemence as Van Til did after him. Voetius opposed Descartes so completely that he was unable to see where it might be possible for confessional Reformed Christians to agree with Descartes on matters relating to astronomy or theories of blood circulation. In other words, the historical evidence is not that Voetius was a rationalist, but rather that he was, as it were, a proto-hyper-presuppositionalist. Voetius reasoned that if Descartes was wrong about first order issues (and he was), then he could not be trusted on penultimate issues. Van Til's approach produced another irony, that despite the adamant and voluminous criticism by Van Til of the Arminians, Amyraldians, and Barthians, he and many of his followers essentially agreed with the Arminian, Amyraldian, and Barthian critique of their own tradition, that classical Reformed theology had become "bogged down" in the "quagmire of rationalism."[117]

Because of such rhetoric, and because Van Til did not always use the traditional Reformed theological vocabulary, he inadvertently helped to

---

orthodoxy. In his syllabus, *A Survey of Christian Epistemology*, vol. 2 of *In Defense of the Faith* (Phillipsburg, NJ: Presbyterian and Reformed, n.d.), 94–102, he moves from a discussion of Calvin's theology to Descartes.

115. Cornelius Van Til, *An Introduction to Systematic Theology*, vol. 5 of *In Defense of the Faith* (Phillipsburg, NJ: Presbyterian and Reformed, 1978), 49.

116. See Aza Goudriaan, *Reformed Orthodoxy and Philosophy, 1625–1750: Gisbertus Voetius, Petrus Van Mastricht, and Anthonius Driessen*, ed. Wim Janse, *Church History* 26 (Leiden and Boston: Brill, 2006), 37–53, which demonstrates positively that Voetius placed Scripture above human reason.

117. Gary North, "Introduction," in *Foundations of Christian Scholarship: Essays in the Van Til Perspective*, ed. Gary North (Vallecito, CA: Ross House, 1979), ix.

create an impression that he was doing something that had never been done before. His ruthless critiques of modernity and less consistent forms of Calvinism were invaluable, but in some ways at least, much of what Van Til did could be described as a restatement of the key ideas of classical Reformed theology. It would be unhistorical and anachronistic to impute the entirety of Van Til's presuppositional system to sixteenth- and seventeenth-century Reformed orthodoxy, but his insight regarding the Creator/creature distinction, which undergirded all his work, was an idea with which all the classical Reformed theologians operated.[118] If presuppositionalism means beginning with the foundational submission to the authority of God and his revelation in Scripture over against human autonomy, hardly a single sixteenth- or seventeenth-century Reformed theologian, at least in the early and high orthodox periods, disagreed.

About the time Van Til's active academic career was ending, the tide began to turn in the academic literature. In the preface to the 1981 reprint of his book *Reformers in the Wings*, David Steinmetz disavowed his earlier "Calvin versus the Calvinists" interpretation of Theodore Beza and his relations to Calvin:

> At the time I wrote on Theodore Beza, he was widely regarded as a speculative theologian who betrayed the insights of the Reformation by fitting them into the alien framework of Aristotelian philosophy. The more recent essays by Moruyama, Raitt, and particularly by Richard Muller have persuaded me that this view is not true and that the image of Beza in particular and of Protestant scholasticism in general need fundamental re-thinking and reinterpretation.[119]

Steinmetz's scholarship has continued in this trajectory of interpretation more recently by arguing that Calvin's relations to medieval scholasticism are much more complicated than usually acknowledged.[120] Certainly, with the publication of Richard Muller's work on Beza, the old caricature of

118. See chapter 4 of this work.
119. David C. Steinmetz, *Reformers in the Wings*, 2d ed. (Grand Rapids: Baker, 1981).
120. Idem, "The Scholastic Calvin," in *Protestant Scholasticism: Essays in Reassessment*, ed. Carl R. Trueman and R. Scott Clark (Carlisle, UK: Paternoster, 1999).

Beza and the Reformed orthodoxy and scholasticism can be repeated only through stubbornness or ignorance.[121]

Becoming familiar and friendly with our own tradition is an important part of recovering the Reformed confession. It is impossible to have the Reformation without orthodoxy, "if only because the intention to identify, present, and preserve Christian orthodoxy in and for the church lay at the very heart of the Reformation. The Reformation without orthodoxy is not the Reformation . . . the severing of piety from scholasticism is also untrue to the historical case."[122] The same men who wrote our theology in the sixteenth and seventeenth centuries also wrote our foundational books on piety. The idea that we can have the Reformation without the Reformed tradition is problematic. According to Muller, "In short, what is desperately wrong with such a project is that it offers us a mythical Reformation as the foundation of our tradition rather than the historical Reformation—and, in order to justify the myth, obscures the historical bridge that connects us to our genuine past."[123]

Far from being a detour, the confessional Reformed tradition offers us a useful and detailed road map toward *semper reformanda*. According to Muller, what we can learn from the classic Reformed theologians, for example, Peter Van Mastricht's *Theoretical-Practical Theology*, is the practice of connecting sensitive exegesis of Holy Scripture to profound theological formulation.[124] From the successors of the classic Reformed theologians we can learn how to relate theology to new learning. For example, whatever one might think of Charles Hodge's conclusions, one must marvel at his intelligent interaction with nineteenth-century science.[125] Muller also notes that the Southern Presbyterian theologian Robert Louis

---

121. For example, see Richard A. Muller, "The Use and Abuse of a Document: Beza's *Tabula Praedestinationis*, the Bolsec Controversy, and the Origins of Reformed Orthodoxy," in *Protestant Scholasticism*. One signal that the tide of opinion about Reformed scholasticism may be turning is the title of an essay by the Princeton theologian and Barth scholar, Bruce L. McCormack, "Confessions of a Reformed Scholastic," *Perspectives: A Journal of Reformed Thought* 13 (June/July 1998): 12–14.

122. Muller, *Scholasticism and Orthodoxy in the Reformed Tradition*, 28.

123. Ibid., 29.

124. Richard A. Muller, "Giving Direction to Theology: The Scholastic Dimension," *JETS* 28 (1985): 184–85.

125. See Mark A. Noll and David N. Livingstone, eds., *Charles Hodge, What Is Darwinism? and Other Writings on Science and Religion* (Grand Rapids: Baker, 1994).

Dabney (1820–98) developed his epistemology in dialogue with Berkeley, Hume, Kant, and Mill.[126] The confessional Reformed tradition provides a model for us as we seek to engage honestly and carefully the questions which we face in our time. "A scholastic method with its careful division of theology into Biblical, historical, systematic and practical theology may well be the best foundation upon which we can produce effective theological synthesis for our times."[127]

Conclusions

In this introduction I have tried to outline the central argument of this book, that all is not well in the Reformed churches, that they are fragmented, and to a remarkable degree have lost their identity. This loss of identity has occurred because the Reformed churches have been affected deeply by two alien impulses: the quest for illegitimate religious certainty (QIRC) and the quest for illegitimate religious experience (QIRE). Both of these impulses are variations on the two major aspects of the Enlightenment: rationalism and irrationalism. The antidote for these diseases is to recover the Reformed confession, that is, Reformed theology, piety, and practice. This part of the argument will be taken up at length in the next two chapters of this book.

The Reformed confession, considered narrowly, can be the only stable and reasonable definition of the adjective "Reformed." As part of this argument, I have offered explanations for why we have come to such a place. Part of the solution is the recovery of a true understanding of *sola scriptura* and a recovery of the role and use of the Reformed tradition in defining our identity. This approach is in contrast to those who seek to perpetuate either the QIRC or the QIRE. It is to these two problems that the book now turns.

---

126. Muller, "Giving Direction to Theology," 187.

127. Ibid., 193. See also Luco J. van den Brom, "Scholasticism and Contemporary Systematic Theology," in *Reformation and Scholasticism: An Ecumenical Enterprise*, ed. Willem J. van Asselt and Eef Dekker (Grand Rapids: Baker, 2001).

PART 1

THE CRISIS

The distance between God and the creature is so great, that although reasonable creatures do owe obedience unto him as their Creator, yet they could never have any fruition of him as their blessedness and reward, but by some voluntary condescension on God's part, which he hath been pleased to express by way of covenant.

—Westminster Confession of Faith 7.1

Many, no doubt, will turn in impatience from the inquiry—all those, namely, who have settled the question in such a way that they cannot conceive of it being reopened. Such, for example, are the pietists, of whom there are still many. "What," they say, "is the need of argument in defence of the Bible? Is it not the Word of God, and does it not carry with it an immediate certitude of its truth which could only be obscured by defence? If science comes into contradiction with the Bible, so much the worse for science!"

—J. Gresham Machen

The Christian church has, consciously or unconsciously, employed the concept in the formulation of its creeds. In these creeds the church does not pretend to have enveloped the fullness of the revelation of God. The church knows itself to be dealing with the inexhaustible God. The creeds must therefore be regarded as "approximations" to the fullness of the truth as it is in God.

—Cornelius Van Til

CHAPTER
2

The Quest for Illegitimate Religious Certainty

QIRC is the pursuit to know God in ways he has not revealed himself and to achieve epistemic and moral certainty on questions where such certainty is neither possible nor desirable. Sometimes this goal is achieved by finding the *one* great insight that gives coherence to and controls all other facts or phenomena. Some Reformed people seem to be reacting to the uncertainty of the age by grasping for this illegitimate sort of certainty. For example, some congregations and denominations, fearful that the rapid growth in the number of English language Bible translations since 1946 (when the Revised Standard Version was first published) signals an erosion of biblical authority in the church, have named the Authorized (King James) Version (1611) as the only accurate, acceptable English translation of Holy Scripture. Having determined the correct Bible translation, they are convinced that it is the standard by which orthodoxy is measured. Other churches, fearing that feminism is eroding the distinctions between male and female roles, issue ecclesiastical legislation forbidding Christian women from serving in the armed services, and still others, despite the fact that we have always said that we do not regard the Bible as a science or psychological handbook, continue to use it as if it were. Consider, for example, the controversy which arose over T. David Gordon's essay "The Insufficiency of Scripture" in *Modern Reformation*.[1] Though provocatively titled and overstated in places (as he later acknowledged in a subsequent interview with the magazine), Gordon made it quite clear that he was simply restating the classical view that the Scripture is not intended to be a textbook for the various intellectual disciplines. When we confess that Scripture is sufficient for "faith and life" (WCF 1.6), we mean to say, in part, that Scripture is intended to be read neither as a manual for mechanics nor a physician's desk reference. A subsequent issue of the magazine published no less than five letters objecting to Gordon's argument. The volume and tone of the criticism illustrate the fact that such an approach is no longer acceptable in some Reformed circles; that some of us really do take the Scriptures as a guide to civil government and moral renewal for American society and not chiefly as the infallible and inerrant revelation of God's saving work and Word in history. This episode is an example of the attempt to achieve epistemic and moral certainty on questions that are properly matters of liberty.

There are other examples of this flattening out of tensions and difficulties that testify to the presence amongst us of the QIRC. The rise and influence of the preterist movement (the claim that Christ returned in A.D. 70) within the Reformed churches has generated a body of literature and response.[2] Whereas traditional amillennialism (which, before the twentieth century, was known as postmillennialism) entailed certain tensions between that which is fulfilled and that which remains to be fulfilled, preterism tidies up the problems rather neatly by explaining them all with the single fact of the sack of Jerusalem in A.D. 70.

1. T. David Gordon, "The Insufficiency of Scripture," *Modern Reformation* 11 (January/ February 2002): 18–23. The letters were published in *Modern Reformation*, 11 (May/June 2002): 3–5, and his interview in the same issue, (46–49). See also T. David Gordon, "Critique of Theonomy: A Taxonomy," *WTJ* 56 (1994): 23–43; Kenneth L. Gentry, *Covenantal Theonomy: A Response to T. David Gordon and Klinean Covenantalism* (Nacogdoches, TX: Covenant Media, 2005); Bryan Estelle, "Review of Covenantal Theonomy," *Ordained Servant* (May 2007): http://www.opc.org/os.html?issue_id=21 (accessed 24 September 2007).

2. For a brief definition of preterism see Cornelis P. Venema, *The Promise of the Future* (Edinburgh: Banner of Truth Trust, 2000), 510. For a response to "full" or "hyper" preterism (which claims that Christ returned in A.D. 70) see also Keith A. Mathison, ed., *When Shall These Things Be? A Reformed Response to Hyper-Preterism* (Phillipsburg, NJ: P&R, 2004). See also Kim Riddlebarger, *A Case for Amillennialism: Understanding the End Times* (Grand Rapids: Baker, 2003), 157–79.

The denial of the free offer of the gospel is another example of the QIRC. Those who advocate the historic Reformed doctrine of the free or "well-meant" or promiscuous (CD 2.5) preaching of the gospel distinguish between the command of God in Scripture to preach and offer free salvation in Christ and the divine decree of predestination which lies behind the ministry of the Word. They assume a fundamental distinction between the way we know things and the way God knows things. The opponents of the free or well-meant offer of the gospel openly deny this distinction.[3] The "problem" of the traditional Reformed theology of the decree and its administration is that there is tension between what we know and what God knows. This tension produces uncertainty. The QIRC denial of the distinction eliminates the tension and with it the uncertainty.

This chapter will focus on three movements in our churches that, by their existence, give evidence of the influence of the QIRC: the movement to make the six-day, twenty-four-hour interpretation (hereafter 6/24) of Genesis 1 a mark of Reformed orthodoxy, theonomy, and covenant moralism.[4] The latter reflects the QIRC by turning to what Martin Luther called the "theology of glory" (*theologia gloriae*).[5] This theology had twin children: moralism and rationalism. Where the confessional Protestant (Reformed) doctrine of justification taught justification *sola gratia, sola fide* with the understanding that the justified, in this life, are never fully, inherently, intrinsically, personally sanctified, that it is *sinners* whom God justifies (Rom. 4:5), the covenant moralists flatten out the tension between our justification and our sanctification by moving toward the old medieval and Roman doctrine of justification by sanctification so that God is said to justify the *godly*.

Unlike much of the surrounding culture, confessional Reformed theology still believes in God, creation, revelation, and salvation. Such convictions necessarily place us at odds with the predominantly non-Christian

3. R. Scott Clark, "Janus, the Well-Meant Offer of the Gospel, and Westminster Theology," in *The Pattern of Sound Doctrine: Systematic Theology at the Westminster Seminaries. Essays in Honor of Robert B. Strimple*, ed. David VanDrunen (Phillipsburg, NJ: P&R, 2004), 149–79.

4. This expression comes from R. Scott Clark, ed., *Covenant, Justification, and Pastoral Ministry* (Phillipsburg, NJ: P&R, 2006), 432.

5. Luther said, "Theologus gloriae dicit malum bonum et bonum malum, Theologus crucis dicit id quod res est." *WA*, 1.354. See also ibid., 17.684–85 and below in this chapter.

worldview. This tension is particularly acute when it comes to social and political questions. For most of the modern period, after Christendom, the Reformed churches have been content to live with this considerable degree of tension between our private and civil lives. It has been understood that, touching matters of Christian faith and practice, we have a definitive revelation. When it comes to matters of politics and policy, we turn to Scripture for specific answers with more hesitation, recognizing that we are not national Israel and we have no theocratic civil mandate as Christians. The theonomic and Christian reconstructionist movements, however, seek to resolve this tension by re-instituting the Mosaic civil laws and using Scripture as a sort of textbook of policy and civil-legal questions.

About the same time Christendom was passing away, giving rise to the possibility of a new sort of civil and religious pluralism, the old science was also collapsing under the challenge of a newly invigorated investigation of the physical world. The rise of modern science has created tension between the way the Bible speaks about the physical world and the way contemporary science speaks about the world. As we will see below, in fits and starts, the majority report of the confessional Reformed churches came to be that the Scriptures speak truly about the physical world but, by intention, not scientifically. In the last forty years, in response to this settlement, a movement has arisen which wants to unseat this arrangement. This movement seeks certainty by eliminating the tension between secular science and the Christian faith in favor of a restoration of the certainties of the old, premodern science.

Liquid Modernity

This search for certainty is a reaction to what Zygmunt Bauman has called "liquidity" or the prevailing sense that nothing is fixed, certain, or reliable any longer.[6] Bauman is correct that premoderns lived in a relatively more stable world. The time and nature of their death were uncertain, but everything else was relatively fixed. One's place in society was determined by birth, the social order was relatively fixed, and the nature of divine-human

6. Zygmunt Bauman, *Liquid Modernity* (Cambridge: Polity, 2000).

relations was assumed to be fixed.[7] Little about late modern life seems to be reliable. Those certainties have dissolved into liquidity. What was unacceptable public behavior or speech only a decade ago is now widely accepted. Social and interpersonal relations are in almost constant flux. In Reformed theology, we have proposals to resurrect something that arguably resembles Charles Briggs's approach to Scripture,[8] radical revisions of the doctrine of the Trinity and equally radical revisions of the doctrine of justification.[9]

7. Idem, "Postmodern Religion," in *Religion, Modernity and Postmodernity*, ed. Paul Heelas et al. (Oxford: Blackwell, 1998), 66–67.

8. I am referring to the controversy surrounding Peter Enns, *Inspiration and Incarnation: Evangelicals and the Problem of the Old Testament* (Grand Rapids: Baker Academic, 2005). See G. K. Beale, "Myth, History, and Inspiration: A Review Article of *Inspiration and Incarnation*," *JETS* 49 (2006): 247–71; idem, "Did Jesus and the Apostles Preach the Right Doctrine from the Wrong Texts? Revisiting the Debate Seventeen Years Later in the Light of Peter Enns's Book, *Inspiration and Incarnation*," *Themelios* 32 (2006): 18–43; Peter Enns, "Response to G. K. Beale's Review Article on *Inspiration and Incarnation*," *JETS* 49 (2006): 313–25. On the Briggs controversy see Gary L. W. Johnson, "Warfield and C. A. Briggs: Their Polemics and Legacy," in Gary L. W. Johnson, ed., *B. B. Warfield: Essays on His Life and Thought* (Phillipsburg, NJ: P&R, 2007), 195–240; Barry Waugh, "Warfield and the Briggs Trial: A Bibliography," in ibid., 241–55.

9. See Cornelius Plantinga, "The Threeness/Oneness Problem of the Trinity," *CTJ* 23 (1988); idem, "Social Trinity and Tritheism," in *Atonement: Philosophical and Theological Essays*, ed. Ronald J. Feenstra and Cornelius Plantinga (Notre Dame: University of Notre Dame, 1989). See also Brian Leftow, "Anti Social Trinitarianism," in *The Trinity: An Inter-Disciplinary Symposium on the Trinity*, ed. Stephen T. Davis, Daniel Kendall, and Gerald O'Collins (Oxford: Oxford University Press, 1991); Sarah Coakley, "Persons in the 'Social' Doctrine of the Trinity: A Critique of the Current Analytic Discussion," in *The Trinity*, ed. Davis, Kendall, and O'Collins.

On proposals to revise the Reformed doctrine of justification see E. Calvin Beisner, *The Auburn Avenue Theology Pros and Cons: Debating the Federal Vision* (Fort Lauderdale: Knox Theological Seminary, 2004); R. Scott Clark, ed., *Covenant, Justification, and Pastoral Ministry*; idem, "Baptism and the Benefits of Christ: The Double Mode of Communion in the Covenant of Grace," *Confessional Presbyterian* 2 (2006): 3–19; Guy Prentiss Waters, *Justification and the New Perspectives on Paul: A Review and Response* (Phillipsburg, NJ: P&R, 2004); idem, *The Federal Vision and Covenant Theology: A Comparative Analysis* (Phillipsburg, NJ: P&R, 2006); Cornelis P. Venema, *The Gospel of Free Acceptance in Christ: An Assessment of the Reformation and the New Perspective on Paul* (Edinburgh: Banner of Truth Trust, 2006); O. Palmer Robertson, *The Current Justification Controversy* (Unicoi, TN: Trinity Foundation, 2003). For treatments of the question sympathetic to the federal vision movement see P. Andrew Sandlin, ed., *Backbone of the Bible: Covenant in Contemporary Perspective* (Nacogdoches, TX: Covenant Media, 2004); Douglas Wilson, *"Reformed" Is Not Enough* (Moscow, ID: Canon, 2002); Steve Wilkins and Duane Garner, eds., *The Federal Vision* (Monroe, LA: Athanasius, 2004); Norman Shepherd, *The Call of Grace: How the Covenant Illumines Salvation and Evangelism* (Phillipsburg, NJ: P&R, 2000).

Instead of turning to the Reformed confession,[10] however, many Reformed folk have turned to a kind of rationalism in an attempt to find certainty by elevating a particular interpretation, application, or use of Scripture above the Reformed faith itself. These folk then use their interpretation of Scripture as a mark of orthodoxy and/or sort of prophylaxis against enemies foreign and domestic, real and perceived. This chapter does not aim to respond to the specific claims of each of the examples of QIRC addressed in this chapter, as that would require three new books, but through them to explore the influence of this sort of rationalism on Reformed theology, piety, and practice.

Thesis: The Search for "Solids"

Why are our theological and ecclesiastical priorities as they are? The answer is that these controversies are responses to direct cultural pressure. In other words, rather than contending for the notion that we are creatures, that there is a creational law to which we are all obligated (Rom. 2:14–15), and rather than pointing to the gospel of grace, many have chosen to draw the line at the length of the days of creation and the Mosaic civil law, and to set up a soteriology of grace *and* works. This chapter argues that, in their own ways, each of these responses to contemporary social pressure is an example of the spirit of QIRC and is not only a nonconfessional marker of Reformed identity but, in some cases, is actually opposed to the Reformed confession. To make the case, this chapter will focus on the function of the creation, theonomy, and justification debates as boundary markers of Reformed orthodoxy.

Unlikely Fundamentalists

The QIRC is a variant of fundamentalism. By using this word we are immediately plunged into difficulties. The literature on fundamentalism is massive.[11] Part of the reason the literature is so large is that the word is so

10. See chapter 1 of this work.

11. Martin Marty and R. Scott Appleby, eds., *The Fundamentalism Project*, 5 vols. (Chicago: University of Chicago, 1991–95), investigates fundamentalism as a transreligious, transdenominational, transcultural, global phenomenon. My understanding of American

hard to define and is used in a wide variety of ways. The discussion over the definition of the word "fundamentalist" is made complicated by the fact that some scholars use it to describe those who hold beliefs they find repugnant. For example, James Barr lists three characteristics: belief in biblical inerrancy, hostility to modern theology and biblical studies, and an "assurance" that those who disagree with them are not really Christians.[12] In her introductory essay on "North American Protestant Fundamentalism," Nancy T. Ammerman lists four characteristics of fundamentalism: evangelism, inerrancy, premillennialism, and separatism.[13] Fundamentalists have held and practiced these, but holding and practicing them does not necessarily make one a fundamentalist. For example, something like the inerrancy of Scripture was held as an article of faith by the patristic, medieval, Reformation, and post-Reformation church. Given that it was not until the Enlightenment that the truthfulness and reliability of Scripture became a crisis, it is remarkable how often premodern theologians affirmed the trustworthiness of Scripture. The Reformed doctrine of Scripture has developed in the last two centuries in order to respond to the modernist critics, but the doctrine of the Trinity underwent the same sort of development in response to the Arian critics in the fourth century. In fact, it is not a belief that the Bible is true which makes one a fundamentalist; rather it is the belief that one's interpretation of Scripture is inerrant which qualifies one as a fundamentalist. In the same way, it is hardly self-evident that calling sinners to faith in Christ is fundamentalist unless the only alternative to modern universalism is fundamentalism.

Further, all of these scholars have neglected, as a category, the existence of confessional Protestantism.[14] Confessional Protestants such as

---

fundamentalism has been shaped particularly by George M. Marsden, *Understanding Fundamentalism and Evangelicalism* (Grand Rapids: Eerdmans, 1981); idem, *Fundamentalism and American Culture* (New York: Oxford University Press, 1982); idem, *Reforming Fundamentalism: Fuller Seminary and the New Evangelicalism* (Grand Rapids: Eerdmans, 1987); D. G. Hart, *Defending the Faith: J. Gresham Machen and the Crisis of Conservative Protestantism in Modern America* (Grand Rapids: Baker, 1995); Bradley J. Longfield, *The Presbyterian Controversy: Fundamentalists, Modernists and Moderates* (New York: Oxford University Press, 1991).

12. James Barr, *Fundamentalism* (Philadelphia: Westminster, 1977), 1.

13. Nancy T. Ammerman, "North American Protestant Fundamentalism," in *Fundamentalism Project*, ed. Martin Marty and Appleby, 1:4–8.

14. On the difficulty scholars have had relating confessionalism to liberalism and conservatism see D. G. Hart, *The Lost Soul of American Protestantism* (Lanham, MD: Rowman and Littlefield, 2002).

J. Gresham Machen (1881–1937), Ned B. Stonehouse (1902–62), and the Lutheran Robert Preus (1924–95) have confessed confidence in Scripture and defended that belief intelligently without falling into obscurantism. Harold Bloom, in his often brilliant book *The American Religion*, gets to the heart of the problem of the definition of fundamentalism. "Real fundamentalists," he says, "would find their archetype in the formidable J. Gresham Machen. . . ." Commenting on Machen's *Christianity and Liberalism* (1923), Bloom says, "I have just read my way through this, with distaste and discomfort but with reluctant and growing admiration for Machen's mind. I have never seen a stronger case made for the argument that institutional Christianity must regard cultural liberalism an enemy of faith." He concluded that if "Machen, a scholar and an intellect, is rightly called a Fundamentalist, then I must insist that Wally Amos Criswell and his swarm be called something else, and Know-Nothings will do very nicely."[15]

In certain important respects, Bloom has identified the problem precisely. J. Gresham Machen, whom D. G. Hart has called "an unlikely Fundamentalist," did make common cause with them against those who wanted to retain the form of Christianity while denying its doctrinal and historical substance.[16] The older fundamentalists were defending the proposition that there are certain irreducible truths that Christians must affirm and teach. Indeed, by some standards, those things that were taught in the famous twelve-volume publication titled *The Fundamentals* (1910–15) would today be considered remarkably broadminded.[17]

In the last fifty years, however, the word "fundamentalist" has taken on another and less worthy sense. It has come to describe an attitude which is needlessly narrow, fearful, and desirous of an illegitimate certainty about things on which it is not only possible to be uncertain, but regarding which, in some cases at least, it may even be more Reformed, that is, more faithful to the Reformed theology, piety, and practice, and to the benefit of the church to be nondogmatic. This is not a new point of view in American Reformed circles. Writing in the mid-1920s and concerned

15. Harold Bloom, *The American Religion: The Emergence of the Post-Christian Nation* (New York: Simon and Schuster, 1992), 228.

16. Hart, *Lost Soul*, 88.

17. R. A. Torrey, ed., *The Fundamentals*, 12 vols. (Chicago: Testimony, 1910–15).

about the growing influence of fundamentalism in Reformed Christianity, R. B. Kuiper admitted to being a fundamentalist in the lower case, but not a "Fundamentalist" in the upper case, because, as he said, "The objection which the Reformed or Calvinistic Christian has to Fundamentalism may, I believe, be stated in these few words: there is in it a rather pronounced strain of Anabaptism."[18] He continued by noting that his concerns were identical to those of Herman Bavinck. Because they devalue nature, or rather conflate nature with the supernatural, the Fundamentalists do not appreciate that God uses ordinary means, and therefore, for instance, they do not "value sufficiently a broad liberal education as the foundation of theological training," that is to say, they are anti-intellectual.[19] They do not understand that the proper antipode and effective antidote to modernism (theological liberalism) is not Fundamentalism, but Calvinism.[20]

6/24 Creation as a Boundary Marker

The modern controversy over the length of the days of creation is a prime illustration of the rise of the QIRC in the Reformed community. This debate is not wrong in itself, and I am not taking sides on the exegetical issues, but I do want to call attention to the meaning of the QIRC use of their interpretation of Genesis 1 as a standard of Reformed orthodoxy.[21] At least one North American denomination has taken an official position in favor of the six-day, twenty-four-hour interpretation of the days of creation in Genesis 1.[22] Three other members of NAPARC have received

18. R. B. Kuiper, *As to Being Reformed* (Grand Rapids: Eerdmans, 1926), 77.

19. Ibid., 78.

20. Ibid., 81. See also Hart, *Lost Soul*, 123–33.

21. See, e.g., David G. Hagopian, ed., *The Genesis Debate: Three Views on the Days of Creation* (Mission Viejo, CA: Crux, 2001); Joseph A. Pipa Jr. and David W. Hall, eds., *Did God Create in Six Days?* (Taylors, SC and Oak Ridge, TN: Southern Presbyterian Press and The Covenant Foundation, 1999). Among the more important essays on this topic are: Meredith G. Kline, "Because It Had Not Rained," *WTJ* 20 (1958): 146–57; Mark D. Futato, "Because It Had Rained: A Study of Genesis 2:5–7 with Implications for Gen 2:4–5 and Gen 1:1–2:3," *WTJ* 60 (1998): 1–21; Robert Letham, "'In the Space of Six Days': The Days of Creation from Origen to the Westminster Assembly," *WTJ* 61 (1999): 149–74.

22. The RCUS position paper adopted by the 253rd Synod in 1999 is available online, "The Days of Creation," RCUS Position Papers, http://www.rcus.org/main/pub_papers. asp (accessed 15 February 2007). See the published minutes in *The Reformed Church in*

lengthy committee reports or adopted positions calling for a conservative pluralism.[23] Creation continues to function as a doctrinal litmus test. Why? For the most part, the debate over the days of creation has had little do with the Reformed confession. Proponents of 6/24 creation as a mark of Reformed orthodoxy have been unable to explain the *theological* reason for making the 6/24 interpretation a standard of orthodoxy. Their first argument seems to be that the Bible teaches the 6/24 interpretation, and if we do not believe the Bible on this matter, then, in principle, we do not believe it anywhere. This argument, of course, is as fallacious today as when Martin Luther made it against Huldrych Zwingli at Marburg (1529). Luther argued that anyone who did not agree with his interpretation of this passage did not believe the Bible. No Reformed theologian, however, should concede this argument, and neither should we concede the use of 6/24 creation as a marker of Reformed orthodoxy.

The second argument appeals to the language of WCF 4.1: "In the space of six days. . . ." David Hall argues that the original understanding of the phrase is determined by what most of the divines believed about the creation days.[24] He argues that they understood Genesis to teach 6/24 creation; therefore the phrase "in the space of six days," if inter-

---

the United States: Abstract of the Minutes of the 253rd Synod (Bakersfield and Shafter, CA: Ebenezer Reformed Church and Grace Reformed Church, 1999), 50–70. The Free Reformed Churches of North America also confess 6/24 creation. See http://www.frcna.org/WhoWeAre/Believe.ASP#13 (accessed 1 September 2007).

23. The report received by the Presbyterian Church in America, "The Report of the Creation Study Committee," PCA Historical Center, is at http://www.pcahistory.org/creation/report.html (accessed 15 February 2007). Also see the published minutes in *Minutes of the Twenty-Eighth General Assembly of the Presbyterian Church in America* (Atlanta: The Presbyterian Church in America, 2000), 122–212. The report received by the Orthodox Presbyterian Church is at http://www.opc.org/GA/CreationReport.pdf (accessed 15 February 2007). Also see the published minutes in *Minutes of the Seventy-First General Assembly: Meeting at Geneva College, Beaver Falls, PA, June 2–8, 2004 and Yearbook of the Orthodox Presbyterian Church* (Willow Grove, PA: The Orthodox Presbyterian Church, 2004), 193–350. In 2001 Synod Escondido of the United Reformed Churches in North America declared, "God created all things good in six days defined as evenings and mornings (Genesis 1 & 2 and Exodus 20:11). This means that we reject any evolutionary teaching, including theistic evolution, concerning the origin of the earth and of all creatures (Heidelberg Catechism, Lord's Day IX)." *Minutes of the Fourth Synod of the United Reformed Churches in North America Held Tuesday, June 5 through Thursday, June 7, 2001 at Escondido United Reformed Church, Escondido, California,* Article 43.

24. See Pipa and Hall, eds., *Did God Create in Six Days?*

preted according to original intent, meant six calendar days. From this Hall concludes that those who do not hold the same view of creation as held by the divines should take an exception to the Standards. William Barker responds by observing that the Westminster divines were probably responding to Sir Thomas Browne's advocacy of Augustine's view of instantaneous creation.[25] In other words, the question Hall is asking and the question the divines were answering are not identical. He further challenges Hall's claim that, in fact, twenty-one divines held the 6/24 view. Barker argues that the divines were familiar with the views of a variety of authors who did not necessarily hold to creation in six twenty-four-hour days. He is willing to concede that only five of the divines actually held Hall's view.[26] He notes other ambiguities, such as John Lightfoot's view that the first day was thirty-six hours long.[27] It seems clear that the intent of the divines was to preclude (what they perceived to be) Augustine's nominalist view of the days of Genesis 1 as a literary device without any genuine connection to the actual acts of creation itself. The fact remains that the language is ambiguous and has not been received by the American Presbyterian churches as precluding non–6/24 views.

The irony of using the 6/24 interpretation as a boundary marker of orthodoxy is that it threatens to let the wrong people in and keep the right people out. Ronald L. Numbers has shown that one of the primary sources of the creationist movement is not orthodox Reformed theology but the Seventh Day Adventist movement, the distinguishing beliefs of which have little in common with the Reformed confession.[28] From the middle of the nineteenth century through the middle of the twentieth century, virtually none of the leading Reformed theologians held or taught that Scripture teaches that God created the world in six twenty-four-hour periods.[29]

25. William S. Barker, "The Westminster Assembly on the Days of Creation: A Reply to David W. Hall," *WTJ* 62 (2000): 115.

26. Ibid., 116–17.

27. Ibid., 118.

28. Ronald L. Numbers, *The Creationists: The Evolution of Scientific Creationism* (New York: Alfred A. Knopf, 1992). This fact does not make the 6/24 view incorrect. The point is that there is nothing distinctively Reformed about the 6/24 view such that it serves as an adequate boundary marker of Reformed orthodoxy.

29. Herman Bavinck's views are published in *Reformed Dogmatics*, vol. 2, *God and Creation*, ed. John Bolt, trans. John Vriend (Grand Rapids: Baker Academic, 2004), 406–39.

There was then no question whether Charles Hodge (1797–1878), B. B. Warfield (1851–1921), Herman Bavinck (1854–1921), and J. Gresham Machen (1881–1937) were sound, orthodox, biblically faithful, confessional Reformed theologians. Today, however, such questions are being raised. The perception of these theologians has changed in the Reformed community. This change in perception suggests that our theological priorities have moved. Any boundary marker, however, that includes the Adventists and excludes Hodge, Warfield, Bavinck, and Machen should not commend itself to confessional Reformed folk as a way to mark out Reformed identity.

Most importantly, one's view of the length of the creation days is an improper boundary marker, because it does not arise from the interests of the Reformed confession itself but has been imported from fundamentalism. The elevation of an extraconfessional, exegetical disagreement to the level of a boundary marker, despite the fact that there is nothing obviously at stake in Reformed theology as confessed by our churches, is a strong indicator of the presence of the QIRC (an anticonfessional fundamentalism) in our midst. Hodge, Warfield, Bavinck, and Machen, however, also came to their views *exegetically*, and they did so in the interests of advancing a Reformed reading of Scripture, and after intelligent and careful interaction with modern claims about the physical world. Arguably, in the fundamentalist reaction to the turn in our culture away from the Judeo-Christian explanation of creation and toward the elevation of evolution as a religio-cultural dogma, some in the Reformed sideline churches have asked questions of the biblical text which the text itself does not seem to answer very clearly. It seems wise to agree with Luther's response to the allegorical interpretation of the days when he said: "If, then, we do not understand the nature of the days or have no insight into why God wanted to make use of these intervals of time, let us confess our lack of

---

See also Charles Hodge, *Systematic Theology*, 3 vols. (New York: Scribner, Armstrong, 1873), 1:557–58, 70–73; B. B. Warfield, "Calvin's Doctrine of Creation," in *Calvin and Calvinism* (New York: Oxford University Press, 1931), 287–349. J. Gresham Machen was one of the founders of Westminster Theological Seminary and the Orthodox Presbyterian Church. His day-age views were published in *The Christian View of Man* (London: Banner of Truth, reprint, 1984), 115–16. Though Meredith Kline did not invent the framework interpretation, he is perhaps the best-known advocate of it.

understanding rather than distort the words, contrary to their context, into a foreign meaning."[30] The great tragedy of the modern creation controversy is that, while we in the Reformed sideline have been arguing about the length of the creation days, many of our congregants, even those in denominations that hold a 6/24-creation view, have stopped believing in "creation" or "nature" altogether. While congregants will confess a 6/24 creation, many of them no longer think of the world as something created by God, with inherent limits on our choices. In Reformed terms, many of us no longer think and live as if we are creatures, as if there are such things as nature and providence.[31]

Anthropologist Thomas De Zengotita has described the late or liquid modern approach to reality by speaking of "options." By "options" he means what Cornelius Van Til (1895–1987) meant by "autonomy."[32] For De Zengotita, in contrast to premodernity, where reality was conceived as the result of divine providence, in modernity we became "haunted by the knowledge that everything could be otherwise."[33] We became uniquely self-conscious, so that it has become increasingly difficult to distinguish the mediated from the real, and this mediated and virtual reality has created a panoply of choices to which we autonomous, reality-creating moderns have become accustomed. He calls the unending collage of options "the Blob."[34] The mediation of modern life ("the Blob") resists limits. "The Blob will not tolerate edges."[35] Modernity or mediation, that is, the self-constructed, self-conscious reality distinct to this age, authorizes eclecticism.[36] "The Blob is all about having it both ways. Or more."[37] In late modernity choice is ultimate and the chooser sovereign.

---

30. *WA*, 1:4.

31. Thomas De Zengotita, *Mediated: How the Media Shapes Your World and the Way You Live in It* (New York and London: Bloomsbury, 2005). The brief account of De Zengotita's argument is borrowed from R. Scott Clark, "Whosoever Will Be Saved: Emerging Church? Meet Christian Dogma," in *Reforming or Conforming? Post-Conservative Evangelicals and the Emerging Church*, ed. Gary Johnson (Wheaton, IL: Crossway, 2008).

32. See, e.g., Cornelius Van Til, *The Defense of the Faith* (Philadelphia: Presbyterian and Reformed, 1955), 34–35.

33. De Zengotita, *Mediated*, 43.

34. Ibid., 23.

35. Ibid., 26.

36. Ibid., 259–60.

37. Ibid., 61.

Friedrich Nietzsche was right about modernity: the point of the entire enterprise was to be done with God and limits.[38] Late modernism is high-tech narcissism.[39] In this context, by obsessing on the length of the days of creation, rather than on the existence of nature itself, in the sideline churches, having strained at gnats, we have swallowed the camel of late modernity. This is all quite opposed to the concerns of the narrative in Genesis 1–2. As shall be discussed in chapter 7, the creation narrative is interested in establishing a creational pattern of work and rest and in the existence of an eschatological blessedness (heaven), not in answering our post-Darwinian questions about the length of the creation days.

The other question before us is what to do with general revelation. The 6/24 view may be the correct interpretation of Genesis 1, but it has not been accepted by inerrantist, Bible-believing, confessional Reformed interpreters, theologians, and churches as the only or even the most obvious view since about the 1840s, about the same time the West was faced most directly with the crisis presented by modern science and the theory of evolution. At issue here is how we ought to relate the two books of revelation, nature and Scripture. There is no question that special revelation (Holy Scripture) always has the priority over general revelation (nature), but it is equally clear that we cannot read Scripture properly without some knowledge of general revelation. When Scripture says that our Lord cursed a fig tree (Mark 11:12–14, 20–24), it does not tell us what a fig tree is, or how it propagates or is best cultivated. The purpose of the account of the cursing of the fig tree is to tell us about the nature of faith and our Lord's expectations of the fruit which comes from faith (BC 24).

The struggle over how to relate the two books of revelation did not begin, however, in the nineteenth century. We faced this very same question earlier in our history, and the way we resolved that crisis may be instructive to us today. It is no longer revolutionary (no pun intended) to hold that our universe is heliocentric, that is, the earth revolves around the sun, but it was not always so. For thousands of years, until the middle of the sixteenth century, the views of Aristotle (384–322 B.C.) and Ptolemy (c. A.D. 100–178) controlled astronomy. They held that we live in a geocentric

38. Ibid., 265.
39. Ibid., 275.

universe, that is, that the sun revolves around the earth.[40] Our unaided sense experience does seem to suggest that the earth does not move and that the sun does. Aristotle's influence over Western culture during this same period was enormous. Until the eighteenth century, every student learned grammar, logic, and rhetoric (the *trivium*) using his *Organon* or some textbook derived from it. Those who advanced to the *quadrivium* (music, math, astronomy, geometry) also studied classical astronomy. The geocentric view was one of those propositions which, until questioned, seemed unassailable to all reasonable minds.

In the sixteenth century, however, some began to question geocentrism. The observations of Nicholas Copernicus (1473–1543) that the earth moves, and that the universe is heliocentric and not geocentric, met with a mixed reaction. Some Protestants, among them Andreas Osiander (1498–1552), supported Copernicus; but others were highly critical, for example, the great Protestant theologian Philipp Melanchthon (1497–1560) criticized the Copernican theory in 1549.[41] John Calvin's attitude toward Copernicus has been the subject of considerable scholarly debate. In his *Warfare of Science with Theology* (1896), Andrew Whyte claimed that Calvin, in his commentary on Genesis, asked in reference to Copernicus, "Who will venture to place the authority of Copernicus above that of the Holy Spirit?"[42] In fact, there is no reference to Copernicus by name in Calvin's lectures on Genesis. The closest thing one can find there is a comment in the *argumentum*: "We certainly are not ignorant that the circuit of the heavens is finite, and earth like a little globe is located in the middle."[43] He probably assumed the geocentric view, but his point was to defend the finitude of creation. Some scholars have argued that there

40. Maurice A. Finochiaro, *Galileo on the World Systems: A New Abridged Translation* (Berkeley: University of California Press, 1997), 1–28. He notes also that Copernicus did not invent heliocentrism. He updated "an idea advanced in various forms by the Pythagoreans, by Aristarchus, and by other astronomers in ancient Greece" (ibid., 29).

41. See Christopher Kaiser, "Calvin, Copernicus and Castellio," *CTJ* 21 (1986): 8–9. On the background of the controversy, see Christopher Kaiser, *Creation and the History of Science* (Grand Rapids and London: Eerdmans and Marshall Pickering, 1991), 120–86.

42. Whyte's claim has been influential. For example, Thomas Kuhn, *The Copernican Revolution: Planetary Astronomy in the Development of Western Thought* (Cambridge, MA: Harvard University Press, 1957), 192, followed him verbatim.

43. "Nos certe non ignoramus finitum esse coeli circuitum, et terram instar globuli in medio locatam esse" (*CO*, 23:9–10).

is no evidence that Calvin had ever heard of Copernicus or the heliocentric astronomy, and others argue that in at least one of his sermons, on 1 Corinthians 10:19–24, he publicly rejected the Copernican, heliocentric view. Christopher Kaiser has argued quite plausibly, however, that Calvin was most likely not referring to Copernicus, but to the heretic Sebastian Castellio in the sermon. Kaiser has concluded that, at most, Calvin was opposed to the idea of a geodynamic universe.[44]

Copernicus's observations were modified by Tycho Brahe (1546–1601) and his student Johannes Kepler (1571–1630). The question of the tenability of the traditional view became more intense. Perhaps in response, in 1575 Calvin's student and Beza's colleague in Geneva, Lambert Daneau (1530–95), published a sort of catechism for his students on *Christian Natural Philosophy*.[45] Writing a sort of apologetic for a biblical view of creation and natural philosophy, Daneau said it is no surprise that the (pagan) philosophers are of divided opinion as to the nature of things, since they are ignorant (*ignaros*) of God's truth (*de veritate Dei*).[46] What is more mysterious is how Christians have become so divided. The reason for the division, he said, was that too many Christians have become imbued and tainted with pagan philosophical ideas.[47] He argued that the early church fathers were unable to overcome their non-Christian philosophical training after their conversion to Christianity. He took it as his mandate to "emend from the Word of God" (*emendandi ex Dei verbo*) the opinions of the philosophers.[48] His primary aim was what we today might call a Christian worldview. He intended to defend certain general principles, for example, "the miracle of the creation of the world" (*miraculam creationis mundi*), which come from Scripture, but also some particulars, for example, that creatures have par-

44. Kaiser, "Calvin, Copernicus and Castellio." To survey the debate see Richard Gamble, ed., *Calvin and Science* (New York: Garland, 1992). Davis A. Young, *John Calvin and the Natural World* (Lanham, MD: University Press of America, 2007), catalogues many of Calvin's comments on the natural sciences and offers a geologist's analysis of them.

45. Lambert Daneau, *Physicē Christiana sive, Christiana de Rerum Creatarum Origine et Usu Disputatio* (Geneva, 1575), in Daneau, *Opuscula Omnia Theologica* (Geneva, 1583). This treatise was translated into English as *The Wonderfull Woorkmanship of the World* (London, 1578).

46. Daneau, *Opuscula Omnia Theologica*, 226.

47. Ibid.

48. Ibid.

ticular natures, which is learned from natural philosophy.[49] As a result of considering such things as a matter of art and theology, we will come to praise God all the more ardently.[50] He argued that, as in every art, distinctions must be made. Theology per se is "the promises of eternal life" (*vitae aeternae promissiones*). Natural philosophy (physics) is the study of the "visible world" (*visibilis mundi*).[51] Nevertheless, he asserted, "a natural philosophy is contained in the sacred Scriptures."[52]

According to Daneau, Scripture confirms our universal sense perceptions, hence his belief in geocentrism. Where he did not believe that Scripture was clear, he was agnostic. For example, he surveyed a variety of ancient opinions about the shape of the earth. The student asks whether any of these opinions (*sententiae*) are true. Daneau replies, "God himself knows. We who read nowhere in his Word these matters clearly defined . . . often fall into contrary opinions and are divided."[53] He adduced biblical passages (Job 22:14; Isa. 40:22) which seemed to him to suggest the world is round (*rotundam*), and he thought the world was round, but he refused to make it a matter of orthodoxy.

The argument intensified when Galileo (1564–1642) publicly attacked the traditional view while advocating his revision of the heliocentric astronomy. The invention of the telescope in 1608 and Galileo's improvement of it in 1609 made things even more difficult for the traditional view. Using the new telescope, Galileo was able to observe the surface of the moon, Jupiter and its satellites, and the phases of Venus, and he marked the rotation of the sun on its own axis.[54] The empirical evidence against the traditional view was mounting. In reaction, the Roman church placed Copernicus's book *The Sidereal Messenger* (1610) on the index of forbidden books (1616) and later arrested, tried, and condemned him (1633).[55]

49. Ibid., 228–29.
50. Ibid., 229.
51. Ibid., 230.
52. "Ergo Physica etiam his ipsiis Literis sacris continentur." Ibid.
53. "Deus ipse novit. Nos autem qui ex eius verbo ista aperte definita nusquam legimus . . . saepe in contrarias sententias discendimus et distrahimur." Ibid., 238.
54. Finochiaro, *Galileo on the World Systems*, 36.
55. On the Roman Catholic reaction to Galileo, see Richard J. Blackwell, *Galileo, Bellarmine and the Bible* (South Bend, IN: Notre Dame University Press, 1991).

Following Daneau, the leading theologian at the University of Utrecht Gijsbert Voetius (1589–1676) opposed not only the radical new epistemology of René Descartes (*cogito ergo sum*),[56] but he also opposed the introduction of the Copernican astronomy to the University of Utrecht.[57] He knew that one's astronomy was not "fundamental to religion," but given that universal sense perception is that the sun moves and earth does not, and given that Scripture seems to speak this way, and given that even Tycho Brahe, who advanced the new astronomy, had recently presented a system which was more compatible to Scripture, there was little reason to accept the Copernican-Cartesian view over the older view.[58]

Even though by the turn of the eighteenth century, Descartes and Christian Wolff (1679–1754) had won the war and modernity was gaining momentum, the respected theologian Herman Witsius (1636–1708), who taught at Franeker and Leiden, expressed skepticism about Kepler's "optical tube" (*tubam opticam*) through which he claimed to have seen not only the moon, but its earthlike geography and even "stupendous" (*stupendae*) men on the moon "working at their labors."[59] The Frisian pastor, Wilhelmus à Brakel (1635–1711), while acknowledging Calvin's principle of accommodation, nevertheless held out for the geocentric view on the

56. See René Descartes, "Meditatio Secunda 2.3," in *Meditationes de Prima Philosophia/ Meditations on First Philosophy, a Bilingual Edition*, ed. George Heffernan (Notre Dame, IN: University of Notre Dame, 1990), 100–101. Though Descartes did not actually *say* "cogito ergo sum," it is a fair summary of his argument. He said, "So that—all things having been weighed enough, and more, this statement were, finally, to be established: '*I* am, *I* exist' (ego sum, ergo existo) is necessarily true so often as it is uttered by me or conceived by the mind" (emphasis original).

57. See J. A. van Ruler, *The Crisis of Causality: Voetius and Descartes on God, Nature and Change* (Leiden: Brill, 1995).

58. Theo Verbeek, "From 'Learned Ignorance' to Skepticism: Descartes and Calvinist Orthodoxy," in *Skepticism and Irreligion in the Seventeenth and Eighteenth Centuries*, ed. Richard H. Popkin and Arjo Vanderjagt (Leiden: Brill, 1993), 42. The primary and secondary literature on this episode contradicts the claim made by John Leith in 1973 and repeated in 1999 by Robert Letham that by the mid-seventeenth century "orthodox theology [was] already being carried on in isolation from the intellectual currents of the day." See Letham, "'In the Space of Six Days,'" 18.

59. "Se laborantes vidisse operarios." Herman Witsius, *Exercitationes Sacrae in Symbolum Quod Apostolorum Dicitur et in Orationem Dominicam*, 3rd ed. (Amsterdam, 1697), 8.78.136.

basis of Hebrews 11:3; Psalms 19:5–6; 104:5; and Joshua 10:13.[60] To be sure, Voetius, Witsius, and à Brakel were not alone in their suspicion of the new science. Maurice A. Finochiaro has pointed out that during the "Galileo Affair" (1613–33), many churchmen sided with Galileo's heliocentric views, or at least his right to hold them, and many natural philosophers (scientists) opposed him.[61]

Thus, because he held what now seems to have been a backward view of science, Voetius should not be considered anti-intellectual. Aza Goudriaan demonstrates that Voetius was anything but anti-intellectual. In his first disputation he defended the harmony of naturally revealed philosophical truth and specially revealed theological truth.[62] He was engaged in a complex argument (epistemology, cosmology, theology) and the theological stakes were high. As J. A. van Ruler's account makes clear, Voetius opposed Descartes root and branch because at stake in the discussion was not just new theories of corpuscular blood circulation but the nature of man and his relations to God. If Descartes was correct, the heart was nothing more than a machine which bore no substantial relations to the human soul. Did God, at creation, establish the nature of things and operate immanently through second causes or not? Did God give things their *quiddity* (that which makes them what they are) or not?[63] Voetius judged the traditional Christian appropriation and revision of Aristotelian vocabulary and categories against the proposed Cartesian mechanist physics "in terms of their ability to define the relation between God, the Creator and Nature, His creation."[64] Descartes' approach did mark a turn to a deistic understanding of the world. He was deliberately

60. Wilhelmus à Brakel, *The Christian's Reasonable Service*, trans. Bartel Elshout, 4 vols. (Ligonier, PA: Soli Deo Gloria, 1992), 275.

61. Finochiaro, *Galileo*, 3.

62. Aza Goudriaan, *Reformed Orthodoxy and Philosophy, 1625–1750: Gisbertus Voetius, Petrus Van Mastricht, and Anthonius Driessen*, ed. Wim Janse, Church History 26 (Leiden and Boston: Brill, 2006), 29–32.

63. Van Ruler, *The Crisis of Causality*, 60. One might take issue with van Ruler's general handling of Voetius. He ignores the contemporary literature on Reformed scholasticism, and as a consequence he juxtaposes Voetius the "neo-Scholastic" with Descartes (e.g., 170), whom he admits to be a scholastic, but does not call him such. His account would have been more helpful had he juxtaposed Voetius's theological or Reformed scholasticism with Descartes's mechanistic or deistic scholasticism.

64. Ibid., 318, 107.

pushing God out of nature, creating a vacuum which was filled in the late seventeenth century with "nature." Voetius understood the potential inherent in the Cartesian system. His concerns about dehumanization were not entirely remote from some being voiced today. Ellen Ullman has recently highlighted the hubris of the search for computerized artificial intelligence and the hope that programmers may soon create a "post-human" yet "spiritual" machine.[65]

As has often happened, Voetius, finding himself in a difficult position, in an apologetic mode, found himself defending his categories and vocabulary in the interests of what was even more important to him, the truth of Scripture and the reality of God's tripersonal transcendence and immanence and providence.[66] As Theo Verbeek has shown, Voetius was arguing for what the medieval theologians had called "learned ignorance" (*doctrina ignorantia*).[67] Learned ignorance means recognizing the limits of the human intellect, but it also requires serious learning and engagement with the issues of the day.[68] Voetius sensed that the autonomous rationalism which we know as modernity was present in Descartes. He was trying to protect the validity of universal sense perception of how the world works and the authority of Holy Scripture. If the Cartesians won the day, not only might the traditional Christian explanation of things be not as compelling, but the very foundation of Christianity, the final authority of Scripture, would be lost.

Though most confessional Reformed Christians today might not find compelling the Christian Aristotelianism of Daneau, Voetius, and others, and though we would blanch occasionally at their use of Scripture, their principles for dealing with the crisis should remain interesting to us.

65. Ellen Ullman, "Programming the Post-Human," *Harper's*, October 2002, 60–70.

66. *Pace* van Ruler, *The Crisis of Causality*, 308, who, though he admits Voetius was defending the faith, argues that he was defending Aristotle even more vehemently. He contrasts Voetius's and Zanchi's use of Aristotle with Daneau's rather more critical appropriation of the philosopher. Setting aside Zanchi for the moment, the comparison may be somewhat unfair to Voetius who was facing a direct threat of the sort that Daneau did not. The difference between 1575 and 1640 is more than just sixty-five years. In 1575, whatever modernity would become, it was still quite inchoate. In 1640, however, its implications were much clearer, and Christian Aristotelianism was virtually Voetius's only refuge in a debate of this sort.

67. Verbeek, "From 'Learned Ignorance' to Skepticism: Descartes and Calvinist Orthodoxy," 34.

68. Ibid., 41.

Scripture, they argued, establishes the general theological principles (e.g., the divine attributes, the Creator/creature distinction, the two natures of Christ, that humans are body and soul) that become the lens through which one interprets general revelation. We learn particulars, however, from the study of general revelation. Just as we learn grammar, logic, and rhetoric from non-Christian classical sources, so we learn science from botanists and biologists. The difference between Daneau and us is that we have learned a different science. We have also modified our use of Scripture. We are using Calvin's principle of accommodation (about which more shall be said in chapter 7), but applying it to different texts than Daneau and Voetius did. Ironically, in this question anyway, we now follow the hermeneutic of Galileo more closely than that of à Brakel.[69]

The passages to which à Brakel appealed in defense of geocentrism or the passages to which Daneau appealed to support his view of the shape of the earth have not changed. Isaiah 40:22 still says that God sits "enthroned above the circle of the earth." Psalm 104:5 still says, "He set the earth on its foundations; / it can never be moved" (NIV). Neither has the confessional Reformed commitment to the truth of these passages changed. What has changed, however, is our interpretation of those passages. It is not mere coincidence that our interpretation of those passages changed at the same time our scientific views changed. As Thomas Kuhn has described it, there was a "paradigm shift" from the geocentric to the heliocentric view and Reformed Christians participated in that shift.[70] As it became more and more untenable to believe that the earth is the center of the universe and that the earth is a flat disc in space, the claim that Psalm 104:5 and Isaiah 40:22 teach those things also became untenable. Over time, the new science changed our interpretation of Scripture. We abandoned geocentrism because the evidence gradually became so overwhelming that we were forced to reconsider our interpretation of

69. Galileo said, "It pleased the Holy Spirit to accommodate the words of Sacred Scripture to the capacities of the common man in such matters as do not concern his salvation." "Galileo's Unpublished Notes," in Blackwell, *Galileo*, 270.

70. Thomas Kuhn, *The Structure of Scientific Revolutions*, 2d ed. (Chicago: University of Chicago Press, 1970). See also Michael Polanyi, *Personal Knowledge: Towards a Post-Critical Philosophy*, corrected ed. (Chicago: University of Chicago Press, 1962); idem, *Science, Faith and Society* (Chicago: University of Chicago Press, 1964).

Scripture. Today, not only would no thoughtful Bible interpreter advance the notion that these passages intend to teach a particular view of the shape of the earth or its relations to the sun, few would think of even using Scripture in such a way. This fact does not shock us anymore, because the process began more than four hundred fifty years ago. We have grown up in a world which takes a heliocentric universe for granted, in much the same way that the classic Reformed theologians grew up in a world which assumed a geocentric or geostatic universe.

It is noteworthy that the views of Copernicus were known when the BC (1561) and the HC (1563) were published. The Westminster divines did their work in the midst of Voetius's controversy with Descartes. Nevertheless, none of the sixteenth- or seventeenth-century confessional standards spoke to the controversy. They left us free to wrestle with the hermeneutical implications of the new learning. In our relative silence, we pursued a different course from our Lutheran friends who made certain scientific claims in their confessions (e.g., garlic ruins the power of magnets) which provoke smiles of embarrassment now.[71]

As it turns out, geocentrism rested upon deductions from Scripture which were not "good and necessary" (WCF 1.6), which accorded with a long and honored tradition, with common sense perception, but which tradition and perception proved to be wrong. Thus, Voetius's "learned ignorance" continues to serve us, even if his astronomy does not. There are certain claims about the physical universe which we are bound to make on biblical and therefore on confessional grounds. The resurrection of Jesus is the most important example of such a problem. Some old-fashioned modernist scientists might tell us that resurrections cannot happen. We could admit that it was unusual, and that even some at the time wanted empirical evidence—which our Lord graciously supplied (John 20:27). Nevertheless, anyone who says "cannot" has not made a purely scientific but rather a religious claim. Only God knows about "can" and "cannot." The unusual is some distance from the impossible.

From the confessional point of view, it is not necessary to do bad science or bad exegesis in order to be Reformed. Despite the fact that there

71. *The Formula of Concord*, The Epitome, 1.15, in Timothy Wengert and Charles Arand, eds., *The Book of Concord* (Minneapolis: Fortress, 2000), 489.

have been scientific revolutions since Copernicus, despite the fact that we now dissent from the scientific views of some of the classic Reformed theologians, we do not dissent from their theology, piety, and practice. What makes us Reformed is not that we agree (or disagree) with their science, but that we still confess the same theology. To use the older category of interpretation: we should accept the *substance* of their theology, that is, that which makes it what it is, but not necessarily its *accidents*, that is, that which can be eliminated without affecting their theology. Thus the creation controversy, unlike the fundamentalist-modernist controversy of the 1920s and 1930s, is not about whether the Christian faith is true or even whether the historic confessional Reformed faith is true, but about which interpretation of the inspired inerrant Scriptures is true. This intramural debate is not between two religions, as Machen had it so brilliantly in 1923, between *Christianity and Liberalism,* and not even between different hermeneutical principles, but rather it is a debate over the application of those principles and specific exegetical conclusions.[72]

Theonomy/Reconstructionism

Another major evidence of the QIRC within the Reformed churches is the rise of theonomic or reconstructionist ethics.[73] In response, at least two North American denominations have erected study committees on theonomy, with one of them taking a strong official stance against it.[74] Nevertheless, the movement continues to attract adherents within and

72. J. Gresham Machen, *Christianity and Liberalism* (New York: Macmillan, 1923).

73. These are distinct movements but they are sufficiently interrelated to allow them to be treated together for the purposes of this work. For a brief account of the Christian Reconstruction movement see R. Scott Clark, s.v., "Christian Reconstruction," in *The New Dictionary of Christian Apologetics,* ed. Walter Campbell Campbell-Jack, Garvin J. McGrath, and C. Stephen Evans (Leicester, UK and Downers Grove, IL: InterVarsity, 2006).

74. In 1979, the Seventh General Assembly of the PCA adopted four points of "definition and recommendations regarding theonomy." They rejected theonomy as a standard of orthodoxy, but they also refused to rule it unorthodox. In 1987, however, the RCUS adopted two recommendations, the second of which says, "It is the position of the RCUS that the Heidelberg Catechism teaches that the ceremonial and judicial laws instituted by Moses have been entirely abolished and done away with by the coming of Christ, as far as it relates to obligation and obedience on our part. The moral law, however, has not been abolished as it respects obedience, but only as it respects the curse and constraint." See Reformed Church

without Reformed churches, and at least one Reformed denomination is closely identified with the movement.[75]

It is a historical fact that when our confession was formed Christendom and the righteousness of theocracy (the civil enforcement of the first table of the Decalogue) were assumed. Theocracy, however, is not theonomy, or "the abiding validity of the law of God in exhaustive detail."[76] Advocates of theonomy have either blurred the distinction between theocracy and theonomy or simply ignored it as they appeal to the premodern Reformed theologians in support of their agenda. When writers such as Calvin and Rutherford are read in their own historical context, they are not found to be arguing for anything like the absolute moral necessity of the application of the Mosaic civil laws and penalties to the postcanonical state.

The first half of the slogan "the abiding validity of the law of God in exhaustive detail" is not controversial among confessional Reformed folk. No confessional churches or theologians doubt or deny the abiding validity of God's law, but the slogan omits crucial distinctions. The formative or mainstream Reformed theologians accepted the medieval distinction between civil, ceremonial, and moral laws or the civil, ceremonial, and moral aspects of the Mosaic law. So the difficulty comes in the second half of the definition, "exhaustive detail." Of course, as Greg Bahnsen argued this, it became clear that the slogan contained a certain amount of hyperbole. After all, even the advocates of the slogan accept that the ceremonial law is abolished in Christ; thus apparently the detail is not exhaustive but selective. As a slogan, however, "the abiding validity of the law of God in selective detail" or "selective application," is probably not going to stir the blood.

The second half of the definition as understood by the theonomic reconstructionist movement is also problematic because it cannot be

in the United States, *Abstract of the Minutes of the Reformed Church in the United States 1987 Synod* (Sutton, NE: Reformed Church in the United States, 1987), 44.

75. John M. Otis, "Reformed Presbyterian Church United States Distinctives and the Westminster Standards," http://rpcus.com/?id=RPCUS_Distinctives (accessed 27 March 2007).

76. Greg Bahnsen, *Theonomy in Christian Ethics* (Phillipsburg, NJ: Presbyterian and Reformed, 1984), 39–86.

squared with the "general equity" clause of the WCF 19.4.[77] The flourishing of this movement in our churches over the last forty years suggests profound alienation from our confession. Article 30 of the Second Helvetic Confession (1566) offers perhaps the most extensive account of the duty of the civil magistrate of any of the Reformed confessional documents.[78] Against the Anabaptists, the Reformed affirmed the legitimacy of civil service as a vocation. The article continues by reaffirming the magistrate's duty to advance the welfare of the institutional church by enforcing both tables of the Decalogue. The magistrate is to perform his duty justly, execute justice on lawbreakers (including blasphemers), and conduct just wars when necessary.[79]

In the middle of the seventeenth century, the WCF reached similar conclusions. It too was written with theocratic assumptions such as the propriety of a state church. In 31.2 it assumed and confessed that magistrates may call ecclesiastical assemblies (such as the Westminster Assembly).[80] Nevertheless, the divines envisioned distinct vocations for the civil magistrate and the institutional church. Ecclesiastical assemblies are competent to address ecclesiastical matters only, and civil matters may be addressed only in extraordinary circumstances (31.4). In no case, however, do the Reformed churches confess anything like the "abiding validity of the law of God in exhaustive detail." One searches them in vain for any instruction or even intimation that the Reformed churches confess that the Mosaic civil law is still in force. Instead, we find something altogether

77. See Craig A. Troxel and Peter J. Wallace, "Men in Combat over the Civil Law: 'General Equity' in WCF 19.4," *WTJ* 64 (2002): 307–18.

78. The Second Helvetic Confession was written by Heinrich Bullinger (1504–75) in 1561 and published in 1566. It was adopted by the Swiss, French, Polish, and Hungarian Reformed churches.

79. *Creeds*, 3:907–9.

80. The American Presbyterian churches, upon adopting the Westminster Standards on 19 September 1729, took exception to "some clauses" in chapters 20 and 23 of the confession concerning the civil magistrate. In 1789, the Presbyterian Church renounced a state church and revised the last paragraph of chapter 20, the third paragraph of chapter 23, and the second paragraph of chapter 31 of the confession, removing from the magistrate the responsibility to see to the peace and purity of the church, to suppress "all blasphemies and heresies." William S. Barker, "Lord of Lords and King of Commoners: The Westminster Confession and the Relationship of Church and State," in *The Westminster Confession into the 21st Century: Essays in Remembrance of the 350th Anniversary of the Westminster Assembly*, ed. J. Ligon Duncan III, 2 vols. (Ross-shire, UK: Mentor, 2003–4), 1:423–26.

different. Despite the frequent theonomic polemic against "natural law," the WCF had no such difficulties.[81]

In contrast to the theonomic movement, the Reformed churches had no difficulty affirming the existence of natural law. Arguing on the basis of the covenant of works (7.2), the WCF says, "God gave to Adam a law, as a covenant of works, by which He bound him and all his posterity to personal, entire, exact, and perpetual obedience; promised life upon the fulfilling, and threatened death upon the breach of it; and endued him with power and ability to keep it" (19.1). This is the second time the confession mentions the covenant of works, by the way. If repetition means anything, it does suggest that this is a fundamental idea in the Reformed confession. Article 2 continues by teaching the republication of "this law": "This law, after his fall, continued to be a perfect rule of righteousness; and, as such, was delivered by God upon Mount Sinai, in ten commandments, and written in two tables; the first four commandments containing our duty towards God; and the other six, our duty to man."[82]

The phrase "covenant of works" in 19.1 is appositive to the noun "law." In this context, the "law" refers to a covenant of works. Thus, when 19.2 establishes "this law" as the subject of the verb "delivered," the reference of "this law" must be nothing but the "law" defined as a covenant of works in 19.1. The law that continues to bind all image-bearers is not said to be the Mosaic civil code but the same law delivered in creation and substantially repeated at Sinai. To be sure, God elaborated upon this law during the Israelite national covenant by giving ceremonial

81. On the natural law doctrine behind the language of the WCF see R. S. Clark, "Calvin and the Lex Naturalis," *Stulos Theological Journal* 6 (1998); David VanDrunen, *A Biblical Case for Natural Law* (Grand Rapids: Acton Institute, 2006); Stephen J. Grabill, *Rediscovering the Natural Law in Reformed Theological Ethics*, Emory University Studies in Law and Religion (Grand Rapids: Eerdmans, 2006).

82. On this article, Thomas Boston said, "How, then, one can refuse the covenant of works to have been given to the Israelites, I cannot see." These same theologians also held that Mosaic law was an administration of the covenant of grace. The doctrine of the unity of the covenant of grace and the doctrine of republication were regarded as complementary not antithetical. See his notes in Edward Fisher, *The Marrow of Modern Divinity* (Scarsdale, NY: Westminster Discount Books, n.d.), 58. The doctrine of the Decalogue as a kind of "republication" of the moral, creational law was widely held in seventeenth-century Reformed theology. See R. Scott Clark, "Letter and Spirit: Law and Gospel in Reformed Preaching," in *Covenant, Justification, and Pastoral Ministry*, 356–57 n. 87.

laws, which he abrogated in the death of Christ. He also gave civil laws to Israel, but the WCF is explicit about the fate of the civil laws. To national Israel, "as a body politic, He gave sundry judicial laws, which expired together with the state of that people, not obliging any other now, further than the general equity thereof may require." We should not miss the two key phrases for the purposes of understanding the confessional Reformed approach to the alleged "abiding validity" of the Mosaic civil law. We confess that the civil laws have "expired." This was standard Reformed doctrine.

Here is the distinction between theocracy and theonomy. The original intent of the confession was theocratic but there is no evidence that it was theonomic. The Mosaic civil laws do not oblige any noncanonical civil authority any more than the "general equity" of the civil laws may require. Whatever "general equity" does mean, there is no evidence that it means anything like "the abiding validity of the law of God in exhaustive detail." The only law that does have abiding, exhaustive validity is the natural or creational law delivered to Adam and restated at Sinai. WCF 19.5 says, in part, "The moral law doth for ever bind all, as well justified persons as others, to the obedience thereof; and that, not only in regard of the matter contained in it, but also in respect of the authority of God, the Creator, who gave it." It is the *moral* law, that is, the law delivered in creation, which survives the expiration of the Israelite national covenant.

Covenant Moralism

Of the three controversies surveyed briefly in this chapter, perhaps none of them better illustrates the diminished influence of the Reformed confession, and the rise of the QIRC in the conservative Reformed churches, than the thirty-year struggle over the doctrine of justification. The history and nature of this controversy have been discussed in detail elsewhere, and those discussions need not be repeated here.[83] What is most significant for the purposes of this essay is that the controversy exists at all, because

---

83. See footnote 9 above for bibliographic references.

there is no single doctrine in the history, theology, and confessions of the Reformed churches since the sixteenth century on which there has been more unanimity of thought and expression. The fact that there have been a controversy involving the dismissal of one faculty member from a major Reformed seminary, several official ecclesiastical committees, reports, and actions, and numerous books and articles is best explained as evidence that the Reformed confession no longer functions as the norm of theology, piety, and practice in conservative Reformed churches. What has taken its place is the QIRC.

Consider briefly the teaching of the Reformed confessions on the doctrine of justification. In BC 22, we confess that faith is something that is kindled in the hearts of the elect, that it "embraces Jesus Christ with all his merits, appropriates him, and seeks nothing more besides him." The confession continues by teaching that "either . . . all things which are requisite to our salvation are not in Jesus Christ, or if all things are in Him, then those who possess Jesus Christ through faith have complete salvation in Him." Either Christ is a complete Savior or he is not. On this basis we confess, according to the BC, that we are justified by faith alone (*sola fide*) "by faith apart from works." Furthermore, our confession is crystal clear that when we confess that we are justified through faith alone we mean to say that faith is "only an instrument with which we embrace Christ our righteousness." In other words, there is nothing intrinsic to the act of faith itself that makes it any part of the ground of justification. Rather, the ground of our justification, according to the BC, is Jesus Christ. "Imputing to us all His merits, and so many holy works which He has done for us and in our stead, [He] is our righteousness." In article 23 the confession clarifies that faith in the active obedience is only "relying and resting upon the obedience of Christ crucified alone, which becomes ours when we believe in Him." In case, however, someone might seek to find a way to redefine the Reformed definition of faith in the act of justification, article 24 asserts that, as important as Spirit-wrought sanctity (good works) is as a fruit and evidence of our justification, they play no role whatsoever as part of the ground or instrument of justification because "it is by faith in Christ that we are justified, even before we do good works."

This doctrine of justification was articulated in stark contrast to that which was propounded at the Council of Trent in 1547. At Trent, Rome declared that our cooperation is necessary toward eventual justification, that justification is a process and not a punctiliar, definitive divine declaration. Trent denied explicitly that faith, in justification, is only confidence in the divine mercy. According to Trent, under the "new law," the law can be kept by grace and cooperation with grace unto final justification. The council explicitly condemned the Protestant doctrine of justification of sinners on the basis of the imputation of Christ's alien righteousness.

If, as it has seemed to the Reformed for more than four hundred years, there is a stark difference between the Roman and Protestant doctrines of justification, and if the Reformed confession is completely clear about what we believe about justification, then there must be other reasons why this controversy exists. The first and most obvious explanation is ignorance. Too many Reformed people, even ministers and elders, are not sufficiently familiar with the basics of the Reformed doctrine of justification, its background, and its intent. Second, and more seriously, this crisis is the fruit of a sincere but misguided desire to produce sanctity among God's people. The method of the revisionists, however, is essentially that of the Romanists and the Remonstrants. In the confessional scheme, sanctity is the logically necessary result of justification. The paradox of the Protestant view is that sanctity, the goal, is not achieved by aiming at it directly, at least not when justification is in view. It was for this reason that, in his 1548 lecture on Galatians 5:6, Calvin said, "When you are engaged in discussing the question of justification, beware of allowing any mention to be made of love or of works, but resolutely adhere to the exclusive particle."[84] The "works" to which Calvin referred are condign merit, that is, Spirit-wrought sanctity that meets the terms of divine justice and congruent merit which God, according to medieval theologians, graciously imputes to our best efforts. The "love" to which Calvin referred is the Roman definition of faith in justification as "faith formed by love" (*fides formata caritate*), that is, the reality of sanctification in the life of the believer. In place of "love" and our merit in justification, Calvin pointed

---

84. "Ergo quum versaris in causa iustificationis, cave ullam caritatis vel operum mentionem admittas: sed mordicus retine particulam exclusivam." CO, 50:247.

readers to Christ's merit for believers, the benefit of which is received through faith alone. It is the qualifier alone to which Calvin referred when he spoke of the "exclusive particle." In other words, Calvin said, in effect, "do not cave into the Roman pressure to add sanctity to the instrument of justification but hold on to *sola fide.*"

According to Luther (and Calvin after him) the temptation to add human cooperation with grace, in justification, is best described as the "theology of glory" (*theologia gloriae*) in contrast to the "theology of the cross" (*theologia crucis*).[85] By this contrast Luther was warning against the confusion of the divine and the human. Christian theology is a theology of the cross. It does not seek to know God apart from his revelation in Christ. In the doctrine of justification, it does not seek to stand before God apart from the imputed righteousness of Christ. Conflation of theology as we know it with the way God knows, the theology of glory, is a form of rationalism because it diminishes the scandal of the cross and of the gospel: the justification of sinners.[86]

It was this very impulse that caused the Council of Trent, Session 6, to declare that the righteousness with which we are infused, and which increases in believers, is "preserved and also increased before God through good works" (canon 24) and that such righteousness (*iustitia*) is not "merely fruits of and signs of justification obtained."[87] In effect, Rome came to agree with Paul's critics in Romans 6:1, "Shall we sin that grace may abound?" The rationalist-moralist answer has always been to preclude anyone from thinking that it might be possible to "sin that grace may abound" by making it very clear that God justifies only good people, but any such doctrine cannot be squared with Paul's unequivocal declaration in Romans 4:5 that God "justifies the ungodly." This is the seductive power of rationalism and moralism. It seems to offer an explanation of the ways things work, but it does so at the expense of all the facts and by smoothing over difficulties. Though it makes Christianity seem more reasonable and a better path to sanctity to say or imply that God justifies the good, that is neither what Scripture teaches nor what we confess.

85. *LW*, 31:225.
86. Chapter 4 of this work is devoted to this problem.
87. H. Denzinger, *Enchiridion Symbolorum*, 30th ed. (Freiburg: Herder, 1955), 298.

Conclusions

The late or liquid modern moral collapse has not left the church untouched. It seems to challenge the very plausibility of the Christian faith and life. In response to this comprehensive sociocultural pressure, some elements with the Reformed churches have sought an illegitimate form of certainty in doctrines and practices that are not confessed by the Reformed churches and that even contradict the Reformed confession. This chapter surveyed three movements that reflect the spirit of fundamentalism, defined as the QIRC, the quest to know God in ways he has not revealed himself and to achieve epistemic and moral certainty on questions where such certainty is neither possible nor desirable. This chapter has offered a partial explanation of the rise of these movements and shown how they illustrate the quest for illegitimate religious certainty. In the next chapter, we turn our attention to the other aspect of the crisis in our churches.

This infallible assurance doth not so belong to the essence of faith, but that a true believer may wait long, and conflict with many difficulties, before he be partaker of it: yet, being enabled by the Spirit to know the things which are freely given him of God, he may, without extraordinary revelation in the right use of ordinary means, attain thereunto.

—WESTMINSTER CONFESSION OF FAITH 18.3

CHAPTER
3

The Quest for Illegitimate Religious Experience

Writing in 1844, John Williamson Nevin (1803–86) attacked the "anxious bench" not only as a "new measure," but also as heresy leading to Pelagianism.[1] Against the new measures of the Second Great Awakening, he juxtaposed the system of the catechism. As Nevin saw things, in the earlier stages of his career anyway, he set the "ordinary means" piety of the Reformed confessions against the new measures piety of revivalism.[2] The new measures against which Nevin railed may also be described as the Quest for Illegitimate Religious Experience (QIRE). This quest is one of the most ancient impulses in Christian theology. One of the great themes of the history of medieval theology is the story of the rise and influence of mysticism, the quest for the vision of God (*visio Dei*), which Luther and Calvin derided as the desire to see God "naked" (*Deus nudus*).[3] This quest to

---

1. John Williamson Nevin, *The Anxious Bench*, 2d ed. (Chambersburg, PA: Reformed Church in the United States, 1844).

2. For a sympathetic account of Nevin see D. G. Hart, *John Williamson Nevin: High Church Calvinist*, ed. D. G. Hart and Sean Michael Lucas, American Reformed Biographies (Phillipsburg, NJ: P&R, 2005).

3. WA, 31²:38.19; 40¹:174.2; 42:9.32–10.2. See also B. A. Gerrish, *The Old Protestantism and the New: Essays on the Reformation Heritage* (Chicago: University of Chicago Press, 1982), 131–59; Walther von Loewenich, *Luther's Theology of the Cross*, trans. Herbert J. A. Bouman (Minneapolis: Augsburg, 1976), 27–49. On Calvin's doctrine of the hiddenness

experience God apart from the mediation of Word and sacrament has always been with us. It manifested itself in the Anabaptist-spiritualist movements in the early sixteenth century, in the spiritualism of the late sixteenth and early seventeenth centuries, in pietism in the seventeenth and eighteenth centuries, and finally in modern revivalism in the eighteenth and nineteenth centuries.[4]

The evidences of the inroads of pietism into contemporary Reformed piety are too numerous to catalogue, but one example illustrates the problem. Perhaps the most pervasive is the apparently benign sort of mysticism which many Reformed people now practice in ascertaining of the providence of God a priori. Many who would never tolerate the modern Pentecostal practices of being slain in the Spirit or tongues have become practical Pentecostalists. We tolerate or even encourage the practice of listening for the "still small voice" (1 Kings 19:12, KJV) of God in order to discern the moral will of God. Such an approach to discerning God's moral will is quite foreign to the Reformed confession. In place of mystical or introspective exercises the WCF counsels us consistently to seek the moral will of God in his Word. In 3.8, regarding the question of how the mystery of predestination is to be handled, we confess that those, "attending the will of God revealed in his Word" and obeying it "may, from the certainty of their effectual vocation," be assured of their eternal election. In 18.3 we are directed to the "ordinary means" and away from "extraordinary revelation." In 19.6 we confess that though we are no longer under the law as a covenant of works, nevertheless, it continues to be a "rule of life informing [us] of the will of God, and [our] duty; it directs and binds [us] to walk accordingly." In 19.7, God's moral will is said to be "revealed in the law." One finds the same pattern in the earlier Reformed

---

of God apart from Christ see *OS*, 3:204.15, 23, 25 (*Institutes* 1.17.2). Calvin did speak of the *nuda essentia* of God but only to say that it exists, not that we know it per se. See *OS* 3:154.23 (*Institutes* 1.14.2); Herman Selderhuis, *Calvin's Theology of the Psalms*, Texts and Studies in Reformation and Post-Reformation Thought (Grand Rapids: Baker Academic, 2007), 179–94.

4. "The Awakening touched the hearts of so many New Englanders because it was essentially an undogmatic, pietistic call for the regeneration of American society." Joseph A. Conforti, *Samuel Hopkins and the New Divinity Movement: Calvinism, the Congregational Ministry, and Reform in New England between the Great Awakenings* (Grand Rapids: Christian University Press, 1981), 2.

confessions. Nevertheless, consistently it seems, whether in hearing professions of faith, in house visitation, or casual conversation, Christian piety is reckoned chiefly in terms of the private and the subjective. If someone asks, "What is God teaching you these days?" one has the sense that the expected answer is not to be a summary of this week's sermon or reflection on the significance of baptism or the Lord's Supper, but an insight derived from a special experience or private revelation.

Perhaps the most outstanding example, however, of the subjective turn in contemporary Reformed piety is in public worship. It would not be hard to find a Reformed congregation today in which the Sunday (or Saturday night) liturgy begins with twenty-five minutes of Scripture songs sung consecutively, each song blending into the next, perhaps augmented by a Power Point or video presentation. In this increasingly popular liturgy, the singing is followed by a dramatic presentation which, in turn, is followed by congregational announcements, most of which focus on the various cell-group programs. Increasingly, the sermon is a brief, colorfully illustrated, emotionally touching collection of anecdotes, in which the hearer is not so much directed to the law and the gospel, but, in one way or another, to one's self. Anxious to intensify the religious experience of parishioners or to make the church accessible to the non-churched, many Reformed congregations have turned to new measures, to drama, dance lessons, and even a service arranged thematically by the name of the local professional sports franchise. Such practices are rather more indebted to eighteenth- and nineteenth-century revivalism than they are to Geneva, Heidelberg, or Westminster Abbey. Such practices are also symptoms of the synthesis of Reformed worship with the emerging modern culture in which, as Philip Rieff noted, hospital and theater replace the church.[5]

How did John Calvin's great-grandchildren come to such a place? A complete answer to this question, of course, would entail several volumes. For our purposes, however, it is enough to understand that these ills are symbolic of the transformation of Reformed piety by ideas that are fundamentally alien to our confessional theology, piety, and practice,

5. Philip Rieff, *The Triumph of the Therapeutic: The Uses of Faith after Freud*, 40th anniversary edition (Wilmington, DE: ISI Books, 2006), 18.

because, to a large degree, we have given ourselves over to a quest for illegitimate religious experience. QIRE describes the desire to achieve an unmediated encounter with God. It also describes religious subjectivism (often part of that quest) and even religious enthusiasm. In the experience of the American Reformed churches, this quest has been fueled by a synthesis of the confessional Reformed soteriology with forms of piety that emerged during the North American revivals of the eighteenth and nineteenth centuries, and it is to that synthesis that we turn our attention.[6] We shall consider in turn the nature of pietism and its influence on modern Reformed theology, piety, and practice; the nature of revivalism in the eighteenth and nineteenth centuries; and the confessional alternative to pietism and revivalism.

Pietism: The Bridge from Reformation to Revival

It is the contention of this chapter that reformation and revival are distinct and largely incompatible models of theology, piety, and practice. The Reformation, which gave us the first- and second-generation Reformed confessions, consistently points the sinner first to the objective divine promises and only secondarily to one's awareness of the Spirit's presence within. Revivalism, however, tends to turn first of all to the subjective. The basic difference between revivalism and reformation is evident in the terms themselves. The first speaks to the interior world of the believer (however conceived), and the latter describes objective institutional change and doctrinal reorganization. *Pietism* is not to be confused with *piety*, which describes the Christian life and worship; pietism describes a retreat into the subjective experience of God. According to one writer, pietism, whether Lutheran or Reformed, is a critique of orthodoxy. Even in its mildest forms, at its heart pietism flows from dissatisfaction with objective religion, with the classical Reformed and Lutheran Word and sacrament piety, from dissatisfaction with the ordinary. Pietism seeks "the

6. D. G. Hart has argued a similar case in "Jonathan Edwards and the Origins of Experimental Calvinism," in D. G. Hart et al., eds., *The Legacy of Jonathan Edwards: American Religion and the Evangelical Tradition* (Grand Rapids: Baker Academic, 2003), 161–80.

life and liveliness of faith" rather than the "truth of fait
said that the "subjectivity of Pietism, or the doctrine of th
Quakerism and the other ecstatic movements, has the cha
diacy or autonomy against the authority of the church. '
sharply, modern rational autonomy is a child of the myst
of the doctrine of the inner light."[8] Dale W. Brown, who ....om a
perspective sympathetic to pietism, identifies five central motifs: 1) a turn
to the practical; 2) a primitivist reading of Scripture, which is described
as biblicism; 3) an emphasis on sanctification and ethics; 4) an emphasis
on religious experience; 5) acts of mercy.[9]

In all its forms then, for pietism, one's experience of the divine presence is ultimately more important than what one believes or knows or
where one attends church or how often one receives the Lord's Supper.[10]
However orthodox a particular pietist might be, if one has to choose
between orthodoxy and experience, the pietist chooses experience. Even
in defending pietism against the charge that it is overly subjectivist and a
revival of late medieval mysticism, F. E. Stoeffler conceded that pietism
"had no one system of theology, no one integrating doctrine, no particular
type of polity, no one liturgy, no geographical homogeneity."[11] Certainly
several of these claims cannot be made of confessional Reformed theology.
We have a theology, an integrating doctrine (covenant theology), a polity,
and a form of worship.

In certain respects, pietism is a more recent expression of older
forms of mysticism that sought union with God or even divinization
(*theosis*).[12] For example, Joachim of Fiore (c. 1135–1202), the devout
Italian Cistercian who had a series of life-changing visions, or Christian Platonists such as the Dominican theologian Meister Eckhart

7. C. John Weborg, "Pietism: Theology in Service of Living toward God," in *The Variety
of American Evangelicalism*, ed. Donald W. Dayton and Robert K. Johnston (Downers Grove,
IL: InterVarsity, 1991), 161.

8. Paul Tillich, *A History of Christian Thought* (New York: Simon and Schuster, 1967),
286.

9. Dale W. Brown, *Understanding Pietism* (Grand Rapids: Eerdmans, 1978), 27–28.

10. D. G. Hart, *The Lost Soul of American Protestantism* (Lanham, MD: Rowman and
Littlefield, 2002), 20–24.

11. F. E. Stoeffler, *The Rise of Evangelical Pietism* (Leiden: Brill, 1971), 13.

12. See Bernard McGinn, *The Foundations of Mysticism* (New York: Crossroad, 1991).

1260–c. 1328) or Ramon Lull (c. 1233–c. 1315), who taught a theology of union with the Godhead. These mystics were working within ontological categories. They analyzed the basic human problem in terms of being and non-being, rather than sin and redemption. These theologians sought union with God, not by way of the incarnation and the cross, but without mediation.

The Anabaptist movement in the early sixteenth century taught a combination of moralism and mysticism. Almost without exception, the Anabaptists from Hans Denck (1500–1527), to probably the most learned of all the radicals, Balthasar Hubmaier (1481–1528), to the most moderate of them all, Menno Simons (1496–1561), rejected the Lutheran and Reformed confessional doctrine of justification, for the same reasons that Rome rejected it, because they thought it would tend to encourage immorality and impiety.[13] Instead, they sought to promote piety primarily through small groups (conventicles), through private devotional exercises and a strong dose of mysticism. The Schleitheim Confession (1527), in which there was no mention of justification *sola gratia, sola fide, solo Christo* but strong emphasis on piety and morality is illustrative of this tendency. The Mennonite Dordrecht Confession (1632) confirms this judgment in article 5, which is headed "The Law of Christ, which is the Holy Gospel, or the New Testament," wherein the law and gospel are related, and justification is described in ways which are much closer to the Council of Trent than to Luther and Calvin.[14] The mystical-ontological tradition continued in the theology and piety of the influential renegade German Lutheran layman, Jakob Boehme (1575–1624), whose theology was organized around immediate experience of and even absorption into the divine Abyss (*der Ungrund*). Andrew Weeks links Boehme's "mystical and pansophic" theology to pietists such as Gottfried Arnold (1666–1714),

13. See G. H. Williams, *The Radical Reformation*, 3rd ed. (Kirksville, MO: Sixteenth Century Publishers, 1992), 251–54. Williams argues that Caspar Schwenkfeld never abandoned the Protestant gospel, but admits he rejected the doctrine of *simul iustus et peccator* which all the Protestants considered essential to the forensic doctrine of justification. See ibid., 200–203.

14. John H. Leith, ed., *Creeds of the Churches*, 3rd ed. (Louisville: John Knox, 1982), 281–307.

Count Nikolaus Ludwig von Zinzendorf (1700–1760), and Philipp Jakob Spener (1635–1705).[15]

To be sure, some orthodox Reformed theologians have been described as pietist.[16] William Ames (1576–1633) and Gijsbertus Voetius (1589–1676) have been described as scholastic *and* pietistic.[17] It is true that Voetius encouraged conventicles, and it is true that they were responsible for what has come to be called the Dutch Second Reformation or Dutch Puritanism (*Nadere Reformatie*), a movement with a strong emphasis on doctrinal and moral precision, but unlike the German Lutheran pietists, the theology and piety of these theologians did not take the ontological-mystical turn. Ames and Voetius, who were both also skilled dogmatic theologians, were committed to a piety oriented around the means of grace.[18] When the adjective "pietist" is applied to Voetius and Ames, it has become so elastic and inclusive as to become meaningless.[19]

15. Andrew Weeks, *German Mysticism from Hildegard of Bingen to Ludwig Wittgenstein: A Literary and Intellectual History* (Albany: State University of New York Press, 1993), 184. See Jacob Boehme, *The Way to Christ*, trans. Peter Erb (New York: Paulist, 1978); idem, *The Signature of All Things* (Kila, MT: Kessinger, n.d.). For an example of von Zinzendorf's doctrine, see N. Count von Zinzendorf, *Nine Public Lectures*, trans. George W. Forrell (Iowa City: University of Iowa Press, 1973).

16. See Martin H. Prozesky, "The Emergence of Dutch Pietism," *Journal of Ecclesiastical History* 28 (1977): 29–37.

17. James Tanis, "Reformed Pietism in Colonial America," in *Continental Pietism and Early American Christianity*, ed. F. E. Stoeffler (Grand Rapids: Eerdmans, 1976); Weborg, "Pietism: Theology in Service of Living toward God," 161; Prozesky, "The Emergence of Dutch Pietism," 34–35; Stoeffler, *The Rise of Evangelical Pietism*, 133, describes Ames as Dutch Reformed pietism's first theologian. For a general introduction to Voetius see Andreas J. Beck, "Gisbertus Voetius (1589–1676): Basic Features of His Doctrine of God," in *Reformation and Scholasticism: An Ecumenical Enterprise*, ed. W. J. van Asselt and Eef Dekker (Grand Rapids: Baker, 2001); Joel Beeke, "Gisbertus Voetius: Toward a Reformed Marriage of Knowledge and Piety," in *Protestant Scholasticism: Essays in Reassessment*, ed. Carl R. Trueman and R. Scott Clark (Carlisle, UK: Paternoster, 1999). On the difficulties of describing Voetius as a pietist, see Joel R. Beeke, *The Assurance of Faith: Calvin, English Puritanism, and the Dutch Second Reformation* (New York: Peter Lang, 1991), 386–87.

18. For a more positive assessment of the relations between pietism and Reformed theology see George Brown, "Pietism and the Reformed Tradition," *Reformed Review* 30 (1977): 143–52.

19. See Stoeffler, *The Rise of Evangelical Pietism*, 121–79, where he provides a detailed account of the pietism of Jean de Taffin, G. C. Udemans, W. Teelinck, Ames, J. van Lodensteyn, T. G Brakel, and J. de Labadie.

Johannes Cocceius (1603–69) is also sometimes described as a pietist, but primarily on the ground that he was a forerunner of the later biblical theology movement, which assumes incorrectly a dichotomy between scholastic and biblical theology.[20] Willem J. van Asselt has shown that Cocceius (who also wrote a dogmatic theology) eludes any reasonable definition of pietist, unless we mean by pietist all who love Jesus and read the Bible for spiritual nourishment.[21]

Theodore Frelinghuysen and perhaps Jonathan Edwards are more aptly called pietists than Voetius and Ames.[22] W. W. Sweet argued that "colonial revivalism was rooted in pietism and not in New England Calvinism; it was only by impregnating his Calvinism with pietism that Jonathan Edwards's gospel was rendered effective in reaching the hearts of his people at Northampton."[23] Edwards and his followers restated Reformed theology in terms of "the immediacy of God's presence and sovereignty" and the "role of man's feelings and will."[24]

The Revivalist Quest for Religious Experience

In his introduction to D. Martyn Lloyd-Jones's *Revival*, J. I. Packer offers a brief definition of what Lloyd-Jones meant by revival:

> Revival for "the Doctor" meant more than evangelism that brings in converts, and more than cheerfulness, enthusiasm, and a balanced budget in the local church. What he was after was the new quality of spiritual life that comes through knowing the greatness and nearness of our holy, gracious Creator—something that in former days would have

20. Prozesky, "The Emergence of Dutch Pietism," 31–32.

21. Willem J. Van Asselt, *The Federal Theology of Johannes Cocceius (1603–1669)*, ed. Robert J. Bast, trans. Raymond J. Blacketer, Studies in the History of Christian Thought (Leiden: Brill, 2001).

22. W. W. Sweet, *Revivalism in America: Its Origin, Growth and Decline* (Gloucester, MA: Peter Smith, 1965), 44–52. See also Joel R. Beeke, *Forerunner of the Great Awakening: Sermons by Theodorus Jacobus Frelinghuysen (1691–1747)* (Grand Rapids: Eerdmans, 2000).

23. W. W. Sweet, *Religion in Colonial America* (New York: Cooper Square, reprint 1965), 282. We will consider Edwards's relation to pietism in more detail below.

24. Lefferts A. Loetscher, *The Broadening Church: A Study of Theological Issues in the Presbyterian Church since 1869* (Philadelphia: University of Pennsylvania Press, 1954), 5.

been called *enlargement of heart*, and usually starts with a deepened sense of the power and authority of God in the preaching of the Biblical message.[25]

Packer's definition is quite faithful to that given by Lloyd-Jones himself. In defending the present need for revival and analyzing the various obstacles to the same, Lloyd-Jones defined revival in terms of the present-day, personal, "experimental" experience of the outpouring of the Holy Spirit. "This is obviously the crucial point with regard to this whole question of revival, because I take it that by definition what a revival means is an outpouring of the Spirit of God; the Spirit of God coming in power upon a person or a number of persons at the same time."[26]

Lloyd-Jones continued his argument by refuting those who dare to dismiss the modern revivals (e.g., the Welsh revival of 1859) as less than apostolic. For Lloyd-Jones, to doubt that they were genuine revivals is blasphemy against the Holy Spirit.[27] He put the problem squarely before us:

> What so many are disputing and denying and ignoring, is what I would call the immediate and direct action of the Holy Spirit. They say that the Spirit only works through the word, and that we must not expect anything from the Spirit apart from that which comes immediately through the word. And so it seems to me, they are quenching the Spirit.[28]

What we have is a clear disagreement about that which we should expect the Spirit of God to be doing in the postapostolic church and therefore how we ought to think about Reformed theology, piety, and practice. Further, Lloyd-Jones's claim rests not upon biblical exegesis, systematic theology,

25. D. Martyn Lloyd-Jones, *Revival* (Westchester, IL: Crossway, 1987), vi. See also J. I. Packer, *Keep in Step with the Spirit* (Old Tappan, NJ: Revell, 1984), 255–58; idem, *The Collected Shorter Writings of J. I. Packer*, 4 vols. (Carlisle, UK: Paternoster, 1998), 2:57–85.

26. Lloyd-Jones, *Revival*, 50.

27. Ibid., 51.

28. Ibid., 53. This was not an isolated theme in Lloyd-Jones's later teaching. See also D. Martyn Lloyd-Jones, *Joy Unspeakable: Power and Renewal in the Holy Spirit* (Wheaton, IL: Harold Shaw, 1984); idem, *The Sovereign Spirit: Discerning His Gifts* (Wheaton, IL: Harold Shaw, 1985).

or examples drawn from classical Reformed theologians, but upon his interpretation of providence. Lloyd-Jones was arguing that anyone who disagrees with his interpretation of the history of the modern revivals is quenching the Spirit.

This line of argumentation on the part of the modern proponents of the theology, piety, and practice of awakening creates a certain awkwardness relative to the Reformed confession. Elsewhere he wrote:

> Calvinism without Methodism tends to lead to intellectualism and scholasticism—that is its peculiar temptation.... Another danger which Calvinism without Methodism is prone to is that *Confessions of Faith*, instead of being subordinate standards, tend to be the primary and supreme standard, replacing the Bible in that position. I am only talking about tendencies, and not saying that this happens to all Calvinists. Officially we say that these Confessions are the "subordinate standard"; the Bible comes first, then these. But there is always a danger that the Calvinist may reverse the order.[29]

Lloyd-Jones spoke for many modern Reformed folk, echoing the concerns of many critics of Reformed orthodoxy. There are many who sympathize with our doctrines of Scripture and predestination, but who are suspicious of the role of ecclesiastically sanctioned confessions of faith and are, frankly, dissatisfied with our means-of-grace piety.[30] Arguably, Lloyd-Jones was calling for Calvinism without Calvin's sacramental piety.

Following the tradition of those eighteenth-century promoters of revival, what Lloyd-Jones saw as indubitable evidence of the present sovereign work of the Spirit, many of our sixteenth- and seventeenth-century theologians might well have regarded as, and many eighteenth-century Old Side Presbyterians saw as, misguided enthusiasm.[31] By "enthusiasm" I

29. D. Martyn Lloyd-Jones, *Puritans: Their Origins and Successors. Addresses Delivered at the Puritan and Westminster Conferences: 1959–1978* (Edinburgh: Banner of Truth Trust, 1987), 209.

30. This passage seems to bring Lloyd-Jones uncomfortably close to the sentiment of Charles G. Finney in his *Lectures on Systematic Theology* (Grand Rapids: Eerdmans, 1964), preface.

31. On the history of competing contemporaneous interpretations of the eighteenth-century awakenings see Frank Lambert, *Inventing "the Great Awakening"* (Princeton, NJ:

mean something like the sort of uncontrolled emotional excess (*intemperies*) practiced by those whom Calvin called "enthusiasts" and of which he was so critical.[32] R. A. Knox's definition of enthusiasm as that religion in which grace obliterates nature is also relevant here.[33]

It is well to begin with Lloyd-Jones, since, unlike some other proponents of revival in the modern period he was consistently predestinarian in his soteriology. Unlike some of the actors in the First Great Awakening and nearly all of the major figures in the Second Great Awakening and through the middle of the twentieth century, Lloyd-Jones never capitulated to the temptation to manipulate his congregation to achieve a selfish end. More recently, Iain Murray has defended the legitimacy of revivals by distinguishing them carefully from "revivalism."[34] For Murray, the revivals associated with the First Great Awakening should be considered proper evangelicalism. Modern historians, because they fail to account for the providence of God, do not distinguish those things that God actually did from those things that were merely the result of human manipulation.[35] He claims without substantiation that "orthodox Christianity at an earlier date protested that revival and revivalism—far from being of the same genus—are actually opposed."[36]

Like Lloyd-Jones before him, Murray has stated the problem well. In contrast to Lloyd-Jones and Murray, I contend, however, that both awakenings were subspecies of the same genus, the QIRE. He appeals to

Princeton University Press, 1999). See also Joseph A. Conforti, *Jonathan Edwards, Religious Tradition, and American Culture* (Chapel Hill: University of North Carolina Press, 1995).

32. *Institutes* 1.9.3 and 3.13.14; *OS*, 1:84.31–35. On Calvin's attitude toward the Anabaptists generally see Willem Balke, *Calvin and the Anabaptist Radicals*, trans. W. J. Heynen (Grand Rapids: Eerdmans, 1981).

33. R. A. Knox, *Enthusiasm: A Chapter in the History of Religion* (Oxford: Oxford University Press, 1950).

34. Iain H. Murray, *Revival and Revivalism: The Making and Re-Making of American Evangelicalism: 1750–1858* (Edinburgh: Banner of Truth Trust, 1994), 2–3.

35. Ibid. One presumes that when Murray says "an earlier date" he is thinking of the Edwardsean or Whitefieldian revivals. If so, he is guilty of begging the question, i.e., assuming what he intends to prove, but by beginning his narrative in 1750, after the close of the First Great Awakening, he has arranged things so that he cannot make his case in a way that convinces those who disagree with him or who do not share his historiographic methods. For an alternative to Murray's account see Harry S. Stout, *The Divine Dramatist: George Whitefield and the Rise of Modern Evangelicalism* (Grand Rapids: Eerdmans, 1991), xix.

36. Murray, *Revival and Revivalism*, 2–3.

providence to explain good revivals (those he likes) but ignores providence when describing the bad revivals (those with which he disagrees). Like all orthodox Calvinists, Murray understands that both Edwards and Finney were the result of the providence of God, but to account for this fact would imply the very connection Murray seeks to deny.[37] According to Murray, what gave power to the Old Princetonians was not the soundness of their doctrine (though that is surely a necessary condition for revival), but the quality of their personal religious experience.[38] The good revivalists were those who achieved a genuine religious experience, whether they were Anglican, Methodist, or Baptist. In the cases he describes, it is not a common theology or even polity that binds together the good revivalists; it is a common heightened personal experience of the divine presence.[39]

As we saw in the case of Lloyd-Jones, it is sometimes said and more frequently assumed that confessional Reformed theology, piety, and practice need to be augmented with the piety and evangelical fervor of the eighteenth- and nineteenth-century revivals. In such a marriage, however, classical Reformed theology and piety are unequally yoked. In the case of Murray's defense of the First Great Awakening as distinguished from most of the Second, some Reformed folk would like to save the predestinarian, Calvinistic revivals (1730s–1770s) while discarding the Arminian revivals (1800–1860). Judged, however, by confessional Reformed theology, piety, and practice, it is more difficult to see them as models for our theology, piety, and practice. Rather, taken individually or as a whole, the revivals represent a subjectivism that is alien to the Reformed confession.

37. Ibid., xx.
38. Ibid., 45. There was a strong connection between Old Princeton and the piety of the First Great Awakening. For example, Archibald Alexander recounted a conversion experience worthy of one of Edwards's journals. See Lefferts A. Loetscher, *Contributions to the Study of Religion*, vol. 8, *Facing the Enlightenment and Pietism: Archibald Alexander and the Founding of Princeton Theological Seminary* (Westport, CT: Greenwood, 1983), 24–26. Mark Noll, however, notes a certain ambivalence toward Edwards in the later history of Old Princeton. See Mark A. Noll, "The Contested Legacy of Jonathan Edwards in Antebellum Calvinism," in *Reckoning with the Past: Historical Essays on American Evangelicalism from the Institute for the Study of American Evangelicals*, ed. D. G. Hart (Grand Rapids: Baker, 1995), 200–17.
39. See Murray, *Revival and Revivalism*, chapter 3. See also D. Martyn Lloyd-Jones, "Revival: An Historical and Theological Survey," in *Puritan Papers, Volume 1, 1956–1959*, ed. D. Martyn Lloyd-Jones (Phillipsburg, NJ: P&R, 2000), 297–99.

This argument might strike some readers as highly unusual and even improbable, but it would not have sounded strange to the orthodox Reformed theologians of the eighteenth century who first faced the question of how to evaluate the New England revivals. This was a substantial part of the Presbyterian debate between the Old Side and the New Side over the First Great Awakening.[40] The confessional ministers and theologians, that is, those identified with the Old Side, were not opposed to the gracious, sovereign extraordinary working of the Holy Spirit through the preaching of the gospel, but they were opposed to preaching *for* revival. They supported George Whitefield's belief in divine sovereignty and justification *sola gratia, sola fide, solo Christo*, but they criticized his extra-ecclesiastical methods, which were deeply affected by his need to draw and keep audiences by excitement. This is not to say that the New Side preachers and Great Awakening revivalists were not sincere, that they were not Calvinist in their soteriology, or even that God, in his wonderful freedom, did not use them to accomplish great things; rather it is only to say that what happened to North American Reformed piety and practice in the eighteenth century constituted a significant shift away from earlier more confessional models, and that shift was fueled by a reaction to the rising tide of modernity and an adaptation to and adoption of ideas foreign to the Reformed confession.[41]

40. Mark A. Noll, *America's God: From Jonathan Edwards to Abraham Lincoln* (New York: Oxford University Press, 2002), 26, identifies the Old Side with Reformed confessionalism. Historians have neglected the Old Side. In the scant literature that exists, Leonard Trinterud's chapter on the Old Side titled "The Withered Branch" has dominated the story. See Leonard Trinterud, *The Forming of an American Tradition: A Re-Examination of Colonial Presbyterianism* (Freeport, NY: Books for Libraries Press, 1949; reprint, 1970). For a much more balanced approach see D. G. Hart and John R. Muether, *Seeking a Better Country: 300 Years of American Presbyterianism* (Phillipsburg, NJ: P&R, 2007), 50–69.

41. On the relations between modern evangelicalism and the Enlightenment generally see D. W. Bebbington, *Evangelicalism in Modern Britain: A History from the 1730s to the 1980s* (London: Unwin Hyman, 1989). Garry Williams criticizes Bebbington's thesis that early-eighteenth-century evangelicalism was a product of the Enlightenment. This chapter argues, however, that the same evidence to which Williams appeals to rescue modern evangelicalism from the Enlightenment, only further condemns it. See Garry J. Williams, "Was Evangelicalism Created by the Enlightenment?" *Tyndale Bulletin* 53 (2002): 283–312. On the pietist (and Edwardsean) reaction to the Enlightenment see James Turner, *Without God, without Creed: The Origins of Unbelief in America*, New Studies in American Intellectual and Cultural History (Baltimore: Johns Hopkins University Press, 1985), 60–63. In making this claim I am not ignoring Leigh

Any discussion of the turn to religious subjectivism by some Calvinists in the American colonies must reckon with Jonathan Edwards (1703–58). It must also reckon with the fact that, for a variety of reasons, criticism of Edwards is difficult to both make and receive. It is difficult to make because Edwards has a singular place in the history of American Reformed theology. He is the American theologian and he was as brilliant as he was prolific. Therefore there is a considerable body of primary literature with which to reckon before saying anything about Edwards. There is also an ever-growing body of secondary literature surrounding the study of Edwards. Finally, it is difficult for those who identify with Reformed orthodoxy to criticize Edwards because many American Calvinists agree with his theology, or at least they think they do. One suspects, however, that confessional Reformed folk might not be so ready to identify with Edwards's theology if they understood its debt to modernity and specifically to certain forms of rationalism and idealism.[42]

Contemporary scholars of Edwards are raising some important, if difficult, questions about the sources, nature, and consequences of Edwards's theology. One example is Michael J. McClymond's conclusion that "Edwards taught a doctrine of divinization. The only thing missing is the word itself."[43] Another cause for concern for those committed to confessional orthodoxy

---

Eric Schmidt's argument that the rise of the lengthy "communion season" in the Scottish Kirk essentially replaced elements in pre-Reformation folk religion. See Leigh Eric Schmidt, *Holy Fairs: Scotland and the Making of American Revivalism*, 2d ed. (Grand Rapids: Eerdmans, 2001), 15–32. Schmidt's work is exceptionally valuable for calling attention to the preconditions of revivalism created by infrequent communion. There is some truth, however, to the criticism of Schmidt's conclusions that actual evidence for a direct connection between the Scottish practice of the seventeenth century and colonial revivalism is "patchy" and requires a "leap of faith." See Eric Crouse, "Review of *Holy Fairs: Scotland and the Making of American Revivalism*, 2nd Edition," *Journal of the Canadian Church Historical Society* 45 (2003): 237–41.

42. Loetscher, *The Broadening Church*, 6. According to Sang Hyun Lee, Edwards was the most modern man of his time. See Sang Hyun Lee, *The Philosophical Theology of Jonathan Edwards* (Princeton, NJ: Princeton University Press, 1988), 3. Lee's principal thesis is that Edwards taught a "dispositional ontology." For a discussion of and response to this claim see Stephen R. Holmes, "Does Jonathan Edwards Use a Dispositional Ontology? A Response to Sang Hyun Lee," in *Jonathan Edwards: Philosophical Theologian*, ed. Paul Helm and Oliver D. Crisp (Aldershot, UK: Ashgate, 2003), 99–114.

43. Michael J. McClymond, "Salvation and Divinization: Jonathan Edwards and Gregory Palamas and the Theological Uses of Neoplatonism," in *Jonathan Edwards: Philosophical Theologian*, ed. Helm and Crisp, 153.

should be Edwards's doctrine of justification about which there have been unresolved questions since the publication of Thomas A. Schafer's 1951 essay.[44] Of course, modern scholarship is not the first to suggest that there might be reasons to be cautious about Edwards's theology. Charles Hodge (1797–1878) offered strong criticism of Edwards's doctrine of original sin and "continued creation." Hodge said, "According to the theory of continued creation there is and can be no created substance in the universe. God is the only substance in the universe."[45] He concluded that this "doctrine, therefore, in its consequences, is essentially pantheistic."[46]

Another reason why some readers may have missed some of the problems in Edwards's theology is the story that has been told concerning the development of his theology. The Princeton theologian Samuel Miller (1769–1850) noted that Edwards, at age fourteen, read John Locke's *Essay on Human Understanding* at Yale and entered into its arguments and philosophy "with delight."[47] Since Perry Miller's 1949 *Jonathan Edwards*,

44. Thomas A. Schafer, "Jonathan Edwards and Justification by Faith," *Church History* 20 (1951): 55–67. More recently, George Hunsinger, W. Robert Godfrey, and others have also raised questions about Edwards's doctrine of justification. See George Hunsinger, "Dispositional Soteriology: Jonathan Edwards on Justification by Faith Alone," *WTJ* 66 (2004): 107–20; W. Robert Godfrey, "Jonathan Edwards and Authentic Spiritual Experience" (paper presented at "Knowing the Mind of God," 2003 Westminster conference); Gary Steward, "Faith and Obedience in Jonathan Edwards' Understanding of Justification by Faith Alone" (unpublished paper, 2006). John Gerstner and Jonathan Neil Gerstner, Samuel Logan, Jeffrey Waddington, and Brooks Holifield have defended Edwards's orthodoxy on justification. See John H. Gerstner and Jonathan Neil Gerstner, "Edwardsean Preparation for Salvation," *WTJ* 42 (1979): 5–71; Samuel T. Logan Jr., "The Doctrine of Justification in the Theology of Jonathan Edwards," *WTJ* 46 (1984): 26–52; Jeffrey C. Waddington, "Jonathan Edwards's 'Ambiguous and Somewhat Precarious Doctrine of Justification,'" *WTJ* 66 (2004): 357–72; E. Brooks Holifield, *Theology in America: Christian Thought from the Age of the Puritans to the Civil War* (New Haven: Yale University Press, 2003), 119–20.

45. Charles Hodge, *Systematic Theology*, 3 vols. (New York: Scribner, Armstrong, 1873), 2:219.

46. Ibid., 2:220. A. A. Hodge later offered more restrained criticism of Edwards when he said, "President Edwards was always brimming over with ideas of his own, which stood in need of regulating"—quoted in C. A. Salmond, *Princetonia: Charles and A. A. Hodge; with Class and Table Talk of Hodge the Younger* (New York: Scribner and Welford, 1888), 179, and cited in David B. Calhoun, *Princeton Seminary*, vol. 2, *The Majestic Testimony 1869–1929* (Edinburgh: Banner of Truth Trust, 1996), 526 n. 25. Lee, *The Philosophical Theology of Jonathan Edwards*, 50, argues that Edwards avoided absolute monism.

47. See Samuel Miller, *Life of Jonathan Edwards* (New York: Harper and Brothers, 1840). For a survey of the modern literature on Edwards see Sean Michael Lucas, "Jonathan

many scholars have interpreted Edwards primarily as an empiricist following Locke.[48] Those who accepted this reading of Edwards had less reason to query his relations to neo-Platonism, idealism, and rationalism. However, several scholars have suggested that Edwards was, in fact, much more influenced by the neo-Platonism and idealism of George Berkeley (1685–1753) and Nicolas de Malebranche (1638–1715). Edwards turned to these sources as part of his attempt to find certainty in response to the skepticism of the sort represented by David Hume (1711–76).[49]

Norman Fiering has argued that Edwards was no empiricist but rather deeply influenced by what Louis Loeb has called the "theocentric metaphysicians."[50] In this school, "the standard of knowledge is strict demonstration based upon intuition and deduction."[51] Edwards "fits perfectly into these criteria . . . whereas Locke hardly belongs at all."[52] According to Fiering, Edwards was a "daring and acute philosophical speculator who shared the (perhaps naïve) trust common in his time that modern philosophy—that is, philosophy beginning with Descartes—could be turned to the advantage of orthodox religion."[53] He could not see the dam-

Edwards: Between Church and Academy," in D. G. Hart, Sean Michael Lucas, and Stephen J. Nichols, eds., *The Legacy of Jonathan Edwards: American Religion and the Evangelical Tradition* (Grand Rapids: Baker Academic, 2003), 228–47.

48. Perry Miller, *Jonathan Edwards* (Westport, CT: Greenwood, reprint, 1973), 52–67; Ned C. Landsman, *From Colonials to Provincials: American Thought and Culture 1680–1760* (Ithaca, NY: Cornell University Press, 1997), 109. On Miller's method see George M. Marsden, "Perry Miller's Rehabilitation of the Puritans: A Critique," *Church History* 39 (1970): 91–105.

49. Landsman, *From Colonials to Provincials*, 108–14; Richard H. Popkin, "Immaterialism in the American Colonies: Samuel Johnson and Jonathan Edwards," in *Columbia History of Western Philosophy*, ed. Richard H. Popkin (New York: MJF Books, 1999), 452–54. Of the Cambridge Platonists Alan Gabbey writes, "Their aim was to ensure that the sceptics' bridles on the natural light of reason would not thereby become bridles also on the progress of the Christian soul toward divine knowledge and understanding." Alan Gabbey, "'A Disease Incurable': Scepticism and the Cambridge Platonists," in *Scepticism and Irreligion in the Seventeenth and Eighteenth Centuries*, ed. Richard H. Popkin and Arjo Vanderjagt (Leiden: Brill, 1993), 71–91.

50. Norman Fiering, "The Rationalist Foundations of Jonathan Edwards's Metaphysics," in *Jonathan Edwards and the American Experience*, ed. Nathan O. Hatch and Harry S. Stout (New York: Oxford University Press, 1998), 77.

51. Ibid.

52. Ibid.

53. Ibid., 78. Conforti, *Samuel Hopkins and the New Divinity Movement*, argues that the New Haven divinity is a direct development of Edwards's theology.

age that Hume's *Dialogues concerning Natural Religion* would wreak on all such projects. "As a man of his time he was captivated by such systems, no less than Malebranche, Leibniz and Henry More."[54] He rejected the traditional Reformed doctrine of *concursus*, that God works fully in every thing but does so through "second causes" (WCF 5.2),[55] which led to his occasionalism whereby the world is said to be re-created (which notion the earlier Reformed orthodox had rejected) moment by moment.[56] The epistemological corollary to his occasionalism was his rejection of Christian Aristotelianism, which was little more than the appropriation and adaptation of Aristotelian categories in the service of Christian theology,[57] in favor of Cambridge Platonism, which led him to conclude, "knowledge in man and God is essentially the same, both existing by ideas."[58] To be sure, he acknowledged that God's ideas are infinite and ours are not, but the analogy between God and man is not consistent. For Edwards, the "created world is an emanation of Christ."[59] There is a divine archetype (e.g., of the conversion experience) of which there is an ectype innate *in the human mind*.[60] Through intuition and mental reconstruction of the

54. Fiering, "Rationalist Foundations," 78.

55. *Creeds*, 3:612.

56. Fiering, "The Rationalist Foundations," 79–81. Lee, *The Philosophical Theology of Jonathan Edwards*, denies but Oliver Crisp affirms that Edwards was an occasionalist. See Oliver D. Crisp, "How 'Occasional' Was Edwards' Occasionalism?" in *Jonathan Edwards: Philosophical Theologian*, ed. Paul Helm and Oliver D. Crisp (Aldershot, UK: Ashgate, 2003), 61–77.

57. On this see R. Scott Clark, *Caspar Olevian, and the Substance of the Covenant: The Double Benefit of Christ*, Rutherford Studies in Historical Theology (Edinburgh: Rutherford House, 2005), 58–63.

58. Fiering, "Rationalist Foundations," 82–83. See *Works*, 13:197, where, in 1723, Edwards wrote of the "universe" being "conscious of its own being." "Now except the world had such a consciousness of itself, it would be altogether in vain that it was." See also ibid., 210, no. 20; 251–52, no. 87.

59. Fiering, "Rationalist Foundations," 83.

60. Ibid., 85. According to Lee, Edwards's morphology of conversion is his way of diagnosing divine activity in the world (*The Philosophical Theology of Jonathan Edwards*, 231). This relation of archetype to ectype is rather different than that envisioned by the Reformed orthodox. See chapter 4 of this work for an extensive discussion of this distinction. On the basis of this sort of language, Fiering argues that Ames and others were also Platonist. His connection of the usage of the terms "archetype" and "ectype" to Platonism fails to recognize the fundamental distinction made by theologians such as Ames between the Creator and the creature. Fiering cites Keith L. Sprunger, *The Learned Doctor Ames: Dutch Backgrounds*

world, these innate ectypes can be recovered and used to explain divine activity in the world. Such an approach demanded a subjectivist theology, piety, and practice.[61]

According to Ned C. Landsman, one important result of the revivalist response to the Enlightenment was to de-emphasize "the subtleties of religious doctrine."[62] The shift toward idealist categories and religious subjectivism created great tensions within early American Presbyterianism, resulting in a seventeen-year split between those who identified with more traditional Reformed theology, piety, and practice, known as the Old Side, and the New Side, that is, those who favored the new preaching and approaches to ministry (e.g., the Tennents, Whitefield, and Edwards). One measure of the subjectivist spirit, even among some Presbyterians, was their willingness to subvert the order of the institutional church, as William Tennent (1673–1745) did via the Log College of the 1730s; another was to attack their opponents as unconverted, as did Gilbert Tennent (1703–65) in his notorious 1740 sermon "The Danger of an Unconverted Ministry."[63] Those who expressed concern about the new approach to the ministry and piety became Pharisees of the same sort that grieved our Lord who saw that his people had no shepherds.[64] In other

---

of English and American Puritanism (Urbana: University of Illinois Press, 1972), 141, to the effect that Ames was a Ramist-Platonist and anti-Aristotelian. Sprunger's account is more complicated than Fiering implies, and the relations between Ramism and Aristotelianism are also more complicated than he implies. See Clark, Caspar Olevian, 38–73.

61. See E. Brooks Holifield, Theology in America, 107–11. Jeffrey H. Morrison, John Witherspoon and the Founding of the American Republic (Notre Dame, IN: University of Notre Dame Press, 2005), 9, says that upon becoming the president of the College of New Jersey, "one of Witherspoon's first tasks was to root out the philosophical idealism that was the legacy of his short-lived predecessor at Princeton." Witherspoon "succeeded in substituting Scottish realism for the New England idealism of Edwards." Stephen J. Nichols, An Absolute Sort of Certainty: The Holy Spirit in the Apologetics of Jonathan Edwards (Phillipsburg, NJ: P&R, 2003), 36–39, concedes Edwards's idealism but seeks to qualify by linking it to Calvin.

62. Landsman, From Colonials to Provincials, 101.

63. Gilbert Tennent, "The Danger of an Unconverted Ministry," in Richard L. Bushman, ed., The Great Awakening: Documents on the Revival of Religion, 1740–1745 (New York: Atheneum, 1970), 87–93. George Whitefield also made similar charges against some of his opponents but later published several apologies, including one to Harvard College in January 1745 for his sometimes intemperate language against his critics.

64. J. I. Packer comes close to doing this same thing in his defense of Edwards's revivalism. See J. I. Packer, A Quest for Godliness: The Puritan Vision of the Christian Life (Wheaton, IL: Crossway, 1990), 318.

words, the measure of one's ministry was no longer whether a minister proclaimed the law and the gospel and administered the means of grace according to the Scriptures as understood by the Reformed confessions. Rather, the measure of one's ministry was now the *result* of that preaching as measured by the New Side, specifically the degree to which it generated a certain religious enthusiasm or experience. To his credit, Tennent later reconsidered his remarks and repented of them. Nevertheless, they stand as a symbol of the revivalist critique of confessionalist Reformed theology and piety.[65]

Arguably then, even the First Great Awakening, which many are accustomed to considering as Reformed as distinct from the Second Great Awakening with its new measures, is also problematic from the perspective of confessional Reformed theology, piety, and practice. It is not that the Reformed confessions and ministers of the sixteenth and seventeenth centuries were opposed to genuine religious experience. Quite to the contrary, they were strongly in favor of a vital religious life, but the sort of religious experience described by Jonathan Edwards and the eighteenth-century revivalists was different from that envisioned by our confessional standards and the classical Reformed theologians.

In his *Faithful Narrative of the Surprising Work of God in the Conversion of Many Hundred Souls etc.* (1737), Edwards described how Northampton (Massachusetts) had slipped into a "degenerate time."[66] A few years after the death of Edwards's grandfather, Solomon Stoddard (c. 1643–1729), reports Edwards, there was a "general awakening" marked by the observation of "satisfying evidences" of saving faith. The pattern which Edwards described and to which he gave his approval is palpably different from the earlier pattern of Reformed piety embodied in the Reformed confessions.[67] For example, he reported that, after a conversation with a young

65. For an account of some of the critics of the Great Awakening see Frank Lambert, *Inventing "The Great Awakening"* (Princeton, NJ: Princeton University Press, 1999), 185–221.

66. *Works*, 4:146.

67. This is an important distinction. Clearly the so-called half-way covenant of 1662, adopted by the Congregationalists of New England, testifies to a significant presence of religious subjectivism well before Edwards. See Robert G. Pope, *The Half-Way Covenant* (Princeton, NJ: Princeton University Press, 1969). See also Solomon Stoddard, *An Appeal to the Learned: Being a Vindication of the Right of Visible Saints to the Lord's Supper* (Boston,

woman, he concluded, "God had given her a new heart, truly broken and sanctified."[68] Those who had already been "converted" were said to be "enlivened and renewed with fresh and extraordinary incomes of the Spirit of God." "Many" who had struggled with a lack of assurance "had now their doubts removed by more satisfying experience, and more clear discoveries of God's love."[69]

Edwards followed accounts of his own ministry with similar reports that revival began to "break forth" in other places under the Tennents and Theodore Frelinghuysen (1691–1748).[70] Edwards observed that the typical pattern involved a heightened conviction of sin, "apprehension of misery," awareness of jeopardy before the divine justice, and fervent repentance.[71] The cry became, "What shall we do to be saved?" According to Edwards, "The place of resort was now altered; it was no longer the tavern, but the minister's house that was thronged for more than ever the tavern had wont to be."[72] After their sometimes prolonged "legal distresses," the true converts were given the grace to think of God's mercy, especially in Christ's death for sinners.[73] His accounts, of course, are quite restrained and properly give all credit for all "shower" of divine blessings to the sovereign working of God's Spirit.[74] The case of Abigail Hutchinson

---

1709). Stoddard, Edwards's grandfather, reacted to the half-way covenant by opening the table to all, even those not in good standing with the church. He described the Lord's Supper as a "converting ordinance" by which he seems to have meant an agency through which Christ raises sinners from death to life. See Jonathan Edwards, *An Humble Inquiry into the Rules of the Word of God concerning the Qualifications Requisite to a Complete Standing and Full Communion in the Visible Church* (Boston, 1749). In contrast, HC Q. 65 says that it is through the preached gospel that the Spirit creates faith, and the Supper is the means used by the Spirit to confirm faith. In his treatise, Edwards rejected his grandfather's position and restricted the Supper not just to those in good standing with the church, but to those who could be judged to have had the necessary religious experience.

68. *Works*, 4:149.

69. Ibid., 4:152.

70. Ibid., 4:156.

71. Ibid., 4:161–70.

72. Ibid., 4:161.

73. Ibid., 4:171.

74. Walter V. L. Eversley makes an excellent point, that Edwards was faced with a terrific tension between his role as revivalist, in which role he advocated conversion, and his role as a pastor, in which role he advocated communion. See Walter V. L. Eversley, "The Pastor as Revivalist," in S. H. Lee and A. C. Guelzo, eds., *Edwards in Our Time* (Grand Rapids: Eerdmans, 1999), 113.

is a prototype for the rest.[75] She experienced an extraordinary sense of God's displeasure with her sins and her jeopardy before him. Her fears and doubts were relieved only by meditation on 1 John 1:7, "The blood of Christ cleanses from all sin," and an equally extraordinary awareness of God's "truth" and "sweetness" which led to a series of intense religious experiences, including "a kind of beatific vision of God."[76]

There are disturbing aspects to even this restrained account of the revival.[77] First, Edwards's approval of these prolonged states of spiritual anguish as evidence of a genuine work of the Spirit, even though he tried to mitigate them, seems to be evidence of the influence of a sort of proto-Romantic turn to religious experience under the influence of Enlightenment psychological categories.[78] We do not need to speculate here. He gave a commencement day sermon at Yale College in 1741 in defense of the revivals in Northampton, "The Distinguishing Marks of a Work of the Spirit of God." Here he drew direct parallels between the various apostolic phenomena and the phenomena accompanying the New England revivals.[79] He admitted that one cannot conclude that an event is a work of God's Spirit necessarily by the "effects on the bodies of men; such as tears, trembling, groans, loud outcries, agonies of body, or the failing of bodily strength."[80] He was at pains to find parallels for several of these in Scripture.[81] The sermon is marked by a search for a justification for the religious subjectivism represented by the revivals. Though he acknowledged formally a distinction between the apostolic period and the

75. *Works*, 4:191–99.

76. Ibid., 4:195. See also the case of Phebe Bartlet in ibid., 4:199–205.

77. Ibid., 4:189. Edwards was careful to explain that though the Quakers had come "hoping to find good waters to fish in," they went away "discouraged."

78. George M. Marsden, *Jonathan Edwards: A Life* (New Haven and London: Yale University Press, 2003), 192.

79. *Works*, 4:226–88.

80. Ibid., 4:230. See also ibid., 4.263. In his 1743 *Some Thoughts concerning the Revival*, Edwards continued this line of argumentation appealing to the conversion experience of his wife, Sarah (Pierpont) Edwards as confirmation of the genuineness of the revival. See Edwards, ibid., 4:69–70, 331–441. See also Marsden, *Jonathan Edwards: A Life*, 239–52.

81. *Works*, 4:232–34. Edwards argued that, if the queen of Sheba, who lived before the incarnation, fainted, how much more appropriate is it for Christians to faint at the direct experience of the risen Christ. He also appealed to the example of the Philippian jailer who fell down before Paul.

revivals, nevertheless, his operating use of Scripture made that distinction in practice quite fluid.[82] Having failed to distinguish clearly between the history of redemption in the apostolic epoch and our postcanonical epoch, he gave himself the nearly impossible task of trying to delineate proper religious experience from improper religious experience. Given his assumptions, he had to defend the right sort of ecstasy from the wrong sort and the right sort of visions and "strong and pleasing imaginations" from the wrong.[83]

Edwards's subjectivism is apparent in his appeal to Song of Songs 2:5, 8, the key phrase being "I am sick of love." As Edwards neared the end of his undergraduate training, he experienced his own religious awakening. He meditated upon this passage of the Song, during which he had a "kind of vision or fixed idea and imaginations of being alone in the mountains or some solitary wilderness, far from all mankind, sweetly conversing with Christ, and wrapped and swallowed up in God."[84] Twenty-one years later, Edwards was using the same biblical passage to explain not only his own conversion experience, but also the entire New England revival. According to Edwards, they had all become lovesick. Abstracted from its context, Edwards's mysticism would be hard to distinguish from Bernard's interpretation of the Song of Songs.[85] In its context, however, it is more than pious mysticism; it is Romanticism. Christ is Savior and Lord to be sure, but he is also an intimate object of romantic, almost erotic religious affection. Considering Edwards's own biography, the influence of idealism and Malebranche's occasionalism,[86] it is not difficult to understand his subjectivist morphology of conversion.[87]

82. Ibid., 4:243–44, 76–79.
83. Ibid., 4:237.
84. Miller, *Life of Jonathan Edwards*, 17.
85. Bernard, *On the Song of Songs*, trans. Kilian Walsh and Irene M. Edmonds, 4 vols., Cistercian Fathers Series (Spencer, MA: Cistercian, 1971), 4:7, 31, 40. See also Etienne Gilson, *The Mystical Theology of Saint Bernard*, trans. A. H. C. Downes (New York: Sheed and Ward, 1940).
86. Marsden, *Jonathan Edwards: A Life*, 80.
87. On Edwards's understanding of and struggle over the "morphology" of his own conversion see Charles Hambrick-Stowe, "The 'Inward, Sweet Sense' of Christ in Jonathan Edwards," in *The Legacy of Jonathan Edwards: American Religion and the Evangelical Tradition*, ed. D. G. Hart et al. (Grand Rapids: Baker Academic, 2003), 79–95.

Edwards's subjectivism was in contrast to the earlier Reformed approach, which regarded the preaching of the law in its pedagogical use as *praeparatio evangelii*, but the terrors induced and the results reflect more romance than Reformation.[88] Because of his neo-Platonism, Edwards established an ideal, a paradigm of conversion and religious experience, to be wrought not only progressively by the ordinary means of grace, but immediately by the Spirit. Thus, the marks of the work of the Spirit are not only faithful attendance to the means of grace and the fruit of the Spirit and dying to self and living to Christ, but specific and special marks so that the "extraordinary influences" of the Spirit become ordinary.[89] He conceded implicitly that the revivals in Northampton did not fit the earlier pattern of Reformed piety and practice, arguing that "what we have been used to or what the church of God has been used to, is not a rule by which we are to judge whether a work be the work of God, because there may be new and extraordinary works of God."[90]

To be sure, Edwards wrote clearly about love toward the brothers as a mark of the Christian. "Divine charity in the heart is the greatest privilege and glory." The "ordinary sanctifying influences of the Spirit of God are the end of all the extraordinary gifts." The closer the church is to its state in heaven, "all extraordinary gifts shall have ceased and vanished away." He did not expect a "restoration" of the apostolic gifts "in the approaching glorious times of the church" nor did he "desire it." He reminded the proponents of revival that human learning is not to be despised and a spirit of judging other Christians should not prevail among them. Particularly in the third section of *Religious Affections*, Edwards wrote as a pastor who had

88. Clark, *Caspar Olevian*, 186, 195.

89. Perry Miller, "Introduction," *Works*, 4:228. Miller argued that "federal theology" was a bilateral covenant theology "requiring assent on both sides" (by God and man) allowing ministers, "even while professing absolute predestination," to "offer to rational men certain inducements for their attempting to open negotiations." He connected this caricature of federal theology to the idea of the "means of grace." "By this adroit and highly legalistic formulation, seventeenth-century New England found a way for human enterprise in the midst of a system of determinism." This federal theology, Miller argued, was "conspicuous" in its "utter absence" from Edwards's 8 July 1731 commencement sermon at Yale. Instead, Edwards's theology is that of direct divine action without means (Miller, *Jonathan Edwards*, 30–31). Miller was utterly confused about the nature of Reformed federal theology but right to notice the *relative* absence of concern for the means of grace in Edwards's theology.

90. Ibid.

to temper enthusiasm and spiritualism among the ("radical New Lights") proponents and participants of revival.[91] Nevertheless, his reflections on the ordinary are rather eclipsed by his extended defense of the unusual, which Edwards called "uncommon operations" in the third section of the *Marks*.[92] In Edwards's scheme, the revivals of Northampton are but a continuation of the revivals which began with the apostles and which reemerged in the Reformation.[93]

To the Old Side criticism that God the Spirit operates by the Word, he responded that the Spirit was effectuating the revival and attending phenomena through the Word.[94] If people got a little carried away in the revivals, well, folk also got carried away in the apostolic church.[95] In other words, though he was too polite to say it, the implication was clear: Edwards' critics were quenching the Spirit. He warned his critics to be careful not to be "guilty of the unpardonable sin."[96] In order to justify his claim that these events were the work of the Spirit, *he had to show that those who experienced them had the right sort of experience.* According to John E. Smith, "the whole of his thought might be viewed as one magnificent answer to the question, *What is true religion?*"[97] For Edwards, true religion was not simply an orthodox profession of faith—Edwards was quite committed to divine sovereignty and thought of himself as an heir of Reformed orthodoxy—accompanied by an ordinary Christian life lived in the communion of the saints. But he demanded more, an extraordinary experience of grace. Edwards described at length the sense of guilt and fear of damnation that the truly converted experienced. Such intense experiences, he argued, could not be anything but genuine.

The fact that Edwards, like all religious subjectivists, was forced to begin to analyze and defend the quality of the religious experience of those involved in the revival should signal to us a problem of large proportions. He had to distinguish his version of religious experience from that,

91. *Works*, 4:280; Marsden, *Jonathan Edwards: A Life*, 283–85.
92. *Works*, 4:268.
93. Ibid., 4:268–69 (1.5).
94. Ibid., 4:239.
95. Ibid., 4:241.
96. Ibid., 4:271. See also Marsden, *Jonathan Edwards: A Life*, 236.
97. "Editor's Introduction," in *A Treatise concerning Religious Affections*, in *Works*, 2:2.

for example, of the Quakers, who had been drawn away from Christ.[98] Attention is no longer on the objective work of Christ for his people and the secret but ordinary work of the Spirit in his elect through the Word and sacraments. We have entered a realm of subjective judgments, in which Edwards believed one can "safely determine" whether and to what degree one has experienced "a deep concern about a future state and eternal happiness," the consciousness of the "dreadfulness of sin."[99] A truly converted man is not likely to be self-deceived; a "man that has been thoroughly terrified with a sense of his own danger and misery, is not easily flattered and made to believe himself safe, without any good grounds."[100] Edwards assumed that his readers will all recognize the signs of a "thoroughly terrified" man.

Though he later warned against it in the *Distinguishing Marks*, it is hard to see how Edwards was not forced to attempt what cannot be done, that is, to interpret the providence of God. For example, in his concluding remarks in *A Faithful Narrative*, Edwards wrote that "in the latter part of May, it began to be very sensible that the Spirit of God was gradually withdrawing from us, and after this time, Satan seemed to be let more loose, and raged in a dreadful manner."[101] If Lloyd-Jones was correct, that to criticize the 1859 revival as hysteria is blasphemy, then what should we say of Edwards's assumption that he could determine, from the appearance or disappearance of certain extraordinary phenomena, the presence or absence of God the Spirit? Does anyone know the secret movement of God's Spirit (John 3:8)? There is no doubt that Edwards knew this truth, but his subjectivism worked against his better theology.[102] Edwards pursued this basic approach to religious affections his entire life. Under the influence of the Cambridge Platonists, but like all pietists, Edwards established a priori tests of religious experience.[103] That was the point

98. *Works*, 4:250.
99. Ibid., 4:251.
100. Ibid., 4:252.
101. Ibid., 4:206.
102. Marsden, *Jonathan Edwards: A Life*, 286–90.
103. Charles Chauncy, "Seasonable Thoughts on the State of Religion," in *The Great Awakening: Documents Illustrating the Crisis and Its Consequences*, ed. Alan Heimert and Perry Miller (Indianapolis: Bobbs-Merrill, 1967), 75, notes that, in reaction to Hobbes's materialism, Edwards concluded that all things exist only in the divine intellect. In Edwards,

of *Religious Affections*. One doubts, however, that the "ordinary means" (WCF 18.3) piety of the Westminster Standards is so easily reconciled with the idealist pietism of *Religious Affections*. In other words, Gilbert Tennent, who, in his notorious 1740 sermon "The Danger of an Unconverted Ministry," attacked his Old Side opponents as unconverted, was wrong.[104] The measure of ministry is not the degree to which it creates religious enthusiasm but rather its faithfulness to the "due use of the ordinary means" (WCF 1.7).

There were genuine differences between the First and Second Great Awakenings. For example, the leading Reformed ministers of the First Great Awakening were strongly committed to the doctrines of absolute divine sovereignty and predestination. On the other hand, the leading voices of the Second Great Awakening (see below) ardently rejected not only predestination, but also the Reformation doctrine of justification. Nevertheless, there were genuine continuities between the two movements. Both were marked by innovative methods, neither was particularly churchly in orientation, and both were ultimately measured by their advocates by the degree of religious experience they fostered. None of these things could be said fairly of the classic Reformed theologians of the sixteenth and seventeenth centuries.[105]

My criticism of Reformed subjectivism in the colonial revivals should not be confused with Charles Chauncy's criticisms of Edwards. In 1743, Chauncy, a Congregationalist minister in Boston and a leader of the Congregationalist "Old Lights," published the most important criticism of the Great Awakening, *Seasonable Thoughts on the State of Religion in New England*. He was an enigmatic figure, applauded by the Arminians of his day, taken by many in the eighteenth century as a rationalist and a universalist.[106] He opposed the awakening, because it offended cool

---

the old Reformed analogy between God and man became ontology which, in turn, fed his quest for religious ecstasy.

104. Edwards agreed with Tennent's judgment against the critics of the awakening. See Marsden, *Jonathan Edwards: A Life*, 210.

105. Ibid., 201–13.

106. Norman B. Gibbs and Lee W. Gibbs describe him as a "kenotic" theologian. See Norman B. Gibbs and Lee W. Gibbs, "Charles Chauncy: A Theology in Two Portraits," *Harvard Theological Review* 83 (1990): 259–70; idem, "'In Our Nature': The Kenotic Christology of Charles Chauncy," *Harvard Theological Review* 85 (1992): 217–33.

reason by its passionate experience of God's presence. My criticism of revivalism is not that it is too passionate (Calvinism has always been one of the hotter religions); rather my criticism is that it is passionate about the wrong things.

My objections are more like those of the Old Side leader, John Thomson (c. 1690–1753).[107] In 1741 he argued in his essay *The Government of the Church of Christ* that the revivalists were guilty of alienating the affections of the congregations for their ministers.[108] The revivalists made life impossible for ordinary ministers by charging that the latter were unregenerate, mentioning Tennent's sermon explicitly.[109] How exactly does one defend oneself against the charge that one is unregenerate, especially when the charge assumes as its major premise that the regenerate will support the revival? If one points to one's piety, then one is guilty of the sin of pride. In other words, the only way to extricate oneself from the complaint that one is not regenerate is to support the New Side.

Thomson was not opposed to genuine religious experience, including a deep penitence for and hatred of sin and a heartfelt love for and gratitude to Christ for his grace to sinners, but he expected that experience to develop and to be nurtured in the context of and "by due use of the ordinary means." He maintained that the New Side had an unnecessarily low view of the visible church. Why should the principle of Reformed church order, that it is wrong to "intrigue to occupy another's place," be set aside on the basis that there is a revival afoot which supersedes good order?[110] He was defending the right use of the means of grace, that is, the proclamation of the Word of God, which he defined as law and gospel, believing that Christ has attached promises to the ordinary preaching of the Word. Thomson was operating upon the conviction that, through

107. John Thomson, *The Government of the Church of Christ, and the Authority of Church Judicatories Established on a Scripture Foundation: And the Spirit of Rash Judging Arraigned and Condemned. Or the Matter of Difference between the Synod of Philadelphia and the Protesting Brethren Justly and Fairly Stated* (Philadelphia, 1741). I am influenced in my interpretation of Thomson by an undated essay by Peter Wallace, "Old Light on the New Side: John Thomson and Gilbert Tennent on the Great Awakening." See also Hart and Muether, *Seeking a Better Country*, 39–67.

108. Thomson, *Government*, 111.

109. Ibid., 112.

110. Ibid., 61.

calling sinners to repent and believe the gospel, God the Spirit sovereignly brings sinners to faith.[111] In effect, Thomson argued, if the Old Side consisted of dead orthodoxy (Tennent had called them Pharisees), the New Side, by teaching that true Christians can distinguish between converted and unconverted ministers, was guilty of a sort of Donatism, that is, making the effect of preaching contingent upon the spiritual condition of the preacher.[112] It was a matter of defining "success." Thomson said, "If crying out in our public Assemblies, to the Disturbance of the Worship of God, and if falling down and working like Persons in Convulsions, I say, if those Things only be reckoned Signs of Success, I must own that I do not understand it."[113]

The Piety of Confessional Orthodoxy

The alliance between revivalism and Reformed churches has not been without fallout. It is true that, in many cases, those who advocate this marriage think that without a touch of revivalism, Reformed theology, piety, and practice are naturally heartless and sterile.[114] Those who think this way have already accepted the revivalist or subjectivist paradigm and its critique of Reformed theology. Consequently they judge Reformed theology, piety, and practice by an alien standard. If revivalism, as an expression of religious subjectivism, desires an immediate experience of the divine presence, then American revivalism is a continuous history of the quest for the immediate encounter with or heightened experience of God, distinguished by different soteriologies (Calvinism in the eighteenth century and Arminianism in the nineteenth century) and only relatively different methods. The moderate showmanship of George Whitefield (1714–70) was really a prototype for Charles Finney's New Measures,

111. Ibid., 116–17. Tennent had alleged that the Old Side ministers did not distinguish properly between law and gospel.

112. Tennent, "The Danger of an Unconverted Ministry," 117. See also Thomson, *The Government of the Church of Christ*, 188.

113. Thomson, *The Government of the Church of Christ*, 118. See also ibid., 123.

114. R. B. Kuiper warned of the danger of "orthodoxism." See R. B. Kuiper, *To Be or Not to Be Reformed: Whither the Christian Reformed Church?* (Grand Rapids: Zondervan, 1959), 32.

Dwight L. Moody's businesslike approach, and the outrageous stunts of Sister Aimee and Billy Sunday.[115]

The revivalist traditions have more than supplemented the theology, piety, and practice of confessional Reformed Christianity; they have supplanted it. Word and Spirit piety is replaced by event and excitement pietism, whether attributed to the direct action of the Spirit in the eighteenth century or to the New Measures of the nineteenth century. Even in its best and most admirable form, the revivalist program is still misguided, because, as Packer, Lloyd-Jones, and Murray define revival, it is fundamentally the quest for a particular religious experience: the immediate encounter with God. This requires us to ask, what is the proper place for religious experience in Reformed theology, piety, and practice? Consider how William Perkins (1558–1602), the father of English Puritanism, described conversion. In his catechism Perkins made it clear that conversion is not ordinarily a momentary or epochal experience and certainly not chiefly a private religious experience, but rather and ordinarily the result of the prevenient grace of justifying faith which comes through the hearing of the preached gospel and the consequent grace of sanctification received in the means of grace administered in the church. It is not as if the Reformed confession is unconcerned with religious experience, but in the sixteenth and seventeenth centuries we were more concerned about the objective manifestations of regeneration and conversion, which the apostle Paul called "the fruit of the Spirit."[116] Perkins characterized the fruit of the Spirit this way:

> Fruits worthy of amendment of life, are such fruits as the "trees of righteousness bear," namely, good works: for the doing of good works there be three things requisite: First, it must proceed from justifying faith. For the work cannot please God except the person please him, and the person cannot please him without this faith. Second, it is to be done in obedience to God's revealed word; "To obey is better than sacrifice, and

115. See William G. McLoughlin Jr., *Modern Revivalism: Charles Grandison Finney to Billy Graham* (New York: Ronald, 1959); Hart, *The Lost Soul of American Protestantism.*

116. William Perkins, "The Foundation of the Christian Religion Gathered into Six Principles," in William Perkins, *The Whole Works of That Famous and Worthy Minister of Christ in the University of Cambridge, M. William Perkins,* 3 vols. (London, 1631), 1:2.

to hearken is better than the fat of rams." Thirdly, it is to be referred to God's glory, "Whether you eat or drink," says Paul, "do all to the glory of God."[117]

The difference between "fruit" and "gifts" is the difference between the "ordinary" and the "extraordinary." Think of the difference between Paul's teaching on the "fruit of the Spirit" (in Gal. 5:22–26) and the "gifts of the Spirit" in 1 Corinthians 12. It has seemed to the Reformed that the apostle was much more concerned about the latter than the former.[118] The classical Reformed theologians spoke of the need for moral *renewal*. Like Calvin, they consistently used terms such as renewal (*renovatio*), conversion (*conversio*), and regeneration (*regeneratio*) for moral renewal or sanctification rather than the initial quickening work of the Spirit through the word.[119] In those cases, they were speaking of the second of Christ's double benefit (*duplex beneficium*), sanctification. They were not speaking, however, of a heightened sense of God's presence, nor were they speaking of extraordinary providences or sudden waves of conversion in their churches and communities. Rather, it was not until the rise of the proto-Enlightenment reaction to the Reformation in the early seventeenth century that pietism (the forebear to modern evangelicalism) really began to gain a foothold among orthodox Protestants. It was not until the Enlightenment was well established that revivalism also became an institutional fact of modern Christian life.

Prima facie, it would seem difficult to oppose a "new quality of spiritual life," since this would seem to be one of the promises of the new covenant as expressed in Jeremiah 31:33–34:

117. Ibid., 1:373.

118. E.g., Richard Owen Roberts describes the first evidence of genuine revival as that "intense spirit of conviction" which is "felt immediately." Richard Owen Roberts, *Revival* (Wheaton, IL: Tyndale, 1982), 23.

119. The use of terms such as *regeneratio* and *renovatio* for this quickening was a later development in Reformed theology. See Richard A. Muller, *Dictionary of Latin and Greek Theological Terms* (Grand Rapids: Baker, 1985), s.v. "renovatio." For an example of the earlier use of the term see Clark, *Caspar Olevian*, 184–85. Outside Olevianus see Calvin, *Institutio* 1.15.4. In later Reformed theology the term denoted "de primo momento, quo primum convertitur, et novam vitam per regenerationem accipit." F. Turretin, *Institutio Theologiae Elencticae*, in *Francisci Turretini Opera*, 4 vols. (Edinburgh, 1847), 15.5.2. See also P. van Mastricht, *Theoretico-practica Theologia*, new ed. (Utrecht, 1699), 657–64.

This is the covenant that I will cut with the house of Israel after those days, declares Yahweh: I will put my law in them, and I will write it on their hearts. And I will be their God, and they shall be my people. And no longer shall each one teach his neighbor and each his brother, saying, "Know Yahweh" for they shall all know me, from the least of them to the greatest, declares Yahweh. For I will forgive their iniquity, and I will remember their sin no more.

Careful consideration of this passage shows that the subjective blessings promised herein, which we know to be the Pentecostal outpouring of the Holy Spirit with all its attendant graces, are inextricably connected to the objective accomplishment of redemption in the incarnation, obedience, death, and resurrection of Jesus Christ. This promise is cast in the language of the Ancient Near Eastern treaty patterns, in this case a "royal grant."[120] This passage is a covenant promise made to God's people corporately, publicly, about benefits that are the result of his making (cutting) of a new covenant. That covenant was cut in the blood of the incarnate Son of God, to which he referred when he said, "This cup is the new covenant in my blood, which is poured out for you" (Luke 22:20). Whatever blessings are entailed in this new covenant, they are bound up with God's decisive covenantal saving work in history. This language does not suggest so much a heightened state of religious experience or awareness of the divine presence as it does the objective establishment of a new state of divine-human relations. In other words, this language is more sacramental, Protestant, and official than it is personal, private, or revivalist.

Although these new covenant blessings are described in old covenant (Mosaic) terms, there is still an indissoluble connection between the Word and the inward work of the Spirit. If we take "Torah" here as a general term for God's Word, rather than as a reference to the killing power of the Law per se, then even in the prophetic idiom God's converting work is associated with his self-revelation. It would also seem that what was promised here was fulfilled in a very public and definitive way at Pentecost. The proof that the apostles were Spirit-filled was in their preaching. The import of

120. For a helpful discussion of the types of Ancient Near Eastern covenants and how they relate to the various biblical covenants see Michael S. Horton, *God of Promise: Introducing Covenant Theology* (Grand Rapids: Baker, 2006), 23–59.

this most central passage for Reformed covenant theology is clear: in the new covenant, as part of the fulfilment of the promises of the covenant of grace in Jesus Christ, God will draw nearer to his people, and they will experience blessings that are peculiar to the new covenant; particularly, according to Hebrews 8:10–11, we have now a sort of knowledge of God that was unavailable under the typological Mosaic covenant (Col. 2:17; Heb. 8:5; 10:1; 1 Peter 1:12; 1 Cor. 10:1–5). The new covenant state of blessedness, with all its rich internal blessings, is nevertheless tied closely to the progress of the *historia salutis* (the history of redemption), to the objective saving acts of God through his Christ and Spirit in history, which have subjective benefits for Christ's people.

One finds the same correlation in the prophecy of the dry bones in Ezekiel 37:1–14. The "hand of Yahweh" presents the challenge of the dry bones to the prophet. The question comes: "Son of man, can these bones live?" How does the Lord answer? He commands the prophet (v. 4) to preach the Word of Yahweh. God in himself (*Deus in se*) is utterly free, and one would be foolish to prescribe to him what he may or may not do. The point here, however, is that we do not know about his secret work (Deut. 29:29), but we know him, as he has revealed himself to us (*Deus erga nos*), and that we have no revealed promise from him to act apart from his Word. With respect to his absolute power (*de potentia Dei absoluta*), God is free to do as he wills. With Calvin, we must say that we know only of his ordained power (*de potentia Dei ordinata*).[121] Yet, for Calvin, it is not as if God is bound to a standard extrinsic to himself.[122] Calvin refused to separate the power of God (*potentia Dei*) from the will of God (*voluntas Dei*).[123] What this means for us Calvinists is that we must acknowledge God's freedom to work extraordinarily, but, in theology, piety, and practice, we must submit ourselves to the ordinary means of grace and consider ourselves shut-up to the revealed will of God (Isa. 55:8–9).

With this distinction in mind, we must distinguish between the new covenant blessings promised through Jeremiah and revival as defined by Packer, Lloyd-Jones, and Murray, and for this reason, the accomplishment

---

121. *Institutes* 3.23.2.

122. R. S. Clark, "Calvin and the Lex Naturalis," *Stulos Theological Journal* 6 (1998): 73. See *Institutes* 2.17.1.

123. *Institutes* 3.23.2.

of redemption and its application by God the Spirit are not well described by the language of revival or revivalism. This is not to belittle genuine Christian religious experience. Rather, I am trying to explain part of the reason for the substantial difference that now exists between the piety and practices of the founders of the Reformed churches and that which has come to largely dominate the Reformed churches today. As Packer, Lloyd-Jones, and Murray describe revival, it is not chiefly the apprehension of Christ by grace alone, through faith alone, flowing from God's electing grace and union with Christ, revealed in the Word of God written and preached, which results in a new life of progressive sanctification. What the neorevivalists have in mind seems more on the order of a second blessing for the Christian, a move to a higher and more intense spiritual experience of the presence of God, which is neither opposed to nor bound to the ordained, ecclesiastically sanctioned preaching of the gospel.

The Gifts of the Spirit or the Fruit of the Spirit

Contrast Edwards's "marks" of revival and his twelve marks of religious affections with the three marks given in the BC.[124] In writing to Philip II, Guido de Brès (1522–67) with the other authors and editors of the BC (1561) sought to explain how the theology, piety, and practice of the Reformed churches differed from Rome and the enthusiastic radical Reformers, whom the confession describes as "sects."[125] In article 29 the

124. On Edwards's marks of revival see Marsden, *Jonathan Edwards: A Life*, 235, 263.

125. The expressions "toutes les sectes" and "toutes autres sectes" (*Creeds*, 3:419) or "omnes sectae" and "omnibus aliis sectis" (Niemeyer, 380) are a little ambiguous. Initially it is not clear to what group the phrase "all sects" refers. The phrase "aliis sectis" might be translated "other sects," in which case the Reformed are just one among a group of sects. The English translation in *Creeds* omits any reference to "other." This is probably correct. If we compare the use of "sectes" in BC 29 to Calvin's usage from the same period, in a very similar context, the meaning becomes clearer. Calvin used the word "sectae" several times in the preface to Francis I (e.g., *OS*, 3:15.1–4) to refer derisively to radical groups such as the Socinians and the Anabaptists who brought the Reformation into disrepute. This sense of the word is confirmed in *Institutes* 1.13.22 (*OS*, 3:137.16) where it refers to anti-Trinitarians such as Servetus and in *Institutes* 3.23.8 (*OS*, 4:402.24) where it refers to Pelagians, Manicheans, Anabaptists, and Epicureans. If these uses are parallel to that in BC 29, then "sects" refers to religious groups distinct from the Reformed and other confessional Protestants (e.g., the Lutherans). This reading seems to fit the flow of the argument in the article that begins with

confession says that there are three marks of true churches and three marks of true Christians. There are two types of churches, true and false. The marks of a true church are "pure preaching of the gospel," the "pure administration of the sacraments as Christ instituted them," and the practice of "church discipline for correcting faults." The false church is marked by arrogating to itself more authority than warranted by God's Word, is not subject to Scripture, does not administer the sacraments biblically, and persecutes believers. In the context in which the confession was drafted, the bloody persecution of the Reformed by Philip II, such can hardly be understood to refer to any other group but the Roman church. What is most important for our purposes is that the confession establishes objective, empirical standards so that, according to the confession, these "two churches are easy to recognize and thus to distinguish." Whatever the virtues of the New England revivals and Edwards's apology for them, they cannot be said to have been "easy to recognize and distinguish." Edwards himself struggled with this question for years. If it was not easy for Edwards to sort out, how much harder is it for those who do not accept his idealistic grid by which to evaluate religious experience?

The marks of the true Christian, are also three: faith, fruit, and fighting against sin. Because the visible church is a mixed assembly composed of believers and hypocrites, the confession, like Edwards, was concerned to establish objective marks to distinguish Christians from hypocrites. Christians are recognized by their "faith," their "fleeing from sin and pursuing righteousness," having received Christ. Christians love their neighbor and God, and they are to "crucify the flesh and its works." They "fight against" sin "by the Spirit . . . all the days of their lives, appealing constantly to the blood, suffering, death, and obedience of the Lord Jesus, in whom they have forgiveness of their sins, through faith in him." Nevertheless, "great

---

a distinction between the "true church" and false "sects" which call themselves churches. The BC distinguishes carefully between the "sects" and unbelievers who are in the visible church and repeats the distinction between the church and sects. Near the end of the article, attention turns to the "fausse Église" (*Creeds*, 3:420) or "falsam . . . ecclesiam" (Niemeyer, 380). The "sects" and the "false church" are, in the last line of the article, ultimately joined together as opposed to the true church, but that does not mean that there is no distinction between them since the "false church" was at least denominated a "church" of sorts whereas the radicals were not even granted that level of recognition.

infirmities remain."[126] The approach of the BC to identifying saints was not the same as the approach followed by Edwards in the eighteenth century. Because it was not suffused with Edwards's idealism and neo-Platonism, the BC was much simpler and less subjective.

The WCF (1647) took the same approach to distinguishing Christians from hypocrites in the visible assembly. Chapter 15.1 described repentance as an "evangelical grace." In 15.2 the evidence of this grace is a sense of God's holiness and righteousness and the jeopardy of the sinner before such. In 16.2 the confession described obedience to God's commandments as "fruits and evidences of a true and lively faith." In 16.4 the confession remarked that even those in whom the Spirit is at work, who "in their obedience, attain the greatest height which is possible in this life . . . fall short of much which in duty they are bound to do."[127]

Another measure of the different conceptions of the Christian's life between Edwards and the Reformed confessions appears in their interpretation of Romans 7. In answer to a question about "forgiveness of sins," HC Q. 56 says that the gospel is that God will "no more remember my sins, nor the sinful nature with which I have to struggle all my life long." This language, of course, is drawn from Romans 7:24–25 ("wretched man that I am"). The framers of the catechism understood Paul to be speaking of the ordinary Christian life.[128] In question 114, concerning whether Christians are able to keep God's law perfectly, the catechism answered in part, "No, but even the holiest men, while in this life, have only a small beginning of this obedience."[129]

The contrast between the Edwardsean marks and those of the Reformed confessions is quite clear. The marks for which the catechism looks are rather more ordinary than those for which Edwards looked. It looks for fruit in the context of Word and sacrament ministry. Edwards's marks are more subjective, experiential, and less ecclesiastical. Written as it was by ministers in the "churches under the cross" in a time of great persecution, the confession breathes of the spirit of the theology of the

126. *Creeds*, 3:420.
127. Ibid., 3:631–34.
128. Ibid. See also Caspar Olevian, *Firm Foundation*, trans. Lyle D. Bierma (Grand Rapids: Baker, 1995), 94–95.
129. Schaff, *Creeds*, 3:349.

cross, but Edwards's vision of the Christian life was more triumphalist. This vision is evident, for example, in the means by which the revival was advanced, however modestly reported. "Continual news kept alive the talk of religion, and did greatly quicken and rejoice the hearts of God's people, and much awakened those that looked on themselves as still left behind, and made them the more earnest that they also might share in the great blessing that others had obtained."[130]

Two things stand out in this passage. First, Edwards did not mention the duly authorized public proclamation of the gospel (though that certainly occurred), but what we might today call the media, or better, the "buzz," that advanced revival and particularly created what could be called a market for the new enthusiasm. What was true of Edwards in small ways became true of the "Grand Itinerant" George Whitefield in much greater ways, setting a pattern for centuries to come.[131] It is also hard to miss the overtones of the second blessing in Edwards's account. Edwards happily recognized two classes of Christians, those who had a special experience of grace and those who had not. In these phenomena, he found providential confirmation of his ministry. Perhaps Edwards was correct, that all these events were nothing but the work of the Spirit, but was his concentration on religious affections and heightened experience of the divine presence consistent with the Reformed confessions?[132] Edwards's language supports the thesis that "revival" is really a code for a heightened subjective experience of the divine presence, rather than a turn to the objective promises of God and a restoration or reformation of the divinely established means of grace.

This brief survey of some of Edwards's language is not meant to be a comprehensive survey or analysis of his theology, piety, and practice, but only to suggest there were ways in which Edwards's interesting experiment, uniting aspects of Reformed theology with religious subjectivism through the epistemological and psychological categories of the Enlightenment, established a trajectory that has been damaging to Reformed theology,

130. *Works*, 4:153–54.

131. Mark A. Noll, "Jonathan Edwards and Nineteenth Century Theology," in *Jonathan Edwards and the American Experience*, 113–32.

132. Edwards was capable of giving sustained attention to the objective saving acts of God in history; see his sermons collected as *A History of the Work of Redemption*.

piety, and practice, by turning our attention away from the objective saving acts and Word of God.[133] Judged by confessional Reformed piety, religious subjectivism (e.g., revivalism or pietism) is illegitimate because it seeks what is by definition an *extraordinary* providence of God, which is not promised in Scripture.[134] This desire for the extraordinary tends not only to devalue the ordinary providence of God but also the expressed promises of God. He is most free to work all manner of wonderful things; there are, for example, instances of an intense sense of the divine presence, a surprising understanding of the application of Scripture to a given situation, or some other blessing; but they cannot define the Christian life, and they are no proper standard by which to measure sanctification or Christian maturity. It is a significant mistake to make the religious experience envisioned by revivalists the organizing principle for Reformed piety.[135]

We can understand the difference between the ordinary and the extraordinary by analogy with the Pauline teaching on the "fruit of the Spirit" and the "gifts of the Spirit." Compare Paul's teaching in 1 Corinthians 12 with his teaching in Galatians 5:22–26. Another way of putting the difference is to distinguish between *feelings* and *fruit* or genuine sanctity. It is not as if they are necessarily opposed, but, in contrast to revivalism, the apostle is much more concerned about the latter than the former.[136] In 1 Corinthians 11–14 the apostle Paul explains to a first-century congregation the proper function

133. Mark Noll, "Jonathan Edwards and Nineteenth Century Theology," in *Jonathan Edwards and the American Experience*, 264, shows the mixed reception that Edwards received at Princeton. "As they saw it, Edwards had too easily tolerated enthusiasm in the colonial Awakening, he had promoted eccentric views of a common humanity in his work on *Original Sin*, he had fostered unsound habits of metaphysical speculation, and his *Dissertation on the Nature of True Virtue* had been misguided in itself and a bad influence on later New England theology." So that by the late nineteenth century, B. B. Warfield "made no use of Edwards's ideas as such. Edwards was an honored figure in Calvinist history, but no longer a resource" (277).

134. Roberts, *Revival*, 318–24, describes Edwards's view of the extraordinary nature of revival. For a contemporary definition of revival as extraordinary see Leigh Eric Schmidt, *Scottish Communions and American Revivals in the Early Modern Period* (Princeton, NJ: Princeton University Press, 1989), 21–22.

135. As Schmidt, ibid., has shown, it is quite possible to turn even the means of grace into an opportunity for revivalism.

136. E.g., E. P. Clowney, *The Church* (Downers Grove, IL: InterVarsity, 1995), 23, describes the first evidence of genuine revival as that "intense spirit of conviction" which is "felt immediately."

of what we regard as the extraordinary gifts of the Spirit. Since the book of the new covenant was in the process of being completed, various persons were authorized by the apostle to bring direct revelations from God the Holy Spirit (1 Cor. 11:5; 12:10, 28; 14:3). So he gave them a doctrinal test (12:3) by which to determine whether someone was actually speaking under the inspiration of the Holy Spirit. If a speaker denied Christ the Lord, he was to be considered a false prophet.

The apostle describes a variety of gifts operating in the Corinthian congregation: healing, wonder working, helping, administration, discernment, the wondrous ability to speak in previously unlearned foreign languages (Acts 2:4–15; 1 Cor. 12:10; 14:2, 4–19), and the gift of interpreting these foreign languages (vv. 11, 28).[137] As B. B. Warfield noted over a century ago, it is virtually impossible to find today any credible, empirically verifiable evidence of the exercise of genuine apostolic power.[138] Because these gifts were so much a part of the administration of the history of redemption, because they were so closely associated with the last great act of redemption before the return of our Savior, that is, the outpouring of the Holy Spirit at Pentecost, the beginning of the reversal of the curse of Babel and the beginning of the creation of the one new man (Eph. 2:15) in Christ, we do not expect them to continue beyond the apostolic epoch of redemptive history, any more than we expect God to send another Noahic flood (Gen. 9:15; 2 Peter 2:5) or part the Red Sea again or bring another ten plagues on the earth, at least not before the judgment.

If the extraordinary work of God is unexpected, the result or the fruit of God's sovereign saving work should always be expected. The essence of all of the extraordinary gifts is love (1 Cor. 13:13), which is a fruit of the Spirit (Gal. 5:22–26). The proper function of all the extraordinary, apostolic-era gifts was to produce the very ordinary (in the fullest sense of the word, ordained by the revealed will of God) fruit of charity. In

137. See Richard B. Gaffin, *Perspectives on Pentecost: Studies in the New Testament Teaching on the Gifts of the Holy Spirit* (Phillipsburg, NJ: Presbyterian and Reformed, 1979), 237–51; idem, "A Cessationist View," in *Are Miraculous Gifts for Today?* ed. Richard B. Gaffin and Wayne A. Grudem (Grand Rapids: Zondervan, 1996), 25–64.

138. B. B. Warfield, *Counterfeit Miracles* (Edinburgh: Banner of Truth Trust, reprint, 1983). Wayne Grudem argues for continuing, noncanonical, fallible revelations, but even if we concede his claims, the phenomena for which he argues are not identical to those attributed to the apostles in Acts.

Galatians 5:22–23 Paul identifies the fruit of the Spirit: "love, joy, peace, patience, kindness, goodness, faithfulness, gentleness, self-control." Paul says that when we manifest these virtues we "live by the Spirit." That is, these are the Spirit-wrought evidences of genuine Christianity. These fruits are the evidence that Christians have "crucified the flesh with its illegitimate lusts and inappropriate desires" (v. 24). In other words, where the extraordinary gifts are limited to the apostolic epoch, the ordinary Christian experience, not limited to the apostolic church, is that of struggle with sin, dying to that sin with the help of grace, and being renewed in the image of Christ by that same grace.

Further, the quest for extraordinary religious experience is illegitimate because it is driven by a false theology. Luther and Calvin described the version of the Christian life that I have sketched briefly as "the theology of the cross." They called the notion that the Christian life moves from triumph to triumph—which we have known since the late nineteenth century as the Higher Life movement—the theology of glory. In Reformation terms, it is a theology of glory to seek to know the hidden things, God's decretive will (Deut. 29:29), or to orient the Christian life around the extraordinary things which are not promised but which God is free to do or withhold. It is the theology of the cross to submit to God's revealed will and to bear patiently with his relative silence, as, for example, during the centuries between the close of the old covenant Scriptures and the revelation of his final Word in the incarnation of the Logos with all its subsequent apostolic revelation. The theology of the cross teaches us that this epoch in the history of redemption, the period between the advents, is a time for patience, hope, and earnest expectation of Christ's return (e.g., Rom. 8:24–25; 1 Cor. 13:7, 13; 15:19; Eph. 1:12, 18; 2:12; Col. 1:5, 27; 1 Thess. 5:8; Titus 2:13). The quest for revival is a subspecies of the theology of glory, which is not content to wait for him who descended and to wait for him especially in his Word preached (Eph. 4:9–10; Rom. 10:5–17)—"The Word is near you, in your mouth and in your heart!" (Rom. 10:8)—but seems to want a sort of glory which is not appropriate for the interadventual pilgrimage.

The reader may be tempted to conclude that, because of my criticism of excessive religious subjectivism and despite my protestations to the contrary, I actually have some interest in downplaying a vital personal piety. Nothing could be further from the truth. Nevin himself urged upon his students such an ardent, heartfelt religious experience that Sam Hamstra Jr. describes him as a "Pietist."[139] The question is not whether we shall have a piety. Rather, the question is, *which* piety shall we have? With its emphasis on the ordinary, the confessional Reformed theology did produce a vital personal and profound piety grounded in the objective saving work of God in Christ and empowered by the Christian's union with the ascended Christ wrought by the Holy Spirit. The very structure of the HC, as indicated in the second question, is indicative of the confessional Reformed approach to piety.[140] From God's holy law we learn first the greatness of our sin and misery and our need for a Savior. From the gospel, we learn how believers are redeemed from sin and misery. Following from our redemption is the Christian life, that is, how we ought to be thankful for such redemption.

Even before the third part of the catechism, there are indications of the sort of piety the classic Reformed theology envisioned. According to HC Q. 32, we are partakers of Christ's anointing, with the result that the Christian life is a "sacrifice of thankfulness," in which we fight against sin and the devil.[141] The same theme recurs in Q. 43. There are two great benefits of Christ's death on the cross. The second of them is that "thereby our old man is crucified, slain and buried with him, that so the evil lusts of the flesh may no more reign in us, but that we may offer ourselves unto him as a sacrifice of thanksgiving."[142] Because of our union with Christ's death, burial, and resurrection, we are "raised up to a new life" (Q. 45).[143] God the Spirit has been given to us as "an earnest, by whose power we

139. Sam Hamstra Jr., ed., *The Reformed Pastor: Lectures on Pastoral Theology by John Williamson Nevin*, Princeton Theological Monographs (Eugene, OR: Pickwick, 2006), xii–xiv.

140. HC Q. 2 asks, "How many things are necessary for you to know that in this comfort you may live and die happily? Three things: First, the greatness of my sin and misery. Second, how I am redeemed from all my sins and misery. Third, how I am to be thankful to God for such redemption." Adapted from *Creeds*, 3:308. The WCF teaches the same doctrine in 21.3. See *Creeds*, 3:646.

141. *Creeds*, 3:318.

142. Ibid., 3:321.

143. Ibid.

seek those things which are above" (Q. 49).[144] God the Spirit has not only effected our union with Christ, but he himself has been given to me, "comforts me," and through him Christ shall abide with me ever (Q. 53).[145] Through Christ's presence with me, I "feel in my heart the beginning of eternal joy" (Q. 58).[146] This same Spirit necessarily works in us the "fruits of thankfulness" (Q. 64).[147]

All this occurs before the catechism actually turns its attention formally to the doctrine of sanctification. The Christian life is the process of being renewed by the Holy Spirit in the image of Christ. Consequently, we must "show ourselves thankful to God" (Q. 86).[148] The theme of the Christian life as a death returns in questions 88–90. The Christian life is the "dying of the old man," that is, mortification of sin, and the "making alive of the new" (Q. 88).[149] Mortification entails hatred for and turning from sin (Q. 89).[150] Spiritual renewal is "heartfelt joy" (*herzliche Freude*, Q. 90) in God and delighting in his revealed moral will.[151] One of the most interesting things, however, about the catechism's view of piety is its definition and use of prayer. Having accounted for sin and death, the gospel, the means of grace, and God's moral will for believers, the catechism turns to prayer (*Gebet*) in its exposition of the Lord's Prayer.[152]

Why is prayer necessary? Because it is the "chief part of the thankfulness (*die Dankbarkeit*) which God requires of us." He has ordered his relations with his people so that "he will give his grace and Holy Spirit (*Gnade und Heilige Geist*) only to such as heartily and without ceasing beg them from him and render thanks unto him for them."[153]

The catechism defines prayer more closely in the subsequent question (Q. 117). Christian prayer comes from the heart (*von Herzen*), according to God's Word, to the only true God, as he "has revealed himself to us."

144. Ibid., 3:323.
145. Ibid., 3:324.
146. Ibid., 3:326.
147. Ibid., 3:328.
148. Ibid., 3:338.
149. Ibid., 3:329.
150. Ibid.
151. Ibid.
152. Ibid., 3:350.
153. Revised from ibid., 3:350.

In order to pray properly, we must be aware of God's majestic presence, we must know our "need and misery and we must pray believing that the Father hears our prayers for Christ's sake." Given the tripartite structure of the catechism, it is significant that prayer appears at the very end. Prayer is the chief way for believers, united to Christ by grace alone, through faith alone, to express their faith and to work out their salvation "with fear and trembling" (Phil. 2:12). It is the evidence and expression of the Spirit's work of gratitude in the heart of the Christian. While, considered narrowly, private prayer is not a "means of grace," it is a wonderfully joyous duty to commune with the Father, through the Son, by virtue of the Holy Spirit's help. It is a great privilege to exercise our personal relationship with Christ by asking of God "all things necessary for soul and body" (Q. 118) according to the pattern revealed in the Lord's Prayer.[154]

The Due Use of Ordinary Means

Just as there is a Reformed approach to religious certainty, there is also a Reformed approach to religious experience. It is a corollary to our Creator/creature distinction. We are not on a quest to experience God apart from the divinely ordained means. This is evident in WCF 1.7:

> All things in Scripture are not alike plain in themselves, nor alike clear unto all: yet those things which are necessary to be known, believed, and observed for salvation, are so clearly propounded, and opened in some place of Scripture or other, that not only the learned, but the unlearned, in a due use of the ordinary means, may attain unto a sufficient understanding of them.[155]

That phrase, "due use of the ordinary means," is at the heart of our piety. The Standards return repeatedly to the notion that it is God's will to use "means" (*media*) to accomplish his will (5.3) and to the necessity of the proper use of the ordained means of grace for the assurance of faith (18.3). WLC 154 says: "The outward and ordinary means whereby Christ

154. Ibid., 3:350–51.
155. Ibid., 3:604.

communicates to his church the benefits of his mediation, are all his ordinances; especially the Word, sacraments, and prayer; all which are made effectual to the elect for their salvation."[156]

No tradition has written more deeply or more carefully about the intimate personal relations between the Savior and his saved; but, unlike Meister Eckhart or Catherine of Siena, we have located our rather modest mysticism in Word and sacrament.[157] The Spirit works a mystical union through the preaching of the gospel by which he creates faith. He strengthens that union through Word and sacrament. The WCF is quite realistic about the nature of the Christian life. Consider the confession's teaching on assurance. In 14.3 we confess: "This faith is different in degrees, weak or strong; may be often and many ways assailed, and weakened, but gets the victory: growing up in many to the attainment of a full assurance, through Christ, who is both the author and finisher of our faith."[158] Assurance begins with the gospel, the objective and gracious promises of God in Christ, so that we confess, "the principal acts of saving faith are accepting, receiving, and resting upon Christ alone for justification, sanctification, and eternal life, by virtue of the covenant of grace" (WCF 14.2).[159] We confess a distinction between the objective work of Christ for us, which we receive and in which we rest, and the subjective work of the Spirit in us. The first is definitive and the second is progressive and gradual. We confess that it is possible to have, in this life,

> an infallible assurance of faith founded upon the divine truth of the promises of salvation, the inward evidence of those graces unto which these promises are made, the testimony of the Spirit of adoption witnessing with our spirits that we are the children of God, which Spirit

156. *Westminster Confession of Faith* (Glasgow: Free Presbyterian Publications, reprint 1997), 246.

157. Schmidt, *Holy Fairs*, 23, appeals to a small collection of sermons by Robert Bruce on the Lord's Supper as evidence of an early form of "conversionist" piety. This analysis seems anachronistic. It is unclear what is "conversionist" about these sermons or how, if they are "conversionist," all confessional Reformed theology is not also conversionist. In fact, these sermons are an excellent example of the sort of Word and sacrament–oriented piety to which I am appealing as a contrast to the piety of the eighteenth-century New Side movement. See Robert Bruce, *Sermons upon the Sacrament of the Lord's Supper* (London, 1591).

158. *Creeds*, 3:631.

159. Ibid., 3:630.

is the earnest of our inheritance, whereby we are sealed to the day of redemption. (WCF 18.2)

We confess a vital religion, but it is not identical to the religion of Edwards's *Affections*. Thus in 18.3 we confess: "This infallible assurance doth not so belong to the essence of faith, but that a true believer may wait long, conflict with many difficulties before he be partaker of it: yet, being enabled by the Spirit to know the things which are freely given him of God, he may, without extraordinary revelation, in the right use of ordinary means, attain thereunto."[160] We confess a living religion that is organized around the means of grace, not an a priori definition of religious experience. Few have dared to accuse the HC of being a cold, academic volume. Indeed, some have alleged that it is too experiential. Thus, it is instructive to compare the sort of Reformed subjectivism we have seen in the eighteenth century with the piety of the HC.

In question 58, the HC says, "inasmuch as I now *feel* (*empfind*) in my heart the beginning of eternal joy."[161] In this case, the catechism is describing for the Christian one of the benefits of believing in eternal life, the internal perception of the existence of joy. In question 129, the catechism asks about the meaning of the word "Amen" in the Lord's Prayer. The answer says that our faith rests less on what we "feel" (*fühl*) in the heart than on the objective promises of God.[162] For the catechism, the feelings of joy which Christians experience are a great gift and not to be despised, but they are not the basis for judging a profession of faith. The basis on which the church evaluates a profession of faith is twofold: first, has one made a credible profession of faith, and second, does one's life correspond to the confession? When the catechism considers the proof, if you will, of one's profession of faith, it looks first to behavior, rather than to religious experience. In answer to the question of why the Christian saved by grace alone, through faith alone, in Christ alone, must do good works, the catechism answers: "Because Christ, having redeemed us by His blood, also renews us by His Holy Spirit after His own image, that with our whole life we show ourselves thankful to God for His blessing,

160. Ibid., 3:638–39.
161. Ibid., 3:326.
162. Ibid., 3:355.

and also that He be glorified through us; then also, that we ourselves may be assured of our faith by the fruits thereof; and by our godly walk win also others to Christ."[163]

There are real benefits to the Christian faith. One of the benefits of being united to Christ is saving faith, which produces in us genuine moral transformation. That moral transformation, or "fruit" (which the catechism describes in subsequent questions as the progressive dying to self and living to Christ), produces in the Christian confidence that he really does have saving faith and does belong to Christ, and these benefits spur the believer to communicate something of Christ's grace to his neighbor.

In contrast to Edwards's narrative, central to the catechism's vision of the Christian life are the means of grace, that is, the preaching of the holy gospel through which the Holy Spirit ordinarily operates to raise dead sinners to life and by which he gives those whom he has raised the grace of justifying faith, and the holy sacraments, through which the Spirit ordinarily operates to give assurance and the grace of sanctification.[164] In the view of the catechism, the fruit of a sanctified heart and life is not the result of an immediate transforming experience (which might happen) but rather the result of the process of being graciously conformed to Christ's image.

Conclusions

In North America, beginning in the early eighteenth century, Reformed theology, piety, and practice were profoundly and adversely affected by synthesis of the Reformed confession with pietism. The result of this synthesis was a turn away from the objective to the subjective. In this chapter, this turn to the subjective is described as the quest for illegitimate religious experience, the desire for an unmediated encounter with God apart from the ordinary means. Gradually, through the eighteenth and nineteenth centuries, as the restraint of confessional orthodoxy was eroded, pietism came to dominate Reformed piety. As we shall see in subsequent chapters, the effect of the turn away from the

163. HC Q. 86 in ibid., 3:338.
164. HC Q. 65, in ibid., 3:328.

objective was a near complete transformation of Reformed piety and worship. In contrast, this chapter has offered a sketch of confessional Reformed piety, Christ-centered, grounded in the gospel of Christ's obedience, death, and resurrection for sinners, and in the operation of the Holy Spirit through the ordained means of grace: the preaching of the gospel and the administration of the sacraments. According to the Reformed churches, Christ has promised to use these means to bring his people to maturity and sanctity.

This chapter ends the first section of the book in which we have considered both the QIRC and QIRE. At bottom, as Phillip Schaff argued, they are really only two aspects of the same impulse. This union is symbolized in Jonathan Edwards, whose idealist pietism forms a connection between QIRC and QIRE. Both seek immediate intersection with the divine. The latter seeks intersection with the divine affections, if you will, and the former seeks intersection with the divine intellect.

The book now turns to the second part, beginning with the path to recovering the Reformed identity.

PART 2

THE RECOVERY

Q. *But why are you called a Christian?*

A. Because by faith I am a member of Christ and thus a partaker of His anointing, in order that I also may confess His Name, may present myself a living sacrifice of thankfulness to Him, and with a free conscience may fight against sin and the devil in this life, and hereafter in eternity reign with Him over all creatures.

—Heidelberg Catechism, Q. 32

The distinguishing characteristic between every non-Christian theory of knowledge, on the one hand, and the Christian concept of knowledge on the other hand, is . . . that in all non-Christian theories men reason *univocally*, while in Christianity men reason *analogically*.

—Cornelius Van Til

CHAPTER
4

Recovering a Reformed Identity (1)

In trying to explain the difference in character between the Scottish and the English, Robert Louis Stevenson once observed that the way each spends the Sabbath is quite distinct. He also observed that the first question of their two catechisms says much about each of them.[1] The Westminster Shorter Catechism (1647) begins with the question, "What is the chief end of man?" whereas the English Catechism (1549) begins, "What is your name?"[2] Amusing as this contrast is, there is more to the first question of the English catechism than might first appear.

The second question asks, "Who gave you this name?" The answer is that we receive our name at our baptism. The practice of naming children is now a private matter and is no longer associated with holy baptism, but no less important. If one's name has been chosen with care, it says something of significance about the one who carries it. For instance, in earlier times Christian children were given a biblical name or the name of a particularly pious or outstanding Christian. In this way Christian parents tried to communicate something of their hopes and prayers for their child. Indeed, the English Catechism continues in this vein.

1. Robert Louis Stevenson, *Memories and Portraits* (New York: Charles Scribner's Sons, 1917), 14–16. I am grateful to Alan Girdwood for calling my attention to this passage.
2. *Creeds*, 3:517.

What did your Godfathers and Godmothers then for you?

They did promise and vow three things in my name. First, that I should renounce the devil and all his works, the pomps and vanity of this wicked world, and all the sinful lusts of the flesh. Secondly, that I should believe all the Articles of the Christian Faith. And thirdly, that I should keep God's holy will and commandments, and walk in the same all the days of my life.[3]

In the words of the HC, the hope of baptism is that we should learn three things:"the greatness of my sin and how I am redeemed from all my sins and misery and how I am to be thankful to God for such redemption" (Q. 3).[4]

The act of naming a child at baptism presumes two things. First, it presumes that it is someone else who says the first definitive word about who I am. Of course, this agrees with reality as we know it, since "In the beginning, God created the heavens and the earth," and that same God spoke all things into existence through the Word of God (Gen. 1:1, 3; John 1:1–3; 2 Peter 3:5–6). If God's speech defines reality, then it is appropriate that I should be defined by Christian speech about me. Second, it presumes that one's identity is not defined in a purely individual manner. If one is named at the moment of inclusion in the visible Christ-confessing covenant community, then one is already a member of one race, that is, Adam's children, in whose fall one is included, and, by God's grace, one is now being recognized as a member of the covenant community.[5]

In a similar way, every Reformed Christian carries a name that says much about the bearer. He who wears it does not define the meaning of the name; the name defines him. Wearing the name "Reformed" means that one is a member of a community of faith which existed and was defined before him. Thus far, I have been arguing that, in a variety of ways and for two main reasons, we Reformed folk are suffering from a sort of amnesia—

3. Ibid.

4. Ibid., 3:308.

5. One form for the baptism of infants says, "And although our children do not understand these things, we may not therefore exclude them from baptism, since they are without their knowledge partakers of the condemnation in Adam, and so again are received unto grace in Christ"— Christian Reformed Church, *Psalter Hymnal: Doctrinal Standards and Liturgy of the Christian Reformed Church*, centennial edition (Grand Rapids: Publication Committee of the Christian Reformed Church, 1959), 85.

we have forgotten our name, the major premise of our theology, and how we define ourselves relative to other folk. In truth, however, we have been baptized, as it were, with a perfectly good Christian name, a name that stands for a biblical and confessional theology, piety, and practice.

Not all those who identify with the Reformed tradition agree that there is something like a distinct Reformed identity or that the Reformed confessions are the best way to determine that identity. Alan P. F. Sell admires the Reformed confessions the way one admires the remaining sections of old Route 66, as relics of a bygone era and road not much traveled today. However quaint they may be, it is the current praxis of modern mainline Reformed churches that defines the Reformed identity, especially the ordination of females to the ministry of Word and sacraments and broad ecumenism.[6] John Frame regards Reformed Christianity as a subset of transdenominational evangelicalism.[7] Richard F. Lovelace, arguing for a place for evangelicals in the mainline, argues that Reformed people ought to define their identity not according to the Reformed confession (considered broadly or narrowly) but according to the eighteenth- and nineteenth-century revivals. The Old School Presbyterians erred by trying to "evict those who disagreed with them" by using the church courts, that is, by acting like confessional Presbyterians.[8]

In contrast to these approaches, this chapter argues that our amnesia is something from which it is possible to recover step by step. To that end this chapter is the first of two parts. In this chapter we begin by relearning our name and the major premise of our theology. In the next chapter we move to the meaning of our name and its relation to confessional boundaries.

Recovering Our Grammar by Overcoming "Translation"

A preliminary diagnosis of the current condition of the Reformed movement is that we have lost our memory, our vocabulary, and, as a

6. Alan P. F. Sell, "Reformed Identity: A Non-Issue of Catholic Significance," *Reformed Theological Review* 54 (2000): 17–27.

7. John Frame, *Evangelical Reunion: Denominations and the One Body of Christ* (Grand Rapids: Baker, 1991).

8. Richard F. Lovelace, "Evangelical Revivals and the Presbyterian Tradition," *WTJ* 42 (1979): 144, 147–48.

result, important aspects of our theology, piety, and practice. William Willimon has commented on the modern need to "translate" the biblical language "into something more palatable" to people who live in a high-tech, fast-moving culture of convenience. "The modern church has been more willing to use everyone's language but its own" with the result that by "the time most of us finish qualifying the scandal of Christian speech, very little can be said by the preacher that can't be heard elsewhere."[9] In the nature of things, these losses create a vacuum which is being filled by views, approaches, and practices which are not only not Reformed, but actually hostile to the Reformed understanding of Scripture, Christian faith, and practice. How did this happen and what can be done about it?

In the modern period, theologians have been, if not quite entirely, mainly preoccupied with theological method. For those who accepted the conclusions of modernity as the assured results of science, and who wished to retain a Christian vocabulary and association with the Christian tradition and church, the question became how to continue speaking like a Christian, how to accommodate or translate Scripture and the premodern, precritical worldview to the modern, critical world, without invoking the categories and convictions of a now discredited faith.[10] Rudolf Bultmann (1884–1976) proposed that we translate the religious conceptions of the Bible into existentialist categories, arguing that the biblical view of the world was necessarily mythological and therefore unintelligible to modern man.[11] In doing so, however, as David Kelsey says, we are not really translating anymore. "The result of the move from one conceptuality to another is not a 'translation' but a 'redescription.'"[12] Paul's account of Christ's death is not exactly equivalent to Bultmann's notion of an "authentic existence."[13]

9. William H. Willimon, *Peculiar Speech: Preaching to the Baptized* (Grand Rapids: Eerdmans, 1992), 9.

10. David H. Kelsey, *The Uses of Scripture in Recent Theology* (Philadelphia: Fortress, 1975). This work is an extended critique of the use of translation as a metaphor for doing theology. See also Michael S. Horton, *Covenant and Eschatology: The Divine Drama* (Louisville: Westminster John Knox, 2002), 184–91.

11. Rudolf Bultmann, *Kerygma and Myth: A Theological Debate*, trans. R. H. Fuller (New York: Harper and Row, 1961), 1–44.

12. Kelsey, *The Uses of Scripture*, 188.

13. Ibid., 189.

More interesting, perhaps, is that even those in the Reformed confessional tradition who rejected the modernist translation project have also wrestled with the proper way to do theology after modernity. Some confessionalists carried on the classic approach to theology, but we have often seemed to forget gradually our own grammar, logic, and rhetoric. Confessional Reformed theology, however, works with some basic beliefs about the nature of relations between God and his creation, beliefs that are derived from Scripture and shape theological method. Chief among these is the notion that God is the "beginning of being" (*principium essendi*) and, as such, the "beginning of knowing" (*principium cognoscendi*).[14] A corollary to this doctrine is the notion that human knowledge of God is analogical.

There are a number of biblical passages which indicate a conceptual framework in which God and human beings are regarded as analogues. This analogical conception is basic to Genesis 1:26, in which Adam is said to have been made in the "image" and "likeness." In verse 27 the same language is repeated, but set in terms of Adam's relations to another, a female person. As a created representation of God, as an image/likeness bearer, Adam was nothing, if not an analogue to God. Not only is Adam's existence as a creature utterly dependent upon the will of the Creator, but his status as a person is contingent upon and derived from the personal God who spoke all things into being, who entered into personal relations with him, and who constituted him a person with faculties (rational, voluntary, affective), enabling him to enter into personal relations with another creature drawn from himself (Gen. 2:21–22).

Thus the conceptual framework of man as analogue to his Creator is the backdrop to many other passages which indicate a parallel, but separate life and existence experienced by God and man. For example, in Exodus 25:9, 40, God commands the Israelites to "make this tabernacle and all its furnishings exactly like the pattern I will show you." The noun here translated as "pattern" is derived from the root "to build." In other words, the "pattern" is something that is built already.

This passage assumes an understanding of reality whereby there is an ultimate, final, consummate reality in the heavens, associated with God and

14. Herman Bavinck, *Prolegomena*, ed. John Bolt, trans. John Vriend, vol. 1, of *Reformed Dogmatics* (Grand Rapids: Baker Academic, 2003), 212–14.

the heavenly beings, of which the earthly tabernacle was but an analogue. Unlike the neo-Platonist ontology, neither Scripture nor the Reformed view of analogy presupposes a continuum of existence with God at one end and humans at the other. In the neo-Platonic scheme, the "pattern" would have more "being" and the "copy" would have less being. This is not at all what Scripture is saying. The tabernacle was real, it was useful, it was divinely ordained, but it was only a copy. The biblical "pattern and copy" structure of reality is not that of the neo-Platonic scheme, since in the biblical pattern both the pattern and copy are real. It is not as if the copy lacks being. Both exist, but in different "ages" (in Pauline terms). The biblical pattern is of analogues, not a continuum of being and nonbeing. Psalm 131:1 seems also to recognize this fundamental structure of reality, that with respect to his transcendence, God exists on one plane and we on another. The psalmist contented himself to meditate on revealed things, rather than God's hidden providential decree.

As a principle of theological method, this distinction is an essential assumption of Deuteronomy 29:29: "The secret things belong to Yahweh our God, but the things revealed belong to us and to our children forever, that we may follow all the words of this law."[15] In context, Moses had rebuked the Israelites for their unfaithfulness during the sojourn. In verse 14, Moses reminds them that, speaking as God's authorized representative, he is not cutting this covenant only with those who are present, but with all the Israelites and their children.[16] He warns them of the danger of breaking covenant with the Lord (v. 21). The principle he announces in verse 29 is a summary of all he has said thus far.

In the prophet Isaiah a similar conceptual structure is at work in Isaiah 55:8–9, in which God contrasts his thoughts with ours. His ways are not ours. The noun translated here, and in Psalm 92:5, as "thoughts" elsewhere denotes "skilled designs" used to work in precious metals (Ex. 31:4), human intentions (Esth. 8:3), human plans (Job 5:12), and God's secret purposes (Ps. 40:5). There are analogies between God's skillful intentions and ours as there are analogies between heaven and earth, but according to verse 9 there is a vast qualitative difference. The difference is

15. This verse appears as 29:28 in MT in *BHS*.
16. V. 13 in the MT in *BHS*.

moral: God's ways, thoughts, and plans are utterly pure and righteous and ours are not. There are also ontological discontinuities. God's skillful ways and intentions are infinite and simple. Ours are not. Our Lord knows the end from the beginning (Isa. 46:10). His thoughts have always existed, from all eternity, without change; thus they are as far removed from our thoughts and ways as the heavens are from the earth.

The truth that God revealed to Moses, and Isaiah revealed to Israel and to us, is that we are not to inquire into God's secret decree and providence, what our theologians called the decretive will or his hidden will. We are to devote ourselves to God's revelation of his will or his preceptive will. It is not that there are actually two wills in God, but that, in the nature of divine human relations, in order to give a true account of God's revelation, we must, for the sake of discussion, make distinctions which do not actually exist in God himself. The only way to avoid doing so would be to become God.

The writer to the Hebrews confirms this understanding of Moses' language in Exodus and the psalmist's conception. Hebrews 8:3–6 argues that the biblical priesthood was ordained by God to perform a particular function (make offerings). The earthly sanctuary at which they serve (v. 5) is nothing more than a "type and shadow" of the heavenly sanctuary. The earthly temple, to which they were tempted to return, was by divine intention only a provisional, temporary, typological illustration of the prototypical temple to which Jesus has already ascended. Like Stephen (Acts 7:44), the writer quotes Exodus 25:40 (as it appears in the LXX) that the Israelites are to make everything in the tabernacle according to the "type" which was revealed on the mountain (Heb. 8:5).

This is why Abraham was looking for a city whose builder and maker is God (Heb. 11:10). The writer to the Hebrews characterizes faith as that which has its ultimate interest not in the copy, but in the original.[17] Faith is the "conviction" or "certainty" of the reality of things that are unseen. Noah believed God's Word about things he had not yet seen. Abraham (v. 8) journeyed to a city he had not seen, trusting God's Word, but he did it with his eyes fixed firmly on the eternal, ultimate, heavenly city. Abraham understood the relations between the heavenly prototype and the

---

17. Thanks to Steve Baugh for his help with this passage.

earthly type. The Canaan to which he traveled was a real place of blessing promised by God, but he did not mistake it for the ultimate destination and promised blessing.

This two-level conception of reality, this pattern-copy scheme, is also found in the Johannine corpus. As Geerhardus Vos noted in 1927, the writings of the apostle John know of "two kinds of truth."[18] The words for "true" and "truth" in the New Testament "possess inherently two distinct connotations." They correspond to the adjectives "veracious" and "veritable." The first belongs to the cognitive sphere, to something extramental.[19] The second sense of "truth," however, has less to do with the cognitive correlation between one thing and another, and more to do with ultimate reality (heaven) as distinct from its real, but earthly analogue. This is what Jesus meant to teach when he said, "I am the true bread" (John 6:32) or when he is called "the true light" (John 1:9). In his interpretation, when Jesus says, "I am the way, the truth, and the life" (John 14:6), he is not saying, "I am the propositional truth which corresponds to objective reality," but rather he is saying, "I am the ultimate reality incarnate, come down from heaven." It is that something (e.g., the heavenly pattern for the temple) that is in heaven or has come from heaven which makes it "true" or "the truth."

This is the force of the contrast between Moses and Christ in John 1:17.[20] It is inconceivable that when Scripture says, "The law came through Moses, but grace and truth came through Jesus Christ," we are to understand that "the law came through Moses," but "propositional truth came through Jesus Christ," as if the entire Mosaic economy were being characterized with propositional falsehood. Rather, Vos's interpretation of this language is superior. The contrast that the apostle intends to communicate is not between propositional truth and falsity, but between an economy in redemptive history marked by intentional incompleteness and the advent from heaven of the ultimate reality on which the copy was based. In other words, what the apostle John says is that the provisional, typical, temporary economy of the history of salvation came through

18. Geerhardus Vos, "'True' and 'Truth' in the Johannine Writings," in *Redemptive History and Biblical Interpretation: The Shorter Writings of Geerhardus Vos*, ed. Richard B. Gaffin Jr. (Phillipsburg, NJ: Presbyterian and Reformed, 1980), 343.

19. Ibid., 343–44.

20. Ibid., 349.

Moses, and this temporary administration was symbolized in the Torah. With the advent of God the Son incarnate, all that Moses typified and foreshadowed has been inaugurated in his person and work in this new administration of God's salvation.

It is against the background of analogical relations that we should understand Paul's bill of indictment, in Romans 1:18–2:17, against all fallen, that is, impious and unrighteous humanity, as the proper object of God's wrath, which is presently being revealed from heaven. Despite the fact that God has revealed himself and some of his attributes (eternity, power, and deity) in creation, and despite the fact that all humans have a genuine analogical knowledge of their Creator (Rom. 1:20), nevertheless, humans are so depraved that they are actively suppressing (Rom. 1:18) this knowledge of God, refusing to glorify him as God or even thank him (Rom. 1:21) for his universal mercies. Because of our fallen condition, all humanity is in a reprobate condition (Rom. 1:24). In verse 25, Paul denounces sinful humanity, which has, because of its fallen state, rebelliously "exchanged the truth for a lie." We worshiped the creature rather than the Creator. Certainly, it is the confusion of the Creator with the creation which animates and concretely represents the human condition in Adam.

Reformed theology generally understands Scripture to require a sharp distinction between the Creator and creature on the principle that the "finite is not capable of the infinite" (*finitum non capax infiniti*).[21] Closely related to this principle is the axiom that creatures cannot know God as he is in himself (*in se*) but only as he has revealed himself to us (*erga nos*). By these expressions and distinctions our theologians did not erect, as some have alleged, a logical a priori by which to lever Scripture. Rather, they sought to account for the biblical revelation of divine-human relations and for the biblical revelation concerning the relation of the two natures of Christ. For example, Theodore Beza (1519–1605), responding to the Gnesio-Lutheran Jacob Andreä (1528–90), defended the Reformed Christology: in the hypostatic union Christ's humanity is not deified but

21. This section follows closely *PRRD*, 1:129–35. On this principle see also David Willis, *Calvin's Catholic Christology: The Function of the So-Called Extra Calvinisticum in Calvin's Theology* (Leiden: Brill, 1966).

remains truly human.[22] In his *Commonplaces* (1647), theologian and delegate to the Synod of Dort Antonius Walaeus (1573–1639) discussed this maxim under the topic "The Church Triumphant."[23] He said that it is true that we cannot see God *in se*, but that we will see God as he accommodates himself to our creaturely capacity.

Francis Turretin (1623–87) said, "When God is set forth as the object of theology, he is not to be regarded simply as *Deus in se*, for thus he is hidden to us, but in so far as he is revealed to us and as he has condescended to make himself known to us in the Word."[24] He continued by polemicizing against Thomas Aquinas by arguing that we do not speak about God as he is in himself as did Thomas and the rest of the Scholastics after him because this sort of knowledge of God is not saving but "deadly to sinners." Rather, "God is to be known as he is our God covenanted in Christ, as he has accommodated himself to us in his Word."[25] Where Luther had spoken of "God hidden," Turretin said "in himself"; where Luther said, "God revealed," Turretin said "God covenanted with us in Christ." Though they used different terms, they were saying substantially the same thing.

At the end of the seventeenth century, Petrus van Mastricht (1630–1706) rejected the Lutheran Christology on the basis of this, now axiomatic, Creator/creature distinction.[26] In the late nineteenth and early twentieth centuries Herman Bavinck reaffirmed this distinction: "This theory of the incomprehensibility of God and the unknowability of his

22. Theodore Beza, *Ad Putidas Quasdam Iacobi Andreae Calumnias Responsio*, 2d ed. (Geneva, 1582), 126. See also R. Scott Clark, *Caspar Olevian and the Substance of the Covenant: The Double Benefit of Christ*, ed. David F. Wright, Rutherford Studies in Historical Theology (Edinburgh: Rutherford House, 2005), 104–36.

23. Antonius Walaeus, *Loci Communes* (Leiden, 1647), 453.

24. "Sed quando Deus proponitur ut Obiectum Theologiae, non spectandus est simpliciter ut Deus in se, sic enim nobis est ἀκατάληπτος; sed quatenus revelatus et ut se in Verbo nobis patefacere dignatus est." Francis Turretin, *Institutio Theologiae Elencticae* (Geneva, 1688), 1.5.4.

25. "Nec praecise considerandus est sub ratione Deitatis, ut vult Thomas & post eum plerique Scholastici; hoc enim modo cognitio eius non potest esse salutaris, sed exitialis peccatoribus. Sed ut est Deus noster id est foederatus in Christo, quomodo se nobis in Verbo patefecit." Ibid; see also 3.19.1.

26. Petrus Van Mastricht, *Theoretico-Practica Theologia, qua, per Singula Capita Theologica, Pars Exegetica, Dogmatica, Elenchtica & Practica, Perpetua Successione Coniugantur*, 2d ed. (Utrecht, 1699), 573.

essence also became the starting point and fundamental idea of Christian theology."[27] Bavinck quickly surveyed the history of the distinction between God as he is *in se* and as he is toward us (*erga nos*), appealing to a wide range of patristic, medieval, and Reformation theologians.[28] In response to modern agnosticism he asserted, "To a considerable extent we can assent to and wholeheartedly affirm this doctrine of the unknowability of God. Scripture and the church emphatically assert the unsearchable majesty and sovereign highness of God. There is no knowledge of God as he is in himself."[29]

Given the importance and centrality of this distinction to Protestant theology generally and to Reformed theology particularly, it is both surprising and illuminating to observe how an influential contemporary Reformed theologian handles this distinction. Reacting to Bavinck's reassertion of the distinction between the knowledge of God *in se* and *erga nos*, John Frame expresses consternation about the fact that "theologians are often terribly adamant in denying that we know 'God in himself.'" He asserts that they "often fail to clarify the meaning of that rather ambiguous phrase" and singles out Bavinck for criticism in this regard, noting that, at one place, Bavinck denies that we know God in himself and in another deals with "God's being as it exists in itself."[30]

A few responses are in order. First, it does not appear that Frame has been entirely fair with Bavinck. On the same page from which Frame quoted Bavinck as saying, "Thus far we have dealt with God's being as it exists in itself," Bavinck continued, "Not in this sense, however, that we conceived of God and spoke of him apart from what he has revealed concerning himself in nature and Scripture. It is altogether impossible for us to think or speak of God except on the basis of his revelation. . . . Nevertheless, in the foregoing we dealt with God, as according to his revelation, he exists in himself."[31] In context it is clear

27. Herman Bavinck, *Reformed Dogmatics*, vol. 2, *God and Creation*, trans. John Vriend (Grand Rapids: Baker Academic, 2004), 36.

28. Ibid., 36–39.

29. Ibid., 47.

30. John M. Frame, *The Doctrine of the Knowledge of God* (Phillipsburg, NJ: Presbyterian and Reformed, 1987), 32.

31. Herman Bavinck, *The Doctrine of God*, trans. William Hendricksen (Grand Rapids: Eerdmans, 1955), 337.

that Bavinck was not contradicting himself as it appears in Frame's account. Further, it is evident that Bavinck's doctrine was exactly that of the classic Reformed theologians.

Second, judging by his discussion of this issue, it does not appear that Frame clearly understands the intent or the scope of the distinction. Rather than asking Bavinck or Turretin what he might have meant by this distinction Frame postulates two possible meanings that have no relation to the intended sense of the phrase *Deus in se*. What Luther, Calvin, Turretin, and Bavinck meant to communicate is that God existed before we did, that he has an existence apart from us and accommodates his revelation to us by speaking to us about himself in analogies that are true enough for us to understand what we need to understand for faith and life (WCF 1.7). In short, as Frame himself acknowledges, it means that we cannot know God as he knows himself.

This seems fairly straightforward. What is it that troubles Frame about this distinction? First, it seems that Frame does not understand that this last sense is all that is intended. Second, as a result, his discussion of this distinction creates unnecessary problems partly by associating ideas with the distinction that are neither inherent nor relevant to it, such as Kant's phenomenal/noumenal distinction.[32] Third, failing to understand what the Reformed intended, Frame seems to think that when Bavinck (or Turretin) says something about God *in se*, somehow he is claiming to know what that something is. He fails to acknowledge the distinction between knowing *that* a thing is (e.g., God *in se*) and *what* a thing is. We know *that* God has attributes, but we do not know their *whatness* (*quidditas*).[33]

Fourth, Frame does not seem to realize that the classical Reformed theologians understood that there is a certain degree of falsehood in human speech about God. Call this the "as it were" principle. We see this at work in Heidelberg Catechism Q. 27. In answer to the question, "What do you understand by the providence of God?" we confess, "The almighty and everywhere present power of God, whereby, *as it were*, by his hand he still upholds heaven and earth."[34] We do not believe or confess that God, con-

32. Frame, *Doctrine of the Knowledge of God*, 33.
33. *Institutes* 1.2.2.
34. Modified from *Creeds*, 3:316.

sidered apart from the incarnation, can be said to have a literal hand. We recognize this as a metaphorical way of speaking about God's providential work in the world. Yet we also recognize that, because of our finitude, in order to say something true about God we must use divinely authorized analogies to say something that entails a certain degree of falseness.[35] We have the same problem when we speak of the divine attributes. According to our older theologians, when we speak about attributes we are not speaking about God *realiter* but as he has revealed himself to us.[36] In contrast, on one hand, Frame correctly denies that we can know God in himself in this "improper sense," but he argues that revealed knowledge of God is knowledge of God "as he really is."[37] In effect, he conflates revelation with knowledge of God in himself. This conflation allows him to claim that we know God's essence.

Though Frame complains about the ambiguity and confusion surrounding the traditional distinction, it is evident that it is he who is actually ambiguous and confusing. In effect, he accuses the traditional Reformed view of the Kantian phenomenal/noumenal distinction.[38] Ironically, there is a relation between the two. Where the Reformed orthodox said that we cannot know *God* in himself, Immanuel Kant (1724–1804) inverted that principle by applying it not to God (whom he denied) but to every created thing (*Ding an sich*). He made all creation, in itself, hidden. Having confused Turretin for Kant, Frame confuses Reformed theology with Kantian skepticism and reacts to his erroneous conception by affirming and contradicting the distinction between God *in se* and *erga nos* at the same time. In fact, the historic Reformed distinction is not, as he suggests, skeptical; it is pious. We confess that we know God truly according to the Creator/creature distinction. For example, properly speaking, God does not have attributes. All his attributes are one in him. We know this is true (Deut. 6:4) and we can say it, but we cannot do more than that. Thus, we must speak of attributes in the plural in order to be able to tell whatever truth we can about God *as he has revealed himself*. In short, this

35. Horton, *Covenant and Eschatology*, 98.
36. Amandus Polanus, *Syntagma Theologiae Christianae*, 13 vols. (Geneva, 1612), 2:14. On this see *PRRD*, 1:164–67, 212–26.
37. Frame, *Doctrine of the Knowledge of God*, 33.
38. Ibid.

as-it-were-ness is implied in all our speech about God. This example of a significant contemporary confusion over the nature and implications of the Creator/creature distinction suggests that, in order to recover the Reformed confession, we must get back to basics.

According to Reformed theology, God alone is infinite, simple, and immutable. Human beings are finite and complex, and we change every moment we live. God, by contrast, considered apart from the incarnation, is precisely the same as he has always been. He is not more or less God than he was last week. Even in the incarnation he did not become less divine; he did not become mutable or complex. God the Son took on our humanity, but his deity remained consubstantial with the Father and the Spirit. The corollary to this distinction was Luther's distinction between the theology of glory and the theology of the cross and Calvin's doctrine of revelation as accommodation. Beginning in the late sixteenth century and continuing through the seventeenth century and into the early eighteenth century, Reformed theologians distinguished between theology as God does it and theology as he reveals it to us.[39] Unfortunately, these categories of explanation have become unfamiliar, and that fact is an indictment of the state of Reformed theology today. With a little study, however, we can recover them in short order.

The Reformed confession holds to this analogy without intersection between the divine and human intellects. As a preface to our confession of the covenant of works, WCF 7.1 speaks of the "distance between God and the creature." It is a fundamental Reformed belief that God exists on one plane, and we on another. He has one understanding of himself and his creation and has given to us another, analogous understanding. This was a fundamental theme in the theology and apologetics of Cornelius Van Til (1895–1987).[40] Van Til argued, "The distinguishing characteristic between every non-Christian theory of knowledge, on the one hand, and the Christian concept of knowledge on the other hand, is . . . that in all non-Christian theories men reason *univocally*, while in Christianity men

39. Willem J. Van Asselt, "The Fundamental Meaning of Theology: Archetypal and Ectypal Theology in Seventeenth-Century Reformed Thought," *WTJ* 64 (2003): 319–35.
40. See, for example, Cornelius Van Til, *The Defense of the Faith* (Philadelphia: Presbyterian and Reformed, 1955), 48–49, 148–51; idem, *An Introduction to Systematic Theology*, vol. 5 of *In Defense of the Faith* (Phillipsburg, NJ: Presbyterian and Reformed, 1978), 160.

reason *analogically.*"[41] If we accept this distinction and apply it consistently, we will realize that Scripture is not meant to give us a QIRC kind of certainty and the QIRE will be less attractive.

This distinction is also a bulwark in our theology against rationalism. Broadly, there are two kinds of rationalism: the first posits an intersection between the divine intellect and the human intellect.[42] The second form of rationalism replaces the authority of divine revelation with human reason. Having begun with biblicism, the mainline churches have now openly embraced the latter form of rationalism. It is, however, the first form of rationalism that feeds the QIRC in the sideline churches. This kind of rationalism, in its strongest forms, says that we can have certainty only by knowing something that God knows, the way he knows it. In effect, we must, if only temporarily, become the Creator. The answer to this QIRC rationalism is to reestablish firmly in our minds the distinction between the Creator and the creature. Let us begin where Scripture begins: "In the beginning God." We are created "in the image." We are analogues of God. Our thinking is therefore to be analogous to God's. Is this not the basic point of Deuteronomy 29:29?

This conviction, though it has not always come to an identical verbal expression, has received continuous support in confessional Reformed theology. To give but one sixteenth-century example, in his exposition and defense of the Reformed *ordo salutis*, writing in 1589, the German Reformed theologian Hermann Rennecher appealed to the Creator/creature distinction:

> ... although God in his eternal essence and majesty is infinite, and contained in no one natural place, nor can be comprehended and perfectly known of any creature, either celestial or terrestrial (for between a thing infinite, and a thing finite, there is no proportion), yet notwithstanding he has so lively and manifestly declared, and laid open his wonderful goodness towards man in his Son, and in his merits

41. Van Til, *An Introduction to Systematic Theology*, 11.
42. On this see R. Scott Clark, "Janus, the Well-Meant Offer of the Gospel, and Westminster Theology," in *The Pattern of Sound Doctrine: Systematic Theology at the Westminster Seminaries. Essays in Honor of Robert B. Strimple*, ed. David VanDrunen (Phillipsburg, NJ: P&R, 2004), 149–80.

... whosoever therefore truly acknowledges and freely confesses his Son to be their redeemer, they not only see the secrets, as it were, the breast of God laid open to them, but also have him as their merciful and loving Father.[43]

As Rennecher continued his arguments, without using the terms, he appealed to Luther's distinction between the theology of glory and the theology of the cross. For Rennecher, because of his emphasis on this distinction, the doctrine of election is meant to be understood as a comfort for the suffering and doubting, not a program for the triumphant and prosperous. To take but one twentieth-century example, no theme was more fundamental to the theology and apologetics of Cornelius Van Til than the distinction between the Creator and the creature.[44]

Because human beings are and can only be creatures, for Calvin, all Scripture is necessarily God's condescending speech to us. The only alternative is to suppose that human beings, if only for a moment, participate in divine self-knowledge in the way that only God can know it, and this would destroy the Creator/creature distinction and our humanity, because it presupposes that the only way to really *know* something is to be divine. Was this not the most fundamental claim of the evil one (Gen. 3:5)? Was it not the case that one of the implicit tests of the covenant of works was to rely solely on God's account of reality and to be content in being his analogue? This analogical approach to theology and to the relations between the divine and the human, however, has not enjoyed continual support in the history of the church. The restoration of the Creator/creature distinction was one of the great accomplishments of the Reformation.

The Reformation of Theology

At the first reading, it seems that Thomas Aquinas taught the same sort of analogical approach to theology for which I have been arguing.

43. Hermann Rennecher, *The Golden Chayne of Salvation*, trans. Peter Allibond (London, 1604), 2–3. See also Hermann Rennecher, *Aurea Salutis Catena: Continens et Explicans Omnes Ejus Causas, et Singula Dei Beneficia* (Herborn, 1589).

44. See, e.g., Van Til, *The Defense of the Faith*, 48–49, 148–51; idem, *An Introduction to Systematic Theology*, 160.

After all, he wrote, "It is impossible to predicate anything to God and creatures univocally."[45] He wrote that the word "God" can be taken equivocally, univocally, or analogically. He ruled out the univocal sense because the word "God" cannot mean the same thing for God and creatures, nor can God and humans be said to speak equivocally since the reference of the word would be utterly different. He argued for an "analogical" way of understanding speech about God.[46] As the image of God, we are like God in significant ways. Take any moral divine property, for example, goodness. God is good relative to his deity as man is good relative to his humanity. Aquinas said quite clearly that we are, however, unlike God qualitatively because God is of a separate genus. Because he exists as another genus, we cannot know his essence.[47]

On closer inspection, however, the story becomes a little more complex. Even as he explained the necessity of analogy, Thomas appealed to the notion of participation in God. This was not, as we might say today, a Freudian slip. When Thomas spoke of analogy, he did not mean what Van Til meant by analogy, at least not consistently. Thomas thought of divine-human relations as analogical *on a continuum*.[48] For Thomas, if the divine and human intellects do not intersect at some point (for which Thomas generally used the noun *ratio*—ground or reason), there can be no real analogy at any point. For this reason Thomas has been rightly described as an "intellectualist," that is, he taught an intersection of the divine mind with the human mind. For Thomas, "God is the author of the intellective power, and by the intellect it is possible to see him." And

45. Thomas Aquinas, *Summa Theologiae*, ed. Thomas Gilby, 61 vols. (London and New York: Blackfriars and McGraw-Hill, 1964–80), 1a.13.5, resp.: "quod impossible est aliquid praedicari de Dei et creaturibus univoce."

46. *ST* 1a.13.10, resp.

47. Brian Davies, *The Thought of Thomas Aquinas* (Oxford: Oxford University Press, 1992), 43–44; *contra ST* 1a.12.1.

48. This is why he and neo-Thomists since have rejected Anselm's ontological argument. They cannot allow his chief assumption, that God really is *sui generis*. Anselm assumed that "God is that than which nothing greater can be conceived" (*aliquid quo maius cogitari non potest*) because he is a class of one. See *Proslogion*, 3. That is why Gaunillo's objection that he could think of an island that did not exist remains irrelevant, as Anselm argued in reply (in *Liber Apologeticus adversus Respondentem pro Insipiente*) that God is not a creature. Modern neo-Thomists continue to make this mistake. For example, see E. L. Mascall, *Existence and Analogy* (Hamden, CT: Archon, reprint, 1967), 25 and n. 2.

since, he continues, that same "intellective power is created, it is not of the divine essence, it remains that it is some sort of participative likeness of him, who is the first intellect."[49]

Further, "being itself" must refer, at some point, to God and us.[50] For example, Aquinas argued that when we predicate "good" of humans and "good" of God, we are not predicating two unrelated or purely analogical things. There is a continuum or, as Thomas puts it, an "analogy, that is, proportion" (*analogiam*, i.e., *proportionem*) between what is predicated of God and man.[51] So he argued both that we are analogues to God *and* on a continuum with him. Thus, the analogical relations between God and man do not *remain* analogical.[52] Brian Davies says that Thomas thought this way because he was "much indebted to the line of thinking" embodied in neo-Platonist writers such as pseudo-Dionysius (Denys).[53] This assumption of a continuum of being between God and creatures made it almost impossible for him to teach consistently with the principle of analogy.

Thus, for Thomas, we can know created things *in se* (i.e., things as they really are in themselves),[54] and by knowing the essence of things we can know universals, properties that are true of more than one thing. There is nothing problematic about this except that, for Thomas, universals are expressions of the divine intellect and being and, as such, consubstantial with the divine nature. So that, when we make empirical observations and deduce universals from them, the active intellect intersects with the divine intellect. The point of contact is univocal

49. *ST* 1a. 12.2, "Manifestum est autem quod Deum et est auctor intellectivae virtutis, et ab intellectu videri potest. Et cum ipsa intellectiva virtus creaturae non sit Dei essentia, reliquitur quod sit aliqua participativa similitudo ipsius, qui est primus intellectus."

50. Mascall, *Existence and Analogy*.

51. *ST* 1a. 13.5, resp.

52. Though one hesitates to disagree with Ralph McInerny about Thomas, and it is ironic that a Reformed confessionalist is agreeing with Cajetan, nevertheless, McInerny's account of Thomas's doctrine of analogy does not seem to account for the profound influence of neo-Platonism on Thomas's conception of divine-human relations. See Ralph McInerny, *Aquinas and Analogy* (Washington, DC: Catholic University Press, 1996), 7, 8, 14, 15, 162–63. McInerny takes Thomas de Vio (Cardinal Cajetan) to task for misreading Thomas's commentary on Lombard's *Sentences*.

53. Davies, *The Thought of Thomas Aquinas*, 43.

54. *ST* 1a. 85, ad 2.

knowledge of being per se. Thomas's neo-Platonism appears quite clearly in his account of the nature of divine grace and salvation:

> Nothing can act beyond its species, since the cause must always be more powerful than its effect. Now the gift of grace surpasses every capability of created nature, since *it is nothing short of a partaking of the Divine Nature (participatio divinae naturae)*, which exceeds every other nature. And thus it is impossible that any creature should cause grace. For it is as necessary that *God alone should deify (Deus deificet)*, bestowing (*communicando consortium divinae naturae*) a partaking of the Divine Nature by a participated likeness, as it is impossible that anything save fire should enkindle.[55]

Thus, for Thomas, God is the beginning (*principium*) but also the end (*finis*). Thus it is evident that, when Thomas wrote about analogy, he did not mean by it what the Reformed confession does.[56] Whereas WSC 1 has the "end of man" to "glorify God and enjoy him forever," Thomas had the purpose of humanity to "return to God," that is, to enjoy the "beatific vision," and not just in the face of Christ. He said, "The ultimate and perfect blessedness is not possible unless it is in the vision of the divine essence."[57]

In the fourteenth century, Duns Scotus (c. 1265–c. 1308) began a reaction to Thomas's theology, which was carried on by more radical Franciscan theologians such as William of Ockham (1285–1347). Scotus was a key transitional figure in the history of medieval theology, standing halfway between Aquinas and Ockham. According to Richard Cross, Scotus agreed with the latter philosophically but with the former theologically.[58] Whereas, for Thomas, theology is partly theoretical and

55. 1a2ae. 112.1 (resp to obj). Emphasis added.

56. Thomas Gilby, *ST* 1:43, observes concerning the structure of the *ST*: "the grand Platonic sweep of the whole work which follows the *exitus* and *reditus* of Creation—the going forth of things from God and their coming back to him, the setting out and returning home." On this same theme see Fran O'Rourke, *Pseudo-Dionysius and Metaphysics of Aquinas* (Leiden: Brill, 1992; reprint, Notre Dame, IN: University of Notre Dame Press, 2005), 41–48.

57. *ST* 1a–2ae.3.8, "ultima et perfecta beatitudo non potest esse nisi in visione divinae essentiae."

58. Richard Cross, *Duns Scotus* (New York: Oxford University Press, 1999), 5.

partly practical, for Scotus, theology is an affective, moral, contemplative science. For Scotus, things are not the way they are because of the nature of things; rather things are as they are because of the divine will, and therefore they could potentially be different than they are.[59] With this turning away from the divine being to the divine will, Scotus distinguished more consistently than Thomas between God as he is "in himself" (*in se*) and as he is "toward us" (*erga nos*). The corollary is the distinction between God's theology (*theologia in se*) and theology as he reveals it to us (*theologia nostra*).[60]

Martin Luther (1483–1546) developed the Scotist distinction between God *in se* and *erga nos* in a dramatic and definite way for Protestant theology. At the 1518 Heidelberg Disputation Martin Luther unveiled what he called his theology of the cross (*theologia crucis*) against Rome's theology of glory (*theologia gloriae*). By the latter he meant to define a complex of ideas, including the notion that one is ultimately justified before God on the basis of graciously infused sanctity, and the notion that the human intellect intersects with God's. In contrast, relying on Scripture as the revelation of God in Christ, the theologian of the cross "says what a thing is," because he relies on divine revelation in Scripture rather than on a rationalist identity of God and man.[61] For Luther, we do not know God savingly in nature. In nature, the sinner learns only law and condemnation. In his seminal work *On the Bondage of the Will* (*De servo arbitrio*, 1525) against Erasmus's appealing rationalism and explaining the distinction between law and gospel in Ezekiel 18:23, 32, Luther taught a distinction between God hidden (*Deus absconditus*) and God revealed (*Deus revelatus*):

> For he is here speaking of the preached and offered mercy of God, not that hidden and awful will of God whereby he ordains by his own counsel which and what sort of persons he wills to be recipients and

59. See the introduction in Duns Scotus, *Duns Scotus on the Will and Morality*, trans. Alan F. Wolter (Washington, DC: Catholic University Press, reprint, 1997).

60. Amandus Polanus, *Syntagma Theologiae Christianae*, 13 vols. (Hanau, 1609), 1.3.3, cited Thomas Aquinas, *Summa Theologiae* 1a; Boëthius, *De trinitate*; and Duns Scotus's commentary on the *Sentences* as examples of this distinction. See also *PRRD*, 1:124.

61. "Theologus gloriae dicit malum bonum et bonum malum, Theologus crucis dicit id quod res est." *WA*, 1:354.

partakers of his preached and offered mercy.... We have to argue in one way about God or the will of God as preached, revealed, offered and worshipped, and in another way about God as he is not preached, not revealed, not offered, not worshipped. To the extent, therefore, that God hides himself and wills to be unknown to us, it is no business of ours.

Luther clearly demarcated between God as he is *in se* and God as he reveals himself to us. The former is the theology of glory, and the latter is the theology of the cross. The medieval theologians (he thinks of Thomas) believed that they had unmediated access to God, apart from his revelation and the incarnation. He continued, "God must therefore be left alone to himself in his own majesty, for in this regard, we should have nothing to do with him, nor has he willed that we should have anything to do with him. But we have something to do with him insofar as he is clothed and set forth in his Word, through which he offers himself to us."[62] For Luther the theology of glory leads sinners to believe that they can present themselves to God, with congruent merit (*meritum de congruo*). The theologian of the cross clings to the foolishness of the gospel.[63]

John Calvin (1509–1564) accepted Luther's fundamental distinction between God hidden (*Deus absconditus*) and God revealed (*Deus revelatus*). In *Institutes* 1.17.2 he argued from Deuteronomy 29:29; 30:11–14; and Romans 11:33–34 (among other places) that there is a distinction to be made between God's will as it is revealed and his will as it is hidden (*voluntatem absconditam*) from us. Whereas the hidden, secret, providential, decretive, mysterious will of God is like an abyss (*abyssus*), such is not the case with God's revealed will, which becomes to us a "school of truth" (*veritatis schola*).[64] The Sophists (i.e., the Roman Catholic theologians of the Sorbonne) argued about God's "absolute will" (*absoluta voluntas*), in which they "separate his justice from his power," but we respect the boundary between the secret and the revealed.[65] Thus, Calvin restricted

---

62. *LW*, 33:139; *WA*, 17:684–85.

63. Paul Althaus, *The Theology of Martin Luther*, trans. Robert C. Schultz (Philadelphia: Fortress, 1966), 25–34. See also Walther von Loewenich, *Luther's Theology of the Cross*, trans. H. J. A. Bouman (Minneapolis: Augsburg, 1976), 27–49; Alister E. McGrath, *Luther's Theology of the Cross* (Oxford: Blackwell, 1985), 148–81.

64. *OS*, 3:204.15, 23, 25.

65. "Separantes eius iustitiam a potentia." *OS*, 3:205.16–17.

the task of the Christian theologian to adhere to the "rule of modesty and sobriety" (*modestiae et sobrietatis regulam*), that is, those things revealed in Scripture.[66]

Calvin described all Scripture as divine accommodation to human frailty; in the same way adults adapt their speech to children, God adapted revelation to our limited ability to understand. In *Institutes* 1.13.1 he said, "Who has so little intellect who does not understand that God, in a certain sense, speaks baby-talk (*balbutire*) with us as nurses do with infants?"[67] Following Augustine's commentary on Genesis, he argued that Scripture "proceeds at the pace of a mother stooping to her child, so to speak, so as not to leave us behind in our weakness" (*Institutes* 3.21.4).[68] So, then, in his account of the creation of angels, "Moses was accommodating himself to the roughness of the common people."[69] And in describing the beginning and ending of each creation day (Gen. 1:5), Calvin argued, Moses did not intend to establish a rule for the ways all days are measured. Rather, he "accommodated his language (as was already said) to the received custom."[70]

In his interpretation of the phrase "the first day" Calvin rejected as a "violent cavil" (*violentum cavillum*) what he understood to be Augustine's view of instantaneous creation revealed as distributed across six days.[71] Nevertheless, for Calvin, it is not that Scripture presents an artificial account of what really happened. Rather, the entirety of the creative act itself must be regarded as an artifice wrought by God for the sake of human weakness.[72] He read Scripture this way because he was zealous, on the one hand, to maintain the truth of what Scripture says, but on the other hand, to recognize that when, for example, Hebrew idiom says that

66. *Institutes* 1.14.4; OS, 3:19.

67. "Quis enim vel parum ingeniosus non intelligit Deum ita nobiscum, ceu nutrices solent cum infantibus, quodammodo balbutire?" OS, 3:109.13–15. See also Ford Lewis Battles, "God Was Accommodating Himself to Human Capacity," *Interpretation* 31 (1977): 19–38.

68. "Quae velut materno incessu submissius graditur, ne infirmitatem nostram deserat." OS, 4:373.22–25.

69. "Moses vulgi ruditati se accommodans." *Institutes* 1.14.3; OS, 3:154.28–29.

70. "Receptae consuetudini (ut iam dictum est) accommodavit sermonem suum." CO, 23:17.

71. CO, 23:17.

72. "Quin potius Deus ipse, ut opera sua ad hominem captum temperaret, sex dierum spatium sibi sumpsit." CO, 23:18.

God's "nose" gets "hot" as it does in Lamentations 2:3, it does not mean that God, in himself, has a nose or that it actually changes temperature. When Genesis 6:6 says that God "repents," we are to understand that "the repentance which is attributed belongs not properly in himself, but is referred to our understanding."[73] Because of the nature of divine-human relations, because God is so utterly transcendent in himself, so other, it is not possible for us to comprehend even what sort (*qualis*) he is, it is necessary (*necesse est*) in a sense to transform (*transfiguret*) himself for our sake (*nostra causa*).[74] Using Hebrew idiom and familiar speech, Scripture means to say that God is morally displeased, and to help us understand this truth, it uses colloquial speech. To read too much or too little into the form of expression is to actually misunderstand the teaching of Holy Scripture. If we ignore this distinction, then we risk following Clark Pinnock down the path of open theism toward not only "Marcion's incompetent God," as Richard Muller said in 1983, but even toward Mormonism.[75]

By his doctrine of accommodation, Calvin was also concerned to distinguish God's mind, considered apart from his revelation to us, from our minds and our understanding of his Word. Calvin avoided the narrow, even bigoted dogmatism which has sometimes afflicted the confessional Reformed movement in our time. For example, in his commentaries one frequently finds him allowing a certain degree of latitude in the interpretation of particular passages of Scripture. In his lecture on John 4:9 (1553), the question arose whether it is the Samaritan woman or the apostle John speaking editorially who says, "For Jews do not associate with Samaritans." Calvin "thinks" (*puto*) that these words were said by the woman.[76] Others, however, explain the passage as having come from the Evangelist.[77]

73. "Poenitentia quae tribuitur Deo non proprie in ipsum competit, sed ad sensum nostrum refertur." *CO*, 23:118.

74. *CO*, 23:118.

75. See Pinnock's discussion of whether God is "embodied" and the ambiguity of his relations to the Mormon view of God in *The Most Moved Mover: A Theology of God's Openness* (Downers Grove, IL: InterVarsity, 2001), 32–35. Richard Muller first, and quite rightly, leveled the charge at open theism twenty years ago that it offers an incompetent God. See Richard A. Muller, "Incarnation, Immutability, and the Case for Classical Theism," *WTJ* 45 (1983): 32.

76. "A muliere dictum puto." John Calvin, *In Evangelium secundum Johannem Commentarius Pars Prior*, ed. Helmut Feld (Geneva: Librarie Droz, 1997), 119.16.

77. "Alii ab Euangelista explicationis vice additum accipiunt." Ibid., 119.16–17.

Indeed, to Calvin it seems best (*optime*) to read the clause as coming from the woman, but if others prefer (*malit*) to think otherwise, Calvin was not willing to argue the point.[78]

In his lecture on Genesis 1:5 (1554), Calvin admitted that there is some ambiguity in the words "And God called the light day." "What Moses says, however," he conceded, "is able to be understood in a double sense."[79] Scripture might be referring to the evening and morning of the first day, or it might be that the first day consisted of evening and morning. "Whichever you choose it makes no difference to the meaning."[80] Calvin was not, however, an exegetical latitudinarian. There are too many places where he gives ample evidence that, were something of substance at stake, he was willing to defend his interpretation of Scripture and criticize and reject others. The point is, however, that Calvin was able to tell the difference between what is important and what is essential. He was willing to concede that there might be a range of correct interpretations of a given biblical passage, within which one can safely reside. He knew that he was *interpreting* not writing Scripture. He understood that we are recipients of and not the font of revelation or theology. Therefore, he was willing to live with relative uncertainty.

The confessional Reformed theologians, following Luther and Calvin, were careful to distinguish between God as he is "in himself" (*in se*) and as he reveals himself toward us. In contrast to Thomas's doctrine of proportional analogy, Johannes Wollebius (1586–1629) taught, "The essence of God is incomprehensible to us. For, of the finite to the infinite, there is no proportion of a small dish to the ocean."[81]

The Parts of Theology

Because revelation is God-given, theology does not begin with us nor is it fundamentally the expression of our religious experience (e.g.,

78. "Si quis aliter malit, non contendo." Ibid., 119.20.
79. "Quod tamen dicit Moses, bifariam verti potest." CO, 23:17.
80. "Utrumvis eligas, nihil refert quoad sensum." CO, 23:17.
81. Johannes Wollebius, *Christianae Theologiae Compendium*, ed. E. Bizer (Neukirchen: Kreis Moers, 1935), 1.1.3.

Schleiermacher's *Gefühl,* i.e., the feeling of absolute divine dependence). For these reasons, Reformed theology distinguishes between theology as God knows it and theology as he reveals it to us. Beginning in the late sixteenth century and continuing through the seventeenth century and into the early eighteenth century, confessional Reformed theologians called theology as God does it *archetypal* (*theologia archetypa*), and theology as it comes to us *ectypal theology* (*theologia ectypa*). By this distinction, Reformed and Lutheran theology meant to communicate that there is an analogy between the way God conceives of reality and the way we conceive of it, but there is no identity.[82]

The categorical distinction between God's theology and ours became the basis for Protestant theological method. The confessional Reformed theologians at the end of the sixteenth century and early in the seventeenth century simply amplified it. In 1594, Francis Junius (1545–1602) published *De vera theologia* in which he first used these categories by name. According to Junius, there are two kinds of true theology: That which God alone knows and can know and that which God reveals.[83] Because we can never have anything other than analogical knowledge of God and his theology, even his account of the two parts of theology is analogical and is not to be imputed to God himself.[84] In other words, the archetypal/ectypal distinction is not *in* God as he is in himself, but he condescends to make the distinction in order to speak to us and so that we can speak about him.

Archetypal theology is that which exists in the mind of God; it is necessarily hidden from and incommunicable to us creatures just as God's immensity or holiness, as it exists in God, is incommunicable to us. Nevertheless, God's theology is the basis for his self-disclosure to us his creatures. So, in Reformed theology, archetypal theology is theology of the first order or original theology, and the revelation we have from God and our account of that revelation is theology of the second order or derivative. Ectypal theology is the accommodated theology of which

82. See Van Asselt, "The Fundamental Meaning of Theology"; *PRRD,* 1:221–69.
83. Francis Junius, *Opera Theologica Francisci Junii,* 2 vols. (Geneva, 1613), 1.1767.
84. Ibid., 1.1768.62–67. See also Amandus Polanus, *Syntagma Theologiae Christianae,* 13 vols. (Geneva, 1612), 1.3.3.

Calvin wrote. It is the theology of the cross of which Luther wrote, and it is "our theology" of which Duns Scotus wrote before them.

Because we are creatures, we do not and cannot know the content of God's archetypal theology. We only know that it exists. We do know, however, the content of revealed, ectypal theology. Our theologians describe it as "habitual," or "infused," or "acquired." Under the heading of ectypal theology, there are four subdivisions: the theology of the angels (*theologia angelorum*), the theology of the blessed (*theologia beatorum*), the theology of union (*theologia unionis*), and the theology of pilgrims (*theologia viatorum*).

The theology of the angels belongs, of course, to creatures who are glorified but nonhuman, spirits who serve the Creator and Redeemer. The theology of the blessed belongs to the church triumphant (*ecclesia triumphans*), to glorified believers. The theology of union belongs to God the Son incarnate and is the Reformed way of accounting for the two natures of Christ. In his deity he has, of course, archetypal theology, but in his humanity he has ectypal theology. This was a point of contention between Lutheran and Reformed theology. Like confessional Reformed theology, the great Lutheran theologian Johann Quenstedt (1617–88) distinguished between archetypal and ectypal theology, so that all of our language about God's essence and attributes is analogical, not univocal.[85] According to John Theodore Mueller (1885–1967), Lutherans confess, as we do, that God, *in se*, is "liable to no change whatsoever, neither as to existence . . . nor as to accidents . . . nor as to will or purpose." He continues by explaining that, wherever Scripture ascribes a change of place or mind to God, it does this "in accommodation to our mode of perceiving. These passages do not teach that God is subject to change as men are . . . but must be understood in a manner becoming God."[86] Because of their doctrine that the attributes of the deity have been communicated to the humanity (*communicatio idiomatum*), confessional Lutherans teach that Jesus has archetypal theology in his human nature. All the confessional

85. Robert D. Preus, *The Theology of Post-Reformation Lutheranism*, 2 vols. (St. Louis: Concordia, 1970–72), 1:172–73; Heinrich Schmid, *The Doctrinal Theology of the Evangelical Lutheran Church*, trans. Charles A. Hay and Henry E. Jacobs, 4th ed. (Philadelphia: Lutheran Publication Society, 1889), 115.

86. J. T. Mueller, *Christian Dogmatics* (St. Louis: Concordia, 1934), 164.

Protestants agree, however, that the theology that we mere creatures, members of the church militant (*ecclesia militans*), have and do is pilgrim theology. Considered generally, it is what we are doing now, getting to grips with God's self-disclosure primarily in Scripture and secondarily in nature.

The Eclipse of the Categorical Distinction

Most of the classic Reformed (and Lutheran) theologians, follow-ing Luther and Calvin, worked explicitly with the categorical distinction between archetypal and ectypal theology, but others, while they assumed the distinction, did not dwell on it, and the distinction was gradually eclipsed by other concerns. For example, one of the great Puritan theo-logians of the late sixteenth and early seventeenth century, William Ames (1576–1633), a student of William Perkins (1558–1602), delegate to the Synod of Dort (1618–19) and the teacher of Gijsbertus Voetius (1589–1676), and profoundly influential in the development of both Dutch Reformed theology and New England Puritanism, gave theology a more subjective turn by defining it as "living to God."[87] It is clear from his section on the doctrine of God that Ames accepted Calvin's Creator/creature distinction, but when it came to the traditional "parts" or "divi-sions" of theology, he said that the two parts of theology are "faith and observance."[88] In contrast, in his *Theological Miscellanies or On the Rise, Development and Study of True Theology* (1661) John Owen (1616–83), the most important English Reformed theologian of the seventeenth century, affirmed the categorical distinction, so that for Owen, theology is, as Carl Trueman has said, "relational"; it is "knowledge of God as he has revealed himself to be towards humans."[89]

87. William Ames, *The Marrow of Theology*, trans. John Eusden Dykstra (Durham, NC: Labyrinth, 1968), 77.
88. Ames, *Marrow*, 79.
89. John Owen, ΘΕΟΛΟΓΟΥΜΕΝΑ ΠΑΝΤΟΔΑΠΑ *sive De Natura, Ortu, Progressu, et Studio, Verae Theologiae*, in *The Works of John Owen*, ed. W. H. Gould, 24 vols. (New York: Robert Carter and Brothers, 1851–54), vol. 17; Carl R. Trueman, *The Claims of Truth: John Owen's Trinitarian Theology* (Carlisle, UK: Paternoster, 1998), 55. See also Sebastian Rehn-man, *Divine Discourse: The Theological Methodology of John Owen*, ed. Richard A. Muller,

Owen's contemporary Francis Turretin (1623–87) made a brief, hurried mention of the categorical distinction in his *Institutes of Elenctic Theology* (1679–85), but did not elaborate on it. He was most anxious to discuss the latter, "our theology" (*theologia nostra*). This might have been due to the fact that his *Institutio* was not meant to be a comprehensive system, but a polemical work, and therefore he wanted to press on to the issues at hand. Nonetheless, through Turretin, the archetypal/ectypal distinction was communicated to the eighteenth and nineteenth centuries as his *Institutes* were made the primary theology text at Old Princeton Seminary, until Charles Hodge began using his own text. One also finds the same pattern in other European theologians of the period, for example, Johannes Cocceius (1603–69) and Peter van Mastricht (1630–1706).[90]

Ironically, though Jonathan Edwards (1703–58) famously praised van Mastricht, he did not follow him in theological method. Rather, in his treatise *Christian Knowledge or the Importance and Advantage of a Thorough Knowledge of Divine Truth* (1756–57), Edwards united Ames and Turretin by defining theology as "the doctrine of the living God by Christ" including "all Christian doctrines as they are in Jesus, and Christian rules directing us in living to God by Christ."[91] This definition tended to push the conception of theology away from the categorical distinction. As we have already seen, there were strong structural impulses, like Aquinas's neo-Platonism, in Edwards's theology, piety, and practice that also pushed him away from the categorical distinction.

Herman Venema (1697–1787), a mild Cartesian who taught in Franeker, made a brief mention and explanation of the categorical distinction in his *Institutes of Theology* published in English posthumously in 1853, but it does not appear that this text was ever used widely or was influential in eighteenth- or nineteenth-century confessional Reformed theology.[92] The terms remained in circulation in the eighteenth century, as

Texts and Studies in Reformation and Post-Reformation Thought (Grand Rapids: Baker, 2002), 57–71.

90. Johannes Cocceius, *Summa Theologiae*, in Johannes Cocceius, *Opera Omnia*, 10 vols. (Amsterdam, 1701), 7.1.3; Van Mastricht, *Theoretico-Practica Theologia*, 1.1.15.

91. *Works*, 2:157–58.

92. Herman Venema, *Institutes of Theology*, trans. A. W. Brown (Andover: Draper Brothers, 1853), 4.

evidenced by Immanuel Kant's use of them in his *Lectures on Philosophical Theology* (1817), but he redefined them radically so that his use of them did not correspond to the earlier orthodox usage.[93]

In the nineteenth century, in his highly stylized account of Reformed orthodoxy, Heinrich Heppe (1820–79) made no mention of the categorical distinction.[94] Charles Hodge (1797–1878), who was well read in Reformed orthodoxy, was surely aware of the categorical distinction, but he did not use it prominently in his *Systematic Theology* (1872–73).[95] This absence may be due to the fact that he simply assumed Turretin's subdued treatment of it. The *Theological Lectures* of William Cunningham (1805–61), published posthumously in London in 1878, contain an intelligent and detailed discussion of theological method, but no mention of the categorical distinction.[96] Likewise, one finds no mention of these categories in B. B. Warfield's essays "The Idea of Systematic Theology" (1896) and "The Task and Method of Systematic Theology" (1910).[97] In his *Dogmatic Theology*, W. G. T. Shedd (1820–94) conducted a detailed defense of theology as science, interacting with a number of eighteenth- and nineteenth-century writers, but made no reference to the categorical distinction.[98]

By the early twentieth century, with a few notable exceptions, the terms seem to have largely disappeared from the confessional Reformed vocabulary. There were exceptions, however. The French Reformed theologian Auguste LeCerf (1872–1943) made brief, positive mention of them in his *Introduction to Reformed Dogmatics*.[99] In the Netherlands,

93. Immanuel Kant, *Lectures on Philosophical Theology*, trans. Allen W. Wood and Gertrude M. Clark (Ithaca, NY: Cornell University Press, 1978), 23.

94. Heinrich Heppe, *Reformed Dogmatics Set Out and Illustrated from the Sources*, ed. Ernst Bizer, trans. G. T. Thomson (London: George Allen and Unwin, 1950), 1–11.

95. Charles Hodge, *Systematic Theology*, 3 vols. (New York: Scribner, Armstrong, 1873).

96. William Cunningham, *Theological Lectures* (London: Nisbet, 1878).

97. B. B. Warfield, "The Idea of Systematic Theology," in *Studies in Theology* (New York: Oxford University Press, 1932); idem, "The Task and Method of Systematic Theology," in *Studies in Theology*.

98. W. G. T. Shedd, *Dogmatic Theology*, 3 vols. (New York: Charles Scribner and Sons, 1889; reprint, Grand Rapids: Klock and Klock, 1979), 1:3–58.

99. Auguste LeCerf, *An Introduction to Reformed Dogmatics*, trans. André Schlemmer (London: Lutterworth, 1949), 21.

in his *Encyclopaedie* (1894) Abraham Kuyper (1837–1920) offered a substantial discussion of the nature of ectypal theology.[100] In a cryptic remark, however, he revealed something of what happened to the categorical distinction. In explaining how theology is dependent upon revelation he commented: "Our earlier theologians explained this by distinguishing between archetypal theology (*Theologia archetypa*) and ectypal theology (*Theologia ectypa*)—a distinction which as it was finally defended could not be maintained but which contains an element of truth that should not be abandoned."[101] He did not explain exactly why it could no longer be maintained, yet he appealed repeatedly to the categorical distinction and used it as the basis of an entire section of the *Encyclopaedie*.[102] Nevertheless, these words signal a loss of confidence in the distinction.

In his *Gereformeerde Dogmatiek* (*Reformed Dogmatics*), published in four volumes and four editions from 1895 to 1918, Herman Bavinck (1854–1921) also used the categorical distinction but did not express Kuyper's reservations. Louis Berkhof (1873–1957) followed Bavinck in building upon this distinction in his *Reformed Dogmatics*.[103] In the 1930s, Berkhof republished his textbook under the title *Systematic Theology*, separating the *Introductory Volume*, in which he discussed the categorical distinction, from the rest of his systematics. As a result, Berkhof's theology was published for decades without a prolegomena, giving readers without an extensive knowledge of confessional Reformed theology a false impression and certainly contributing to the loss of the categorical distinction. Only in 1996, under the sponsorship of Richard Muller, was his system reprinted with the original *Introductory Volume* included within the same cover.

At Westminster Seminary, from its founding in 1929 until the late 1960s, though John Murray (1898–1975) taught most of the systematic theology, Cornelius Van Til (1895–1987) was chiefly responsible for teaching theological prolegomena and method. Though his entire approach to

100. Abraham Kuyper, *Principles of Sacred Theology*, trans. J. H. de Vries (Grand Rapids: Eerdmans, 1954), 248–58.

101. Ibid., 248.

102. Ibid., 253–54, 57–92.

103. Berkhof, *Introductory Volume to Systematic Theology*, rev. ed. (Grand Rapids: Eerdmans, 1932), 93–95. Writing at the same time in France, Auguste LeCerf, discussed the categories only briefly. See LeCerf, *An Introduction to Reformed Dogmatics*, 21.

theology and apologetics, between which he made no strong distinction, was premised on the notion of the categorical distinction, he did not always use the traditional vocabulary,[104] perhaps because, as he said, "to my beginning students, coming from all sorts of backgrounds, I must stress the basic points of theology and make them plain."[105] Against his contemporaries Gordon Clark (1902–85) and Herman Hoeksema (1886–1965), Van Til maintained the archetypal/ectypal distinction.[106] He saw an analogy between God's theology and ours as a "two-layer theory of reality."[107] "Christians," he said, "believe in two levels of existence, the level of God's existence as self-contained and the level of man's existence as derived from the level of God's existence. For this reason, Christians must also believe in two levels of knowledge, the level of God's knowledge which is absolutely comprehensive and self-contained, and the level of man's knowledge which is not comprehensive but is derivative and re-interpretative."[108]

Despite his vociferous criticism of Friedrich Schleiermacher (1768–1834) and his adoption of some of the categories of analysis used by the confessional Reformed theologians, Karl Barth (1886–1968), the most influential Reformed theologian of the twentieth century, made no great use of the categorical distinction in his greatest work, *Church Dogmatics*. Perhaps he did not discuss it because he read no discussion of it in Heppe? It also seems likely that the distinction did not fit Barth's theology, since, ironically, having accepted Kant's phenomenal/noumenal distinction, he also accepted (despite his protests against Schleiermacher and the turn to the ostensibly objective revelation event) a subjective turn. The categorical distinction was premised on the Scriptures as the objective Word of God grounded in a belief in actual historical facts of redemption. In contrast, for Barth, Scripture is not the objective Word of God grounded in an objective history (in the premodern sense) of salvation, but rather Scripture becomes the possibility of an existential

104. See, for example, Van Til, *An Introduction to Systematic Theology*, 203.

105. Van Til, *The Defense of the Faith*, 235–36. It is not clear, however, how the vocabulary of idealist philosophy is more straightforward than the classical Reformed vocabulary of the seventeenth century.

106. Idem, *An Introduction to Systematic Theology*, 203. For more on the controversy between Van Til and Clark and its relations to this discussion see Clark, "Janus, the Well-Meant Offer of the Gospel, and Westminster Theology," 149–80.

107. Van Til, *The Defense of the Faith*, 29.

108. Ibid., 12.

encounter with the "Word." Scripture becoming God's Word in the revelation event is a subjective affair.[109] For example, Barth rejected explicitly Turretin's definition of theology.[110] For Barth, theology can never be the task of assembling, repeating, and defining the teaching of the Bible.[111] Consequently, rather than a public discipline making claims about public revelation and objective historical reality, for Barth, theology became a private discipline.[112] He defined theology as something done solely by the church (the community of faith) and solely for the church, as language about a shared existential encounter that defeats the purpose of the categorical distinction.[113]

Conclusions

In this chapter I have argued that the name "Reformed" is something we are given; it is received. As heirs of a family name we do not get to define it as much as it defines us. A major part of what we have inherited is the biblical distinction between God and the creature. Though this may seem like a theological ABC, it is remarkable how often it is ignored today. The notion that human beings exist on some continuum with God is widely held, and the Reformed community is not immune to the influence of this idea, especially when it is clothed in traditional Reformed terminology.

The archetypal/ectypal distinction is essential. It is this distinction that distinguishes Reformed theology from Rome in soteriology, the entire force of which is salvation through divinization. It distinguishes us from our fellow confessional Protestants, the Lutherans, because they predicate the attributes of the deity to Jesus' humanity. In so doing, they must create a unique kind of humanity (one which is ubiquitous) that tends to separate the Mediator from his people who rely on his righteousness and consubstantiality with our humanity for their salvation and assurance.

109. Karl Barth, *Church Dogmatics*, trans. Geoffrey W. Bromiley, 13 vols. (Edinburgh: T&T Clark, 1936–69), 1.1:15, 41.

110. Ibid., 1.1:6.

111. Ibid., 1.1:16.

112. Ibid., 1.1:10. It is the case that either God spoke creation into existence, and Adam fell in time and space, in *Historie* or not. Either Christ rose or he did not. How can Barth regard the latter as historical and marginalize the creation narrative as saga?

113. Ibid., 1.1:4.

The categorical distinction also undermines the two illegitimate quests criticized in chapters 2 and 3 of this book: QIRC and QIRE. It undermines the latter by breaking down the intersection between the divine and human which was the unstated premise behind much of the theology, piety, and practice of the First Great Awakening. The Reformed understanding of things is that we do not have immediate access to God's being. We have *mediated* access through God the Son incarnate and through the preaching of the gospel and the administration of the sacraments. The goal of our theology is to think God's thoughts *after* him, as his image-bearers, as analogues.

The categorical distinction also subverts the QIRC by putting us creatures in our place. It relocates our center of gravity, as it were, away from biblicism or our private understanding and application of Scripture, back toward the church. It changes the questions. Rather than asking how we can apply the Mosaic civil penalties, determine the length of the creation days, or reengineer Reformed doctrine to create a better product, we can now ask how the Reformed churches understand the Scriptures. What questions do the Reformed churches think are important and why? Put negatively, if the Reformed churches have not confessed or taught the application of the Mosaic civil law to post-Mosaic societies, or if they have not confessed the nature of the creation days in detail, perhaps it is because Scripture does not teach these things. If Scripture does not teach them, then perhaps the theology of the cross (ectypal theology) and our status as image-bearers constrain us from teaching and confessing them too. Positively, where the Reformed churches, having given sustained and prayerful attention to a locus of doctrine, *have* confessed something in detail, for example, covenant theology and the doctrine of justification, perhaps as those who identify with the Reformed confessions we would do well not to fundamentally alter that confession without the consent of the churches.

The Reformed churches define the "Reformed" reading of Scripture, what it is to be Reformed, and they have codified that definition in public ecclesiastical documents. It is to those documents and the nature of our relations to them that we now turn.

If there be such a thing as "lying to the Holy Ghost," here it is. It is destroying the very intention of a creed; the object of which, as all allow, is to ascertain and secure concurrence of faith. If the system of doctrine taught in the Confession be wrong, let it by all means be changed. But as long as we profess to hold certain doctrines, let us really and honestly hold them. I would unspeakably rather discard the Confession altogether, than adopt a principle which would render its use a solemn mockery.

—SAMUEL MILLER

CHAPTER
5

~~~~~~~~~~~~

Recovering a Reformed Identity (2)

The argument of this chapter is that there is a Reformed identity that in important ways has been lost and must be recovered. To argue that there is a single, unifying Reformed identity is to fly in the face of the *Zeitgeist*. The spirit of our age is to think and speak almost exclusively about those things that distinguish one person, congregation, theology, piety, or practice, or reading of a text from another. The earlier modern period was a time in which there was great emphasis on the "one." There developed a misguided but rather solid consensus about God (the universal fatherhood of God) and man (universal fraternity and human perfectibility). Modern philosophy was the quest for the one universal rational truth or empirical fact that all reasonable persons could know, the starting point for Truth. In the late/liquid modern period, that quest has dissolved into a million subjectivities: "your truth," "your experience," and "your (e.g., feminist, Marxist, deconstructionist) reading" of a text.

As Reformed Christians, just as we are obligated to query and challenge the hubris of the earlier stage of modernity, so we are equally obligated to query and challenge the skepticism of our age. As Cornelius Van Til reminded us, as creatures made in God's image, we must always account for "the one and the many."[1] As I understand the Reformed theology, piety, and practice, however, there has always been unity amidst

1. This was such a pervasive theme in his theology that it seems impossible to cite one text, but one could start with Cornelius Van Til, *The Defense of the Faith* (Philadelphia: Presbyterian and Reformed, 1955), 42–63.

diversity. That unity has been expressed in our confessional documents and in the mainstream of Reformed theology, piety, and practice. There was a remarkable degree of agreement on the main lines of Reformed theology. Judging by the theology of the classical period of Reformed theology, when our vocabulary and categories were developed, we can speak of a Reformed doctrine of Scripture, a Reformed understanding of the nature of theology, and Reformed doctrines of God, man, Christ, salvation, church, and sacraments. There was a Reformed piety organized around the Word, the sacraments, and prayer. There was common Reformed understanding of the principle by which worship was to be conducted, when, and even how often. Thus there can even be said to have been a Reformed practice.

In the previous chapter we observed the effect of forgetting our grammar, our name, and the most basic distinction of our theology. In the introductory chapter this book has argued that the Reformed confession considered narrowly as public, ecclesiastically sanctioned documents can be the only stable and reasonable definition of the adjective "Reformed." In this chapter, we consider the nature of the act of confessing the faith formally and how we ought to relate to the church's confessional documents. It will be argued that if we are to recover our confession, we must enter into an honest, binding relation to those documents and the tradition in which they were composed, and if we are to be genuinely confessional, we must recover the practice of confessing our faith.

Confessing the Faith with the Reformed Tradition

We confess our faith and catechize our covenant children because the Scriptures themselves not only record various confessional formulae, but they teach us by command and by example to confess our faith. One of the fundamental articles of the Christian religion was stated within the Scriptures themselves in confessional form (Deut. 6:4): "Hear, O Israel, Yahweh our God, Yahweh is one." At the high occasion of the dedication of the temple (1 Kings 8:31–35), we find King Solomon standing before Yahweh and the covenant assembly as convener of the covenant assembly.

In the midst of his prayer he placed "confessing the name" of Yahweh in a corporate, covenantal, and oath-taking context (v. 33).

There is indirect evidence for the practice of corporate and individual confession among the early Christian communities in the Gospel of John. In his indictment of the parents of the man born blind, John mentions that that they were afraid to confess (9:22) Jesus as the Savior because they feared exclusion from the synagogue. The narrative functions as an admonition to the early Christian community to continue confessing Jesus as God the Son incarnate despite whatever opposition they may be encountering. The same concern seems to lie behind the narrative recorded in Matthew 10:32, where Jesus says, "Therefore whoever confesses me before men, I will also confess him before my Father in heaven."

The apostle Paul taught the same thing, that we both "confess with the mouth" and "believe with the heart" that Jesus is Lord (Rom. 10:9–10). The apostle urged "faithful" or "trustworthy sayings" to the young pastor Timothy four times and once to Titus (1 Tim. 1:15; 3:1; 4:9; 2 Tim. 2:11; Titus 3:8).[2] Certainly the form and language of 1 Timothy 3:16 seem confessional. The apostle John even used a confessional test to determine whether one is a Christian. Whoever refuses to "confess" that Jesus is God the Son incarnate is not to be regarded as a Christian (1 John 4:1–3). According to John Webster, one of the fundamental purposes of the confession is to publicly repudiate falsehood. It is a "move against falsehood," and any confession worthy of the name will include "an anathema, an assertion that a teaching or practice is outside the church."[3]

The practice and theory of confession are closely connected to the biblical notions of covenant and oath-taking. Webster says that creeds and confessional formulae are means "*through which the church affirms its allegiance to God.*"[4] Modern biblical scholarship shows the parallels between the oath-taking rituals of the Ancient Near East and the oath-taking rituals instituted among God's people.[5] The ideas of oath-swearing

2. See George Knight III, *Faithful Sayings in the Pastoral Letters* (Grand Rapids: Baker, 1979), 240.
3. John Webster, *Confessing God* (Edinburgh: T&T Clark, 2005), 78.
4. Ibid., 76 (italics original).
5. See Kenneth A. Kitchen, *Ancient Orient and the Old Testament* (Downers Grove, IL: InterVarsity, 1966); Meredith G. Kline, *The Structure of Biblical Authority* (Grand Rapids:

and covenant-making are closely linked in Scripture. In Genesis 21:31–32 we find a human contract between Abimelech and Abraham described with a verb of oath-swearing and the noun "covenant." The same sort of procedure is evident on a national scale in the ratification of the national covenant with Israel in Exodus 24:7–8. In response to the reading of the law, the terms of the national covenant, Israel swears: "All that Yahweh has spoken we will do, and we will be obedient" (ESV). To seal the relation, Moses effectively baptizes them in the blood of the covenant (v. 8). The ideas of covenant and oath-taking are linked explicitly in Ezekiel 16:59, where Yahweh Elohim prosecutes Israel for despising the "oath" by breaking the national covenant. This same conceptual connection is repeated throughout Ezekiel 17 (vv. 13, 16, 18–19).

The idea of confession as a covenantal act also flows from our doctrine of God. Yahweh is a covenant-making, oath-taking, and oath-keeping God. In the Ancient Near Eastern world, the act of "cutting a covenant" (in the bodies of animals or in human flesh; Gen. 17:1–10) implied the imprecation "may it be to me as it is to these slaughtered animals if I break this covenant." It was an oath sworn solemnly against one's own life. Oath-taking, confession of truths, and the formal ratification of a relationship are intertwined in the act of covenant-making. A similar sort of connection between confession, covenant, and oaths is evident in Leviticus 16:21 where the verb "to confess" is used in conjunction with the symbolic placing of the sins of Israel on the scapegoat. The scapegoat ritual was recognition of Israel's oath-bound relation to Yahweh and the demand for holiness and righteousness inherent in Israel's national covenant with the Lord. The ritual also acknowledged the fact and consequences of Israel's covenant-breaking.

Two of the clearest examples of such oath-taking rituals are the passing of Yahweh himself between the pieces of the slaughtered animals (Gen. 15:7–21) and his prosecution of Israel for breaking a covenant made by this sort of oath-taking procedure (Jer. 34:18–20). In the first case (Gen. 15), having put Abraham to sleep, in which case Abraham

Eerdmans, 1972); idem, *Treaty of the Great King* (Grand Rapids: Eerdmans, 1963); George E. Mendenhall, *Law and Covenant in Israel and the Ancient Near East* (Pittsburgh: Presbyterian Board of Colportage, 1955); Michael S. Horton, *The God of Promise: Introducing Covenant Theology* (Grand Rapids: Baker, 2006), 23–50.

could do nothing, God is said to have gone between the pieces and, by implication, taken an oath and the attending curses upon his own head, as it were. In the history of redemption, Yahweh is always faithful to his oath, but Israel, who had sworn at Sinai, "All the words that Yahweh has spoken we will do" (Ex. 24:3 ESV), did not keep their oath. Repeatedly, as we see in the second case, Yahweh prosecutes Israel for failing to live up to the "word of the covenant."

In the second instance, in Jeremiah 34:18–20, the Lord says,

> The men who have violated my covenant and have not fulfilled the terms of the covenant they cut before my face, I will treat like the calf they cut in two and then walked between its pieces. The leaders of Judah and Jerusalem, the court officials, the priests and all the people of the land who walked between the pieces of the calf—I will hand over to their enemies who seek their lives. Their dead bodies will become food for the birds of the air and the beasts of the earth.

Here the connection between oath-taking and covenantal relations is immediate and clear. When the leaders of Judah and Jerusalem walked between the pieces of a calf, they swore a blood-oath of loyalty to Yahweh. They promised unequivocally to obey him. More than that, by walking between the pieces, they declared before the Lord that they were as good as dead. As a consequence of their infidelity, Yahweh promises to bring upon them the sanctions to which they agreed when they made the covenant.

The oath-taking aspect of covenant-making is reflected in the New Testament in Paul's curse against the enemies of the gospel (Gal. 5:12) and in the corporate implications of abusing the Lord's Supper (1 Cor. 11:29–30). This oath-taking conception of covenantal life is evident in Hebrews 6:4–6 where the writer reminds those baptized Christians who had made public professions of faith, who had been admitted to the Lord's table, of the dangers inherent in membership in the covenant assembly.[6]

6. It is not that all the baptized members of the congregation were elect, united to Christ, or regenerate, from which state some fell away. Rather, this passage, read against the backdrop of the history of redemption, is another example of what Herman Witsius called "the double mode of communion" in the covenant of grace. For more on this see R. Scott Clark, "Baptism and the Benefits of Christ: The Double Mode of Communion in the Covenant of Grace," *The Confessional Presbyterian* 2 (2006): 3–19; idem, "Election and Predestination:

The language of verse 6 is particularly frightening where the condition is "if they then fall away," and the consequence is "they are crucifying once again the Son of God to their own harm and holding him up to contempt." This same accusation occurs with equal force in Hebrews 10:29 where the writer accuses apostates of having "trampled underfoot the Son of God and having regarded as common the blood of the covenant." This is the same blood foreshadowed by Moses when he baptized the Israelites in blood (Ex. 24:3–8). There too the visible people of God entered into an oath-bound covenant with promises, obligations, and sanctions. When the Israelites, covered with blood, swore fidelity to Yahweh, they made a blood-oath covenant.

Whatever difficulties adhere to these passages, it is clear enough that we are to consider that in each case the members of the congregation had entered into formal external relations to the administration of the covenant of grace, and with those relations came jeopardy brought by oath-taking and covenant-making.[7] It is also clear that our justification and salvation depend upon Christ's fulfilment of and bearing for us the consequences of our oath- and covenant-breaking. The covenant of grace is nothing but God's oath and acts graciously to save his elect through faith alone in our covenant-keeping Messiah alone. In response to his grace, he calls us to take covenant oaths when we come into formal external relations with him and his people.

In the Christian tradition these oaths have taken the form of confessions and catechisms. Confession concerns the preservation and transmission of that faith handed down once for all to the saints (Jude 3). Certainly the ancient church had a pattern of catechesis and confession. The confession known as the Apostles' Creed was originally a Roman baptismal formula that developed over several centuries. Converts were expected to confess the faith upon baptism, and baptized covenant children were expected to confess the faith after instruction. Catechumens, that is, those who were being instructed in the faith, who were not yet in communion, were dismissed from the service before the administration of the Supper.

The Sovereign Expressions of God," in *A Theological Guide to Calvin's Institutes: Essays and Analysis*, ed. David Hall and Peter Lillback (Phillipsburg, NJ: P&R, 2008), 90–122.

7. The sacredness and inviolability of such oaths is the ground of our Lord's caution regarding oaths in Matt. 5:34–37 and James's warning in James 5:12.

The universal pattern of Christian catechesis was to teach the Apostles' Creed, the Lord's Prayer, and the Decalogue. The Reformation continued the ancient pattern. The Reformed tradition has always been confessional. From the earliest days of the Reformation all the Protestants confessed their faith. From Huldrych Zwingli's Sixty-Seven Articles of 1523 to the Helvetic Consensus Formula (1675) the Reformed churches produced no fewer than twenty-five major, and many more minor confessions and catechisms.[8] On average between 1523 and 1675, accounting only for the major confessional documents, the Reformed produced a significant confessional document every six years.

There are two difficulties to face immediately. First, confessions, however limited they may be, are inescapable.[9] Even "no confession" is a confession of sorts. Everyone who associates with a "no confession" church confesses that there is "no confession." Anyone in a "no confession" congregation who attempted to impose a longer or different confession would run into opposition from all those who confess "no confession." Second, the creation and use of any such document to norm the reading of Scripture are necessarily problematic. What is the status of a confessional document? Does it necessarily or implicitly subvert the normative status of Scripture? Is Scripture the "unnormed norm" (*norma non normata*)? The answer is that, among classical, confessional Protestants, Scripture is indeed the norm which norms all norms. Nevertheless, that norm must be read and understood within a given community (i.e., the church), and that community must come to some agreement about what Scripture teaches and implies and how it is to be read and applied within the church. Any such agreement or covenant is a confession. John Webster is right to say,

8. E.g., Sixty-Seven Articles (1523); Ten Conclusions of Bern (1528); Zwingli's Confession of Faith (1530); Tetrapolitan Confession (1530); Confession of Basel (1534); First Helvetic Confession (1536); Calvin's Catechisms (1537, 1541); Genevan Confession (1536–37); Zürich Consensus (1549); Confession of the English Congregation in Geneva (1556); Forty-Two Articles (1553); Thirty-Nine Articles (1562–71); Gallic Confession (1559); Scots Confession (1560); Belgic Confession (1561); Second Helvetic Confession (1566); Heidelberg Catechism (1563); Second Scots Confession (1580); Irish Articles (1615); Canons of Dort (1619); Westminster Confession and Catechisms (1647–48); Consensus Helvetica Formula (1675).

9. This point has been made many times by confessional Protestants. See, e.g., Daniel R. Hyde, *The Good Confession: An Exploration of the Christian Faith* (Eugene, OR: Wipf & Stock, 2006), 7–10.

In making its confession, the church lifts up its voice to do what it *must* do—speak amazement of the goodness and truth of the gospel and the gospel's God. Creeds and confessional formulae exist to promote that act of confession: to goad the church towards it, to shape it, to tie it to the truth, and so to perpetuate the confessional life and activity of the Christian community. In this way, creeds and confessional formulae are the servants of the gospel in the church.[10]

To be sure, the community's understanding of Scripture may change, and when it does, if there is consensus regarding that change, the confession may and should be changed to reflect that consensus. What exactly is the relation between the community and the secondary authority, its confession? The idea that Christians should be, in their interpretation of Scripture, in theology, piety, and practice, held accountable to a human document strikes some Christians as flatly wrong and a violation of conscience, a violation of *sola scriptura*, or both. We have seen, however, that this view of ecclesiastical authority is not tenable among those who would be Reformed. Among the Reformed churches, our confessional documents have always been recognized as a *"public and binding indication of the gospel."*[11]

Among confessional Protestants there have been primarily two approaches to subscribing confessions. The earlier approach has been called the *quia* (because) approach. The confession is said to norm and bind subscribers *because* it is biblical. The second approach is *quatenus* (insofar as), in which the confession is said to norm and bind subscribers only *insofar as* the confession is biblical.[12] The confessional Lutheran approach was *quia*. As Peter Lillback notes, one Lutheran prince required all his ministers and teachers to subscribe not only the Formula of Concord (1570), but also everything written by Martin Luther and Martin Chemnitz.[13] According to the Lutheran writer E. H. Klotsche, *quatenus* is

10. John Webster, *Confessing God*, 69 (italics original).
11. Ibid., 74 (italics original). Webster is using "gospel" in the broad sense of "the Christian faith," as opposed to the narrower sense of "the good news."
12. E.g., Webster, *Confessing God*, 81–82, reflects this approach.
13. Peter A. Lillback, "Confessional Subscription among the Sixteenth Century Reformers," in *The Practice of Confessional Subscription*, ed. David W. Hall (Oak Ridge, TN: The Covenant Foundation, reprint, 1995), 39.

no real subscription because it introduces too much subjectivity into the relations between the subscriber and the confession.[14] The early Reformed practice was also *quia* subscription. This was true among the English under Edward VI in 1553 and under Elizabeth in 1566 when ministers were to subscribe the Forty-Two Articles and the Second Helvetic Confession.[15] This was also true regarding the subscription of the Thirty-Nine Articles in 1571 and for other minor documents through 1604.[16]

Calvin's Ecclesiastical Ordinances of 1541 required that children make profession of faith, and be tested by the Genevan catechism. Parents were required to bring their children to catechism on Sunday afternoon. The child had to recite the catechism and make profession of faith to the congregation. The consistory prescribed an oath (1542) in which ministers promised and swore to set forth "purely his Word for the edification of this Church," to uphold the Church Order and constitution of the city, and to submit to the polity. Following Geneva, the continental Reformed practice was to subscribe the BC and the HC and, after 1618, the CD (explicit in the vow of subscription imposed by the synod in the *Post-Acta*), without exception or *quia*. There are two key provisions. The subscribing minister must "heartily agree with" (*corde sentire*) and "believe" (*credere*) the three forms. Second, he confesses that the Forms of Unity "agree" (*consentire*) "entirely with the Word of God" (*per omnia Verbo Dei*). Further, all ministers vowed "to teach and faithfully to defend the aforesaid doctrine, without either directly or indirectly contradicting the same by our public preaching or writing," and to "declare, moreover, that we not only reject all errors that militate against this doctrine and particularly those which were condemned by the above mentioned Synod, but that we are disposed to refute and contradict these and to exert ourselves to keeping the Church free from such errors."[17] Synod allowed, however,

14. E. H. Klotsche, *Christian Symbolics; or, Exposition of the Distinctive Characteristics of the Catholic, Lutheran and Reformed Churches as well as the Modern Denominations and Sects Represented in This Country* (Burlington, IA: The Lutheran Literary Board, 1929), 15–16, cited in Lillback, "Confessional Subscription among the Sixteenth Century Reformers," 35–36.

15. Lillback, "Confessional Subscription," 40–41.

16. Ibid., 41.

17. H. H. Kuyper, ed., *De Post Acta of Nahandelingen van de Nationale Synode van Dordrecht in 1618 en 1619 Gehouden* (Amsterdam: Höveker & Wormser, 1899), 186–88.

that if, after ordination and subscription to the Three Forms of Unity, a minister "should harbor a different consideration or sentiment against this doctrine," he promised that he would "neither publicly or privately propose, teach, defend the same, either in preaching or writing." Instead, he promised first to "disclose the same to Presbytery, Classis and Synod."[18] The Form of Subscription details the process by which the minister's change of view might be publicly and ecclesiastically evaluated to see whether he could still subscribe the standards of the churches.

The Scots also took the *quia* approach to the 1560 Scots Confession, though they allowed exceptions to the Second Helvetic Confession (1566), which they subscribed as an ecumenical act.[19] When it came to their own documents, however, the early Reformed churches did not allow exceptions, and they were quite ready to use them as tests of orthodoxy.[20] With the approval of the Westminster Standards in 1647 by the Scottish General Assembly (and their February ratification by Parliament), all ministers were required to subscribe them without qualification.[21] This had been the pattern of the Scots Presbyterians since 1560.[22] They were to subscribe them, however, "as ratified and expounded in the Act of Approval."[23] Here a little light appears between subscription and the original document. Now the *animus imponentis* (the intent of the one imposing) of the ratifying body is definitive of the status and nature of subscription. This, however, was not system subscription, but a move to

18. Ibid.

19. Lillback takes this fact as evidence of an incipient *quatenus* approach to confessional subscription. See Lillback, "Confessional Subscription among the Sixteenth Century Reformers," 59. He makes the same argument relative to Calvin's subscription of the *Augustana Variata* (1541). See Lillback, "Confessional Subscription among the Sixteenth Century Reformers," 46–47. It is not clear, however, that the conclusion is necessary. It is true that the Scots and Calvin did allow exceptions, but not to their own documents. They allowed exceptions only to documents which were more or less alien to their churches. In other words, they signed them as ecumenical acts. It does not follow that if they allowed exceptions to alien documents, they set the stage for exceptions to proper symbols.

20. Lillback, "Confessional Subscription among the Sixteenth Century Reformers," 43, 50.

21. Ligon Duncan, "Owning the Confession: Subscription in the Scottish Presbyterian Tradition," in *The Practice of Confessional Subscription*, ed. David W. Hall (Lanham, MD: University Press of America, 1995), 81.

22. Ibid.

23. Ibid.

account for the lack of an explicitly Presbyterian ecclesiastical polity in the WCF and to impose upon the Scottish Kirk a particular understanding of WCF 31.2. Oral subscription was the norm until 1690, after the Glorious Revolution and after the "killing times." The written formula of 1693 mentions nothing of exceptions or "system subscription."[24] There were no exceptions allowed or envisioned.[25]

In the eighteenth century, however, greater distance between the confession and the Scriptures began to appear. In 1720 the Irish Presbyterians adopted a version of the *quatenus* approach requiring ministers to hold to the "substance of doctrine" when subscribing the WCF. *Quia* subscription was the rule in the Netherlands until the Nederlands Hervormde Kerk (Dutch Reformed Church) allowed *quatenus* subscription in 1816.[26] The turn by the NHK to *quatenus* subscription was one of the issues that prompted the *Afscheiding* (separating) of 1834.[27]

Among colonial American Presbyterians there were two approaches to subscription. Led by Jonathan Dickinson (1688–1747), some of the New Side questioned whether confessional subscription was biblical.[28] In 1727, John Thomson (c. 1690–1753), one of the leaders of the Old Side, introduced an overture on subscription, which, if enacted, would have bound Presbyterians to a form of subscription not very different from that adopted by the Synod of Dort. Defending the Irish "substance" view, Dickinson attacked Thomson's approach to subscription in 1729 as a way of "horrible schisms, convulsions, and confusions."[29] In the Preliminary Act of 1729, Synod declared that by subscribing the Standards, Synod was declaring its "agreement in and approbation of" them "as being in all the essential and necessary articles, good forms of sound words and systems of

---

24. Ibid., 82.

25. See Iain Hamilton, *The Erosion of Calvinist Orthodoxy: Seceders and Subscription in Scottish Presbyterianism*, ed. David F. Wright, Rutherford Studies in Historical Theology (Edinburgh: Rutherford House, 1990), 5.

26. W. Robert Godfrey, "Subscription in the Dutch Reformed Tradition," in *The Practice of Confessional Subscription*, ed. David W. Hall (Lanham, MD: University Press of America, 1995), 71.

27. Ibid.

28. C. A. Briggs appealed to Dickinson as his model. See Charles Augustus Briggs, *American Presbyterianism: Its Origin and Early History* (New York: Charles Scribner's Sons, 1885), 208–23.

29. Ibid., 212.

Christian doctrine."[30] In contrast to the stance to be taken later by mainline Presbyterian and Reformed churches in Britain, Europe, and America, by which confessional documents were reduced to mere historical witnesses, by this language Synod intended to "adopt the said Confession and Catechisms as the confession of our faith."[31] The Standards were intended to govern who could be admitted to the church's ministry. No candidate could be admitted unless he "declares his agreement with all the essential and necessary articles of said confession." Any candidate who found himself with "any scruple" with respect to *any article* of the Standards must (as with the Dort formula of subscription) "declare his sentiments to the Presbytery or Synod." The judicatory may admit a candidate with a scruple about the Standards only if it judges that "scruple or mistake to be only about articles not essential and necessary in doctrine, worship or government."[32] Any candidate failing this test must be judged ineligible for ministry in the Presbyterian Church. Ministers with differences over extraconfessional, or "extra-essential and not necessary points of doctrine," were to be treated with "the same friendship, kindness and brotherly love, as if they had not differed from us in such Sentiments."[33]

Such was the level of trust that subscription in 1729 was merely verbal. In the afternoon session, all the ministers of Synod but one, "after proposing all the scruples that any of them had to make against any articles and expressions" in the Standards, agreed unanimously "in the solution of those scruples, and in declaring the said Confession and Catechisms to be the confession of their faith." The unrecorded scruples aside, the only exceptions taken to the Standards by the Synod were to "some clauses in the twentieth and twenty-third chapters,"[34] about which Synod declared "that they do not receive those articles in any such sense as to suppose the civil magistrate hath a controlling power over Synods with respect to the exercise of their ministerial authority; or power to persecute any for

30. Guy S. Klett, ed., *Minutes of the Presbyterian Church in America 1706–1788* (Philadelphia: Presbyterian Historical Society, 1976), 103.

31. Ibid.

32. Ibid., 104.

33. Ibid.

34. Ibid.

their religion, or in any sense contrary to the Protestant succession to the throne of Great Britain."[35]

The spirit of the Synod in adopting and subscribing the Standards in 1729 might be paraphrased thus: "we believe the substance of everything in the Standards, except for the doctrine of the civil magistrate's role in church government." In other words, "We are confessional Presbyterians, but we are also colonial Americans." The American revisions to the Standards support this interpretation. In 1788, Synod amended WCF 20.4, striking the expression "and by the power of the civil magistrate." In WLC 109 they struck the phrase "tolerating a false religion."[36] The question, however, of the nature of confessional subscription arose repeatedly in the eighteenth century. The minutes of the next Synod, in 1730, reflect ongoing tension. An overture adopted by Synod stipulated that "some persons have been dissatisfied at the manner of wording" of the 1729 agreement regarding the Standards as not strict enough. The 1730 Synod declared that they understood those clauses to oblige ministerial candidates "to receive and adopt the Confession and Catechisms at their admission, in the same manner, and as fully as the members of Synod did, that were then present."[37]

In 1734 the matter arose again. This time Synod ordered an annual inquiry whether the ministers who had been received during the year had adopted the Standards along with "the Directory" according to the acts of Synod "made some years since for that purpose" and whether that inquiry had been duly recorded in the minutes.[38] Again in 1736 the Synod recognized that there was some dissatisfaction with the language of the preliminary act of 1729.

> That in order to remove said offence, and all jealousies that have arisen
> or may arise in any of our people's minds, on occasion of said distinctions
> and expressions, the Synod doth declare, that the Synod have adopted,
> and still do adhere to the Westminster Confession, Catechisms, and

35. Ibid.
36. Briggs, *American Presbyterianism: Its Origin and Early History*, 364.
37. Klett, ed., *Minutes of the Presbyterian Church in America 1706–1788*, 108.
38. Ibid., 131.

Directory, without the least variation or alteration, and without any regard to said distinctions.

As in the modern period questions arose about the Synod's intent in adopting the Standards: "And we do further declare, that this was our meaning and true intent in our first adopting of said Confession. . . . And we hope and desire, that this our Synodical declaration and explication may satisfy all our people, as to our firm attachment to our good old received doctrines contained in said Confession, without the least variation or alteration."[39]

Twenty-two years later, as part of the Plan of Union reuniting the Old and New Sides in 1758, Synod declared that both Synods "having always approved and received" the Standards "as an orthodox and excellent system of Christian doctrine . . . we do still receive the same as the confession of our faith." Synod also pledged its continuing adherence to the place of worship, government, and discipline of the DPW, "strictly enjoining it on all our members and probationers for the ministry." Ministers were to preach according to the "form of sound words" in the Standards and "avoid and oppose all errors contrary thereto."[40] In less than thirty years, the gentlemanly agreement of 1729, tested repeatedly in the church courts and by the Old Side/New Side schism, became a rather more vigorous form of subscription now "strictly enjoining" the Standards upon members of presbytery and requiring more than mere toleration of the Standards but rather a stout defense of the same.

By the middle of the nineteenth century, however, serious questions were arising in the Church of Scotland and elsewhere challenging both *quia* and conservative *quatenus* subscription; and, as a result, the Church of Scotland moved to a liberal *quatenus* position. In 1900, foreshadowing developments to come in North America, the Kirk of Scotland required only that ministers subscribe with the understanding that the WCF was the confession of the Church of Scotland and that by signing it they were declaring that they "believe the fundamental doctrines of the Christian

---

39. Ibid., 141.
40. Briggs, *American Presbyterianism: Its Origin and Early History*, 319–20.

faith contained therein." Obviously, one could drive a truck through such verbal holes, and that has been done for a century.[41]

In the modern period, mainline American Presbyterians, following the Church of Scotland, reduced the Westminster Standards to the status of a mere witness to the historic faith of the church. With the adoption of the Confession of 1967, which supplanted whatever remaining authority the Westminster Standards had to that point, all confessional documents were reduced, in the second ministerial vow taken at ordination, to mere "guidance," to "historic and faithful witnesses to the Word of God." In the words of John Muether, the mainline approach turns the confession into "an expression of the historically conditioned experience of faith."[42] It is not that the mainline does not appreciate what is happening. The preface to the *Book of Confessions* makes it clear that the modern mainline stance is deliberate. The mainline Presbyterians recognize that

> Reformed Christians are put in a difficult position with their self-limiting, self-relativising confessions. On the one hand they are bound: so long as they are faithful members of a Reformed church they are not free to interpret Christian faith and life (or even Scripture itself) however seems best to them personally, but are committed to submit themselves to the authority and guidance of the confessional standards of their church.[43]

At the same time, having embraced and internalized the quest for illegitimate religious experience (now in the form of the Barthian doctrine of revelation as existential encounter), the preface insists that Presbyterians are "free" and even required by the confessions themselves "to remember the human limitations and fallibility of their church's confessional standards," which entails revision according to "a new and perhaps different word from the living Lord" in the

41. Duncan, "Owning the Confession: Subscription in the Scottish Presbyterian Tradition," 84–85.

42. John Muether, "Confidence in Our Brethren: Creedal Subscription in the Orthodox Presbyterian Church," in *The Practice of Confessional Subscription*, ed. David W. Hall (Lanham, MD: University Press of America, 1995), 303.

43. Presbyterian Church (U.S.A.), *The Constitution of the Presbyterian Church (U.S.A.). Part I, Book of Confessions* (New York and Atlanta: Office of the General Assembly, 1983), xviii.

"light of further study of Scripture."[44] Those who oppose this approach to the Standards are characterized as having "contradicted the very Reformed tradition they confess" by making of the Standards "absolute, infallible, unchangeable truth and authority" in the same way that "the Roman Catholic church has traditionally claimed for its official teaching."

Doubtless, there have been some who have thought this way, but none of the sideline churches holds such a view of the confession, nor does the General Assembly offer any evidence demonstrating that such an abuse of the confession was widespread among the classical Reformed theologians who formed our tradition. This language seems to be more a caricature than characterization. The stance of the mainline seems reasonably clear, however, when the preface continues by arguing that

> both Scripture and the confessions teach us to have confidence in the Holy Spirit's continuing guidance of the church through the centuries as the Spirit enables the church to hear the Word of God through Scripture in every new time and situation. Therefore when there are differences between the confessions, initial priority should be given to contemporary confessions. This is only initial preference because further reflection may reveal that at some points the church in earlier times was more able and willing to be guided by the Spirit than the contemporary church.[45]

It would be good to know whether, since 1967, and in what particulars, the mainline Presbyterians have decided that the Westminster Assembly was correct and modern theology is wrong.

Finally, according to the mainline, the church's historic confession of the faith, its reading of Scripture since the early sixteenth century regarding the very things that define what it is to be Reformed, for example, the theology, piety, and practice of the Reformed faith, may all be set aside in favor of continuing illumination, if not exactly continuing revelation. While formally affirming the necessity of a confession, the mainline ruthlessly relativizes any particular confession at any time by the ongoing illuminating work of the Spirit. It seems that the mainline Presbyterians are saying that unless one consents to their doctrine of "continuing guid-

44. Ibid., xviii–xix.
45. Ibid., xxiv.

ance," one is not really Reformed. This is a bit like arguing that unless one consents to the Wesleyan doctrine of sinless perfection, one is not Reformed. According to the mainline Presbyterians, in principle, therefore, there can be no fixed definition of what it is to be Reformed, but only a temporarily fixed address locating what most mainliners think the Spirit is saying at a given point.[46]

Among the Dutch Reformed churches in North America, the Reformed Church in America in the 1970s adopted a new "Declaration for Ministers of Word and Sacrament," in which the minister declares that he or she believes "the gospel of the grace of God in Jesus Christ as revealed in the Holy Scriptures of the Old and New Testaments and as expressed in the Standards of the Reformed Church in America." He further accepts the "Scriptures as the only rule of faith and life."

In borderline churches such as the Christian Reformed Churches in North America the vows and stance toward the confession adopted by the Synod of Dort (1619) were replaced in 1976 with guidelines which conditioned *quia* subscription. The minister now subscribes the Three Forms of Unity "without mental reservation," affirming that "all the doctrines contained in the standards of the church" are taught in the Word of God. This commitment, however, does not mean that all "these doctrines are all stated in the best possible manner" or that the standards are comprehensive or exhaustive. The CRCNA also recognized that subscription obligates one only to those "doctrines confessed" and not to "the references, allusions, and remarks that are incidental to the formulation of these doctrines nor to the theological deductions which some may draw from the doctrines set forth in the confessions." These qualifications, which were probably implicit from the beginning, do not seem harmful.

In 1998, however, the CRCNA adopted what could be fairly construed as a slightly broader form of subscription, a move that has attracted little

---

46. It is mystifying how an appeal to what is tantamount to ongoing revelation can be thought to be more faithful to Reformed theology than the classical Reformed approach to Scripture and confession. The appeal of the mainline Presbyterians to the ongoing leading of the Spirit seems more Anabaptist than Calvinist in character. For more extensive criticism of the Confession of 1967 see Edmund P. Clowney, "The Broken Bands: Constitutional Revolution in American Presbyterianism," in *Scripture and Confession: A Book about Confessions Old and New*, ed. John H. Skilton (Phillipsburg, NJ: Presbyterian and Reformed, 1973), 158–216.

attention.[47] Even more recently, however, Synod 2005 commissioned a task force to reconsider the form of subscription. As of this writing, the task force has submitted its report to the churches for review.[48] The spirit of the report may be evident in these words: "office bearers today desire to be more guided and less silenced by the confessional documents."[49] The task force recommends that the vow of subscription be revised to read: "We accept the historic confessions: the Belgic Confession, the Heidelberg Catechism, and the Canons of Dort, as well as Our World Belongs to God: A Contemporary Testimony, as faithful expressions of the church's understanding of the gospel for its time and place, which define our tradition and continue to guide us today."[50]

The similarity of this language to that adopted by the mainline Presbyterians in 1967 is striking. In both instances, the historic confessional documents are reduced to testimonies to past belief with ongoing relevance. This vow is hardly a resounding reaffirmation that the HC, the BC, and the CD remain the vital confession of the CRCNA. In the new vow, one is no longer bound closely to the language and intent of the confessions, but rather one promises "to be shaped by them" and to "continually review them [sic]" in the "light of our understanding of the Scriptures."[51] If this vow is adopted, it seems that ministers will no longer be reading the Scriptures with the Reformed churches since the sixteenth century, but checking to see if the Reformed churches agree with them.

Contemporary Approaches to Subscription in Confessional Churches

As distinct from the earliest Presbyterian and Reformed practice, virtually all American Presbyterians have accepted since the middle of the

47. See Article 51.IV in the Minutes of Synod 1998 in *Christian Reformed Church in North America: Acts of Synod* (Grand Rapids: Christian Reformed Church in North America), 425–26.

48. http://www.crcna.org/site_uploads/uploads/resources/2007_formofsubscription. pdf (accessed 18 September 2007).

49. Ibid., 2.

50. Ibid., 7.

51. Ibid.

nineteenth century the assumption that ministerial candidates will take some exception to the Standards. Samuel Miller argued in 1833 that the question to be asked is:

> "How is this public subscription, or assent to the Confession of Faith, to be understood?" Is it to be considered as precluding all variety of opinion whatever, as to the mode of explaining the doctrines of the Confession? Is it the design of this subscription to secure entire and perfect uniformity in the manner of construing every minute article, as to censure and exclude every possible diversity of exposition on any point? To *expect* such perfect uniformity, among two thousand ministers of the gospel, is a chimera. It never was or can be realized. And to attempt to *enforce* such a principle, would be worse than useless.[52]

Miller continued by arguing that it was the intent of both the Synod of Dort (1618–19) and the Westminster Assembly to be so inclusive. He cited the diversity of views at the Synod of Dort on the extent of the atonement, and the diversity of views at the assembly on the question of the logical order of the decree (i.e., supralapsarianism or infralapsarianism), and the assembly's toleration of the minority who denied the imputation of the active obedience of Christ as examples of such breadth of opinion.[53]

For Miller, the most relevant questions were: how many exceptions may be taken and to what effect? When do exceptions vitiate subscription? At stake in this argument was the meaning of the second ordination vow, used by American Presbyterians since 1788: "Do you sincerely receive and adopt the Confession of Faith and Catechisms of this Church, as containing the system of doctrine taught in the Holy Scriptures?"[54] The question concerns the meaning of "system of doctrine." There are three competing

---

52. Samuel Miller, *Doctrinal Integrity: On the Utility and Importance of Creeds and Confessions and Adherence to Our Doctrinal Standards* (Dallas: Presbyterian Heritage, 1989), 77 (italics original).

53. Ibid., 77–78. On the question of active obedience and how the Westminster Confession should be read, see R. Scott Clark, "Do This and Live: Christ's Active Obedience as the Ground of Justification," in *Covenant, Justification, and Pastoral Ministry: Essays by the Faculty of Westminster Seminary California*, ed. R. Scott Clark (Phillipsburg, NJ: P&R, 2006), 331–64.

54. George W. Knight III, "Subscription to the Westminster Confession and Catechisms," in *The Practice of Confessional Subscription*, ed. David W. Hall (Oak Ridge, TN: Covenant Foundation, 2001), 126.

contemporary approaches to subscribing the Westminster Standards: "system subscription," "full subscription," and "good faith subscription." I will explain each of these briefly and then analyze them toward drawing some conclusions for this section of the book.

In 1858 Charles Hodge criticized both the Irish "substance" approach and "strict subscription" in defense of "system subscription," a position more conservative than the Irish view and more liberal than the strict view held by some Scots and American Presbyterians. All of these, however, were varieties of *quatenus* subscription. Hodge argued that the Irish "substance of doctrine" view was too subjective. Against the strict view of some of the Scottish Presbyterians he argued in favor of a "system of doctrine" subscription which allows exceptions and even expects them, but which does not permit exceptions that would contradict the Reformed faith.[55] He argued that the words "system of doctrine" must be understood in "their plain, historical sense."[56] According to Hodge, the expression "system of doctrine" does not mean Christianity generically. He argued that its meaning is defined by the *animus imponentis*. The intent of the Synod of Philadelphia was to understand "system of doctrine" to refer to the Reformed faith as understood historically. He appealed to the Adopting Act of 1729 of the Synod of Philadelphia. When Synod spoke of "all the essential articles," it referred to the system of doctrine contained in the Standards.[57] It is not enough to say one holds the "substance of doctrine," since the church knows that only when it comes to expression in a form, which is defined by the Standards.[58]

Hodge himself held every proposition taught in the confession. He estimated that he was one of a dozen ministers in the American Presbyterian church who could do so, but he did not think it necessary to do

55. Charles Hodge, "Adoption of the Confession of Faith," *The Princeton Review* 30 (1858): 669–92.

56. Charles Hodge, *Discussions in Church Polity*, reprint ed. (Seoul and New York: Westminster, 2001), 318.

57. Ibid., 323.

58. Ibid., 325. John Murray observes that we do not subscribe the system of truth contained in the confession, but the confession as the system of truth contained in the Scriptures. See John Murray, "Creed Subscription in the Presbyterian Church in the U.S.A.," in *The Practice of Confessional Subscription*, ed. David W. Hall (Lanham, MD: University Press of America, 1995), 259.

so.[59] According to David Calhoun, because system subscription allowed for such latitude, Hodge did not regard the New Haven or Hopkinsian theology as "beyond the pale."[60] Against the strict approach, he argued that "system" does not entail "every proposition" in the Standards. The confession "may contain many propositions by way of argument or inference, or which lie entirely outside the system, and which may be omitted, and yet leave the system in its integrity."[61] For Hodge, the phrase "system of doctrine" denoted an objective known quantity and defined and limited the extent to which the confession is adopted. He rejected as "unfounded" the objection that "system subscription" is too subjective. Every honest person knows what Reformed churches teach. In Hodge's world, any educated nineteenth-century Lutheran could say what constitutes the Reformed "system of doctrine."[62] When, however, he gave his own summary it was, in effect, the five heads of doctrine from the Synod of Dort. That is, he reduced the system to soteriology. He argued that, had the Presbyterian Church intended in 1729 to require a ministerial candidate to adopt every proposition in the confession, she would have said so.[63] According to Hodge, when the Synod adopted the confession in 1729, she did not take exception to WCF 20 and 23 but, rather, asked, "Do you receive that Confession" or "the system of doctrine in that Confession?" There was no need for an exception because "system" excludes the strict or "every proposition" view.[64]

In his mind, Hodge was defending a qualified subscription over against an unqualified subscription. The "every proposition" view leads to false subscription, or hypocrisy. It contradicts the "plain, historical meaning of the words which the candidate is required to use and . . . the mind of the church in imposing a profession of faith." Further, it is impractical, since almost no minister in the Presbyterian Church holds every proposition. On such a standard, the Presbyterian Church would

---

59. David B. Calhoun, "'Honest Subscription': Old Princeton Seminary and Subscription to the Westminster Standards," in *The Practice of Confessional Subscription*, ed. David W. Hall (Lanham, MD: University Press of America, 1995), 239.

60. Ibid., 240.

61. Hodge, *Church Polity*, 326.

62. Ibid., 333.

63. Ibid., 327.

64. Ibid., 328.

be bereft of ministers.[65] If the Presbyterian Church tried to impose "every proposition" on its ministers, the Presbyterian Church would soon "split into insignificant sects."[66] In 1867, with reunion between the Old and New Schools in view, he reasserted his defense of "system."[67] He opposed the reunion, on the grounds that the New School was too latitudinarian.[68]

The only new point Hodge made in 1867 was to argue that system subscription is the Old School approach. He went on to defend it from being confused with the "every proposition" or strict view. This is essentially also how B. B. Warfield approached the confession.[69] Frederick W. Loetscher followed Warfield in 1929, though his son would not.[70] Warfield argued that the system approach gives enough latitude to preclude the need for a new confession.[71] Later, John Murray (1888–1975) argued on the basis of the acts of the 1736 Synod that the eighteenth-century Presbyterian Church had not rejected any part of the confession. Rather, it was a question of the intent of the body in adopting the Standards (*animus imponentis*).[72]

The contours of the debate have not changed fundamentally since the eighteenth century. In our time several writers (e.g., Morton Smith, Joseph Pipa, George W. Knight III) continue to defend a version of the "every proposition," or full or strict subscription view. They complain that

65. Ibid., 330.

66. Ibid., 335. This is also how Hodge argued in 1831. See Calhoun, "'Honest Subscription,'" 239. John Murray argued that Hodge changed his view between 1839 and 1858 or that he offered two different interpretations of the second ordination vow. See Murray, "Creed Subscription in the Presbyterian Church in the U.S.A.," 260.

67. Charles Hodge, "The General Assembly," in *Discussions in Church Polity* (New York: Westminster, reprint, 2001), 335–42.

68. Calhoun, "'Honest Subscription,'" 242.

69. B. B. Warfield, "The Confession of Faith as Revised in 1903," in *Selected Shorter Writings of Benjamin B. Warfield*, ed. John E. Meeter, 2 vols. (Nutley, NJ: Presbyterian and Reformed, 1973), 2:396–98.

70. Frederick W. Loetscher, *Address on the 200th Anniversary of the Adopting Act* (Philadelphia: Presbyterian Church in the U.S.A., 1929). See also Lefferts A. Loetscher, *The Broadening Church: A Study of Theological Issues in the Presbyterian Church since 1869* (Philadelphia: University of Pennsylvania Press, 1954).

71. B. B. Warfield, "The Presbyterian Churches and the Westminster Confession," *The Presbyterian Review* 10 (1887): 646–57.

72. Murray, "Creed Subscription," 260.

the system view allows too much latitude to officers and presbyteries in determining what is the system of doctrine.[73] The full subscription view defines system to mean not just the system of truth in the confession, but rather it means subscribing the documents themselves.[74] The documents themselves constitute the system.

According to the proponents of full subscription, this does not mean that all doctrines in the Standards "are of equal importance" since, even in Scripture, there is a hierarchy of doctrines.[75] They argue that full subscription does not require subscription to every word or expression in the system. Nevertheless, Joseph Pipa argues that the full subscription view envisions "no conflict between the Bible and the Standards." His "personal confession" is that the Standards summarize what the Bible teaches. According to Pipa, the Standards are a faithful summary of the teaching of Scripture. In distinction from the system subscription position which argues that once an exception has been registered and approved, a presbyter may teach it publicly, Pipa argues that should one later conclude that the Scriptures contradict the Standards at a given point, "he may and should write exegetical and theological papers advocating the necessary changes in the Standards, circulating such papers among fellow presbyters, but he should not teach or write publicly on his position." If he succeeds, the church will amend the Standards.[76] According to the full subscription position, "system subscription is in effect no subscription." He argues that "system" paved the way for the elimination of Calvinism from the Standards in the PCUSA.[77]

73. Their views are argued in detail in several essays in David W. Hall, ed., *The Practice of Confessional Subscription* (Lanham, MD: University Press of America, 1995). See also Morton H. Smith, *The Subscription Debate: Studies in Presbyterian Polity* (Greenville, SC: Greenville Presbyterian Theological Seminary, n.d.).

74. Joseph A. Pipa Jr., "The Practice of Subscription" (paper presented at the 29th General Assembly of the Presbyterian Church in America, Dallas, TX, 2001). See also Morton Smith, "The Case for Full Subscription," in *The Practice of Confessional Subscription*, ed. David W. Hall (Lanham, MD: University Press of America, 1995).

75. Pipa, "Practice," no pagination; Smith, *The Subscription Debate*, 5–6.

76. Pipa, "The Practice of Subscription."

77. On this point Pipa and Knight seem to make a straw man of the system view by confusing the system subscription and substance subscription views. Smith connects system subscription with the rise of New School Presbyterianism. See Smith, *The Subscription Debate*, 10–11. This connection seems unhistorical. Samuel Miller and Charles Hodge were decidedly Old School *and* proponents of system subscription.

George W. Knight III argues that system subscription leads to liberalism. Should the PCA adopt the full subscription approach, all office bearers already ordained, who do not fully subscribe, would be grandfathered but not allowed to teach contrary to the Standards.

The third approach to confessional subscription in American Presbyterianism, which advocates call the "good faith" approach to subscription, was approved at the Thirtieth General Assembly (2003) of the Presbyterian Church in America. The Book of Church Order (21–4) now says that it is the

> right and responsibility of the Presbytery to determine if the candidate is out of accord with any of the fundamentals of these doctrinal standards and, as a consequence, may not be able in good faith sincerely to receive and adopt the *Confession of Faith* and *Catechisms* of this Church as containing the system of doctrine taught in the Holy Scriptures. (cf. BCO 21–5, Q. 2; 24–6, Q. 2)

In order to determine whether a candidate can "receive and adopt" the Standards in "good faith," a presbytery is obligated to investigate a candidate's views, and the candidate is required to "state the specific instances in which he may differ with the *Confession of Faith* and *Catechisms* in any of their statements and/or propositions." A presbytery has the right to "grant exception" so long as presbytery judges that the candidate's exception is "not out of accord with any fundamental of our system of doctrine because the difference is neither hostile to the system nor strikes at the vitals of religion."

Good faith subscription rejects the assumption of the full subscription approach that the Standards are the system. It assumes that the system is less than the Standards themselves, but it is broader and more tolerant than the system subscription approach, but like system subscription it assumes that ministerial candidates will take exception to the Standards. It enlarges the role of presbyteries in determining the acceptability of exceptions. Proponents of good faith subscription argue that they intend that ministerial candidates should be faithful to Scripture, but they also argue that the Adopting Act of 1729 intended to prevent subjectivism in subscription and to keep the confession from gaining canonical status.

John Murray shared this concern.[78] This approach to subscription seems to move closer to the old Irish substance view than it does to Hodge's system view.

T. David Gordon makes a helpful observation, distinguishing between "plenary" subscription and "floating" subscription (whereby every exception allowed becomes a part of the confession de facto). He argues for a tertium quid, distinguishing between what church courts say acting "jointly" and what ministers say acting "severally."[79] The denomination (PCA) says one thing jointly or corporately, but ministers may say something else severally or individually. A minister may teach his exception so long as he notes it as an exception, that it is not the church's view.[80]

On Becoming Confessional

The first step toward becoming confessional again is to recover the proper use of the confessions as boundary markers. This may not be easy. There has been resistance to such a use of the confessions for a long time in conservative Reformed circles. For example, R. B. Kuiper, who had connections not only to old Westminster and the Orthodox Presbyterian Church, but also to Calvin Theological Seminary and the CRCNA, warned in the 1920s about the dangers of confessionalism. "The Christian Reformed people on the whole have a profound respect for their Confessions. May that ever be the case! But God forbid that their regard for the Confessions ever degenerate into *Confessionalism*."[81]

Kuiper noted that none of those who had "departed from the Confessions" submitted his views to the church for study and ecclesiastical judgment. This, he argues, would have required the church to go back to Scripture and, "no matter to what conclusions it might have come, by so doing to express that the Bible stands above the Confessions."[82] Because

78. Murray, "Creed Subscription," 259.
79. T. David Gordon, "The Church's Power: Its Relation to Subscription," in *The Practice of Confessional Subscription*, ed. David W. Hall (Lanham, MD: University Press of America, 1995), 297.
80. Ibid., 298.
81. R. B. Kuiper, *As to Being Reformed* (Grand Rapids: Eerdmans, 1926), 64.
82. Ibid.

this did not happen, "all the church had to do" to dispose of a certain case was "to appeal to the Confessions."[83] "I am afraid that in consequence at least a few people are under the impression that the authority of the confessions in matters of doctrine is very nearly tantamount to that of Scripture itself. But that, of course, is confessionalism."[84] He qualified this warning by commending an ecclesiastical committee for the way it handled the "Danhof-Hoeksema" case at Classis Kalamazoo for "disproving the erroneous views of these brethren not only from the Confessions and the writings of leading Reformed theologians, but from the Bible as well. Technically, it was not at all obliged to do that. But to do so was the part of wisdom. The danger of confessionalism was lessened."[85] He continued by openly expressing worry about the degree to which his own perceptions were "blurred by confessionalism."[86]

One understands Kuiper's concerns, but as the Reformed churches have historically understood the nature and function of the Reformed confessions as boundary markers, and as the Reformed churches have understood the nature of our relations to the confessions, Kuiper understated things. It is not that the authority of the confessions is "very nearly tantamount to that of Scripture," but it *is* tantamount to that of Scripture, assuming that a given confession *is* biblical and intended to be subscribed *because* (*quia*) it is biblical. If a confession is not biblical, it should be revised so that it is biblical, or it should be discarded in favor of a confession that is biblical.

Second, what is needed is a confession that can be subscribed *because* it is biblical.[87] Tim Keller is probably correct when he says that the current

83. Ibid.
84. Ibid.
85. Ibid., 65.
86. Ibid., 66.
87. *Pace* J. V. Fesko, "The Legacy of Old School Confession Subscription in the OPC," *JETS* 46 (2003): 694–97. Fesko uses the archetypal-ectypal distinction (see chapter 4) as a way to deny *quia* subscription. He appears to suggest that *quia* subscription is an attempt to attain archetypal theology. Such a criticism is hard to understand since what is being subscribed is itself ectypal not archetypal theology. He denies the logical possibility of a "one to one correspondence" between the doctrines of the Bible and the doctrines of the confession on the ground that it violates the distinction between archetypal and ectypal theology. This does not follow. *Quia* subscription assumes that Scripture is ectypal theology, and that is why a close correspondence is possible. The criticism seems to assume an identity between Scripture

tensions with the PCA (and, one might add, within NAPARC) will not be resolved even by coming to "a consensus of *subscription-with-no-exceptions*—it would not really get to the heart of our rift."[88] Three things are necessary. First, what is needed is an agreement on how the Reformed churches will subscribe their confession; second, they must come to agree as to what confession they are subscribing; and third, they need to embrace a confession that can be subscribed by all confessional Reformed Christians without regard to their ordination to special office or their status as unordained laity. Let us begin with the last point.

George Knight observes that the practice of the American Presbyterian church has always been to distinguish between "what was required in a confession of faith ... for salvation and church membership and what was required in a confession of faith" for ordination to special ecclesiastical office.[89] As a matter of history this seems to be the case in modern times, but it is also true that it has not always been the case. It is not obvious that establishing two levels of subscription, one for laity and another for ordained officers, is either biblical or consistent with the Reformation. From where in Scripture would one deduce that God expects one level of subscription for officers and another for laity? Certainly it is possible for one to be a Christian without affirming every proposition in the Reformed confession, but that is beside the point. On that rationale, why should we bother establishing Reformed congregations at all? If the Reformed confession defines what it is to be Reformed, then establishing two distinct relations to the same constitutional document would seem to be a recipe for confusion and effectively two churches within one.

Second, the modern American Presbyterian approach to confessional subscription seems to assume the *quatenus* view. From 1647 to the beginning of the ambiguity in the American Presbyterian church in 1729, however, the Westminster Confession was subscribed *quia*. Further, the fact that the American practice has been some version of

---

and archetypal theology, and if so, it rests, at the point at least, on a misunderstanding of the archetypal-ectypal distinction. On this distinction see chapter 4 of this book.

88. Timothy Keller, "How Then Shall We Live Together? Subscription and the Future of the PCA," in *29th General Assembly of the Presbyterian Church in America* (Dallas: n.p., 2001).

89. Knight, "Subscription to the Westminster Confession and Catechisms," 142.

quatenus subscription does not mean that it must remain the case. In the European Reformed tradition, ministers and members alike have been expected to subscribe the confessions in the same way. The history of the American Presbyterian discussion about how the Westminster Standards should be subscribed is prima facie evidence that there must be a better way. It is evident that few American Presbyterians in the confessional churches actually subscribe the confession without taking exception to something. Even the full subscription approach allows for exceptions.

Every *quatenus* approach to subscription necessarily assumes some distance between the confession and Scripture. This way of relating Scripture and confession raises significant questions. Why should a church adopt a confession that some or even most of the church believes to be at least partly unbiblical? Why should a church not draft and adopt a confession she believes to be wholly biblical? The question becomes more complex when different subscribers find different parts of the confession unbiblical. Wherever there are exceptions, then it is no longer clear which document is being subscribed. Every time an exception is taken, the document being subscribed functionally changes at least for that subscriber and arguably (Gordon's distinction notwithstanding) for the body permitting the exception. At least the idea of a whole, integral confession has become theoretical. Imagine there are three hundred propositions in a confession. If one hundred ministers each take only one different exception from the confession, in the aggregate, one third of the confession is no longer functioning as a norm in the church. Further, it is not at all clear that there is any consensus as to how the Standards should be subscribed.

Third, what is needed is a document that can be subscribed by all Reformed people in the same way. Here I agree with R. B. Kuiper when he argued in 1926:

> When our Reformed fathers wrote the Confessions, they intended that these documents should be revised from time to time with a view to heresies that might in the future arise, and in accordance with the additional light on the truths of Scripture which the Holy Spirit might

be pleased to give the church. I believe that the time has come for us to do something along this line.[90]

In fact, in the 1560s the Dutch Reformed churches, meeting in regional synods, reread the BC each year to see if it needed to be revised. From the perspective of classic Reformed orthodoxy, writing a new Reformed confession that is consistent with the spirit and intent of the earlier Reformed confessions but that speaks to the issues that have arisen since the seventeenth century, issues to which the Reformed churches should properly speak, is the Reformed thing to do. To be Reformed is to be confessional, to subscribe ecclesiastically sanctioned documents, but to be Reformed is also to be *confessing*. There are two senses in which we are confessing. In the first instance to be confessing is to actively teach, uphold, and defend the faith as we confess it. This is what ministers, elders, deacons, and in the Dutch and German Reformed traditions, the laity, promise to do when they become members or officers. In the second instance, the participle "confessing" suggests a continuous activity. I contend that, as important as our current confessions are—they are the major preoccupation of this work— it is not enough only to confess them.

At the outset of this chapter, I noted the remarkable number of confessions and the remarkable rate at which they were produced in the sixteenth- and seventeenth-century Reformed churches. This fact is even more remarkable when we consider that, in the period of almost four centuries since the adoption of the Canons of Dort and three-and-one-half centuries since the adoption of the Westminster Standards by the Kirk of Scotland, though there have been many documents adopted by the mainline churches, those who most strongly identify with the confessional tradition have been strangely silent. It is doubtless true that the reluctance of the confessional Reformed churches to write and adopt new confessions reflects the quality of and Reformed satisfaction with the Three Forms of Unity and the Westminster Standards. These documents are indeed worthy of admiration, and we have been quite naturally and rightly hesitant to revise them. It is also the case that, in the modern period, proposed revisions (such as those proposed at the turn of the twentieth century and

90. Kuiper, *As to Being Reformed*, 66.

opposed by the likes of B. B. Warfield) could not all be judged happy or in the spirit of the original documents.

Nevertheless, the relative reluctance of modern Reformed folk to confess the faith in their own words to their own generation since Dort and Westminster suggests a certain weakness in the post-Westminster understanding of the importance and necessity of confession. Just after the Westminster Assembly substantially finished its work, René Descartes died. By the middle of the eighteenth century the rationalism of Christian Wolff was fundamentally displacing Christian revelation as the locus of authority for many. In the nineteenth century that trend continued with Immanuel Kant. The rationalism and empiricism of the Enlightenment necessitated the development of a highly sophisticated apologetic and massive prolegomena to theology. The rationalism, empiricism, and skepticism of the modern period gave life to the higher-critical movement of the eighteenth and nineteenth centuries. Yet our confessions were all written before the crisis prompted by modernity was in full force. There can be little doubt whether the delegates to the Synod of Dort or the Westminster divines, facing the same circumstances, would have articulated explicitly the ministerial role of reason relative to revelation. Faced with the fundamental challenge to the authority and reliability of Scripture, there can be little doubt that the Reformed orthodox would have said more or less what Warfield, Hodge, and Old Westminster said about the nature of biblical inspiration and the reliability and essential unity of Holy Scripture.

In the modern period we have faced the questions concerning the so-called death of God, open theism, the nature of humanity and the image of God,[91] the historicity of Jesus, the nature of justification, the doctrine of the church,[92] and the nature of the final state.[93] We could adduce a list of major questions in virtually every locus of theology, as well as questions

91. Not that ecclesiastical assemblies should be pronouncing on social questions, but the nineteenth-century debate over slavery was in some measure a debate over theological anthropology, as is the contemporary abortion debate, as is the debate over cloning. Theologians have also raised serious questions over the nature of the body/soul dualism and the state of the human person after death.

92. E.g., what are the ecumenical responsibilities of the church?

93. There is a large-scale loss of confidence in the traditional doctrine of personal eschatology.

touching the piety and practice of the Reformed churches, that have not been addressed consistently, confessionally, formally, and ecclesiastically in the modern period.

The question remains why we, the heirs of the confessional tradition, did not answer these questions in ecclesiastical confessions. Certainly the earlier documents were still serviceable for answering, in principle, many of these questions, but this is beside the point because those who wrote our sixteenth- and seventeenth-century confessions might have made the very same argument, but they did not. The origin of the Westminster Standards can be explained by largely external forces. The developing English empire needed a common statement of faith for the English and Scottish churches. The chaos of the English church(es) before and during the civil war also wanted a common confession. The HC was also the product of necessity. Frederick III inherited a religiously confused electorate. As he was imposing the third religious confession (*cuius regio, eius religio*) since the 1555 on the Palatinate, the need for a new catechism was self-evident. None of these explanations, however, accounts for the rise of the BC.

The French Confession was published in 1559. Guido de Brès (1522–67) began drafting the Belgic Confession almost immediately after the appearance of the French Confession.[94] The French Confession, whether written by Calvin himself, certainly reflected his theology and influence. Further, it had ecclesiastical sanction as it was adopted by the French Reformed Church. The situation of the French Reformed Church was a little different than that faced by the French Reformed Christians in the southern Netherlands, but was it so different as to warrant an entirely new confession to be presented to the world just two years later? Could not the Reformed churches of the Netherlands have adapted the French Confession to their own needs? Certainly there were no new major theological or ecclesiastical issues since 1559 that would have justified a new confession. To top all of these, De Brès and the editors of the Belgic Confession had to work hard to earn Calvin's reluctant approval for their document. All of these would seem to be perfectly good

94. On the Belgic Confession see Daniel R. Hyde, *With Heart and Mouth: An Exposition of the Belgic Confession* (Grandville, MI: Reformed Fellowship, 2007); Nicolaas H. Gootjes, *The Belgic Confession: Its History and Sources*, Texts and Studies in Reformation and Post-Reformation Thought (Grand Rapids: Baker Academic, 2007).

reasons for not producing another confession, but apparently they were not sufficient. De Brès and the Reformed Christians of the Netherlands not only produced a confession (under extreme duress) but they adopted it, and not the French Confession, in multiple ecclesiastical assemblies until the Belgic Confession was adopted by the Synod of Dort as one of the Three Forms of Unity.

Why did De Brès and the Reformed churches of the Netherlands persist with the BC? N. H. Gootjes provides a partial answer. When the BC was published in 1561 it appeared anonymously.[95] The confession was not to be taken as De Brès's (or the committee's) but as that of the Reformed churches of the Netherlands. It was not sufficient to take over the French Reformed Confession (even though De Brès and the others borrowed significantly from the French Confession with the result that in many places they are indistinguishable). The BC was not merely the product of nationalism. The rest of the answer lies in the nature of Reformed theology, piety, and practice. There are several English-language collections of ecclesiastical confessional documents. Most of them, however, because they do not focus solely on the Reformed confessions or because they are limited in scope, fail to communicate the number and consistency of the Reformed confessions from the mid-sixteenth century until the late seventeenth century. Seemingly every German duchy (there were dozens of them) and Swiss canton produced its own confession, and they did so repeatedly. They did so because that is what Reformed churches did. They understood something we have forgotten: the faith must be confessed anew in every generation and in every place, or it will be lost or deformed. That this is manifestly true is obvious from the history of modern Reformed theology, piety, and practice and from the sorts of elementary questions, for example, the doctrine of justification and the administration of the Lord's Supper, that presently trouble the Reformed churches.[96] The rise and influence of QIRC and QIRE is directly explicable, at least in part, by the refusal of Reformed churches since the classical period to follow the example of the sixteenth- and seventeenth-century churches.

95. N. H. Gootjes, "The Earliest Report on the Author of the Belgic Confession," *Nederlands Archief voor Kerkengescheidnis* 82 (2002): 86–94.
96. E.g., the federal vision and paedocommunion controversies.

There are three principal objections to writing a new confession: 1) the Westminster Standards and Three Forms are sufficient; 2) modern confessions have been unorthodox; 3) we are not capable of writing confessions. I address these serially in reverse order. First, those who argue that Reformed churches are not presently capable of writing a Reformed confession today both overestimate those who wrote our confession and underestimate the potential latent in the contemporary Reformed churches. Consider the primary authors of the Three Forms of Unity. Guido De Brès, the primary author and editor of the BC, was thirty-nine when the confession was published. He had a university education and was a gifted preacher, but like many sixteenth-century Protestants he probably did not have an extensive formal theological education. Zacharias Ursinus (1534–83) was twenty-nine and Caspar Olevianus (1536–87) was twenty-seven when the Heidelberg Catechism was published. Ursinus studied for several years with Philipp Melanchthon (1497–1560) before being called to Heidelberg, and Olevianus studied briefly in Zurich and Geneva before beginning his ministry in Trier and then being called to Heidelberg. Ursinus's internship with Melanchthon was invaluable, but after Melanchthon's death he studied only briefly before taking the call to Heidelberg. Neither of them had extensive formal training by modern standards. What they had that many have not had since the eighteenth century in the United States was a good classical education in the *trivium* (grammar, logic, and rhetoric). They became very good, significant theologians, but the HC was produced relatively early in their careers. The BC and the HC were the results of judicious borrowing, good editing, and a fine pedagogical sense as much as theological acumen.

Because of the analogies in the way they were produced, for the purposes of this argument, the Westminster Standards and the CD may be considered together. To be sure, there were genuine differences between the two assemblies and their products. The CD were the product of a remarkable and fairly unique international synod attending to a pressing international crisis symbolized by the Dutch Remonstrants. As such, the history of the CD (and the Westminster Standards are like them in this regard) is much more complicated than that of the BC and HC.[97] The Westminster Standards, of course, unlike the CD, were intended to provide a comprehensive statement of and catechesis in the Reformed theology, piety, and practice for the Churches of England and Scotland. Nevertheless, despite their differences, both the Westminster Assembly and the Synod of Dort were ecclesiastical assemblies and the result of hard, diligent, thoughtful, and prayerful committee work.

However remarkable their products, they were not inspired by the Spirit of God. They were the result of wise deliberation and the application of the Reformed confession to particular problems in a particular time and place. In other words, though there were remarkably gifted and outstanding delegates, it is not as if such work could not possibly be replicated today. Such thinking is more romantic than historical or realistic. Because the CD and Westminster Standards were formed long ago in a faraway place, we tend to think of them not in high-definition color but in sepia and tintype. Such romanticism has helped to create a mythology around the formation of our ecclesiastical confessions which has contributed to our reluctance to continue actively restating the Reformed faith in every generation and place. The chief difference between the sixteenth- and seventeenth-century confessional Reformed churches and the contemporary confessional Reformed churches is not ability but will. It is not as if we do not know or cannot learn what orthodox Reformed Christians confess, how they worship, or how they practice their faith. We can and have done so. We seem to have forgotten that Reformed orthodoxy is not magic. It is an act of the intellect, affections, and will, and it is the last faculty that seems absent in this regard.

One can anticipate the response to the second objection. It is quite true that, judged by the standard of the classical Reformed confessional documents, many of the modern confessions have been unorthodox. Implicit

---

97. For background on the formation of the Canons see W. Robert Godfrey, "Tensions within International Calvinism: The Debate on the Atonement at the Synod of Dordt 1618–1619," Ph.D. diss. (Stanford University, 1974). Donald Sinnema, "The Issue of Reprobation at the Synod of Dort (1618–1619) in the light of the History of This Doctrine," Ph.D. diss. (University of St Michael's College, 1985). Peter Y. DeJong, ed. *Crisis in the Reformed Churches: Essays in Commemoration of the Great Synod of Dort 1618–1619* (Grand Rapids: Reformed Fellowship, 1968).

in this objection, however, seems to be the assumption that such must necessarily be the case. Of course when put on paper, the fallacy becomes obvious. The two chief differences between the confessions drafted and adopted during what has been called "the confessional age" and the contemporary confessions are illustrated by Edward A. Dowey's explanation of the Confession of 1967 adopted by the Presbyterian Church U.S.A. He observed that the first difference between it and the Westminster Standards is that "with the *Confession of 1967* . . . a strong *social*-ethical hermeneutic of faith obedience is introduced into a Reformed confessional document."[98] He rightly acknowledged the 1934 Barmen Declaration as a precedent, and it is true that these two documents marked a shift away from the historic Reformed pattern. That pattern was this: that as ecclesiastical documents, it does not belong to confessional documents to speak directly to particular social, political, or civil questions any more than it belongs to the ministry of the gospel to comment on such questions. The minister is called and ordained to preach the law and the gospel and to administer the sacraments and to bring counsel and comfort to God's people. In his capacity as a minister, he is not elected to civil office, nor is he called any more than the apostles were called in their office to work, as ministers, toward social reform. This is the clear teaching of WCF 31.4: "Synods and councils are to handle, or conclude nothing, but that which is ecclesiastical: and are not to intermeddle with civil affairs which concern the commonwealth, unless by way of humble petition in cases extraordinary; or, by way of advice, for satisfaction of conscience, if they be thereunto required by the civil magistrate."[99] Unlike the modern mainline churches, however concerned the authors of the classical confessional documents were about the social conditions of their day, they did not give in to the temptation to confuse the civic and ecclesiastical kingdoms.[100]

Second, Dowey was also right to further observe that the Confession of 1967 was an attempt to "overcome the orthodox dichotomy between

98. Edward A. Dowey, "Confessional Documents as Reformed Hermeneutic," *Journal of Presbyterian History* 79 (2001): 55.

99. *Creeds*, 3:670.

100. On these topics see David VanDrunen, "The Two Kingdoms: A Reassessment of the Transformationist Calvin," *CTJ* 40 (2005): 248–66; D. G. Hart, *A Secular Faith: Why Christianity Favors the Separation of Church and State* (Chicago: Ivan R. Dee, 2006).

justification and sanctification," though those who still believe the old confession must dissent vigorously from his claim that this was a positive development grounded in Calvin's theology.[101] Barth's inversion of the distinction between law and gospel, the basis for the move in the Confession of 1967 to change the relations between justification and sanctification, was nothing less than a repudiation of the Reformation. It is hard to see how, as those who claim to be heirs of the Reformation, we can view this as a happy development.[102] The difference between those Reformed churches that have been described throughout this book as confessional and the mainline churches (represented by Dowey) is not that the mainliners do not confess anything, they certainly do, and in that sense may be called "confessional." Rather, the difference is that, having fundamentally rejected Reformed orthodoxy in favor of modernity, the mainline churches confess a different faith.[103]

There is nothing about the confession-drafting and -adopting process that necessitates that those churches that still believe the same faith confessed in the sixteenth and seventeenth centuries, and that will confess that same faith about the issues we have faced in modernity (and late modernity), change fundamentally their theology, piety, and practice. Rather than being an opportunity for mischief, why could it not be an opportunity for relearning what we confess in our present confessions and the intent and purpose behind those confessions? This is not to say that every contemporary attempt to restate the faith for our time will be successful. It does not appear, for example, that *Our World Belongs to God: A Contemporary Testimony*, adopted by the Christian Reformed Churches in 1986, has gained widespread acceptance or use.[104] *The Testimony of the Reformed Presbyterian Church of North America* adopted in 1980 by the

101. Dowey, "Confessional Documents as Reformed Hermeneutic," 55–56.

102. On this problem see R. Scott Clark, "How We Got Here: A Brief History of the Current Controversy," in *Covenant, Justification, and Pastoral Ministry: Essays by the Faculty of Westminster Seminary California*, ed. R. Scott Clark (Phillipsburg, NJ: P&R, 2006), 16.

103. See J. Gresham Machen, *Christianity and Liberalism* (New York: Macmillan, 1923). Machen's judgment now finds open support in the PCUSA. See, e.g., James M. Moorehead, "Redefining Confessionalism: American Presbyterians in the Twentieth Century," *Journal of Presbyterian History* 79 (2001): 72–86.

104. Synod of the Christian Reformed Church, *Our World Belongs to God: A Contemporary Testimony*, in *Psalter Hymnal* (Grand Rapids: CRC Publications, 1987), 1019–38.

RPCNA might be regarded as a slightly more successful attempt to restate the Reformed faith for our time,[105] but both documents seem somewhat idiosyncratic. *Our World* seems like a neo-Kuyperian restatement of the faith; and the RPCNA *Testimony*, though a step toward doing the work of a new confession inasmuch as it begins to address a number of questions raised since the Enlightenment, will not likely find support beyond the RPCNA, if only because of its strong insistence (e.g., 23.4) on the supposed continuing national covenant between postcanonical nations and God whereby "every nation ... should enter into covenant with Christ and serve to advance his kingdom on the earth."[106]

Finally, it is difficult to know how to answer the objection that the Reformed churches in the late modern period are not capable of writing a confession, since it is a negative argument. To begin, however, it is true, as has already been observed, that some of the contemporary attempts to restate the faith have not been a smashing success. It is true that there was an abortive attempt to write a new Reformed confession in the 1980s that foundered, perhaps because it was laden with some aspects of the QIRC. If, however, "is" does not entail "must," and if the premise is true that Reformed people are a confessing people, then it would seem to be a duty that obligates us whatever our present state. As already argued, if we do not assume too much of those who wrote our classical confessions, and if we follow the same guidelines and process as they, it is hard to imagine that we could not produce something of long-term benefit and use of the confessional, sideline, and borderline Reformed churches.

To that end a humble suggestion is offered. Rather than having each Reformed denomination and federation of NAPARC draft and adopt its own contemporary testimony (which, in their nature, tend to carry less authority), perhaps the member bodies of NAPARC could send properly prepared and duly authorized delegates to a confessional convention to

105. Reformed Presbyterian Church of North America, *The Testimony of the Reformed Presbyterian Church of North America*, in *The Constitution of the Reformed Presbyterian Church of North America* (Pittsburgh: Reformed Presbyterian Church of North America, 1989).

106. *The Constitution of the Reformed Presbyterian Church of North America*, A-70. This imperative might strike most Reformed readers as odd if only because in the one instance of a national covenant, between Yahweh and Israel, it was the former who approached the latter to initiate a covenant relationship.

meet to draft, present, and adopt a new confession of the historic Reformed faith for our time. It is unreasonable to think that the member bodies of NAPARC could not find within their ranks a sufficient quantity and quality of pastors and theologians ready to take on such a task. This NAPARC confession would be an ecumenical Reformed document, and it should be subscribed by all members *because* (*quia*) it is biblical. It should contain nothing from which anyone who genuinely holds the historic confessional Reformed faith should need to dissent. The creation, adoption, and (*quia*) subscription of the NAPARC confession would advance not only real confessional Reformed ecumenism (based on a shared understanding of a shared confession in which all the NAPARC bodies would have ownership), but it would also promote a more profound understanding of the existing Reformed confession.

There is informal evidence to support this claim. Since 1995, I have assigned students annually to write a brief confession of faith. Over the years, those students who have completed this exercise have testified almost universally that it was one of the most difficult projects they completed in their education but also one of the most profitable. It is difficult partly because of the necessary brevity of the assignment. The imposed brevity forces students to decide on theological and confessional priorities. In the nature of the case, it is a zero-sum game. If they wish to elaborate on one topic, they must necessarily say less about another. This forces them to reckon with what is genuinely important in Reformed theology, piety, and practice. The assignment is rewarding in the way learning to build cars is rewarding. There are two types of automobile drivers in the world: those who only drive and those who also repair their own cars. Those who build their own computers or model airplanes come to an understanding of both their product and the craft behind it. They understand not only *that* it works but also *why* and *how*. There are many in our churches today who have some understanding of the Reformed confession, but they do not appreciate or understand *why* the confession says what it does and *how* the confession is constructed. Because the mainline denominations either did not understand Reformed orthodoxy or rejected their theology, they were unable to do in our day what the orthodox did in theirs. There is nothing preventing those who are orthodox, however, from doing in our day what they did in theirs.

Conclusions

This and the previous chapter have argued that there is a Reformed identity, and it is defined by the Reformed confession. We have considered the nature of confessing the faith and of subscribing that confession. We have seen that confessing the faith is a biblical practice and imperative. We have considered the history of confessional subscription, and it has been argued that, if a confession is to perform its intended function as an ecclesiastical constitution and covenant, the best way to subscribe an ecclesiastical confession is to subscribe it because it is biblical, not to the degree it is thought to be biblical. Toward advancing that agenda it has been argued that in order to regain our confessional identity we need to take up our responsibility to confess the Reformed faith again in our time.

It is clear, however, in our time that there are many who are either unfamiliar with the Reformed churches and confession or who confuse it with QIRC and/or QIRE, or who are in Reformed churches and are tempted to wander to another confession. There remain many reasons either to take up or to reembrace with heart and soul the Reformed confession, and it is to some of these reasons that we now turn.

Q. *What is the making alive of the new man?*

A. Heartfelt joy in God through Christ, causing us to take delight in living according to the will of God in all good works.

—Heidelberg Catechism, Q. 90

CHAPTER
6

~~~❧⸎❧~~~

The Joy of Being Confessional

I n nineteenth-century America the Mercersburg Movement was a major reaction to revivalism and fundamentalism. The effect of this movement, whether intended is a matter of debate, was to marginalize the Reformation either by appeal to pre-Reformation theology or by looking to future developments by an appropriation of a Hegelian philosophy. In our age there have been a series of analogous reactions to revivalism and fundamentalism. In the 1970s Thomas Howard signaled his discontent with evangelicalism by converting to the Roman Catholic Church.[1] In the wake of Howard's conversion a number of other evangelicals (e.g., Scott Hahn) followed the Roman Road.[2] Robert Webber chronicled restlessness with the evangelical status quo, describing the movement of evangelicals to Anglicanism.[3] In the 1990s, with the collapse of the Berlin Wall, American evangelicals came into direct contact with forms of Christianity hitherto unknown to most American evangelicals. One of those evangelicals, Peter Gilchrist, found in Eastern Orthodoxy things he was missing and converted, taking a number of other evangelicals with him.[4] A recent report by the Associated Press on the growth of the Orthodox Churches

1. See Thomas Howard, *Evangelical Is Not Enough* (Nashville: Thomas Nelson, 1984).
2. Scott Hahn and Kimberly Hahn, *Rome Sweet Home: Our Journey to Catholicism* (San Francisco: Ignatius, 1993).
3. Robert E. Webber, *Evangelicals on the Canterbury Trail: Why Evangelicals Are Attracted to the Liturgical Church* (Waco, TX: Word, 1985).
4. Peter E. Gilchrist, *Coming Home: Why Protestant Clergy Are Becoming Orthodox* (Ben Lomond, CA: Conciliar, 1992).

in the USA claims that "since the mid-1990s, about 850,000 Americans have been drawn to more than a dozen different divisions of Orthodoxy that have congregations in the U.S." To put this number in perspective, there are about 500,000 confessional Reformed people represented in NAPARC (North American Presbyterian and Reformed Council) denominations.

The most recent evangelical trend, however, eliminates the need to change addresses altogether. Like their older evangelical brothers and sisters, the emerging church movement also rejects (at least elements of) fundamentalism and revivalism. In their place, they are constructing a cross-traditional, eclectic synthesis. *Christianity Today* writer Andy Crouch describes the approach to worship and theology of Mars Hill Bible Church (Grand Rapids) as simultaneously "echoing and subverting a fashion-driven culture of cool."[5] This hip veneer covers an intentional theological synthesis. As pastor Rob Bell puts it, "We're re-discovering Christianity as an Eastern religion, as a way of life. Legal metaphors for faith don't deliver a way of life. We grew up in churches where people knew the nine verses why we don't speak in tongues, but had never experienced the overwhelming presence of God."[6]

An eclectic approach to Christianity, with somewhat different results, also marks Brian McLaren's *A Generous Orthodoxy*, in which he describes himself simultaneously as a "missional, evangelical, Post/protestant, liberal/ conservative, mystical/poetic, biblical, charismatic/contemplative, fundamentalist/Calvinist, Anabaptist/Anglican, Methodist, catholic, green, incarnational, depressed-yet-hopeful, emergent, unfinished Christian."[7]

Scot McKnight cites the definition of the movement given by Eddie Gibbs and Ryan Bolger:

> Emerging churches are communities that practice the way of Jesus within postmodern cultures. This definition encompasses nine practices. Emerging churches (1) identify with the life of Jesus, (2) transform the secular realm, and (3) live highly communal lives. Because of these

5. Andy Crouch, "The Emergent Mystique," *Christianity Today*, November 2004, 38.
6. Ibid.
7. From the cover of Brian McLaren, *A Generous Orthodoxy* (Grand Rapids: Zondervan, 2004). For a critique of McLaren's attempted synthesis see R. Scott Clark, "Whosoever Will Be Saved: Emerging Church? Meet Christian Dogma," in *Reforming or Conforming?: Post-Conservative Evangelicals and the Emerging Church*, ed. Gary Johnson and Ronald Gleason (Wheaton, IL: Crossway, 2008).

activities, they (4) welcome the stranger, (5) serve with generosity, (6) participate as producers, (7) create as created beings, (8) lead as a body, and (9) take part in spiritual activities.[8]

McKnight gives his own list of five characteristics. The emerging churches (which he distinguishes from "emergent" churches) are "prophetic" (or at least provocative). They are "postmodern," "praxis-oriented," "post-evangelical," and "political."[9] Judging by the accounts given by the proponents of the movement, its characteristics are virtually identical to elements of forms of Anabaptist radicalism and pietism. Having rejected fundamentalism, younger (and some not so young) "postevangelicals" are embracing an informal, eclectic style of worship and church life that maximizes what I have described as the quest for illegitimate religious experience.[10] From the outside, from the Reformed confession, the emerging church movement looks like late or liquid modern pietism.[11]

In response to the exodus out of evangelicalism, this chapter renews the invitation to evangelicals proffered in the first chapter, to consider relocating theologically and ecclesiastically not to Rome, or to Constantinople or even to the Emergent Village,[12] but rather to Geneva. In renewing this offer, one is also conscious that there are Reformed folk who, though they are members of ostensibly Reformed congregations, are on the edge of following the evangelical and postevangelical trails. Thus, this chapter is particularly addressed to them. It is argued that the evangelical and postevangelical relocation notwithstanding, there are at least five good reasons for embracing the Reformed confession.

8. This is condensed from Eddie Gibbs and Ryan Bolger, *Emerging Churches: Creating a Christian Community in Postmodern Cultures* (Grand Rapids: Baker Academic, 2005), 43–44.
9. Scot McKnight, "Five Streams of the Emerging Church," *Christianity Today*, February 2007, 36–39.
10. See chapter 3 of this work.
11. I put "postmodern" in so-called scare quotes in order to draw attention to the relatively naïve use of the word by proponents of the emerging and emergent movements. In fact, very little about these movements is genuinely postmodern but would be better described as late or liquid modern. See Zygmunt Bauman, "Postmodern Religion," in *Religion, Modernity and Postmodernity*, ed. Paul Heelas et al. (Oxford: Blackwell, 1998); idem, *Liquid Modernity* (Cambridge: Polity, 2000).
12. http://www.emergentvillage.org/ (accessed 21 September 2007).

The Virtues of Being Confessional

The evangelical and postevangelical discontent is the result of the two quests that have dominated American evangelical religion for more than two centuries. This explanation accounts for the relatively easy movement of evangelicals into what might seem to be foreign territory. With respect to the QIRE, having grown up with flannel graphs of the Second Person of the Trinity, it is really only a short step to traditional icons. With respect to the QIRC, once one overcomes the predominating ignorance of and bigotry against Rome that permeate North American fundamentalism, once one discovers that Roman Catholics love Jesus and read the Bible, it is not a great step to trade the authoritarianism of fundamentalism for the magisterial authority of the Roman communion. In other words, though they occur in a different setting, Rome, Constantinople, and the Emergent Village each offer to fundamentalism and evangelicalism a more ancient and better-looking version of what already animates them.

It seems clear from at least some of the testimony of the evangelical pilgrims, especially from the proponents of the emerging church, that it is simply assumed that Calvinism or the Reformed faith is synonymous with American fundamentalism or revivalism. The pilgrims from evangelicalism seem to assume that, in rejecting fundamentalism and revivalism, they must also reject the Reformation. It is true that, in modernity, the Reformed churches have not always been good witnesses to their own tradition. We have too often looked and sounded and acted as though we were revivalists or fundamentalists. Nevertheless, if the adjective "Reformed" is defined by the Reformed confession, then we are not simply another version of those things evangelicals and postevangelicals are fleeing. Judged by what it confesses about its theology, piety, and practice, the Reformed confession possesses several virtues. The word "virtue" is a Latin word derived from the noun *vis*, that is, strength. In recent years, there has been a renaissance in the study of moral virtue.[13] The virtues that we shall consider below are theological and ecclesiological. They are attributes that should attract

13. See Alasdair C. MacIntyre, *After Virtue: A Study in Moral Theory*, 2d ed. (South Bend: University of Notre Dame, 1984); Oliver O'Donovan, *Resurrection and Moral Order: An Outline for Evangelical Ethics*, 2d ed. (Grand Rapids: Eerdmans, 1994); David F. Wells, *Losing Our Virtue: Why the Church Must Recover Its Moral Vision* (Grand Rapids: Eerdmans, 1998).

anyone interested in the historic Christian faith and especially those who are dissatisfied with contemporary evangelicalism and fundamentalism.

It Is Biblical

It is an article of the historic Christian faith that God reveals himself. The Reformed churches, as catholic churches (holding the faith revealed in Scripture, believed and practiced by Christians in all times and places), hold that God has revealed himself in two books. The Belgic Confession (Art. 2) calls creation a "most elegant book" designed to lead us to contemplate "the invisible things of God" and some of his attributes.[14] This affirmation of the truth and universality of natural revelation is in contrast to the Barthian (neoorthodox) theology of revelation which denies natural revelation.[15] Natural revelation is sufficient only to leave humans "inexcusable" before the bar of divine justice (WCF 1.1).

Nonetheless, however elegant natural revelation, the effects of sin are such that "neither the light of nature, nor the law" (CD 3/4.1) is capable of "giving that knowledge of God and of his will, which is necessary for salvation" (WCF 1.1).[16] Thus, the historic Christian tradition has taught that the Scriptures are the font of all saving knowledge of Christ and all true theology.[17] In the judgment of the Reformed churches, the medieval church was not faithful to that principle. The patristic, medieval, and Reformed churches also taught that the Scriptures, inspired by God the Spirit, are true, without error, and because they are inspired by God, infallible. The Reformed confession agreed with the patristic and medieval church in holding a high view of Scripture. In so doing, we are only accepting what the Scriptures say about themselves, that they are God's Word, that they "cannot be broken" (John 10:35), that they are "profitable

14. *RCH*, 8.
15. Emil Brunner et al., *Natural Theology: Comprising "Nature and Grace" by Professor Dr. Emil Brunner and the Reply "No!" by Dr. Karl Barth* (London: G. Bles Centenary Press, 1946).
16. *RCH*, 9.
17. For example, in the prologue to his *Breviloquium*, Bonaventure said that the "source" (*ortum*), "progress" (*progressum*), and "state" (*statum*) of Holy Scripture "is called theology" (*theologia dicitur*), in Bonaventure, *Tria Opuscula . . . Breviloquium, Itinerarium Mentis in Deum et De Reductione Artium ad Theologiam* (Florence: Collegii S. Bonaventurae, 1944), 7.

for correction, rebuke and training in righteousness" (2 Tim. 3:16), and that God the Spirit also used the created gifts of the writers of Scripture, so that it must be regarded as fully inspired by God the Spirit (2 Peter 1:20–21; 2 Tim. 3:16). In this view, we are not only following our Lord Jesus and the apostles, but we are also following the historic Christian church. With them we confess the Scriptures to be the only final authority in faith and life.

Thus, the Reformed churches confess that Scripture was not "sent or delivered by the will of man," but by the Holy Spirit operating through human beings. The writers of Scripture committed God's Word to writing at his command (BC 3).[18] The canonical Scriptures are God's Word and as such have authority of themselves. Their authority is not derived from the church (WCF 1.1). Because Scripture is holy and wholly God's (i.e., it belongs principally to him), it cannot be revised (WCF 1.2). From it Christians should learn "true wisdom and godliness, the reformation and government of churches." From Scripture we learn the "only rule of faith and obedience" (WSC 3).[19]

It is one thing to have a high view of Scripture. It is another thing, however, to have a theology, piety, and practice which are *actually* biblical. It is not widely known today, but the theologians and pastors who set the framework for the confessional Reformed reading of Scripture and theology were devout, passionate, sophisticated, and serious students of the Bible. I do not mean to suggest that merely because the classic Reformed theologians produced a great deal of published biblical study, their theology was therefore biblical. The Roman, Lutheran, Arminian, and Amyraldian scholars of the age also produced a considerable amount of biblical scholarship, and yet the confessional Reformed community would be reluctant to say that those works were biblical, at least not in the same sense. By biblical, I mean that the Reformed theologians have taken Scripture as the primary and unique authority for their theology, in the way that was discussed earlier. They read Scripture with considerable sophistication and sensitivity and insight, in part because they typically refused to segregate their theological concerns from their reading

18. *RCH*, 10.
19. *RCH*, 10–11.

of Scripture. They asked theological questions of the text as they read it. Indeed, in many Reformed writers of the period, one is more likely to find detailed theological reflection on Scripture in their biblical commentaries. This reflection was sometimes harvested postmortem to produce a volume of *Common Places*, as in the case of Martin Bucer.[20] Sometimes, the theologians included topical theological discussion within the covers of their commentaries. Their theology was biblical because, though it was often arrayed in systematic or topical or dogmatic form, its concerns were driven by the concerns of Scripture itself. Even when they used the older Aristotelian philosophical language, they used that language in the service of the exposition and defense of the Scriptures and their teaching.[21]

Second, because the Reformed churches take seriously the Holy Scriptures as the true and reliable Word of God, we have always taken seriously the art and science of Bible interpretation. We believe that though the Scriptures contain difficulties, to be sure, they are clear enough to be understood for salvation. In the words of the WCF (1.7): "Yet those things which are necessary to be known, believed, and observed for salvation, are so clearly propounded, and opened in some place of Scripture or other, that not only the learned, but the unlearned, in a due use of the ordinary means, may attain unto a sufficient understanding of them."[22] We reject the skepticism of those (e.g., Rome) who say that the Scripture and extracanonical oral tradition form a unified source of authority such that the church is not *ministerial* but *magisterial* relative to Scripture. We also reject the late modern skepticism of those who argue that texts have no meaning except that which the reader imputes to them. Without denying the difficulty of interpreting texts and Scripture in particular, we nevertheless believe the Scriptures to be sufficiently clear to learned and unlearned readers so that from them, with the illumination of the Spirit, we may come to a sufficient understanding of them for saving faith and the Christian life.

20. *Common Places of Martin Bucer*, ed. D. F. Wright (Abingdon, UK: Sutton Courtenay Press, 1971).

21. On this see R. Scott Clark, "The Authority of Reason in the Later Reformation: Scholasticism in Caspar Olevian and Antoine De La Faye," in *Protestant Scholasticism: Essays in Reassessment*, ed. Carl R. Trueman and R. Scott Clark (Carlisle, UK: Paternoster, 1999), 58–73.

22. *RCH*, 15.

The same Holy Spirit who created the world (Gen. 1:2) and inspired the Scriptures also helps his people interpret the Scriptures. His orchestration of the divine plan of salvation unifies God's Word. The Reformation and post-Reformation Reformed theologians agreed particularly with the patristic argument against the Jewish and Gnostic critics of Christianity, that God has one covenant of grace and that God the Son incarnate, Jesus Christ, is the focus of God's saving acts and revelation in history. We confess that this one covenant of grace has been "differently administered" throughout redemptive history, that under Moses it was administered through "promises, prophecies, sacrifices, circumcision, the paschal lamb, and other types and ordinances... all foresignifying Christ to come" (WCF 7.5).[23] All of the Hebrew (and Aramaic) Scriptures look forward to the coming of Christ. Reformed hermeneutics are, in this way, covenantal and christocentric.[24] Thus, in the HC we confess that God himself revealed the gospel first in paradise and published the gospel successively through redemptive history (HC Q. 19).[25]

We understand that from all eternity, the persons of the Godhead made a covenant within the Trinity (*pactum salutis*) that God the Son should become the covenant head of his people (WCF 8.1), that he should earn salvation for and mediate salvation to them, and that salvation should be applied to them through the person and work of the Holy Spirit. In history we recognize two great covenants, the covenant of works (WCF 7.2) between God and Adam and the covenant of grace (WCF 7.3; CD, Rejection of Errors 2.2) between God and his people.[26] Because of this covenantal and christocentric approach which Scripture itself requires, we not only recognize the variety of literary conventions in Scripture (narrative, wisdom literature, didactic, poetic, and semipoetic), we also recognize that within those conventions there are two great hermeneutical categories in Scripture, that is, law and gospel.[27] A passage is considered

23. *RCH*, 53.

24. The adjective "christocentric" is used in a variety of ways such that it has become problematic. On this see Richard A. Muller, "A Note on 'Christocentrism' and the Imprudent Use of Such Terminology," *WTJ* 68 (2006): 253–60. Nevertheless, in this context other adjectives seem inadequate.

25. *RCH*, 10.

26. *RCH*, 52–53.

27. HC QQ. 2–3, 21, 60, 65; CD 5.14. See Phillip Schaff, ed., *The Creeds of Christendom*, 3 vols. (Grand Rapids: Baker, 1983), 3:308, 13, 26, 28; R. Scott Clark, "The Catholic-Calvinist

law when it makes a demand and gospel when it makes a promise. Thus, for us, the covenant of works is law. It says, "Do this and live" (Luke 10:28). The covenant of grace says, "Come to me, all you who are weary and heavy burdened, and I will give you rest" (Matt. 11:28).[28]

Obviously, hermeneutics are intricately related to theology. Christian theology must be driven by the Scriptures, but no one reads the Scripture without a theology. So we must be constantly submitting our theology, that is, our understanding of Scripture, to the Scriptures themselves for revision and correction. Thus, we also work hard at the practice of theology. Some, of course, say that we take theology, particularly systematic or dogmatic theology, too seriously so that we let it ride roughshod over the Scriptures. If one evaluates this claim, however, against the actual record of Reformed theology since 1540, it is hard to see how this is actually the case. The research of Richard Muller has made it very difficult indeed to sustain such a claim.[29] Reformed theology might be wrong about a given question, and it is true that our theologians have made exegetical mistakes or drawn false conclusions, some of which have been described in this work, but such could be said about any tradition. Ironically, some have criticized Reformed theology as being shot through with paradox and mystery. Thus depending upon the set of critics to which one listens, either Reformed theology is rationalist, forcing God into a box of our making, or we are irrational mystics, who refuse to use our God-given intellects.

In fact, judged by our confession, Reformed theology is neither. On the one hand, we do believe that, in the Scriptures, through which the Holy Spirit works, is to be found the very voice of God (*vox Dei*). We believe that God speaks to us as rational creatures, and he expects us to think about what he says and to try to relate one place in Scripture to all the other places in Scripture. At the same time, we understand that it is not our business to tell God what he should say. If one reads our theologians carefully, however, there is precious little evidence that the mainstream of our tradition has created a priori definitions and then forced the Scriptures

---

Trinitarianism of Caspar Olevian," *WTJ* 61 (1999).

28. See R. Scott Clark, "Letter and Spirit: Law and Gospel in Reformed Preaching," in *Covenant, Justification, and Pastoral Ministry: Essays by the Faculty of Westminster Seminary California*, ed. R. Scott Clark (Phillipsburg, NJ: P&R, 2006), 331–64.

29. See e.g., *PRRD*.

into them.[30] Rather, we have long recognized that there are a number of apparent paradoxes in Scripture—apparent because they are mysterious to us but not to God.

For example, as Christians we are trinitarians. We confess that, on the one hand, Scripture teaches that God is one. Deuteronomy 6:4 was the fundamental Hebrew confession about Yahweh the Redeemer: "Hear, O Israel, Yahweh our God, Yahweh is one." At the same time, we also confess that God is three persons, so that the Father is God, the Son is God, and the Spirit is God, not three gods but one, not one person, but three (2 Cor. 13:14). How this can be is a great mystery, but we confess with the catholic church that it is so.[31]

We also confess, on the one hand, that human beings were created after God's "own image and likeness, good, righteous, and holy, capable in all things to will agreeably to the will of God" (BC 8).[32] Because we were created so, we are morally responsible for all we do. At the same time we confess that God is completely sovereign such that nothing occurs outside of his decree (WCF 3.1). How can God be sovereign and the first cause of all that happens, and human beings be held morally culpable for all they do? It is hard to say, but Scripture clearly teaches it, so we confess it (Rom. 9:15–29; James 1:14–17). The list of biblically required mysteries could go on, but these suffice to illustrate the classical Reformed commitment to follow the Scriptures faithfully, wherever they may lead, even if it creates difficulties for our systematic understanding of Scripture.

As suggested above, Reformed theology has always been derived from the Scriptures. John Calvin is most famous for his *Institutes*, but he spent much of his time lecturing on and preaching from Scripture. Indeed, it was his weekday lectures and Sabbath sermons in the Scriptures that caused him to revise his *Institutes* most substantially from the 1539 edition toward the form in which we know them today.[33] The great period

30. R. Scott Clark, *Caspar Olevian and the Substance of the Covenant: The Double Benefit of Christ*, ed. David F. Wright, Rutherford Studies in Historical Theology (Edinburgh: Rutherford House, 2005), 52–73.

31. See BC 8; HC QQ. 24–25; WCF 3. See also Richard A. Muller, *The Unaccommodated Calvin*, Oxford Studies in Historical Theology (New York: Oxford University Press, 2000), 15–39; idem, *Post-Reformation Reformed Dogmatics*, vol. 4.

32. *RCH*, 46.

33. T. H. L. Parker, *Commentaries on the Epistle to the Romans* (Edinburgh: T&T Clark, 1986), 118–58.

of biblical study did not end with the death of Calvin. As a matter of fact, the theologians and pastors who followed in the footsteps of Luther and Calvin carried on their practice of regular and careful lecturing and preaching in and through the Holy Scriptures.

One of the reasons it might seem that Bible study declined after Calvin is that we do not have on our shelves or find in bookstores the same number of published commentaries or books (particularly in English) by our theologians, but that does not mean they were not doing such work. By focusing, though not exclusively, on their study of Romans, one can begin to get an idea at least of the quantity of the labors which they undertook in expositing Scripture. Their study of Romans was enormous.[34] For example, though we think of Caspar Olevianus mainly as a contributor to the development of covenant theology and thus focus on his more systematic works,[35] nevertheless, Olevianus's largest volume (760 pages) was his *Commentary on the Epistle to the Romans* (*In Epistolam ad Romanos Notae*, 1579).[36] He published three other New Testament commentaries in the same period.[37] His commentary on Romans is only one of many that could be cited.[38] Lectures on Romans were a commonplace among Reformed theologians. For example, Martin Bucer (1491–1551) published his commentary in 1536. Peter Martyr Vermigli (1499–1562) published his Oxford lectures on Romans.[39] Wolfgang Musculus

34. See Heinrich Heppe, *Reformed Dogmatics Set Out and Illustrated from the Sources*, ed. Ernst Bizer, trans. G. T. Thomson (London: George Allen and Unwin LTD, 1950).

35. Caspar Olevianus, *In Epistolam D. Pauli Apostoli ad Galatas Notae*, ed. Theodore Beza (Geneva, 1578).

36. In Caspar Olevianus, *In Epistolam ad Romanos Notae, ex Gasparis Oleviani Concionibus Excerptae* (Geneva, 1579).

37. Caspar Olevianus, *In Epistolas D. Pauli Apostoli ad Philippenses & Colossenses Notae*, ed. Theodore Beza (Geneva, 1580); idem, *Notae Gasparis Oleviani in Evangelia* (Herborn, 1587). His lectures on the Gospels were published by his son Paul in Herborn. See Caspar Olevianus, *In Epistolam D. Pauli Apostoli ad Ephesos Notae* (Herborn, 1588). His lectures on Ephesians were published posthumously (1588) by his son-in-law, J. Piscator, in Herborn. See David C. Steinmetz, "Calvin and Abraham: The Interpretation of Romans 4 in the Sixteenth Century," *Church History* 57 (1988).

38. See Parker, *Commentaries on the Epistle to the Romans*, 443–55. This list has been developed independently of Steinmetz. For a detailed discussion of commentaries earlier in the sixteenth century see Peter Martyr Vermigli, *In Epistolam S. Pauli ad Romanos D. Petri Martyris Vermilii Florentini, Professoris Divinarum Literarum in Schola Tigurina, Commentarii Doctissimi* (Basle, 1558).

39. *In Epistolam S. Pauli Apostoli ad Romanos D. Petri Martyris etc.* (Basle, 1568). J. P. Donelly and R. M. Kingdon, *A Bibliography of the Works of Peter Martyr Vermigli* (Kirks-

(1497–1563) also published his in 1559.[40] Calvin's commentary on Romans appeared in 1540.[41] It was revised in 1551 and again in 1556 for style and to reflect the controversies over predestination with Bolsec and Pighius.[42]

After Calvin and Bucer, the Reformed continued publishing biblical commentaries. For example, Johannes Piscator (1546–1625), famous for his turn to chiliasm and his rejection of the doctrine of double imputation (i.e., the imputation to believers of Christ's active obedience), published a *Logical Analysis of the Epistle of Paul to the Romans.*[43] Two years later, he published lectures on Romans again, together with lectures on 1 and 2 Corinthians, Galatians, Ephesians, Philippians, Colossians, 1 and 2 Thessalonians, and observations on doctrinal topics.[44] Other orthodox Reformed theologians were equally hard at work commenting on Paul. The Lutheran turned Reformed theologian, Johann Jakob Grynaeus (1540–1617), published a *Brief Chronology of Gospel History: A Logical Declaration Arrangement of the Apostle Paul's Epistle to Romans.*[45] Peter Martyr Vermigli not only commented on Romans, but also wrote a *Commentary on 1 Corinthians* (1567).[46] Craig Farmer has written extensively on the exegetical work of Wolfgang Musculus and particularly on his com-

ville, MO: Sixteenth Century Journal Publishers, 1990). It was translated into English and published in London, 1568.

40. W. Musculus, *In Epistolam Apostoli Pauli ad Romanos, Commentarii* (Basle, 1559).

41. The critical edition is T. H. L. Parker, ed., *Commentarius in Epistolam Pauli ad Romanos*, CO 13, Series II: Ioannis Calvini Opera Exegetica (Geneva: Droz, 1999). There is some uncertainty as to the exact origins of the commentary on Romans. He was appointed "doctor of the sacred letters" (*sacrarum litterarum doctor*) "with the task of expounding Scripture in lectures" (*CO*, 21:126). There is some evidence that he began his lectures in the Pauline epistles by lecturing through Romans. According to Parker, these lectures likely formed the basis of the commentary that he completed in Strasbourg in 1539. See ibid., xiii. See also R. Scott Clark, "Election and Predestination: The Sovereign Expressions of God," in *A Handbook of Calvin's Institutes*, ed. David Hall and Peter Lillback (Phillipsburg, NJ: P&R, 2008).

42. *Commentarius in Epistolam Pauli ad Romanos*, xiii–xix.

43. Johannes Piscator, *Analysis Logica Epistolae Pauli ad Romanos* . . . (Herborn, 1589).

44. Johannes Piscator, *Analysis Logica Epistolae Pauli ad Romanos, Corinthios, Galatas, Ephesos, Phillipenses, Colossenses, Thessalonicenses, una cum Scholis et Observationes Locorum Doctrinae* (London, 1591). In 1594, these lectures were augmented with commentary on 1 and 2 Timothy, Titus, Philemon and Hebrews.

45. Johann J. Grynaeus, *Chronologia Brevis Evangelicae Historiae: Logicque Artificii in Epistola Apostoli Pauli ad Romanos, Declaratio* (Basle, 1580).

46. Peter Martyr Vermigli, *In Selectissimam S. Pauli Priorem ad Corinth. Epistolam D. Petri Martyris . . . Commentarii Doctissimi* (Zürich, 1567).

mentary on the Gospel of John.[47] His lectures on Romans were published in 1600.[48] The lectures on Romans by Benedict Aretius (1505–74), the successor to Wolfgang Musculus in Bern, were published posthumously in 1579.[49] Girolamo Zanchi published a massive *Commentary on the Epistle of the Apostle Paul to the Ephesians* in 1594.[50] Robert Rollock, famous for importing into Scotland the federal theology he learned in Heidelberg, published his lectures on Romans in 1595.[51]

By the turn of the seventeenth century, Roman Catholic commentaries on Romans were emerging in defense of the Tridentine soteriology, and Reformed theologians and Bible scholars responded. For example, David Paraeus (1548–1622), most famous for editing and publishing Ursinus's lectures on the Heidelberg Catechism, published a commentary on Romans promising to controvert textual and theological claims of the Jesuit theologian Robert Bellarmine as well as sundry other heretics.[52] One of the heretics at whom Paraeus aimed was the Italian rationalist Faustus Socinus (1539–1604), whose disputations on Romans were published in 1618.[53]

Not only did the Reformed orthodox now face renewed theological and exegetical challenges from Roman Catholic and Lutheran opponents, but also from within their own movement. Arminius's *Dissertation on the True and Genuine Sense of Romans 7* appeared in 1612.[54] The lectures of

47. Craig S. Farmer, *The Gospel of John in the Sixteenth Century: The Johannine Exegesis of Wolfgang Musculus* (New York: Oxford University Press, 1997).

48. Wolfgang Musculus, *In Epistolam D. Apostoli Pauli ad Romanos Commentarii* (Basle, 1600).

49. Benedict Aretius, *Commentarii in Epistolam D. Pauli ad Romanos, Facili et Perspicua Methodo Conscripti* (Lausanne, 1579).

50. G. Zanchi, *In D. Pauli Epistolam ad Ephesios Commentarius* (Neustadt, 1594). The modern critical edition is D. Hieronymous Zanchii, *Commentarius in Epistolam Sancti Pauli ad Ephesos*, ed. A. H. Den Hartog (Amsterdam: J. A. Wormser, 1888).

51. Robert Rollock, *In Epistolam S. Pauli Apostoli ad Romanos . . .* (Geneva, 1595).

52. David Paraeus, *Ad Romanos s. Pauli Apostoli Epistolam Commentarius. Quo praeter accuratam textuus sacri analysin atque interpretationem de quaestionibus controversis dubia CLXXIX, explicantur: et antiqua Romanarum fides adversus nunc Romanistarum opiniones, praecipue Roberti Bellarmini jesuitae argutias, et Thomae Stapletoni antidota; nec no Socini, Eniedini et Ostrodii haereticorum Samosatenianorum blasphemias vindicatur* (Frankfurt, 1608).

53. Faustus Socinus, *Fausti Socini Senensis Defensio Disputationis Suae de Loco Septimi Captis Epistolae ad Romanos sub Nomine Prosperi Dysidae . . . ante 12 annos ab se editae* (Racow, 1618).

54. Jacob Arminius, *J. Arminii . . . de Vero et Genuino Sensu Cap. vii Epistolae ad Romanos Dissertatio* (Leiden, 1612).

the Remonstrant leader, Simon Episcopius (1583–1643), were published posthumously.[55] Even more challenging to the Reformed confessionalists, Moïse Amyraut published his *Thoughts on Chapter 7 of Paul's Epistle to the Romans* in 1648, and his Amyraldian colleague Louis Cappel also published on Romans a few years later in 1655.[56] To end our survey, it is fitting to note the commentary by Johannes Cocceius (1603–69) on Romans, published in 1665, just a little more than a century after Calvin's death.[57]

Just by this limited survey of Reformed commentaries, primarily on Romans, it is clear that the classic Reformed theologians were as busy lecturing and writing on Scripture as they were writing dogmatic works. Indeed, though the divines of the Westminster Assembly are most famous for the WCF, several of them also produced the *Annotations upon All the Books of the Old and New Testament* (1645), following in the tradition of the Geneva Bible and the Dutch Statenvertaling (Annotations) published in the wake of the Synod of Dort, "an exegesis of the entire Bible, in two volumes, over twenty-four hundred folio pages in length in the final edition."[58] Because they were not as specialized in their work as we have become today, the two vocations, theology and biblical exegesis, were much more closely linked then than they are now. Just as Calvin revised his *Institutes* after lecturing on (and perhaps preaching through) Romans, so too the Reformed orthodox read Romans theologically and derived their theology from their study of Scripture. This survey is only suggestive of the work which continued through the rest of the seventeenth century and just scratches the surface of the tremendous amount of biblical study produced by the classic Reformed theologians. This is not to say that today, were we to read the biblical commentaries of the classic Reformed theologians, we would always agree with

55. Simon Episcopius, *Paraphrasis et Observationes in Caput vii, ix, x et xi Epistolae S. Pauli ad Romanos* (Amsterdam, 1644).

56. Moïse Amyraut, *Mosis Amyraldi Considerationes in Caput vii Epistolae Pauli Apostoli ad Romanos* (Saumur, 1648); Louis Cappel, *Lud. Cappeli Chronologia Sacra: A Condita Mundo ad Eundem Reconditum per Dominum Nostram I. Christum* (Paris, 1655).

57. Johannes Cocceius, *S. Pauli Apostoli Epistola ad Romanos cum Commentario* (Leiden, 1656).

58. See Richard A. Muller, "Scripture and the Westminster Confession," in Richard A. Muller and Rowland S. Ward, *Scripture and Worship: Biblical Interpretation and the Directory for Public Worship*, The Westminster Assembly and the Reformed Faith (Phillipsburg, NJ: P&R, 2007), 9. See also ibid., 11–29.

their every judgment, but we would be impressed with the care with which they handled Scripture and the maturity and wisdom of their judgments.

It Is Catholic

In the Apostles' Creed all Christians confess, "I believe ... the holy catholic church."[59] In BC 27 we confess, "one catholic or universal Church, which is a holy congregation of true Christian believers, all expecting their salvation in Jesus Christ, being washed by His blood, sanctified and sealed by the Holy Spirit."[60] The Reformed churches understood from the beginning that their theology, piety, and practice did not develop overnight in the sixteenth century. They intentionally harvested the best theology, piety, and practice of the Eastern and Western church from the fathers through the Middle Ages.

We have always been conscious that the visible, institutional church has "been from the beginning of the world, and will be to the end." We have always understood that though the Reformation began in Western Europe, "this holy Church is not confined, bound, or limited to a certain place or to certain persons, but is spread and dispersed over the whole world; and yet is joined and united with heart and will, by the power of faith, in one and the same Spirit" (BC 27).[61] According to the WCF, the catholic church is both visible and invisible. When the church is considered as the "whole number of the elect," it is invisible (WCF 24.1). The church invisible, however, exists within the visible assembly, which is also catholic as it transcends any one era or nation (WCF 24.2). The visible church is the locus of God's saving grace in this world, so that outside of it "there is no ordinary possibility of salvation."[62] It is to the catholic visible church that "Christ has given the ministry, oracles, and ordinances of God" (WCF 25.3). The visible catholic church is "sometimes more, sometimes less visible." Visible expressions of the catholic church are marked by the purity of the administration of the gospel, sacraments, and worship (WCF 25.4; BC 29).[63]

59. "Credo . . . sanctam ecclesiam catholicam." Schaff, ed., *The Creeds of Christendom*, 2:45; Geerhardus Vos, "The Eschatological Aspect of the Pauline Conception of the Spirit," in *Biblical and Theological Studies* (New York: Charles Scribner and Sons, 1912).
60. *RCH*, 188.
61. *RCH*, 188. See also HC Q. 54.
62. *RCH*, 189. See also BC 28; *RCH*, 190.
63. *RCH*, 189–190.

The English word "catholic" comes to us from Latin and was derived from the Greek adjective *katholikos*, which simply meant "universal." Thus Reformed churches dispute the claim by the Roman see to be *the* catholic church. In the nature of the case, Roman Catholic is an oxymoron. As the father of the English Puritans, William Perkins (1558–1602) noted in 1597, in his work *Reformed Catholic*, the Roman church is not, according to our understanding of Scripture, really catholic at all, certainly not since her condemnation of the gospel at the Council of Trent (Session 7, 1547).[64]

On the biblical pattern (e.g., 1 Tim. 3:16), the Reformed churches have confessed the ecumenical or catholic creeds (i.e., the Apostles' Creed, Nicene-Constantinopolitan Creed, the Athanasian Creed, and the Definition of Chalcedon). To say that classic or confessional Reformed theology is catholic is also to say that it is deeply connected to the broader history of the church. This fact alone should make our tradition attractive today. Another way of putting it is to say that we are not sectarian, in the pejorative sense of the word. The Reformed tradition has never assumed that it alone is true or has spoken the last word on everything, or that something is true simply because the Reformed theologians or confessions taught it. Not only are the judgments of the tradition subject to Scripture, but they are also subject to review by the broader church. In the Second Helvetic Confession (1566), the Swiss Reformed churches confessed that because Scripture is given by the Holy Spirit, "we do not allow all kinds of interpretation." At the same time, we are not arrogant. We "do not despise the interpretation of the holy Greek and Latin fathers, nor reject their disputations and treatises as far as they agree with the Scriptures; but we do modestly dissent from them when they are found to set down things differing from, or altogether contrary to, the Scriptures" (Chapter 2).[65]

Calvin made extensive, if selective, use of the fathers and the medieval theologians to vindicate his claim to be reforming the faith and the church

64. William Perkins, "A Reformed Catholicke or a Declaration Shewing How Neere We May Come to the Present Church of Rome in Sundry Points of Religion: And Wherein We Must Forever Depart from Them," in *The Workes of That Famous and Worthy Minister of Christ in the University of Cambridge* (Cambridge, 1616), 1:558–636. A modern abridged edition is published in *The Work of William Perkins*, ed. Ian Breward (Appleford, UK: Sutton Courtenay, 1970).

65. *RCH*, 14.

according to the Scriptures and the ancient church. The seventeenth-century theologians made even more extensive and more careful use of the fathers and the medieval theologians. Confident that the Reformed answers to the great theological questions are well grounded in Scripture, the Reformed confession has always been willing to dialogue with the great minds of the church, whether Tertullian on faith and reason or Jerome on the canon or Boethius on anthropology or Thomas on relations between divine grace and human cooperation.

Our catholicity is seen most clearly in our doctrine of God. Our theology, piety, and practice have always been organized by our trinitarian doctrine of God.[66] This fact has sometimes escaped our critics, but it is nevertheless true. In contrast to most modern theology and all modernist theology, confessional Reformed theology understands God's Word to teach that the triune God is alone God, there is none beside him (Ps. 86:10). He alone is the God who is (Ex. 3:14; Rev. 1:8). Our theology does not begin with a generic idea of God, but rather with the God who is one in three. BC 8 begins with God who is "one single essence, in which are three persons, really, truly, and eternally distinct, according to their incommunicable properties."[67] The Father is "the beginning of all things," the Son is the "word, wisdom and image of the Father," and the Holy Spirit is the "eternal power and might, proceeding from the Father and the Son."[68]

Calvin's *Institutes of the Christian Religion* (1559) is a good example of how important the doctrine of the Trinity is to our theology. When Calvin first wrote his *Institutes* for theology students, it had a bipartite structure, law and gospel. In this, he was a faithful student of Luther and Melanchthon. Over the following years, however, as he lectured (and perhaps preached) through the book of Romans, the *Institutes* grew, and as they did, he restructured them into four books.[69] He retained his commitment to the distinction between law and gospel, and the *Institutes* can be still read as having that structure since he moves from natural

66. Clark, *Caspar Olevian*, 74–103.
67. *RCH*, 20.
68. Ibid.
69. On the development of the *Institutes* see Richard A. Muller, *The Unaccommodated Calvin*, Oxford Studies in Historical Theology (New York and Oxford: Oxford University Press, 2000), 129.

revelation, to our need for a redeemer, to Christ our Savior, to the application of redemption by the Holy Spirit, and finally to the church as the place where the means of grace are to be found. The *Institutes*, however, also have a trinitarian structure. The first book concerns God the Father. Book Two is organized around God the Son, and books three and four concern the work of God the Spirit, so that fully half of the *Institutes* are organized around the person and work of the Spirit. For this reason, the great Princeton theologian B. B. Warfield called Calvin "the theologian of the Holy Spirit," and so he was.[70] He might just as well have been called the "theologian of the Trinity." Since Calvin, Reformed theology has continued to organize its theology along trinitarian lines, at least relative to the economic Trinity, that is, according to the assignment, in broad terms, of creation to the Father, redemption to the Son, and the application of redemption to the Spirit. More than that, Reformed piety has always recognized the centrality of Christ as Mediator and the Spirit as the "energy" of God.[71] Because of the consubstantiality of the trinitarian persons, these roles are not absolute.

Relative to the life of the Christian, Christ may be said to become the "mediated" and the Spirit may be the Mediator. For example, in answering a question about how the elements of the Lord's Supper are "the communion of the body and blood of Christ," HC Q. 79 answers that Christ's crucified body and shed blood are the true meat and drink of our souls." They are not so metaphorically but actually. "We are as really partakers of His true body and blood by the working of the Holy Spirit, as we receive by the mouth of the body these holy tokens in remembrance of Him." Believers "really" eat his "true body and blood" only by the working of the Spirit.[72] BC 35 likewise says that, in the Supper, believers eat and drink the "proper and natural body, and the proper blood of Christ." Despite the fact that the "operations of the Holy Spirit are hidden and

70. B. B. Warfield, *John Calvin the Theologian* (Philadelphia: Presbyterian Board of Education, 1909).

71. On this see Michael S. Horton, *Covenant and Salvation: Union with Christ* (Nashville: Westminster John Knox, 2007), where this idea is discussed repeatedly.

72. *RCH*, 226 (revised). On the Spirit in Reformed theology see Daniel R. Hyde, "The Holy Spirit in the Heidelberg Catechism," *Mid-America Journal of Theology* 17 (2006): 211–37.

incomprehensible," nevertheless, our communion or partaking is "by the Spirit through faith."[73]

The Spirit operates not only or even chiefly in creation and redemption but perhaps principally in glorification. The Princeton theologian Geerhardus Vos (1862–1949) described "the eschatological state" as "preeminently a pneumatic state." Vos was not saying that the consummate state is immaterial, but that it is the state in which everything is utterly conformed to the Holy Spirit. In that state the tension between the Spirit (the age to come) and the flesh (this age) is resolved (2 Cor. 4:17).[74]

It Is Vital

As a theology of the Spirit of creation and re-creation, a piety that is suffused with the work and witness of the Spirit through the Word and sacraments, and a practice that worships "in the Spirit" (John 4:23–24), the Reformed confession is not only a subtle and exciting truth, but it is a living (and life-giving) piety and practice. We have not accepted a facile distinction between orthodoxy and orthopraxis or between piety and truth. Orthodoxy means "right thinking" or "right worship." These two concepts are not far separate. Romans 12:2 in the Geneva Bible (1599) speaks of our "reasonable serving" of God.[75] In more contemporary translations, the adjective is usually translated "spiritual." The ambiguity of the word is probably intentional, and it signals the nearly inseparable reciprocity between orthodoxy and piety. That is to say that dead orthodoxy is an oxymoron. One cannot be truly orthodox and spiritually dead. Only when one has stopped believing the historic faith does one become dead. Certainly, it has happened that there are those who are baptized, who have made an orthodox profession of faith, who are members of Christ's church in good and regular standing, and yet who have not laid hold of the Savior by faith alone. This is, one supposes, what most people mean by "dead orthodoxy." Scripture is aware of this phenomenon. Paul distinguished those who are Jews "inwardly"

73. RCH, 224.
74. Geerhardus Vos, "The Eschatological Aspect of the Pauline Conception of the Spirit," in *Biblical and Theological Studies* (New York: Charles Scribner and Sons, 1912), 209–59.
75. *1599 Geneva Bible* (White Hall, WV: Tolle Lege, 2006).

from those who are Jews "outwardly" (Rom. 2:28–29)[76] Our Lord himself warned us that in the interregnum the visible, institutional church would always be mixed (Matt. 13:30). He also instituted a procedure for church discipline (in Matt. 18:15–20; BC 29). In this life, before the judgment and the resurrection, we live in a mixed, disciplined church.

Whatever problems may attach to the existence of dead orthodoxy, dead heterodoxy raises even greater problems. Dead heterodoxy refers to the spurious claims to Christian faith by those whose lives or professions are incongruous with the faith. Though much has been written from the pietist side about the dangers of dead orthodoxy, there have not been so many works written against the dangers attending to emotionally satisfying, perhaps even thrilling religious ecstasy which ultimately cannot be squared with any recognizable form of Christianity. If vitality is measured by body temperature, confessional Reformed theology, piety, and practice may fail the test. If, however, it is measured against the biblical standard, against the standard of the historic catholic faith, then Reformed orthodoxy is as vital a religion as exists.

It Is Evangelical

There has been an ongoing discussion for about twenty-five years over the question "who is an evangelical?" In the early stages, the debate focused on whether Reformed or non-Reformed people were more genuinely evangelical.[77]

It might be objected that Reformed Christians *are* evangelicals, and that it is not a matter of *whether* they will be a subset of evangelicalism, but *how*. The response is that it depends on the notoriously difficult definition of "evangelical" as it describes American Protestants since 1720. There are three competing interpretations of the nature of contemporary evangelicalism. The first and dominant view is that American evangelical-

76. See R. Scott Clark, "Baptism and the Benefits of Christ: The Double Mode of Communion in the Covenant of Grace," *The Confessional Presbyterian* 2 (2006): 3–19.

77. The first part of this section is revised from R. Scott Clark, "How We Got Here: A Brief History of the Current Controversy," in *Covenant, Justification, and Pastoral Ministry: Essays by the Faculty of Westminster Seminary California*, ed. R. Scott Clark (Phillipsburg, NJ: P&R, 2006), 5–11.

ism is defined by its relations to the sixteenth-century Protestants and Reformed orthodoxy as it came to expression in old Princeton. George F. Marsden has argued this case in a number of well-researched and highly influential books. He interprets the rise of early-twentieth-century fundamentalism in relation to old Princeton and the rise of neoevangelicalism (post-1946) relative to old Westminster. Donald Dayton describes this as the "Presbyterian paradigm." For his part, Marsden argues that his interpretation is more complex than Dayton allows and that his view is complementary to Dayton's.[78] This approach has been associated with the Institute for the Study of American Evangelicalism (ISAE) and may be seen in the work of Mark Noll and many others.

A second view, advocated by Donald Dayton, is that American evangelicalism is rooted in the sixteenth-century Anabaptist movement and has been more "Methodist" or "Pentecostal" than classically Protestant. He argues that American evangelicalism is normed by the revivals of the eighteenth and (especially) the nineteenth centuries. He contends that Marsden's "paradigm" (in the sense that Thomas Kuhn uses the term) unfairly omits the socially radical and theologically deviant (from the Reformed point of view) Wesleyan and Pentecostal (i.e., pietist) mainstream of evangelicalism. In this view, Princeton and Westminster are on the margins of evangelicalism. Dayton calls this a "Pentecostal paradigm" for interpreting American evangelicalism.[79]

78. See George F. Marsden, *The Evangelical Mind and the New School Presbyterian Experience* (New Haven: Yale University Press, 1970); idem, *Fundamentalism and American Culture: The Shaping of Twentieth-Century Evangelicalism: 1870–1925* (Oxford: Oxford University Press, 1980); idem, ed., *Evangelicalism and Modern America* (Grand Rapids: Eerdmans, 1984); idem, *Reforming Fundamentalism: Fuller Seminary and the New Evangelicalism* (Grand Rapids: Eerdmans, 1987).

79. See Donald W. Dayton, *Discovering an Evangelical Heritage* (New York: Harper and Row, 1976); idem, "The Limits of Evangelicalism: The Pentecostal Tradition," and "Some Doubts about the Usefulness of the Category 'Evangelical,'" in *The Variety of American Evangelicalism*, ed. Donald W. Dayton and Robert K. Johnston (Downers Grove, IL: InterVarsity, 1991). Dayton and Marsden (and others) have been engaged in a long-running debate about the roots and nature of modern evangelicalism. See George Marsden, "Demythologizing Evangelicalism: A Review of Donald W. Dayton's *Discovering an Evangelical Heritage*," *Christian Scholar's Review* 7 (1977): 203–211, and the *Christian Scholar's Review* 23 (1993): 12–89, which features essays and responses by Marsden and Dayton, and comments by several evangelical observers.

The final and perhaps most provocative approach is that of D. G. Hart, who has argued most recently that there is no such thing as "evangelicalism." It was a convention, an artificial construct which scholars only recently created and which defies definition.[80] Ironically, the "Pentecostal" Dayton may agree with the Presbyterian iconoclast Hart. Dayton too signaled his dissatisfaction with "evangelical" as an adjective in 1991.

To have real meaning, evangelicalism as a universal must have particulars, but it is exceedingly difficult to find those particulars, and even when some are nominated, there are multiple filters for determining which are included and which are not. If one uses recognized institutions as a barometer (e.g., the Evangelical Theological Society, *Christianity Today*, Wheaton College, or Fuller Seminary) and measures contemporary evangelical theology by something like Reformed orthodoxy, then one will likely agree with the criticisms of evangelicalism (as being in a sort of Babylonian captivity) made by David Wells.[81] Given that the original evangelicals were certainly the sixteenth- and seventeenth-century Protestants who routinely described themselves as evangelicals, Wells has a point. When Reformed people call themselves evangelicals, they are thinking of the sixteenth and seventeenth centuries, but almost no one today who might be included under the adjective "evangelical" defines "evangelical" according to sixteenth- and seventeenth-century usage. The "Protestant paradigm" is not holding. According to the Institute for the Study of American Evangelicals there are about 100 million American evangelicals.[82] By contrast, there are no more than 700,000 confessional Reformed Christians (including the borderline denominations outside of NAPARC) in the United States. If, for the sake of discussion, we include this group under the rubric of evangelicalism, and if more than 99 percent of American evangelicals do not define themselves by the

80. See D. G. Hart, *Deconstructing Evangelicalism: Conservative Protestantism in the Age of Billy Graham* (Grand Rapids: Baker, 2004). See also idem, *The Lost Soul of American Protestantism* (Lanham, MD: Rowman and Littlefield, 2002); idem, *That Old-Time Religion in Modern America: Evangelical Protestantism in the Twentieth Century* (Chicago: Ivan R. Dee, 2002).

81. See David F. Wells, *No Place for Truth* (Grand Rapids: Eerdmans, 1993), and idem, *God in the Wasteland* (Grand Rapids: Eerdmans, 1994).

82. "Defining Evangelicalism," http://www.wheaton.edu/isae/defining_evangelicalism. html#How%20Many (accessed 21 September 2007).

Reformed confessions or the convictions of sixteenth- and seventeenth-century Protestantism, then perhaps "evangelical" is no longer a useful adjective to describe those who are confessionally Reformed.

Reformed Christianity defines itself by its confessional theology, piety, and practice. Obviously, given the variety of evangelical theological and ecclesiastical possibilities, neither doctrine nor practice defines evangelicalism. Rather, religious experience defines evangelicalism. What unites evangelicals across ecclesiastical and theological boundaries and defines the movement (to the degree one exists) is their common quest for the immediate (literally, "without instruments") experience or knowledge of God.

To see the truth of this definition, one must only ask, what is that which unites all those, excluding confessional Protestants for the moment, who call themselves evangelical? There are evangelical charismatics, Pentecostals, Roman Catholics, Anglicans, Presbyterians, Baptists, Methodists, evangelicals, and postevangelicals with no formal ecclesiastical affiliation whatever. These may all be considered evangelicals, because those who embrace this identity do so on the basis of a shared religious experience. Naturally, if it is religious experience that unites evangelicals within each of these communions to each other, there can be no common ecclesiology or agreement on soteriology among them. Indeed, it has been a matter of policy of modern evangelicalism to ignore or work around the institutional church and sacraments. For the last sixty years, the major leaders of modern evangelicalism have not been men primarily associated with a visible, institutional church, but rather with transdenominational evangelical entities, such as Carl F. H. Henry of *Christianity Today* and Fuller Seminary, Billy Graham, and Bill Bright of Campus Crusade. In contrast, Reformed Christians have always had the highest regard for the doctrine of the church and sacraments.

By contrast, what defines Reformed Christianity is not the *immediate* experience of God. Rather, the Reformed confession teaches mediation: the mediation of revelation in God's covenants and chiefly through the Mediator of the covenant of grace, Jesus Christ the Word of God incarnate. Reformed Christianity is nothing if not doctrinal and churchly. To the degree we are defined by our theology and practice, we are not evangelicals, as defined above. Therefore, Reformed people do better

215

to distinguish between Christians who are confessional and those who are nonconfessional.[83] By the former I mean "those who are defined by Scripture as understood by the historic Protestant confessions and catechisms."[84] According to this category, there are Lutheran confessionalists, Reformed confessionalists, and perhaps others. In the nonconfessional category, one shall find liberals, that is, those who identify with modern autonomy, and conservatives, who are more traditional. What unifies liberals and conservatives is their relative autonomy to historic symbols of the Reformed and Lutheran churches. Confessionalists, on the other hand, define themselves, their theology, their piety, and their practice according to public, ecclesiastically sanctioned symbolic documents. Because the Reformed churches have used the wrong categories to identify themselves, the QIRC and the QIRE have become more plausible than they might otherwise have been.

How then should Reformed Christians (defined by a theology, piety, and practice) relate to evangelicals? If the precondition for fellowship with evangelicals (as defined in this discussion) is a common religious experience, then our discussion may be brief. Then there is the problem of the existence of "evangelicalism." Assuming, for the sake of discussion, that it exists, would it help if we could change its definition? Until recently, the reigning metaphor for describing evangelicalism has been the "Big Tent." In this metaphor, there must be some universals that define all "evangelicals." In that case there will necessarily be disagreement over what those universals are or should be and who should determine them. In recent years, some have asked the Evangelical Theological Society to function as a quasi-ecclesiastical gatekeeper for the Big Tent of evangelicalism,[85] but as an extraecclesiastical, academic society, with a starkly minimalist

83. See D. G. Hart, *The Lost Soul of American Protestantism.*

84. The Roman communion does not appear to be a strictly confessional body inasmuch as, since Vatican II at least, she is quite latitudinarian on doctrine and practice. It is not necessary to adhere strictly to the magisterial doctrine as embodied in the conciliar pronouncements or the Catechism of the Catholic Church to be regarded as a faithful Roman Catholic. What is essential is to remain in submission to the Roman see. In a similar way, though Anglicans confess the Thirty-Nine Articles, it is not essential to hold them to be regarded as a "faithful" Anglican or Episcopalian.

85. E.g., in the controversy over open theism.

theological basis, it is ill equipped to serve such a function.[86] For those who identify with historic, confessional Protestantism, this metaphor has become increasingly uncomfortable. In its place Michael S. Horton has proposed another metaphor: the "Village Green."[87] In this scheme, evangelicalism would not be reckoned so much on the basis of a shared faith or religious experience but rather on the basis of shared interests. In a tent, some are in and some are out and there is, to switch metaphors, a gatekeeper. In contrast, a village green is a commons shared by all and owned (or controlled) by none in particular.[88]

Decades ago, Cornelius Van Til anticipated the fragmentation and religious subjectivism of contemporary evangelicalism. He warned that the Reformed are not really evangelicals in the modern sense at all, and that despite the appearance of family relations, there are deep-seated differences. The Reformed, Van Til said, begin with the triune God, with divine revelation, and the objective work of Christ for sinners. The evangelicals, he warned, begin with religious experience.[89] In 1990 Robert Brow proved Van Til right and signaled the end of the temporary hegemony in evangelicalism enjoyed by those with some connection to Reformed theology, piety, and practice. Brow was offering nothing more than an elixir made of evangelical pietism, old-fashioned liberal universalism with a dash of moralism added for flavor. Condemned by many as a seducer, it turns out

86. The doctrinal statement of the Evangelical Theological Society requires members to affirm the doctrine of the Trinity and the inerrancy of Scripture as understood by the 1968 Chicago Statement on Biblical Inerrancy.

87. "A piece of public or common grassy land situated in or near a town or village, from which it often takes its name; a 'village green.'" S.v. "green," *The Oxford English Dictionary*, 2d ed., *OED* Online (Oxford: Oxford University Press, 1989), http://dictionary.oed.com/cgi/entry/50098386 (accessed 2 April 2007).

88. See Michael Scott Horton, "Reflection: Is Evangelicalism Reformed or Wesleyan? Reopening the Marsden-Dayton Debate," *Christian Scholar's Review* 31 (2001): 131–55; Roger E. Olson, "Response: The Reality of Evangelicalism: A Response to Michael S. Horton," *Christian Scholar's Review* 31 (2001): 157–62; Michael Scott Horton, "Response to Roger Olson's Reply," *Christian Scholar's Review* 31 (2001): 163–68.

89. For example, he argued in 1930 that instruction in Westminster Seminary must be "more than evangelical." See also Cornelius Van Til, "Wanted—a Reformed Testimony: A Common Witness of Reformed and Evangelicals Inadequate for Our Time," *Presbyterian Guardian* 20.7 (July 16, 1951): 125–26 and 136–37. In some contexts, however, he did occasionally describe the Reformed as "evangelicals" as against liberalism.

that Brow was a prophet of baby-boomer evangelicals and postevangelical "emerging" Christians.[90]

Nevertheless, as suggested above, the Reformed confession may be called genuinely evangelical. In the earliest English sense of the word, evangelical simply meant "Protestant," that is, those who held to the biblical message that Christ died for sinners and that sinners are justified by sovereign grace alone (*sola gratia*) through faith alone (*sola fide*), that Christ alone is the proper object of saving faith (*solo Christo*), and that the unique and chief rule for faith and life is Scripture alone (*sola scriptura*). To say that confessional Reformed theology is evangelical is to say that it is vitally concerned about the evangel or the good news that God the Son has come, taken on humanity in history, bringing with him God's kingdom, grace, salvation, and righteousness (Matt. 4:23; 9:35; 24:14). This is what God the Spirit promised in Isaiah 52:7. The feet of those who "carry good news" are beautiful because they are announcing something of great importance, that God's relation to sinners has changed. There is *shalom* with God; there is salvation. All these blessings are grounded, of course, in the faithfulness and obedience of the "servant" (Isa. 52:13) who "acts wisely" on our behalf, pierced for our sins, crushed for our iniquities (Isa. 53:5). Therefore the good news for the poor (Isa. 61:1) is that there are healing for the brokenhearted and freedom for the captive. According to the apostle Paul, the "good news of God" (Rom. 1:1) is that all that God promised through Isaiah and the other prophets, types, and shadows in the Scriptures, has come to fulfilment in Christ, who in his resurrection was "declared" to be the Son of God "in power." To the Corinthians Paul characterized his gospel, that by which we are saved, as the account of Christ's actively suffering obedience in his death, the confirmation of his death in his burial, and his resurrection and ascension (1 Cor. 15:1–8).

There are many ways in which we could accurately characterize the Reformed confession, but it is certainly a theology, piety, and practice of the gospel, of the Father's love for sinners, of the Son's saving acts for sinners, of the Spirit's work within sinners applying to them Christ's

---

90. The departure of Clark Pinnock from a predestinarian theology to a radical post-Arminian, late Remonstrant rationalism is evident in his publishing since the late 1970s and especially in his recent advocacy of open theism in Clark Pinnock, *Most Moved Mover: A Theology of God's Openness* (Grand Rapids: Baker, 2001).

work for them, operating through the preaching of the holy gospel and the holy sacraments (HC 65).[91] Though we are known for our strong doctrine of divine sovereignty, there would be little point of maintaining such doctrines without their intimate connection to the good news. In other words, if the Reformed churches were to strip away their doctrine of justification, so that they were left with the doctrines of divine sovereignty and providence, they would be no better off than those medieval predestinarian theologians, for example, Gottschalk (c. 804–c. 869), or Thomas Aquinas (c. 1224–1274), Thomas Bradwardine (c. 1295–1349), John Wycliffe (c. 1330–1384), or Gregory of Rimini (c. 1300–1358), each of whom taught a doctrine of God, providence, and the decree quite similar to ours in many respects, except that they lacked the Protestant hermeneutic and doctrine of justification.

We are evangelical in another sense, in that we have always believed in the free or well-meant offer of the gospel.[92] This has been true since the sixteenth-century Reformation, in which, for example, the Genevan Calvinists sent dozens of church-planting missionaries to Roman Catholic France and elsewhere to preach Christ to the nations. The evangelical spirit of confessional Reformed theology, piety, and practice is evident in the Canons of the Synod of Dort (1618–19). One of the chief concerns of the orthodox about the Remonstrant position was that it did violence to the gospel. The Remonstrant soteriology taught, in effect, that "ought" equals "can," so that, if God has commanded one to do something, it must be possible for one to do it. Such a position, of course, devalues the biblical doctrine of sin and depravity and vitiates the law of its killing power (Rom. 7:8; 1 Cor. 15:56). The Remonstrants also taught a doctrine of prevenient grace something like that taught by the Franciscan nominalist theologian William of Ockham: that God has an "antecedent will" to save whoever is willing to be saved. In response, the confessional Reformed theologians reasserted the biblical doctrines of sin, of divine sovereignty,

91. HC Q. 65 in *Creeds*, 3:328.
92. See John Murray, *The Collected Writings of John Murray*, 4 vols. (Edinburgh: Banner of Truth Trust, 1976–82), 4:113–32; R. Scott Clark, "Janus, the Well-Meant Offer of the Gospel, and Westminster Theology," in *The Pattern of Sound Doctrine: Systematic Theology at the Westminster Seminaries. Essays in Honor of Robert B. Strimple*, ed. David VanDrunen (Phillipsburg, NJ: P&R, 2004), 149–80.

and that God has decreed not only sovereignly and efficaciously to save freely and not on the basis of "foreseen faith and the obedience of faith," and to reprobate, but also to use certain means to save those whom he has chosen in Christ from all eternity, namely the foolishness of the free offer of the gospel.[93] Under the first head of doctrine synod declared:

> And that men may be brought to believe, God mercifully sends the messengers of these most joyful tidings to whom He will and at what time He pleases; by whose ministry men are called to repentance and faith in Christ crucified. "How, then, can they call on the one they have not believed in? And how can they believe in the one of whom they have not heard? And how can they hear without someone preaching to them? And how can they preach unless they are sent?" (CD 1.3).

In the second head of doctrine (art. 5) the international Reformed community said with one voice that the "promise of the Gospel (*promissio Evangelii*) is that whosoever believes (*credit*) in Christ crucified (*Christum cruxifixum*) shall not perish." The law and the gospel, that is, repentance and faith (*resipiscentia et fides*) are to be "declared and published to all nations promiscuously (*promiscue*) and indiscriminately (*indiscriminatim*) to whomever God in his good pleasure (*beneplacitum*) sends the Gospel."[94] In short, the controversy with the Remonstrants was fueled as much by the questions "what is the good news?" and "what should be preached?" as by the questions of the nature of the divine decree. Though confessional Reformed theology has not always been credited with a passion for lost souls, it is difficult to read these statements and others and fail to see that the pastors who gathered at Dort were concerned about doctrinal precision *because* they cared for the welfare of both the lost *and* the found.[95]

---

93. Canons of Dort 1.9; Rejection of Errors 1.5 in *Creeds*, 3:583, 557. An English translation of the Rejection of Errors is printed in the *Ecumenical Creeds and Reformed Confessions* (Grand Rapids: Board of Publications of the Christian Reformed Church, 1979).

94. CD 2.5 in *Creeds*, 3:561.

95. In the early twentieth century, part of J. Gresham Machen's controversy with the "modernists" concerned the question of the nature of the gospel to be preached by foreign missions.

It Is Churchly

One of the tensions experienced by pilgrims leaving evangelicalism and postevangelicalism is created by the approach shared by fundamentalism and revivalism to the relations between nature and grace. The dominant approach to nature and grace in these two movements creates a crisis for thoughtful souls, a crisis that demands resolution. The Reformed confession is most helpful here. In the Christian tradition there have been three approaches to the relation of nature to grace or of salvation to creation. The first holds that grace perfects nature. This was the view of the mainstream of the medieval church represented by Thomas Aquinas. In explaining the nature of theology, Thomas argued that "grace does not destroy nature but perfects it."[96] As we have already observed, for Thomas and for Rome following him, grace is not the unmerited divine favor but participation in the divine being.[97] In the words of Brian Davies, it is "God's action in us leading us to union with him."[98] Thomas says,

> Nothing can act beyond its species, since the cause must always be more powerful than its effect. Now the gift of grace surpasses every capability of created nature, since it is nothing short of a partaking of the divine nature (*participatio divinae naturae*), which exceeds every other nature. And thus it is impossible that any creature should cause grace. For it is as necessary that God alone should deify (*Deus deificet*), bestowing a partaking of the Divine Nature (*communicando consortium divinae naturae*) by a participated likeness, as it is impossible that anything save fire should enkindle.[99]

For Thomas (as for Rome today) created finitude is reckoned as a fundamental problem which grace (i.e., divinity) is intended to overcome. In other words, in this view, the problem is not sin but nature itself and therefore it must be overcome. Therefore, grace transforms nature into

96. "Cum enim gratia naturam non tollat, sed perficiat." *ST* 1a.1.8.
97. *Catechism of the Catholic Church*, 2d ed. (Vatican City: Libreria editrice, 1997), para. 34.
98. Brian Davies, *The Thought of Thomas Aquinas* (Oxford: Oxford University Press, 1992), 262.
99. *ST* 1a2ae.112.1 (resp to obj).

deity. H. Richard Niebuhr (1919–62) called this scheme the "Christ above culture" model.[100]

The second approach is most closely identified with the Anabaptists and pietist movements. In this view, grace more or less obliterates nature. The second- and third-century Marcionite movement held this view. Under the influence of Gnosticism, the Marcionites imagined an absolute ontological dualism between good and evil, between the evil, material demiurgic god of Moses and the good, benevolent God of Jesus. In response, Tertullian (c. 155–230) and Irenaeus (c. 130–202) defended the unity of salvation in Christ alone in all ages and the essential goodness of creation. It is a milder version of this spirit that says "do not handle, taste, or touch" (Col. 2:21), that regards much of creation per se with suspicion and fear as something to be painted over. Niebuhr described this model as "Christ against culture."[101] As the Thomist scheme is the product of neo-Platonic dualism, this approach is the child of middle- and neo-Platonic dualism. Instead, however, of a gradual perfection of nature, this approach has, in the words of Eric Voeglin, "immanentized the eschaton."[102]

In contrast to these two views, the confessional Reformed approach to nature/grace relations is to deny the neo-Platonic scheme altogether. The WCF (26.3) says that no matter how intimate our union with Christ is, it does not make believers in any way "partakers of the substance of his Godhead; or to be equal with Christ in any respect: either of which to affirm is impious and blasphemous."[103] In distinction to the other views described here, we confess that grace "renews" nature. Much of

100. H. Richard Niebuhr, *Christ and Culture* (New York: Harper & Brothers, 1951), 130–41.

101. Niebuhr, *Christ and Culture*, 51–57. Ironically, Niebuhr placed Tertullian in this category because he misunderstood Tertullian's approach to faith and reason. When Tertullian asked, "What has Athens to do with Jerusalem?" (*De praescriptione* 7; English translation in *Ante-Nicene Fathers*, 3:246), he was not arguing that faith is irrational. Rather, he was arguing that faith begins with divine revelation as its starting point. He was contrasting the pagan stoa (porch; a reference to the students of Zeno the philosopher) with Solomon's porch. The entire passage is an argument against compromising Christianity for the sake of credibility, not a rejection of the rational defense of Christianity.

102. See e.g., Eric Voeglin, *Science, Politics, and Gnosticism* (Chicago: Henry Regnery, 1968), 83–114.

103. *RCH*, 197.

the Reformed doctrine of sanctification is taken up with the doctrine of "renewal."[104] For example, HC Q. 86 says that Christ "having redeemed us by his blood, also renews (*erneuert*) us by his Holy Spirit."[105] In CD 5.7 we confess that God "by his Word and Spirit ... certainly and effectually renews (*renovat*)" the elect to repentance.[106] In the same way, the WCF (10.1) says that God calls the elect out of sin and death, makes them alive, gives them faith, "renewing their wills."[107] Therefore, Reformed theology confesses, as Richard Muller says in describing the Reformed orthodox approach, "nature and grace are not opposed."[108] In the late nineteenth and early twentieth century, Herman Bavinck summarized the Reformed consensus: "And that, too, was what the Reformation wanted: Christianity that was hostile, not to nature but only to sin. ... Coming again into its own in the Reformation was the old adage: nature commends grace; grace emends nature."[109]

We confess that we were created "good" (Gen. 1:31). The HC asked the same question that Marcion (and the neo-Platonists) asked, but we confess a quite different answer: "Did God create man thus wicked and perverse? No, but God created man good and after his own image, that is, in righteousness and true holiness." The human problem has never been finitude. The human problem has always been sin. It is true that this approach to nature and grace makes the fall even more inexplicable. How is it that Adam, so constituted, chose sin and death over life and glory? This is a mystery that the Reformed confession leaves to the providence and mind of God.[110]

104. See Clark, *Caspar Olevian and the Substance of the Covenant*, 181–209.
105. *Creeds*, 3:338.
106. Ibid., 3:572, 594.
107. *RCH*, 91.
108. Muller, *Post-Reformation Reformed Dogmatics*, 1:280.
109. Herman Bavinck, *Reformed Dogmatics, Prolegomena*, trans. John Vriend, ed. John Bolt (Grand Rapids: Baker Academic, 2003), 362. I am grateful to William Chellis for pointing me to this reference.
110. Some Reformed orthodox theologians did verge on the medieval and Roman doctrine of the *donum superadditum*, i.e., the doctrine that God gave Adam restraining grace before the fall and that the fall was due in part to its removal. See Zacharias Ursinus, *Commentary on the Heidelberg Catechism* (Phillipsburg, NJ: P&R, reprint 1985), 34–35. This view, however, was not held universally nor is it confessed formally by the Reformed churches. BC 14 does say of Adam, "being in honor he understood it not, neither knew

Because, against the spirit of the age (*Zeitgeist*), we confess that grace renews nature, we also confess in HC Q. 35 that in the incarnation, God the Son "took upon him the very nature of man, the flesh and blood of the Virgin Mary, by the operation of the Holy Spirit."[111] From the "blessed Virgin Mary," he took not only his humanity but also a "true human soul, that he might be a real man" (BC 14).[112] The BC explicitly contrasts this Christology with that of some of the Anabaptists, for example, Caspar Schwenkfeld (1489–1561) and Menno Simons (1496–1561),[113] which held that Jesus had a "celestial flesh," reflecting the desire for grace to obliterate nature.[114]

The Reformed churches confess that as Jesus has a true human body, so he has also established a real, human church through which he graciously and powerfully operates through his established means, the preaching of the holy gospel and the administration of the holy sacraments.[115] Through this most fallible of institutions, God is pleased to work wonderful things: sinners are brought to saving faith in Christ, and saints are built up and encouraged in their Christian life. This body is the "communion of saints" (*communio sanctorum*). In the Westminster Confession (26.1) we confess that all "saints are united to Jesus Christ their Head, by his Spirit, and by faith, have fellowship with him." We are also, however, "united to one another in love" and have "communion with each other's gifts and graces." As members of the same body, we are obligated to each other (in a way not too distant from marriage) not only spiritually but physically and materially. We are to aid one another "in outward things, according to [our] several abilities and necessities" (WCF 26.2).[116]

---

his excellency, but willfully subjected himself to sin" (*RCH*, 46). Though this passage is difficult and does appear to lay the cause of sin at Adam's finitude, in context it probably intends to describe the doctrine of probation and Adam's failure to keep what the confession calls "the commandment of life."

111. *RCH*, 74.

112. Ibid.

113. George Huntston Williams, *The Radical Reformation*, 3rd ed. (Kirksville, MO: Sixteenth Century Publishers, 1992), 597.

114. Ibid., 199.

115. *Creeds*, 3:328.

116. *RCH*, 197.

Conclusion

The Reformed theology, piety, and practice are an alternative to the QIRC and QIRE. Because the Reformed churches came to be profoundly influenced by these movements, it is not altogether surprising that as the broader evangelical world looked for alternatives to the manifestations of the QIRC and the QIRE in their movement, they looked at us (to the degree that they even considered the Reformed churches to be an alternative to Rome and Constantinople) and saw more of what they were seeking to escape. Now the postevangelical, post-baby-boomer generations appear to be synthesizing Rome, Constantinople, and Wheaton into a liquid version of evangelicalism, mirroring late modernity.

To the postevangelicals this chapter has tried to signify that, at their best, the Reformed theology, piety, and practice are not just another version of fundamentalism or revivalism, that we belong to neither of these movements. Rather, our roots, our confession, our theology, piety, and practice are not well classified as "evangelical" or "fundamentalist" in the modern sense. As Darryl Hart has argued repeatedly, there is a third party in American religion: confessionalists.[117] Further, I have tried to sketch briefly, and somewhat arbitrarily, five virtues of confessional Reformed theology, piety, and practice. These are virtues which should be attractive to postevangelicals, if they are willing to reconsider their continuing indebtedness to evangelicalism and fundamentalism.

To those who profess the Reformed theology, piety, and practice, this chapter has attempted to outline some of the reasons why one ought to remain Reformed, why there is no need to move, as it were, to Rome, Constantinople, or the Emergent Village. These are just some of the virtues possessed by the Reformed confession. Whereas this chapter has, to some degree, focused on some of the qualities that the Reformed churches share with the church catholic, in the next chapter we turn to that which distinguishes us as we gather in corporate worship.

117. See Hart, *The Lost Soul of American Protestantism.*

We believe that those Holy Scriptures fully contain the will of God, and that whatsoever man ought to believe unto salvation is sufficiently taught therein. For since the whole manner of worship which God requires of us is written in them at large, it is unlawful for any one, though an apostle, to teach otherwise than we are now taught in the Holy Scriptures.

—Belgic Confession 7

But the acceptable way of worshipping the true God is instituted by himself, and so limited by his own revealed will, that he may not be worshipped according to the imaginations and devices of men, or the suggestions of Satan, under any visible representation, or any other way not prescribed in the holy Scripture.

—Westminster Confession of Faith 21.1

The much-sought-after Urban Young People found the Hip Church-man to be an embarrassment, if they noticed him at all.

—Tom Wolfe

Recovering Reformed Worship

There can be little question whether Reformed worship is in trouble in North America and perhaps everywhere. As Frederick W. Schroeder says, "Cultus reform is in the ecclesiastical air of our time. Liturgical alterations and embellishments are the order of the day."[1] W. Robert Godfrey writes that the "last thirty years or so have seen the most dramatic and speedy changes in Protestant worship in any time since the Protestant Reformation."[2] I. John Hesselink, lamenting the loss of psalm singing, says, "In the modern era, this rich heritage has been sold for a mess of pop-pottage, especially in the more conservative Reformed/ Presbyterian Churches."[3] D. G. Hart laments that one might think that someone

> looking for traces of John Calvin's liturgy would have a better chance of finding it in those denominations that look to the past for examples of faithfulness rather than in those that have endeavored to adapt Christianity to modern times. But such a seeker would be sadly misinformed

1. Frederick W. Schroeder, *Worship in the Reformed Tradition* (Philadelphia and Boston: United Church Press, 1966), 20.
2. W. Robert Godfrey, "The Psalms in Contemporary Worship," in *The Worship of God: Reformed Concepts of Biblical Worship* (Ross-shire, UK: Mentor/Christian Focus Publications, 2005), 101.
3. I. John Hesselink, *On Being Reformed: Distinctive Characteristics and Common Misunderstandings*, 2d ed. (New York: Reformed Church Press, 1988), 24.

because more congregations in the PCUSA are likely to follow the Genevan order of service than those in the OPC or PCA.[4]

The importance of the question of how God is to be worshiped is clear. First, it concerns how creatures should approach their Creator and how the redeemed should speak to their Redeemer in public assembly. Second, as Terry Johnson notes, "the way we worship today will determine the shape and substance of our piety for generations to come."[5] The fact that many Reformed Christians alive today have never seen or participated in a worship service that Calvin, the Heidelberg Reformers, or the Westminster divines would recognize does not bode well for the future of Reformed theology, piety, and practice.[6]

For these reasons, in this chapter I argue that an essential part of recovering the Reformed confession is to recover the Reformed principle and practice of worship. On the Reformed approach to worship, Zacharias Ursinus (1534–1583), the primary author of the HC and student of the Lutheran theologian Philipp Melanchthon (1497–1560), said that the Reformed principle of worship is "that we sacredly and conscientiously keep ourselves within the bounds which God has prescribed, and that we do not add anything to that worship which has been divinely instituted, or corrupt it in any part, even the most unimportant."[7] The Reformed principle of worship has come to be known as the "regulative principle of worship" (hereafter, RPW).[8] Briefly, the RPW is that, in stated Lord's Day services, God may be worshiped only as he has commanded and in no other way. Horton Davies says: "The real difference between the Lutheran and

4. D. G. Hart, *Recovering Mother Kirk: The Case for Liturgy in the Reformed Tradition* (Grand Rapids: Baker, 2003), 181.

5. Terry Johnson, "The Regulative Principle," in *The Worship of God: Reformed Concepts of Worship* (Ross-shire, UK: Mentor/Christian Focus Publications, 2005), 11.

6. For a short account of these revisions see John M. Barkley, *The Worship of the Reformed Church: An Exposition and Critical Analysis of the Eucharistic, Baptismal, and Confirmation Rites in the Scottish, English-Welsh, and Irish Liturgies*, ed. J. G. Davies and A. Raymond George, Ecumenical Studies in Worship (Richmond: John Knox, 1967), 37–40.

7. Zacharias Ursinus, *Commentary on the Heidelberg Catechism*, trans. George W. Williard (Phillipsburg, NJ: P&R, 1985), 517.

8. This expression is of recent vintage (like the term "amillennialism") but the idea that it signifies is much older.

the Calvinist reforms in worship may be summed up as follows: Luther will have what is not specifically condemned by the Scriptures; whilst Calvin will have only what is ordained by God in the Scriptures."[9]

The remarkable thing is that this characterization of the RPW is entirely uncontroversial. There is no serious question in the secondary literature on the history and theology of Reformed worship about what the RPW is. Nevertheless, those denominations that actually continue to practice the RPW as it was formulated and practiced in the sixteenth and seventeenth centuries constitute a small minority in the American Presbyterian and Reformed denominations. Often the RPW seems to be regarded as a quaint relic or sometimes it is just ignored. In other cases, however, it is being radically revised so as to become unrecognizable.

For Calvin and the confessional Reformed tradition, this principle has been nothing other than the specific application of the formal principle of the Reformation, *sola scriptura*. Ursinus addressed this very issue in his exposition of the second commandment. He summarized and rejected the Lutheran (and Anglican) principle that the congregation may do whatever is not forbidden on the ground that Christ had rejected this very notion implicitly when he rejected the Jewish tradition of hand washing as a part of worship, "because they associated with it the idea of divine worship, although it was not sinful in itself."[10] Ursinus argued that things that are in themselves indifferent (*adiaphora*), that are "neither commanded nor prohibited by God, if they are prescribed and done as the worship of God, or if it is supposed that God is honored by our performing them, and dishonored by neglecting them, it is plainly manifest that the Scriptures in these and similar places condemn them."[11] Calvin, Ursinus, and the Westminster divines after them understood that the Reformed principle of worship is *sola scriptura* applied to the act of corporate worship. Unless one can demonstrate that Scripture requires that something be done, it may not be done.

The classical and confessional understanding of this principle led the Reformed churches to distinguish between two aspects of wor-

---

9. Horton Davies, *The Worship of the English Puritans* (Morgan, PA: Soli Deo Gloria, reprint, 1997), 16.
10. Ibid., 519.
11. Ibid.

ship: element and circumstances. This distinction was a corollary to the distinction between a substance and an accident.[12] A substance is that which makes a thing what it is. An accident is something that is temporarily connected or related to the substance but such that it can be changed without changing the substance. I am typing at a computer. The actual processor is essential to the computer but the color of the case containing the computer is not. An element, therefore, is essential to worship. The WCF identifies two elements of worship: God's Word (21.5) and prayer (21.3–4). It treats the sacraments under the heading of the Word because they are the gospel made visible.[13] By contrast, the confession speaks (in 21.6–7) of those things, such as place, time, dress, and posture, that may be changed according to culture and wisdom without effecting any change in worship itself.[14] Such things are described as circumstances.[15] These categories are discussed more fully through the course of this chapter.

Having rediscovered the Reformed principle of worship, there is no reason why we cannot recover the Reformed practice of worship. Once we have discovered *what* Reformed worship is, then we must decide *whether* we are willing to act according to our confession. Despite the apparently overwhelming odds, there are some reasons to expect that this might happen. In the last two decades there has been genuine renewal of interest in more classically and confessionally Reformed theology. Radio and Internet broadcasts such as the White Horse Inn and magazines such as *Modern Reformation* attract thousands of subscribers and listeners. Other organizations such as Ligonier Ministries and the Alliance of Confessing Evangelicals are reaching even larger numbers of broadly evangelical Christians with Reformation theology and finding space on the village green of evangelicalism.[16]

12. On the early Reformed use of Aristotle see R. Scott Clark, *Caspar Olevian and the Substance of the Covenant: The Double Benefit of Christ*, Rutherford Studies in Historical Theology (Edinburgh: Rutherford House, 2005), 58–63.

13. *Institutes* 4.14.1.

14. See also *Institutes* 4.10.30.

15. See also Second Helvetic Confession 18 in *Creeds*, 3:880–84 for the English translation. The Latin text is on pages 283–85.

16. See the discussion of this metaphor in chapter 6 of this work.

Contemporary Reformed Discussions of Worship

As a matter of historiography, virtually no conspiracy theory is credible, if only because no conspiracy theory adequately explains all the facts in a given situation or accounts for the complexity of human motives and behavior and human sinfulness. Humans often have difficulty cooperating successfully on simple public projects, let alone on secret projects. Nevertheless, there is a sort of unintentional conspiracy that occurs when most people look at the same question from the same point of view, with the same assumptions, coming to the same conclusions. Judging from the modern literature on worship, one might think that there was a conspiracy to create the impression that worship has always been as it is today. Indeed, a reasonable person well read in the modern literature on worship might be forgiven for coming to such a conclusion, but that conclusion would be wrong nevertheless.[17]

In much of the modern literature the original understanding of the RPW is either rejected or ignored. For example, in his magisterial study on the *Patristic Roots of Reformed Worship*, Hughes Oliphant Old adduces a good deal of evidence that seems to demonstrate that the RPW was a fundamental principle of Reformed worship from the earliest stage of the Reformed Reformation.[18] He interprets the same evidence, however, to indicate only a mere "preference" by Bucer, Oecolampadius, and Calvin for the singing of psalms in worship.[19] The evidence, however, to which he appeals seems to indicate rather more than a preference.[20] Indeed, by assigning the RPW entirely to the Puritans, and by speaking of Calvin's

17. For more comprehensive surveys of the relevant literature see Thomas G. Reid Jr., "'The Acceptable Way of Worshipping the True God': Recent Writings on Worship of Particular Interest to Reformed Christians," in *Worship in the Presence of God*, ed. David Lachman and Frank J. Smith (Greenville, SC: Greenville Seminary Press, 1992); Frank Joseph Smith and Chris Coldwell, "The Regulative Principle of Worship: Sixty Years in Reformed Literature. Part One (1946–1999)," *The Confessional Presbyterian: A Journal for Discussion of Presbyterian Doctrine and Practice* 2 (2006).

18. Hughes Oliphant Old, *The Patristic Roots of Reformed Worship* (Zürich: Theologischer, 1975), 24–25.

19. See also Hughes Oliphant Old, "Calvin's Theology of Worship," in *Give Praise to God: A Vision for Reforming Worship*, ed. Philip G. Ryken et al. (Phillipsburg, NJ: P&R, 2003), 412–35.

20. Old, *The Patristic Roots of Reformed Worship*, 259–63.

"preference" for psalmody in worship, and by arguing that Calvin did not favor the psalms over hymns as a matter of principle,[21] Old gives the impression that Calvin was more of a forerunner of the mainline liturgical renewal rather than a forerunner of the Reformed confessional tradition.[22] Perhaps most puzzling of all, however, is his claim that "the so-called 'regulative principle' is not Reformed in origin but rather Anabaptist."[23] The phrase "regulative principle" did not arise with Bucer or Calvin, but the view that it describes certainly did.[24]

Writing in the mainline United Methodist context, James F. White's survey of Reformation worship uses the categories of "left-wing," "central," and "right wing," to describe differences among the Reformers over worship.[25] The use of these categories, rather than Reformed and Lutheran (which had different principles of worship) or confessional and nonconfessional, which would account better for the relative unity of the Protestants over against the Anabaptist radicals, leads White to ignore the RPW and to mischaracterize Reformed worship generally. Writing in the context of the Presbyterian mainline and advocating ecumenical liturgical renewal, Donald Macleod does not even mention the RPW. The only opposition he can imagine to his account of worship must come from "the closed mind of some cult or ecclesiastical negativism."[26]

Among more conservative Presbyterians, the RPW has received more attention, if not always favor. Robert G. Rayburn, writing from the confessional Reformed tradition to the broader evangelical world, offers some

21. Ibid., 263.

22. See, however, Hughes Oliphant Old, *Guides to Reformed Tradition: Worship* (Atlanta: John Knox, 1984), 3–4, where he says that true "worship is an act of obedience to the law of God." He also acknowledges that Reformed worship is organized by the principle that "the worship of the church should be according to Scripture." For a response to this movement see Donald Macleod, "Calvin into Hippolytus," in *To Glorify God: Essays on Modern Reformed Liturgy*, ed. Bryan Spinks and Iain Torrance (Grand Rapids: Eerdmans, 1999).

23. Old, *Patristic Roots*, 185.

24. He summarizes Calvin's principle of worship quite accurately when he says, for Calvin, "Let us worship God as he has directed us in his word." This seems to me to be nothing other than the RPW as understood by the Reformed churches. See Old, "Calvin's Theology of Worship," 425.

25. James F. White, *A Brief History of Christian Worship* (Nashville: Abingdon, 1993), 107.

26. Donald Macleod, *Presbyterian Worship: Its Meaning and Method*, rev. ed. (Atlanta: John Knox, 1980), 4.

valuable insights into worship, and an entire chapter devoted to uninspired hymnody, but no discussion of the RPW.[27] Rayburn's approach to worship is typical of the modern conservative approach to worship that is not controlled by the confessional principles or oriented to the Directory for Public Worship.[28] Though he speaks highly of the psalms, he makes some unfortunate arguments for the use of uninspired hymnody. For example, he argues from Pliny the Younger's letter (c. A.D. 111) to the emperor Trajan that the early postapostolic church sang uninspired hymns.[29] This conclusion begs the question. It is true that Pliny mentioned the singing of a "song" (*carmen*), but it does not follow that the congregation described sang uninspired songs. How would Pliny know the difference between an uninspired hymn and a canonical song? Further, we do not even know the source of Pliny's information nor can we impute to him any significant knowledge of the Scriptures. What did the Roman elites actually know about Scripture and Christianity other than rumors? Surely he interpreted what he saw (or the report he received) in the context of Roman hymns of allegiance and military songs and the like.[30] Further, to suggest on the basis of this scanty evidence that the early postapostolic church sang uninspired songs ignores the fact (to which Rayburn alludes) that the Psalter was the songbook of the church for a millennium.

In his 1996 book on worship, John Frame, who also writes from the confessional Reformed tradition, addresses the RPW, directly acknowledging that Presbyterian and Reformed Christians have differed with Roman Catholics, Lutherans, and Anglicans on the principle governing worship.[31] He summarizes the RPW accurately, relating it closely to the sufficiency of

27. Robert G. Rayburn, *O Come, Let Us Worship: Corporate Worship in the Evangelical Church* (Grand Rapids: Baker, 1980), 223–41.

28. There are a couple of different archaic spellings of the word "Public" in the title of the DPW. Because this is not chiefly a historical essay the modern spelling is used here.

29. Ibid., 232–33. Pliny wrote, "essent soliti stato die lucem convenire carmenque Christo quasi deo dicere." Constantine E. Pritchard and Edward R. Bernard, eds., *Selected Letters of Pliny the Younger* (Oxford: Clarendon, 1896), 10.96 (p. 124, lines 30–31).

30. He invoked Roman military imagery when he wrote of the early Christians swearing a "testamentum" (oath). Pritchard and Bernard, eds., *Selected Letters of Pliny the Younger*, 124 (line 34).

31. John M. Frame, *Worship in Spirit and Truth* (Phillipsburg, NJ: P&R, 1996), 38–49. These arguments are also found in John M. Frame, "Some Questions about the Regulative Principle," *WTJ* 54 (1992): 357–66.

Scripture, and even appeals to the same sorts of examples (e.g., Nadab and Abihu, Lev. 10:1–2) to support it as do supporters of the original understanding of the RPW.[32] Given these facts it would seem incorrect to list Frame as an opponent of the RPW. The reason, however, for categorizing Frame's account of the RPW as a denial is found in his radical revision and understanding of it. He recognizes that the traditional understanding of the RPW entails a distinction between elements and circumstances, but he rejects the premise on which the distinction was made, that is, that there is a distinction between that which is secular and that which is sacred.[33] He argues, "surely in God's world nothing is purely secular; nothing is entirely devoid of religious significance."[34] He continues, "I agree with the confession that there is room for judgment in matters that are 'common to human actions and societies' [WCF 1.6]. But I do not believe that this is the only legitimate sphere of human judgment. In my view, the term best suited to describe the sphere of human judgments is not *circumstance*, but *application*."[35] Thus understood, the regulative principle for worship is no different from the principles by which God regulates all of our life. In every case, then, both generally and in worship, "everything we do must be done in obedience to God's commands. In both cases, application determines the specifics in accordance with the general principles of the word."[36]

Frame recognizes that this view of the RPW varies not only from the historic understanding of it, but also from the confession's own assumption.[37] He argues, however, that his view does not contradict the confes-

32. Frame, *Worship*, 39.

33. On this distinction see the helpful account in Joseph A. Pipa Jr., "Reformed Liturgy," in *The Worship of God* (Ross-shire, UK: Christian Focus, 2005), 124–34.

34. Frame, *Worship*, 40.

35. Ibid., 41. Italics original.

36. Frame, *Worship*, 42. In this Frame follows Norman Shepherd, "The Biblical Basis for the Regulative Principle," in *The Biblical Doctrine of Worship*, ed. Philip W. Martin, John M. McMillan, and Edward A. Robson (Pittsburgh: Reformed Presbyterian Church in North America, 1974), 50.

37. He cites WCF 20.2: "God alone is Lord of the conscience, and hath left it free from the doctrines and commandments of men, which are, in anything, contrary to his Word; or beside it, if matters of faith, or worship. So that, to believe such doctrines, or to obey such commands, out of conscience, is to betray true liberty of conscience: and the requiring of an implicit faith, and an absolute and blind obedience, is to destroy liberty of conscience, and reason also."

sion but "goes beyond it."[38] Thus the RPW, as Frame understands it, also applies equally to private gatherings and stated services. The RPW is not primarily a limit on church power, but about worship in all its forms.[39]

How does Frame apply his version of the RPW? Because God has given us a general command to preach the Word, because biblical preaching and teaching have a dramatic element, because the RPW does not require a specific command to include drama in worship, because drama can be a form of preaching, because God often teaches his people through dramatic and symbolic acts, and because teaching can be done through dialogue as well as monologue, he concludes that "we cannot object to drama as a form of teaching." He adds, "I am not an advocate of the use of drama ... nevertheless I do believe that Scripture gives us the freedom to use drama; we may not dogmatically restrict the proclamation of the word in worship to the traditional monologue form."[40]

R. J. Gore argues a similar case from a more historical point of view. He gives a reasonable summary of the traditional understanding of the RPW. He also explains that the RPW was intended to govern worship specifically and that it was not intended to govern life beyond worship.[41] His proposed revision begins to emerge when he argues from the diversity of opinion on the nature of what constitutes a circumstance, as distinct from an element of worship. He begins to find difficulties in the *application* of the RPW.[42] He argues that these difficulties "do not vitiate the Puritan regulative principle," but they do suggest it needs to be reformulated.[43] He finds other reasons why the RPW needs to be reformulated. For example, he argues that neither the WCF nor the DPW is entirely consistent with the "Puritan" RPW.[44]

The beginning of his solution is to juxtapose Calvin with the Puritans, a remarkable move, given the state of Calvin studies and the study of Reformed orthodoxy. In particular, he sets Calvin against the

38. Frame, *Worship*, 43.
39. Ibid., 44.
40. Ibid., 92–94.
41. R. J. Gore, *Covenantal Worship: Reconsidering the Puritan Regulative Principle* (Phillipsburg, NJ: P&R, 2002), 26–28.
42. Ibid., 29–32.
43. Ibid., 32.
44. Ibid., 50.

"Puritans" (as if that term described a monolith) on the question of adiaphora (those things morally indifferent).[45] He notes that Calvin used "both leavened and unleavened bread" in the Supper whereas departing "from the tolerant spirit of their mentor, the Puritans . . . opposed the use of the wafer, insisting instead on the use of common (leavened) bread."[46] His argument continues in this vein without pausing to recognize the rather different situation in which Calvin and the English Reformed found themselves. For Gore, "Puritanism steadily embraced increasingly radical positions."[47] They did so because they had a tendency toward "rationalism," that is, worship for the Puritans was chiefly an intellectual exercise born of their view that the intellect has a certain primacy.[48] Even John Flavel and John Owen cannot escape Gore's judgment of rationalism, because Stoicisim and neo-Platonism "exerted some influence on their thinking."[49] Gore seems unaware that Owen in particular was aware of these movements and had adopted theological positions specifically designed to prevent such rationalism, chiefly the distinction between archetypal and ectypal theology.[50] He also criticizes the biblical interpretation of some of the Puritans, concluding that their RPW cannot account for Jesus' own practice and the institution of the voluntary feasts. In other words, in their attempt to be strictly, positively biblical in their approach to worship, they became unbiblical.[51]

45. He cites Patrick Collinson, *The Elizabethan Puritan Movement* (London: Jonathan Cape, 1967), 36, and Horton Davies, *The Worship of the English Puritans*, 37, as proof of this point. Gore cites different editions, but the pagination of my editions seems to match the editions he cites, and neither volume is saying quite what he suggests. Collinson was remarking about the Puritan resistance to the imposition of certain practices, and Davies is describing the Puritan willingness to disagree with Calvin when necessary.

46. Gore, *Covenantal Worship*, 76.

47. Ibid., 92. That these movements were part of the European intellectual milieu is not in question, but Gore gives no evidence of any particular influence on any particular thinkers. By contrast, this work has offered concrete evidence for the influence of Cambridge Platonism upon Jonathan Edwards.

48. His chief authority for this claim is Gregory Dix (93).

49. Gore, *Covenantal Worship*, 95.

50. Sebastian Rehnman, *Divine Discourse: The Theological Methodology of John Owen*, ed. Richard A. Muller, Texts and Studies in Reformation and Post-Reformation Thought (Grand Rapids: Baker, 2002), 57–71.

51. Gore, *Covenantal Worship*, 110.

Gore's alternative to "the Puritan" RPW is what he describes as "covenantal worship" which leads him to follow Frame by erasing the distinction between "cult" (worship) and "culture" (daily life).[52] According to Gore, the Puritans failed to recognize that "all of life is worship," and they failed to cultivate a "healthy respect for and sober use of the concept of *adiaphora* as applied to the question of circumstances."[53] Having concluded that the RPW "as formulated by the Puritans and as adopted by the divines at Westminster Assembly, is unworkable," he proposes to help us by expanding the category of adiaphora.[54] In the place of the historic confessional understanding of the RPW, Gore proposes a "covenantal principle" of worship. Within this "covenantal principle" he includes the elements of worship, for example, "praying, celebrating the sacraments, preaching, and singing of Psalms."[55] He further proposes that the RPW should continue to be defined to include "good and necessary consequences." Finally, he says, "the covenantal principle of worship includes the freedom to worship in any manner warranted by the Scriptures" so that "whatever is consistent with the Scriptures is acceptable in worship."[56] Gore admits that, in this last point, he has proposed a major break with the RPW. This is his answer to the problem of things indifferent.

Despite the bad press about and radical revisions proposed for the RPW, there has been a steady interest in confessional Reformed worship in the modern period. At the beginning of the twentieth century, there was a flurry of interest in the historic and confessional Reformed doctrine of worship. This interest is evident in the conferences and collection of essays sponsored by the Synod of the United Presbyterian Church of North America.[57] This collection, though dated in some of its biblical scholarship, presents cogent and coherent responses to many of the most common objections to Reformed worship. Whatever its

52. Ibid., 112–31.
53. Ibid., 135.
54. Ibid., 137.
55. Ibid., 138.
56. Ibid., 140.
57. John McNaugher, ed., *The Psalms in Worship: A Series of Convention Papers Bearing on the Place of the Psalms in the Worship of the Church* (Pittsburgh: The United Presbyterian Board of Publication, 1907), 77–87. This volume was reprinted by Still Waters Revival Books (Edmonton, 1992).

weaknesses, this collection reflects faithfully the historic view of the nature of Reformed worship.

In the late 1950s, Reformed writers such as William Young were articulating and defending the RPW as part of the "Puritan Conference" held at Westminster Chapel.[58] In the last quarter of the twentieth century, one could find periodic restatements of the RPW in defense of exclusive psalmody that intensified as the "worship wars" erupted.[59] In recent years, however, the situation has changed. There is renewed interest in the RPW. For example, Darryl Hart and John Muether not only explain the RPW as the expression in worship of *sola scriptura*, but defend it from some of the more common caricatures (e.g., it is a Puritan invention and strictly an old covenant idea) and advocate its benefits as a "guardian of Christian liberty."[60] Michael Horton's treatment of worship implies the RPW and argues for the reapprehension of historic liturgies of the Reformed

---

58. William Young, "The Puritan Principle of Worship," in *Servants of the Word: Puritan Conference Papers 1957*, ed. D. M. Lloyd-Jones (London: Banner of Truth Trust, 1957).

59. See e.g., Horace T. Allen, *A Presbyterian Congregation at Worship* (Philadelphia: Geneva and John Knox, 1975); Reformed Presbyterian Church of North America, *The Biblical Doctrine of Worship: A Symposium to State and Clarify the Scriptural Teachings concerning Worship with Emphasis on the Use of the Biblical Psalms in Christian Worship* (Pittsburgh: Reformed Presbyterian Church of North America, 1974); John W. Beardslee, "Some Implications for Worship in Traditional Reformed Doctrine," *Reformed Review* 30 (1977); James J. Farley, "The Presbyterian Tradition of Worship, Applied to Today's Churches" (San Francisco Theological Seminary, 1978); Robert D. Jarman, "The Regulative Principle of Scripture: The Origin of a Cardinal Doctrine in the Early Elizabethan Puritan Movement" (Trinity Evangelical Divinity School, 1977); Duncan Lowe, "Biblical Worship: The Place of the Psalms," in *The Book of Books: Essays on the Scriptures in Honor of Johannes G. Vos*, ed. John H. White (Philadelphia: P&R, 1978); Jack Martin Maxwell, *Worship and Reformed Theology: The Liturgical Lessons of Mercersburg* (Pittsburgh: Pickwick, 1976); Old, *The Patristic Roots of Reformed Worship*; Reformed Presbyterian Church of North America, *Symposium on the Biblical Doctrine of Worship* (Pittsburgh: Reformed Presbyterian Church in North America, 1973); Shepherd, "The Biblical Basis for the Regulative Principle." William Young expanded his defense of the RPW in an article reprinted in Edward A. Robson, ed., *The Biblical Doctrine of Worship* (Pittsburgh: The Reformed Presbyterian Church of North America, 1974), and later in "The Second Commandment: The Principle That God Is to Be Worshipped Only in Ways Prescribed in Holy Scripture and That the Holy Scripture Prescribes the Whole Content of Worship, Taught by Scripture Itself," in *Worship in the Presence of God*, ed. David Lachman and Frank J. Smith (Greenville, SC: Greenville Seminary Press, 1992).

60. D. G. Hart and John R. Muether, *With Reverence and Awe: Returning to the Basics of Reformed Worship* (Phillipsburg, NJ: P&R, 2002), 77–87.

churches.[61] Sean Michael Lucas identifies several streams of thought over worship and a generational conflict over the nature of worship with the result that the baby boomers, once liturgical renegades, have made "contemporary worship" the new tradition, ironically making advocacy of the RPW the loyal opposition to the status quo rebellion.[62] He restates the RPW and affirms WCF 21.1, grounding it in the second commandment.[63] Like Frame, he appeals to the example of Nadab and Abihu but implies a rejection of Frame's revision of the RPW.[64] He restates the distinction between elements and circumstances, admits the difficulty modern Presbyterians have had in applying the RPW, and moves to a discussion of how to choose between uninspired hymns.[65] Terry Johnson has defended the RPW by appealing again to the classical scriptural loci (Gen. 4:3–8; Ex. 20:4; 32; Lev. 10; Deut. 4:2; 12:32; Jer. 19:6; 32:35; Mark 7:7; Col. 2:22–23) and adducing several arguments from Reformed theology. Like most of the contemporary defenders of the RPW, however, he does not reach the same conclusions as the DPW.[66] Derek W. H. Thomas, though wishing to defend the RPW, concludes that the musical instruments are not contrary to the RPW since they are warranted by their use in the temple.[67]

A brief response is in order. Frame says that "surely in God's world nothing is purely secular."[68] This is both true and a red herring. The RPW as originally understood and confessed in the Reformed churches does not assume the sort of secularism that Frame implies. It simply distinguishes the way God rules over different spheres of human life. We cannot drive our cars by asking whether the Lord would have us turn left or

61. Michael S. Horton, *A Better Way: Rediscovering the Drama of God-Centered Worship,* (Grand Rapids: Baker, 2002), 142–62.

62. Sean Michael Lucas, *On Being Presbyterian: Our Beliefs, Practices, and Stories* (Phillipsburg, NJ: P&R, 2006), 115–16.

63. Ibid., 118–19.

64. Ibid., 119.

65. Ibid., 126–29.

66. Terry L. Johnson, "The Regulative Principle," in *The Worship of God* (Ross-shire, UK: Christian Focus, 2005), 9–29.

67. Derek W. H. Thomas, "The Regulative Principle: Responding to Recent Criticism," in *Give Praise to God: A Vision for Reforming Worship,* ed. Philip Graham Ryken et al. (Phillipsburg, NJ: P&R, 2003), 92.

68. Frame, *Worship,* 40.

right. Such questions are matters of wisdom and discretion of the sort described in the book of Proverbs. Unlike driving, in determining what may be done in sacred worship we are meant to ask only "what does God require?" because God has revealed his precise will for every *element* of worship. Of course, Frame rejects this distinction as well, blurring the line unnecessarily between circumstance (questions of time, place, posture, etc.) and element (that which is essential to worship). By rejecting the central distinctions on which the RPW is premised, and by applying the RPW to that to which it was never intended to be applied, to which in its nature it cannot be applied (namely, everything), Frame has made the RPW apply to nothing in worship in particular.

The RPW says that we may do nothing in worship except that which is commanded or implied in God's Word. Frame changes the terms of the RPW by redefining worship to refer not to stated assemblies but to all of life. Certainly it is true that, in one sense, all of life is an act of worship, but the RPW was formed and intended to govern worship conceived narrowly, that is, to what occurs during a stated service. It was not intended to govern every aspect of life. Frame also subverts the RPW by redefining the notion of "command." According to Frame's definition of theology, there is no real distinction between what Scripture says and one's *application* (an essential term in his theological method) of Scripture to a given situation by a given person. This application has the same force as a divine "command." As a result, every application of Scripture or even general revelation is a command. Thus the principle that we must do only what we are commanded now becomes: We can do whatever one concludes from one's application of revelation to any circumstance. What began as a principle of restriction has become a license. Under Frame's hand, the question is no longer: what must I do according to the preceptive revelation in God's Word or according to good and necessary inferences, but, in effect, what may I do by my application of revelation to a situation? Thus, what began ostensibly as an endorsement of the RPW, by the time it is finished, has reversed field entirely and become a subversion of it. This is the same logic that led a U.S. Marine colonel during the Vietnam War to declare to a reporter, "We had to destroy the village to save it."[69]

69. As quoted by Mark McNeilly in *Sun Tzu and the Art of Modern Warfare* (New York: Oxford University Press, 2003), 12.

Gore's proposals, though more historically informed than Frame's, suffer from the same logical fallacies. Further, because they propose the same sort of radical revision of the RPW in the light of some historical study, his apparent ignorance of the study of Reformed orthodoxy in the last twenty-five years is even more remarkable. When he speaks of scholars in the 1970s and 1980s arguing for a paradigm shift between Calvin and Reformed orthodoxy, he is surely thinking of writers such as R. T. Kendall, but he cites none and gives no evidence that he is aware of any of the contemporary scholarship in Reformed orthodoxy such as Richard Muller's monumental *PRRD* or other more introductory works already discussed in this work that have answered the Kendall thesis.[70] The "Calvin v. the Calvinists" argument is central to his program for rescuing Reformed worship from the hands of the Puritans, but it fails for the same reasons that the earlier versions did.[71]

Further, it is quite difficult to see what is distinctively covenantal about Gore's proposed revisions of the RPW. After all, one of the great motivating factors behind the development and articulation of the RPW in the sixteenth and seventeenth centuries was Reformed covenant theology, and the same theologians and churches that developed our covenant theology formulated our principle of worship in the light of our covenant theology. The Reformed confessions are covenantal, and the Westminster Standards are especially influenced in their form and content by Reformed covenant theology. Thus it is not at all clear why one should concede the adjective "covenantal" to Gore's revisions any more than one should be prepared to concede that adjective to the revisers of the Reformed doctrine of justification.[72]

Finally, Gore's revision of the RPW, to allow in worship whatever is consistent with the Scriptures, is the death knell for Reformed worship. Which Lutheran or Roman or Anglican theorist would disagree with this

70. Gore, *Covenantal Worship*, 54.

71. The whole of chapter 5 of his book assumes the validity of the Calvin v. the Calvinists paradigm. See R. J. Gore Jr., "Covenantal Worship: Reconsidering the Critics," *WTJ* 67 (2005): 363–79. In his response to T. David Gordon's review, he continues to assume the validity of this paradigm (371–72).

72. Gore is using the adjective "covenantal" in a way analogous to Norman Shepherd's use of the term to describe his revision of the Reformed doctrine of justification. See Gore, "Response," 373.

principle of worship? Who in the entire history of the Christian church (or in the history of redemption) has ever argued that we should institute a practice that is inconsistent with Scripture? Did Aaron propose anything he thought to be inconsistent with God's will at Sinai (Ex. 32)? In reaction to the Puritans, who, for Gore, so narrowed the category of adiaphora as to exclude almost everything, Gore expands it to include almost anything. The point of the Reformed distinction between elements and circumstances was to prevent the very sort of approach to worship advocated by Frame and Gore.

The modern approach toward the RPW can be categorized in two ways: confessional and nonconfessional. Among nonconfessional writers, whether conservative or liberal, the RPW is ignored, dismissed, or reconfigured beyond recognition. Among most confessional writers, the RPW is defended in principle but typically modified to allow the use of uninspired songs in worship. Those who defend the RPW as understood by the DPW and the Reformed tradition continue to uphold the argument for exclusive psalmody in worship. In what follows, however, I take issue with all three conclusions.

The nonconfessional writers typically reason from theological principles that are not amenable to Reformed theology and naturally draw conclusions regarding the practice of worship that are not compatible with the RPW. Most confessional supporters of the RPW, however well-intended, typically do not go far enough in their application of the RPW, stopping short of the original understanding of the RPW. The reason for this hesitation is unclear. It seems to be assumed that the singing of inspired canonical texts only is wrong, but that conclusion is not often stated explicitly or defended. There seems to be an unstated assumption that the Reformed churches, since the seventeenth century, have discovered some significant flaw in the original understanding of the RPW. Those, however, who uphold exclusive psalmody may go too far. This essay agrees with the New England Puritan theologian John Cotton (1584–1652) and the Westminster Seminary theologian John Murray (1898–1975) who concluded that the argument that, out of the entire canon of Scripture, only psalms may be sung, is a conclusion that does not seem to be so well supported by Scripture that it is inescapably true.

Instead, the essence of the RPW is that we must do in worship only that which is required and what is required is that God's people respond to his Word with his Word.[73] Therefore, in public worship, God's people ought to respond to his Word by singing from the whole canon of God's Word and not just the Psalter.

At the outset of the chapter the connection was observed between the doctrine *sola scriptura* and the RPW. Implicit in the RPW is another corollary: Christian liberty. One of the great concerns of the Reformed churches since the sixteenth century has been to respect the conscience of the worshiper. Where those who would ask worshipers to sing uninspired songs might think that they are exercising Christian liberty, in fact, they are impinging on the liberty of Christians.

Since the 1540s there had been tension in the English church over the question of whether ministers could be required to wear certain vestments. In 1550, the debate heated up. John Bishop (c. 1495–1555), who was martyred during the reign of bloody Mary Tudor,[74] refused to be made to wear the surplice and rochet as part of his ordination as bishop of Gloucester. Having been influenced by Heinrich Bullinger (1504–75) in Zurich, he embraced the formal principle of the Reformation and began to apply it to worship.[75] John Hooper argued that the church can impose only those practices which have explicit biblical warrant or are indifferent, but he defined "adiaphora" quite narrowly as those things which whether used or not detract nothing.[76] If the church is going to require vestments,

73. John Cotton, *The Singing of Psalmes a Gospel Ordinance* (London, 1647); John Murray, "Song in Public Worship," in *Worship in the Presence of God*, ed. David Lachman and Frank J. Smith (Greenville, SC: Greenville Presbyterian Theological Seminary Press, 1992), 191. This argument is elaborated below.

74. The surplice is usually a white vestment reaching to the knee. The rochet is similar to the surplice with narrower sleeves. For more vestments see Janet Mayo, *A History of Ecclesiastical Dress* (New York: Holmes and Meyer, 1984), 49–50. On the vestments controversy see John H. Primus, *The Vestments Controversy: An Historical Study of the Earliest Tensions within the Church of England in the Reigns of Edward VI and Elizabeth* (Kampen: J. H. Kok, 1960). For references to some of the secondary literature on this period see R. Scott Clark, "Ridley, Latimer, and Cranmer: The Oxford Martyrs," *Reformation and Revival: A Quarterly Journal for Church Leadership* 7 (1998): 167–79.

75. Hooper's view of the second commandment in 1550 is on display in John Hooper, *Early Writings of John Hooper, D.D.*, The Parker Society (Cambridge: Cambridge University Press, 1843), 316–22.

76. Primus, *The Vestments Controversy*, 17.

then they are not truly adiaphora. The principle at stake in this question is this: the church may not burden the conscience of the believer by requiring anything in worship not required by Scripture.

A Brief History of Christian Worship

It is also necessary to answer an important question: how did it happen that our principle of worship fell into neglect? It is not possible to survey the history of Christian worship here in any depth, but some context is necessary. First, we have a choice to make: We will pattern Christian worship after either the temple or the synagogue. As the medieval patterns of worship developed, the church turned progressively to the Mosaic, ceremonial, temple cultus as the pattern. Whatever the ambiguity surrounding the origin of the synagogue, it clearly influenced the New Testament church. It was their experience of worship apart from the temple.

Second, it is ill advised to use the temple as the pattern for Christian worship, for the temple was instituted under Moses as part of the typological system that was temporary by divine intention. It was at the center of the cultus that Paul describes as "fading" (2 Cor. 3:7–11). Given the history of Christian worship and the language of the New Testament, it is hard to imagine a compelling reason for us to use the temple as the paradigm for Christian worship. It is beyond dispute, of course, that the New Testament uses temple imagery to describe the new covenant people (e.g., 1 Cor. 3:16; 2 Cor. 6:16; Eph. 2:21; 1 Peter 4:14). It is true that in Christ the temple, Christians are now said to be the temple of God. It does not follow, however, that therefore we ought to pattern Christian worship on the temple in any but metaphorical ways. The New Testament draws theological and moral, not liturgical consequences from our status as the temple.

Further, to use the center of the ceremonial worship that was inherently defective (Heb. 8:1–10:18) as our pattern is bound to attach to Christian practice that which is also fading. The history of Christian worship teaches us this. It was not coincidental that musical instruments returned to Christian worship at the same time Christians began to conceive of ministers in sacerdotal categories. With the ascension of Christ and particularly with the destruction of the second temple in A.D. 70, any return to the Mosaic-theocratic cultic system was impossible.

It is true, as Gore argues, that the synagogue was a human institution, but this fact is largely irrelevant since we have already seen that the temple is not and cannot be the pattern for Christian worship.[77] Further, as C. W. Dugmore argued in the 1940s, it is also a fact that the synagogue was the context in which the new covenant worship developed and evidently shaped apostolic and early Christian worship.[78] A synagogue was formed by a quorum of ten adult males. Each Sabbath two (or possibly three) services were held.[79] According to the Mishna, there were two parts to the synogogic liturgy, the *Shema* (Deut. 6:4: "Hear, O Israel, Yahweh our God, Yahweh is one") with the blessings ("Bless the Lord who is to be blessed") and prayer. The first part "might almost be described as the Jewish Creed."[80] As part of the morning service, a portion of the Pentateuch was read and a portion from the Prophets may have been read in the afternoon service.[81] There were variations in the liturgy to account for the cultic calendar (e.g., the day of atonement).[82] According to some accounts, there were eighteen benedictions (some of which have become notorious) followed by the Aaronic benediction (Num. 6:24–26). There were an exposition of Scripture (Mark 1:21–22; 6:2; John 6:59) and the singing of psalms. Worship was formal but simple and, with the possible exception of the sacraments, the elements of worship (Word and prayer) were present.

We will consider New Testament worship below, so we turn now to patristic worship which was, like the worship of the apostolic church, organized around three basic elements: word, prayer, and sacraments. As in temple and synagogic worship, services were held twice on the Christian Sabbath.[83] It appears that the early postapostolic church sang

77. Gore, *Covenantal Worship*, 102–6.
78. C. W. Dugmore, *The Influence of the Synagogue upon the Divine Office* (London: Oxford University Press, 1944).
79. Dugmore lists a morning, afternoon, and evening service. See ibid., 13.
80. Ibid., 16.
81. Ibid. There was debate among the rabbis over the afternoon reading.
82. Ibid., 15.
83. "Christian Sabbath" is the language of WLC 116.

only inspired songs without accompaniment.[84] Johannes Quasten says that the patristic church, though in favor of the use of music in worship, was quite opposed to the use of instruments in worship. The Sibylline Oracles rejected musical instruments as pagan.[85] "This repudiation of all instrumental music is also most apparent in Tertullian," who substituted "psalms and hymns" for instruments.[86] Chrysostom regarded the use of instruments under the Mosaic covenant as "concession of God to the weakness of the Jews."[87]

Scripture was read and expounded, prayers were offered, and the two divinely ordained sacraments were administered. This much is clear from the Didache (c. A.D. 110), where explicit directions were given regarding the apostolic injunction against eating meat offered to idols (Didache 6:30) and regarding the administration of baptism in the name of the Trinity (7:1–8:1). The Lord's Prayer was used (privately or publicly, 8:2–3) thrice daily; fellowship meals were held and the Lord's Supper was observed (9:1–4; 14:1), and discipline was exercised (9:5; 14:1). The Word was read and expounded (11:1–12).[88] Similar patterns are suggested in the fragmentary evidence of the letter of Pliny the Younger to the emperor Trajan. Writing as a pagan observer of Christian rites, Pliny noted that the Christians observed what we understand as the elements of worship. The same pattern is evident in Justin Martyr's *Apology* (c. A.D. 140).

Gradually, over the course of the thousand years before the Reformation, the medieval church reinstituted progressively aspects of the Mosaic ceremonial cultus including the introduction of musical instruments which

84. On the latter claim see David W. Music, *Instruments in Church: A Collection of Source Documents*, vol. 7, *Studies in Liturgical Musicology* (Lanham and London: Scarecrow, 1998), 27. Music's account of patristic worship is interesting because he has no personal interest in appealing to the fathers in support of the RPW.

85. Johannes Quasten, *Music and Worship in Pagan and Christian Antiquity*, trans. Boniface Ramsey (Washington, DC: National Association of Pastoral Musicians, 1973), 60, 72–75.

86. Ibid.

87. Ibid., 64. Quasten also notes that the early church did not sing in parts because they did not use instruments, and because singing in parts suggested a sort of individualism that was contrary to the divine unity and the "communion of souls" (ibid., 66–67).

88. "The Didache," in *The Apostolic Fathers in English*, trans. and ed. Michael W. Holmes, 3rd ed. (Grand Rapids: Baker Academic, 2006), 163–71.

had been suppressed in churches until the tenth century.[89] Their reintro-
duction was highly controversial. In the eleventh and twelfth centuries,
Baldric, the archbishop of Dol (northern France), argued that instruments
should be used in worship in order to make worship more emotionally
moving and interesting to the youth. In the same period Alred of Rievaulx
argued vehemently against the introduction of instruments of worship.
Though confessional Reformed folk would not sympathize much with
his arguments, it is worth noting how controversial the introduction of
musical instruments was in the eleventh century.[90] It is also important to
observe how the introduction of instruments in worship accompanied
the rise of sacerdotalism in medieval worship.

The Reformation saw itself as recovering not only the biblical pattern of worship, but the praxis of the early postapostolic church.[91] The
reformation of worship happened in stages. The first stage of the reformation of worship established the formal principle of the Reformation: *sola
scriptura*. The Reformed churches applied the Scripture principle most
thoroughly to the practice of worship. They did so by asking a different
question from what had been asked in the early days of the Reformation.
The Lutheran and Anglican question was, "what may we do?" Implicit in
this question is the notion that Christians may do in worship whatever is
not forbidden or, as Frame and Gore would have it, whatever is consistent
with Scripture. The Reformed reformation of worship beginning in 1537
in Geneva meant the institution of a capella psalmody as the predominant
music used in worship.[92] In some cases the Reformed congregations
sang the Decalogue and the Song of Simeon.[93] According to Elsie Anne
McKee, unlike "other Protestants, Calvinists (and most other Reformed)
did not sing human compositions, but they made use of the Psalter as a
treasury of public and private worship."[94]

89. Music, *Instruments in Church*, 43.
90. See ibid., 47–51.
91. See Old, *The Patristic Roots of Reformed Worship*.
92. John D. Witvliet, *Worship Seeking Understanding: Windows into Christian Practice*
(Grand Rapids: Baker, 2003), 203–29.
93. Ibid., 209.
94. Elsie Anne McKee, "Reformed Worship in the Sixteenth Century," in *Christian
Worship in Reformed Churches Past and Present*, ed. Lukas Vischer (Grand Rapids: Eerdmans, 2003), 28.

Contrary to Gore's account, and though it is sometimes overlooked, the principle of worship was one of Calvin's greatest concerns. In his response to the Leipzig Interim (1548) he summarized his understanding of the law of worship: "Who sees not that in this way the [will worship] condemned by Paul is opposed to the commandment of God? I deny, therefore, that any worship of God is legitimate, save that which is required according to his will."[95] He had before argued, "First, we must hold that the spiritual Worship of God does not consist either in external ceremonies, or any other kind of works whatsoever; and, secondly, that no Worship is legitimate unless it be so framed as to have for its only rule the will of him to whom it is performed. Both of these are absolutely necessary."[96]

Calvin's response to the principle of worship at work in the Interim anticipated many of the contemporary discussions. The proponents of the Interim argued from the example of David's dancing before the ark that what is not forbidden is permitted. Calvin responded that the narrative was not given in order to establish "fictitious modes of worship." Rather, David was "led to this by a special inspiration of the Spirit, which is always to be observed in the extraordinary actings of the saints."[97] In other words, things happened in the history of redemption, in the formation of the canon, that were extraordinary, illustrative of the history of redemption, typological, but not normative for us. He summarized his conviction in the 1559 *Institutes* by saying, "We gather that a part of the reverence that is paid to Him consists simply in worshiping Him as He commands, mingling no inventions of our own."[98] In contrast to Gore's reading of Calvin, it seems certain that at every point, Calvin articulated the substance of the RPW, and his successors applied that same principle to their circumstances.

Calvin's convictions were not unique. Among others, John Knox articulated them quite clearly in the Book of Discipline (1564) appended to his *History of the Reformation in Scotland.*[99] One of the errant assumptions

95. *The True Method of Giving Peace to Christendom*, in OS, 3:263. On "will-worship" see Ursinus, *Commentary on the Heidelberg Catechism*, 517–18.

96. Calvin, *True Method*, 3:260.

97. Ibid., 3:263.

98. *Institutes* 4.10.23.

99. See "The First Head of Doctrine," in William Croft Dickinson, ed., *John Knox's History of the Reformation in Scotland*, 2 vols. (New York: Philosophical Library, 1950), 2:281.

on which Gore premises his revisions seems to be that Calvin is the sole source of the Reformed tradition. This perception is unwarranted. In fact, streams flowing from across Europe fed the Reformed confession and practice of worship. Gradually, beginning with Zwingli,[100] Oecolampadius, Bucer, and the Swiss-German Reformers and continuing with Calvin, the French Reformed, the German Reformed, the Dutch Reformed, and culminating with English and Scottish Presbyterianism and Puritanism, the Reformed churches came to a remarkable consensus on the principle by which worship was to be guided, on the question to be asked, and on the understanding of that principle.

Considerable attention has been given to and a significant degree of disagreement exists over the nature of the adoption of the Westminster Standards by the American Presbyterians in 1729.[101] Less attention, however, has been paid to the fate of the 1644 Westminster Directory of Public Worship. Drafted and adopted before the Standards were complete, it represents the consensus of the Westminster divines and the mainstream of the seventeenth-century understanding of the RPW.[102]

The preface to the DPW says that there were three reasons for the creation of the Directory: First, as beneficial as the Book of Common Prayer (hereafter BCP) was to the Reformation, nearly a century later, the BCP had become a tool of oppression rather than liberation. The "prevailing Prelatic party in England under Archbishop Laud was bent on strict conformity, and on extending it to Scotland."[103] The Prelatic party was, in the words of the DPW, "urging the reading of *all* the prayers" (emphasis

---

100. The old judgment that Zwingli rejected all congregational singing has been overturned by the researches of Oskar Farner (1957) and Markus Jenny (1966). For a summary see Gottfried W. Locher, *Zwingli's Thought: New Perspectives*, Studies in the History of Christian Thought 25 (Leiden: Brill, 1981), 61. Locher does not speak directly to the principle by which Zwingli organized his service. This seems to be more a function of the task Locher set for the book, rehabilitating Zwingli for modern readers, and the sorts of questions he asked, than it is a reflection of Zwingli's own understanding of worship.

101. For a thorough discussion of these issues see David W. Hall, ed., *The Practice of Confessional Subscription* (Lanham, MD: University Press of America, 1995).

102. There is a modern language version of the DPW in Richard A. Muller and Rowland S. Ward, *Scripture and Worship: Biblical Interpretation and the Directory for Public Worship*, The Westminster Assembly and the Reformed Faith (Phillipsburg, NJ: P&R, 2007), 141–75.

103. Rowland Ward, "The Directory for Public Worship," in Muller and Ward, *Scripture and Worship*, 87.

added) so that "the many unprofitable and burdensome ceremonies" in it had become an occasion of "much mischief."[104] As a result of the imposition of the BCP, Christians were being kept from the table and ministers deprived of their living. The *de iure divino* Anglicans (e.g., Richard Hooker and Adrian Saravia) "have labored to raise the estimation of it to such a height, as if there were no other worship, or way of worship of God."[105] The second reason is that the BCP tended to give aid and comfort to the Roman critics of the Reformation as validating the mass.[106] Third, it had the unintended consequence of fostering "an idle and un-edifying ministry."[107] Rather than giving themselves to prayer, ministers were relying on the forms. The Directory laid claim on being a continuation of the work of the "first reformers," of whom "we are persuaded, that, were they now alive, they would join with us in this work."[108]

The DPW enjoined prayer, the reading and preaching of the Word, and the use of the sacraments. There should be little doubt about the original intent of the DPW regarding congregational singing. The divines wrote, "It is the duty of Christians to praise God publicly, by singing of psalms together in the congregation, and also privately in the family."[109] Everywhere congregational singing is mentioned in the DPW, only the psalms are mentioned. The word "hymn" does not occur in the DPW. A psalm is to be sung after the reading of the Word, before the sermon.[110] If anything is to be sung after the prayer following the sermon, it is to be a psalm.[111] In describing the interim between the first and second services, the DPW prescribes the singing of psalms.[112] So interested were the divines that the psalms should be sung that the DPW required that "every one that can read is to have a psalm book." They even instituted a system of "lining out" the psalm to be sung whereby a minister or precentor (literally, "foresinger") would

104. *A Directory for Publique Worship of God* (London, 1644), 1–2.
105. Ibid., 3.
106. Ibid., 4.
107. Ibid., 5.
108. Ibid., 6.
109. Ibid., 83.
110. Ibid., 14.
111. Ibid., 38–39.
112. Ibid., 57.

sing one line at a time, to be imitated by the congregation, so that the illiterate could sing along.[113]

However clear the intent of the divines in the DPW might seem to us today, by the early eighteenth century American Puritanism was becoming, in George Marsden's words, "Calvinistic evangelicalism."[114] In England, Isaac Watts's paraphrase of the psalms was finding an audience, and he argued that hymns and songs need only be based on "scriptural *themes*."[115] According to Julius Melton, the shift in English and American practice less than a century after the close of the Westminster Assembly created ambiguity about the intent of the synod in its adoption of the DPW in 1729.[116] By 1786 the general assembly had created a commission to revise the DPW to make it more amenable to American Presbyterian practice, which already included the singing of uninspired songs.[117] The revised DPW expressed no underlying "theory of worship."[118] Though there was a heated controversy over the proposed changes to Reformed worship, in the end the synod sided with the revisionists.

In principle, the RPW died in the late eighteenth century in the American Presbyterian Church.[119] Revivalism was exercising a radical influence upon Reformed worship.[120] According to both Julius Melton and Darryl Hart, it was revivalism that brought the RPW into question in the Presbyterian congregations in New York City. On his preaching tours in the area, George Whitefield had recommended that congregations use Isaac Watts's (1674–1748) paraphrase of the

113. Ibid., 84. George Marsden notes that, in time, in the American colonies, memories of the psalm tunes conflicted so that precentors struggled to keep the congregation on the same tune. See George M. Marsden, *Jonathan Edwards: A Life* (New Haven and London: Yale University Press, 2003), 143.

114. Marsden, *Jonathan Edwards*, 143.

115. Ibid., 144. Emphasis original.

116. See Julius Melton, *Presbyterian Worship in America: Changing Patterns since 1787* (Richmond: John Knox, 1967), 17.

117. Ibid., 18–28. Hart, *Recovering Mother Kirk*, 220, notes that the first American Presbyterian hymnal appeared in 1831.

118. See Melton, *Presbyterian Worship*, 28.

119. Ibid., 11–23; Hart, *Recovering Mother Kirk*, 220–35.

120. Hart, *Recovering Mother Kirk*, 190–94. For a brief survey of the literature on the effect of democratic American populism upon Reformed worship in the nineteenth century see Witvliet, *Worship Seeking Understanding*, 168–75.

psalms in place of the Psalter. The revivalists also advocated the use of uninspired songs in divine services on the ground that they fostered a deeper religious experience than the psalms.[121] Along with the introduction of uninspired songs in worship, Congregationalists and Presbyterians introduced instruments into Reformed services in the late eighteenth century.[122]

In the early nineteenth century, musical instruments were introduced in prominent Presbyterian churches, and by the middle of the nineteenth century the battle for exclusive a capella psalmody was essentially lost among American Presbyterians. Old School theologians such as Samuel Miller and Charles Hodge and their successors spent the rest of the century fighting a rearguard action.[123] The condition of the RPW was so dire in the late nineteenth century that it fell to Charles Augustus Briggs (1841–1913), whom the Old School had charged with heresy for his view of Scripture, to call for a return to the 1644 DPW.[124] According to Melton, the original DPW having been discarded, even the revised DPW received little attention from American Presbyterians through the nineteenth and into the twentieth centuries. Even among intentionally confessional breakaway denominations such as the Orthodox Presbyterian Church (1936) and the Presbyterian Church in America (1973) the original DPW has no official standing.

Among the Dutch Reformed churches, the move away from the RPW was more gradual, at least in North America. Article 69 of the Church Order of the Synod of Dort (1619) required:

> In the Churches only the 150 Psalms of David, the Ten Commandments, the Lord's Prayer, the Twelve Articles of Faith, the Song of Mary, that of Zacharias, and that of Simeon shall be sung. It is left to the individual Churches whether or not to use the hymn "Oh God! who art our Father." All other hymns are to be excluded from the Churches,

121. Marsden, *Jonathan Edwards*, 145.
122. Music connects this phenomenon with the influence of pietism. See Music, *Instruments in Church*, 127–29. For example, Justus Falckner (1672–1723) defended the use of instruments on the basis of their utility for fostering a more intense religious experience and church growth.
123. See Melton, *Presbyterian Worship*, 35–48.
124. Ibid., 118.

and in those places where some have already been introduced they are to be removed by the most suitable means.[125]

The original church order of the Dutch Reformed churches allowed only inspired songs to be sung in congregational worship, with two exceptions. It is fair to note that, in principle, the synod did not impose a canon of "inspired songs only" or exclusive psalmody. Nevertheless, the clear intent of the original Dutch Reformed church order was that Reformed congregations should sing inspired texts. That this was the assumption behind the 1619 Church Order becomes manifest when we remember that the Synod of Wezel in 1568 had ordered the singing of Dathenus's setting of the Psalter, and when we consider that the rejection of uninspired songs in stated services came amidst a wide-ranging reformation of worship and piety also including the rejection of icons as a violation of the second commandment.[126]

The Synod of Dordrecht of 1574 explicitly forbade the singing of any "hymns which are not found in the Bible." This rule was followed by Dordrecht in 1578, the Synod of Middleburg (1581), and the Synod of Gravenhage (1586).[127] Thus, by the time the Synod of Dort promulgated its Church Order it was still trying to implement the RPW (*semper reformanda*) among recalcitrant congregations.

It should be remembered that, in many cities in the Netherlands, the Reformation was still virtually a novelty as late as the early 1570s; thus congregations were being asked to move from the Roman mass to

125. "En Ecclesijs canentur CL Psalmi Davidis, Decalogus, Oratio Dominica, Symbolum Fidei, et hymni Mariae, Zachariae, Symeonis. Canticum autem *O God die onse Vader bist* etc. relinquitur in Ecclesiarum libertate, ut eodem utantur vel non utantur, prout visum fuerit. Reliqua Cantica ab Ecclesijs arcenuntur, et si quae forte in Ecclesias jam introducta sint, et ratione quam commodissima ex iisdem eliminabuntur." H. H. Kuyper, ed., *De Post-Acta of Nahandelingen van de Nationale Synode van Dordrecht in 1618 en 1619 Gehouden Een Historische Studie* (Amsterdam: Höveker & Wormser Boekhandel, 1899), 147.

126. Phyllis Mack Crew, *Calvinist Preaching and Iconoclasm in the Netherlands 1544–1569* (Cambridge: Cambridge University Press, 1978), 12–38, 140–81.

127. Hendrick DeCock, *According to the Command of the Lord: Rev. H. DeCock's Case against Hymns*, trans. J. A. Wanliss and W. L. Bredenhof (Surrey, BC: By the Editors, 1998). See also Idzerd Van Dellen and Martin Monsma, *The Church Order Commentary, Being a Brief Explanation of the Church Order of the Christian Reformed Church* (Grand Rapids: Zondervan, 1941), 2821–83.

the RPW in one step. Further, local congregations were often controlled by "churchwardens who were appointed by the town magistrates, and who frequently were not Reformed."[128] Educated Reformed ministers were in short supply. Many of the congregations had little knowledge of the Reformed faith.[129] Thus, for pastoral reasons, congregations were permitted to sing two inspired texts but "all other hymns" were restricted. Whatever one makes of the synod's approach to a thorny problem, their intent was the elimination from worship of all uninspired songs. That this is the case becomes clearer when one considers that the delegates to synod had no idea that national synods would become virtually impossible for many years. Thus, the reformation of worship undertaken at Dort was left incomplete not by principle but by political circumstances.[130]

After pressure to abandon the RPW began mounting in the early seventeenth century,[131] the Hervormde Kerk in the Netherlands, mother of the Reformed Church in America (RCA), gave up strict subscription to the Three Forms of Unity in the early eighteenth century and, with it, the RPW. The introduction of 192 uninspired songs into worship services of the Dutch Reformed churches in 1807 was one of the causes of the secession of 1834.[132] By the mid-nineteenth century the Reformed immigrants from the Netherlands to the USA found the RCA too liberal, partly due to their use of uninspired songs in public worship, so the immigrants formed the Christian Reformed Church in North America in 1857 by seceding from the RCA. Confessional Reformed practice dominated in the CRCNA "for a long time."[133] In 1876, when "a subscriber wrote to De

128. Richard Fitzsimmons, "Building a Reformed Ministry in Holland, 1572–85," in *The Reformation of the Parishes: The Ministry and the Reformation in Town and Country*, ed. Andrew Pettegree (Manchester: Manchester University Press, 1993), 176.

129. Ibid., 177–82.

130. Karel Blei, *The Netherlands Reformed Church 1571–2005*, trans. Allan J. Janssen (Grand Rapids: Eerdmans, 2006), 37; K. H. D. Halley, *The Dutch in the Seventeenth Century* (London: Thames and Hudson, 1972), 100–114.

131. A. C. Duke, *Reformation and Revolt in the Low Countries*, (London: Hambledon, 1990), 262.

132. John Kromminga, *The Christian Reformed Church: A Study in Orthodoxy* (Grand Rapids: Baker, 1949), 199; Gerrit J. tenZythoff, *Sources of Secession: The Netherlands Hervormde Kerk on the Eve of the Dutch Immigration to the Midwest*, Historical Series of the Reformed Church in America 17 (Grand Rapids: Eerdmans, 1987), 50–51.

133. Kromminga, *Christian Reformed Church*, 200.

Wachter [a Dutch-language church newspaper in the CRC] defending hymns," the confessional practice was stoutly defended in response.[134] Concessions to the use of uninspired hymns began in the 1880s and 1890s.[135] The preparation for official revision of the church order began in the 1920s, and in 1932 Article 69 of the church order was revised by synod to allow for the use of uninspired hymns that have been "approved and adopted by Synod."[136] The use of musical instruments seems to have gained acceptance in the CRCNA about the same time. Today, the use of uninspired songs and musical instruments has become so entrenched in most Dutch Reformed congregations that when the United Reformed Churches in North America (URCNA) were constituted in 1995, though many of the revisions introduced by the CRCNA in the twentieth century were rejected, the new church order (Art. 39) stipulates only that the "150 Psalms shall have the principal place in the singing of the churches. Hymns which faithfully and fully reflect the teaching of the Scripture as expressed in the Three Forms of Unity may be sung, provided they are approved by the consistory."[137]

There seems to be no question any longer in the CRCNA or URCNA whether hymns and instruments are appropriate or even how their use can be squared with the RPW. It is to be noted that, in this article, the URCNA church order does not *require* the singing of uninspired songs.[138] Only the psalms are required to be sung, but neither does it follow the original church order of Dort very closely. This is the language of conservative settlement not *semper reformanda*. Recent history, however, suggests that conservative settlement has not served the churches very well. Writing in 1937, J. L. Schaver pointed out that, though the use of uninspired hymns was now accepted in the CRC, the intention was that the denomination should remain "chiefly a Psalm-singing church."[139] Consider R. B. Kuiper's arguments in 1926 in favor of the introduction of uninspired hymns and musical instruments into Reformed worship. He conceded that the

134. Ibid.
135. Ibid.
136. Ibid., 203.
137. http://www.urcna.info/page.php?18 (accessed 22 September 2007).
138. Van Dellen and Monsma, *The Church Order Commentary*, 281.
139. J. L. Schaver, *Christian Reformed Church Order* (Grand Rapids: Zondervan, 1937), 77.

Reformed practice was exclusive psalmody, but he did not demonstrate a sound grasp of the RPW as confessed by the Reformed churches.[140] He argued that since ministers have long quoted hymns from the pulpit and since practice has been inconsistent with the RPW, and because the singing of uninspired hymns is the best way to acknowledge progressive revelation, "I submit the question whether a New Testament church may rest satisfied with these Old Testament songs. To do so strikes me as a serious, not to say sinful, lack of appreciation of the fuller revelation of God which we possess in the New Testament."[141]

Kuiper observed that "just now choir singing in public worship threatens to become a bone of serious contention" in the CRC. He knew of no objection to using a choir to lead congregational singing, but observed that their use in place of congregational singing led to the "evil" of sloth in congregational worship.[142] He defended the "solemn, stately music of the pipe organ" as "especially adapted for public worship" and recognized that, having admitted one instrument, it was difficult to forbid others. "There can hardly be any objection from principle to the playing of an orchestra, or even a band, on various occasions." He appealed to the use of the instruments in Psalm 150 and chided a fellow who objected to the dedication of a new organ.[143]

This same author, however, published what might be considered a companion volume in 1959, in which he attempted to restrain the forces he arguably helped to unleash thirty-three years earlier.[144] Nowhere in Kuiper's discussion of worship in 1926 does one find a clear, coherent statement of the principle by which Reformed churches had governed their worship since the sixteenth century. Having abandoned the confessional and historic Reformed understanding of the Reformed principle of worship, Kuiper attempted to preserve a "principle place" for the psalms. He insisted on "tasteful" music, and a limited place for the choir in public worship. Without the bedrock of the RPW, however, Kuiper's conserva-

---

140. R. B. Kuiper, *As to Being Reformed* (Grand Rapids: Eerdmans, 1926), 195–96.
141. Ibid., 197.
142. Ibid., 199–200.
143. Ibid., 201.
144. R. B. Kuiper, *To Be or Not to Be Reformed: Whither the Christian Reformed Church?* (Grand Rapids: Zondervan, 1959).

tism rested solely upon the good will and intentions of consistories and pastors. On the face of it, this seems like a strange and futile position for Calvinists (who confess the doctrine of total depravity) to take, as the existence of Kuiper's later volume suggests. Calvin, Ursinus, the Dutch Reformed churches, the Scottish Presbyterians, and the Westminster Divines understood this problem. This is why the only two choices they knew were the RPW and "will worship." It is hard to see how Kuiper was not offering a conservative version of the latter.

Scripture

This essay is quite satisfied with the traditional understanding of the RPW, but not with the way it has been neglected in the modern period. Neither is this essay entirely satisfied with the way the RPW has been appropriated by those who have been most faithful to it in our time. Thus, in this section I offer some considerations that might cause us to reconsider the RPW as confessed by the Reformed churches.

It is interesting that R. Kent Hughes warns that RPW "inclines those in the Reformed tradition" to draw from the cultus of the old covenant.[145] In contrast, we should think that the danger lies not in paying too much attention to the principle of worship under Moses, but, rather, too little attention to it. It should be recalled that, for a millennium, the Western church reinstituted the ceremonial cultus. In the sacerdotal system, the medieval church gradually reinstituted the Mosaic ceremonies. They did so because they did not appreciate the distinction between the substance or the elements of worship under Moses (Word, sacrament, and prayer) and the circumstances. Further, the medieval church did not appreciate the typological nature of the sacramental system under Moses and its fulfilment in Christ.

On this point, Paul's instruction in 1 Corinthians 10:11 is programmatic: "Now these things happened to them as an example, but they were written down for our instruction, on whom the end of the ages has come" (ESV). Paul regards the history of the old covenant as instructive for life

---

145. R. Kent Hughes, "Free Church Worship," in *Worship by the Book*, ed. D. A. Carson (Grand Rapids: Zondervan, 2002), 140.

and worship in the new covenant, which Paul characterizes as partaking in the consummate (eschatological) state. Indeed, he says in verse 4 that the "Rock" from which Israel drank in the wilderness was "Christ." Paul treats the Israelites as a Christian congregation from whom we should learn. For Paul, there is one covenant of grace: "I will be your God, you will be my people" (Gen. 17:1–14; Ex. 6:7; Jer. 7:23; 31:31–34). There is only one Lord, one faith, and one baptism, that is, one covenant of grace under different administrations (Eph. 4:5). Thus, even as we recognize that the administration of Word, sacrament, and prayer was shrouded in types and shadows (Heb. 8:5; 10:1: Col. 2:17), we should not introduce more discontinuity between Moses and Christ than did the apostle Paul. With this principle of substantial continuity (we worship the same God, are saved by the same grace, through the same faith alone, in the same Savior alone), and the administrative differences, we can learn profitably from the history of redemption before Christ.

Throughout Scripture, the act of worship is shaped by and related to God's acts of redemption in the closest possible way. This is evident at the Passover (Ex. 12) when Israel, seeing their redemption through the last and most horrible judgment against their oppressor, "bowed down and worshiped" their Redeemer in awe (Ex. 12:27). According to Exodus 3 when Moses met the angel of Yahweh at Horeb, God revealed himself as the God of Abraham, Isaac, and Jacob; that is, he revealed himself as a covenant-making and covenant-keeping God. He also revealed himself as a holy God. He demanded that Moses recognize his moral purity, uniqueness, and transcendence by removing his sandals. His special presence made the ordinary (the secular) into the sacred. To Moses, Yahweh promised that he would signify to Israel that it was indeed he, Yahweh, the God of the covenant, who had delivered Israel, when they gathered in formal worship before him at "the mountain of God." In Exodus 4, Yahweh instructs Moses as to what is to be said to Pharaoh: "Thus says Yahweh . . . let my son go that he may worship me" (Ex. 4:23; cf. 7:16; 8:1, 20; 9:1, 13; 10:3, etc.). That meeting at Sinai was to be the culmination of redemption whereupon Yahweh was to formalize his relation to Israel as his adopted "son," and his national, covenanted people. He would reveal his law, and they would swear absolute fealty to him.

The Sinaitic law was constitutional for their relations to him. The law not only stipulated whom Israel was to worship (Ex. 20:2), Yahweh their gracious deliverer and sovereign God, but how (Ex. 20:4–5). The God of Abraham, Isaac, and Jacob, the God of Moses, will not be worshiped in any other way than he has revealed in his Word. This much is clear from the example of Jeroboam (1 Kings 12). His first act of governance was the establishment of an alternative system of worship. To keep the people from going to Jerusalem to worship Yahweh in the city of David, he set up golden calves in Bethel and Dan and declared, "Behold your gods, O Israel, who brought you up out of the land of Egypt" (1 Kings 12:28). The people were to worship Yahweh by means of the calves. First Kings condemns this act for the sin that it was (1 Kings 12:30). It was as much a violation of the RPW as it was idolatry. Israel had been warned about this very thing. In preparation for the invasion of Canaan, the Lord of the covenant promised to destroy the nations before his people (Deut. 12:29). His chief complaint against the nations was their pagan worship.[146] He warned,

> And after they have been destroyed before you, be careful not to be ensnared by inquiring about their gods, saying, "How do these nations serve their gods? We will do the same." You must not worship Yahweh your God in their way, because in worshiping their gods, they do all kinds of detestable things Yahweh hates. They even burn their sons and daughters in the fire as sacrifices to their gods. (Deut. 12:29–31)

Here Scripture connects both the first and second commandments. Not only are we not to worship the pagan gods; we are to worship the true God truly. It is significant, then, that to this warning he added, "See that you do all I command you; do not add to it or take away from it." This principle is not confined to the old covenant because God's gracious salvation of his people through faith in Christ the Mediator is not

---

146. Some of the material for this section is revised from an ecclesiastical document I drafted at the request of the Escondido United Reformed Church, "Principles of Reformed Worship," adopted by the consistory on 19 September 2000 (accessed 23 September 2006), available from http://www.wscal.edu/clark/principlesofreformedworship.php. The use and revision of this material does not imply ecclesiastical sanction for the opinions expressed here.

confined to the old covenant. Indeed, it seems clear from the New Testament that it was with the preincarnate Christ that believers had to do throughout the old covenant. God the Son has always been the mediator and revealer of the Father. He is "the Word" (John 1:1). Moses wrote of Christ (John 5:46).

According to Hebrews 12, Moses ascended Mount Sinai but, in Christ, we have come to Mount Zion. We have not come to an empirical mountain (Heb. 12:18), but we have come to "the city of the living God . . . to angels, to the spirits of the righteous" (Heb. 12:18–24). The imagery from Sinai is unmistakable (Ex. 19:16–20). The parallelism between the two mountains is clear. The writer to the Hebrews takes us, as it were, to the foot of Sinai and to the terror that it produced. At the top of Sinai dwells Yahweh in unapproachable glory (1 Tim. 6:16). Hebrews 12:22 reminds us, however, that in the new covenant, we have come to "Mount Zion and the city of the living God." At the top of Mount Zion is "Jesus the mediator of a new covenant" (Heb. 12:24). According to Hebrews, we are to picture Jesus ascended to the glory he enjoyed with the Father before the incarnation (John 17:5).

Given that neither our faith, nor our salvation, nor the object of our worship has changed substantially since Mount Sinai, we should not expect our Lord's revealed will concerning the principle by which he is to be worshiped in public assembly to have changed either, and there is every evidence in the New Testament that it has not. Nowhere do we see any repealing of the principle announced under Moses. The circumstances of worship have changed with the change in the administration of the covenant of grace. The typological and shadowy ceremonies, having been fulfilled, are abrogated, but the principle by which we appear corporately before Yahweh in public assembly has not, because he has not changed.

Further, wherever we see the apostolic church gathered in worship (e.g., Acts 2:42; 13:2), we are to assume that it is conducted with the same reverence and according to the spirit of the same principle announced under Moses. This explains Paul's metaphorical use of ceremonial language to describe the new covenant people of God (Rom. 12:1–2). Even the charismatic worship of the Corinthian congregation is to be orderly (1 Cor. 14:26). Hebrews, which spends eleven chapters arguing for the superiority of the new covenant over the old (Mosaic) covenant, invokes implicitly the RPW: we are to offer God "acceptable" worship "with reverence and awe" (Heb. 12:28). Embedded in the adjective "acceptable" in this context is the notion that worship is strictly regulated by the revealed will of God. The writer to the Hebrews invokes a category of thought familiar to his readers. In Exodus 28:38 (in the LXX) Aaron is said to bear the guilt of the people so that their offerings would be "acceptable" or "approved" or "favorable" to Yahweh (e.g., Lev. 1:3; 19:5). That which is "acceptable" is what is prescribed and ordained by God himself. God's people were not entitled to decide for themselves what they would offer or how. To be sure, we are "acceptable" to God only on account of the righteousness of Christ imputed and received through faith alone. Nevertheless, we are no freer to decide how we will worship Christ now than God's people were under Moses. We have been freed from the Mosaic ceremonies but we are not free to will-worship. It is these passages and many others like them from which the Reformed churches have deduced the RPW, which is nothing but the application of that Scripture or canonical principle to the act of corporate worship.

Confession

Contrary to the impression left by some contemporary discussion, the RPW is not the product of the fevered imaginations of the British Reformed churches. It was the universal confession of all the Reformed churches in the sixteenth and seventeenth centuries. BC 7 says in part, "For since the whole manner of worship which God requires of us is written in them at large, it is unlawful for any one, though an apostle, to teach otherwise than we are now taught in the Holy Scriptures."[147] Because we regard the Scriptures as the sufficient rule for faith and life (*sola scriptura*), we do only that in worship that is taught explicitly or required implicitly in God's Word. BC 32 also says in part: "Therefore we reject all human innovations and all laws imposed on us, in our worship of God, which bind and force our consciences in any way."[148] One of the great functions

147. *Creeds*, 3:388.
148. Ibid., 3:423.

of the Reformed confession regarding worship is that it liberates believers from the tyranny of subjectivism in public worship. No one can require of God's people that they do anything in worship that does not have express or implied positive warrant from God's Word. The exact same doctrine is taught in HC Q. 96: "What does God require in the second Commandment? A: That we in no wise make any image of God, nor worship Him in any other way than He has commanded us in His Word."[149] According to the HC, the same moral will that prevents us from making any representations of the deity (including, as the subsequent questions make explicit, representations of the Second Person of the Trinity) establishes a test. This is generic Reformed theology, piety, and practice.

The way in which this principle was understood in the Netherlands and in Heidelberg is clear from history. The early Reformed churches were a capella singers of God's Word. Upon the introduction of a Reformed church order in the Palatinate in 1563, all the organs were removed and only psalms were sung.[150] The Reformed churches of France and the Lowlands (Belgium) followed the same practice. As they gathered at night or in secret to worship, while Philip II's troops searched for them, they sang psalms.[151]

The Westminster divines adopted the very same principle of worship in the mid-seventeenth century. WCF 21.1 says: "But the acceptable way of worshiping the true God is instituted by himself, and so limited by his own revealed will, that he may not be worshiped according to the imaginations and devices of men, or the suggestions of Satan, under any visible representation, or any other way not prescribed in the Holy Scripture."[152] How the divines themselves understood this articulation of the RPW is clear from the DPW. The way this principle was understood is clear from the history of the period. As Rowland Ward notes, on "Scriptural grounds singing was unaccompanied by instruments in Scotland and in almost all other Reformed Churches, and in May 1644 Parliament ordered the

---

149. Ibid., 3:343.

150. J. I. Good, *The Origin of the Reformed Church in Germany* (Reading, PA: Danel Miller, 1887), 147–48; Wilhelm Niesel, ed., *Bekenntnisschriften und Kirchenordnungen der nach Gottes Wort Reformierten Kirche* (Zürich: Evangelischer Verlag A. G. Zollikon, 1938), 209.

151. For an account of one example see Crew, *Calvinist Preaching*, 68–70.

152. *Westminster Confession of Faith* (Glasgow: Free Presbyterian Publications, reprint, 1997), 89–90.

removal of organs from all churches in England which had them. Hence the Confession had no need to refer to that subject."[153]

The difference between the original and the modern understanding of this principle is illustrated by A. A. Hodge's comments on this section of the confession. He observed that the confession forbids "all manner of *will-worship*, of self-chosen acts and forms of worship." Such, he said, "are an abomination to God."[154] So far, he writes like one of the divines. The next sentence, however, is concessive. "At the same time, of course, there are, as the Confession admits, chapter i., §6 '*some circumstances* concerning the worship of God, and the government of the Church, common to human actions and societies."[155] This is all true and part of the Reformed confession, but one wonders whether the rhetorical force of such concession (which was followed by a strong reaffirmation of the RPW), in 1869, was not to carve out space for a conservative revision of the RPW since the original understanding of the RPW two centuries earlier was hardly observed in American Presbyterianism. After all, when the Westminster divines worked out the DPW in 1644 (before the confession and catechisms were even complete), they did not mention the word "circumstance."

One reason for this was almost certainly that the idea of "circumstances" and "adiaphora" has often been an opportunity for mischief. We have already observed how Frame and Gore, to name but two authors, have proposed a radical revision of the notion of "circumstances," so that it is now to be used to leverage the very notion of elements, with the result that what was once intentionally forbidden (e.g., drama and dancing in public worship) can now be admitted.

Another reason for recovering the classical Reformed understanding of the RPW, already suggested, is the matter of Christian liberty. Worship is not an optional assembly for the Christian. When God's people are gathered on the Christian Sabbath, the day of "sacred assembly" (Lev. 23:3), and the Word and sacraments are administered, the Christian must

153. Rowland Ward, *The Westminster Confession of Faith: A Study Guide*, new expanded ed. (Wantirna, Australia: New Melbourne, 2004), 188.
154. A. A. Hodge, *The Confession of Faith: A Handbook of Christian Doctrine Expounding the Westminster Confession* (Edinburgh: Banner of Truth Trust, reprint, 1983), 272. Emphasis original.
155. Ibid., emphasis original.

attend. If he must attend, then the church must not burden his conscience with any ceremony, rite, or element that God has not required. Thus the principle at stake here is the freedom of the Christian to worship only as God has revealed.

Judging by much of the contemporary literature on Reformed worship, there seems to be insufficient care for the consciences of God's people. Certainly our sixteenth- and seventeenth-century forebears were more conscious of this problem, since they were either emerging from Rome or resisting the imposition of ostensibly indifferent practices—if they were truly indifferent, why did the authorities wish to impose them? They had experienced the crisis created when those in ecclesiastical authority demanded acts of congregants in worship (e.g., adoration of the consecrated host) that clearly contradicted God's Word. As a matter of history, the DPW was intended to liberate Reformed Christians from exactly the sorts of practices the Prelatic party wanted to impose upon them and which some would reimpose on Reformed congregations today. Henry Hammond, in his 1645 exposition of the DPW, explained that the Directory intentionally avoided "six basic characteristics": "(1) a prescribed form or liturgy, (2) outward or body worship, (3) uniformity in worship, (4) the people having a part through responses in prayers, hymns, and readings, (5) the division of prayers into several collects or portions, and (6) ceremonies such as kneeling in communion, the cross in baptism, and the ring in marriage."[156] By recovering the understanding of the Reformed principle of worship embodied in the DPW, confessional Reformed churches in the sideline and borderline denominations may begin to implement the principle *ecclesia reformata, semper reformanda* in its true sense, by recovering the Reformed theology and practice of worship.

Recovery

We are at something of a stalemate. Most of the Reformed community no longer practices in worship what it confesses, at least as that confession

---

156. Rowland S. Ward, "Elements and Practice," in Richard A. Muller and Rowland S. Ward, *Scripture and Worship: Biblical Interpretation and the Directory for Public Worship*, The Westminster Assembly and the Reformed Faith (Phillipsburg, NJ: P&R, 2007), 117–18.

was understood originally. Nevertheless, if we are to keep faith with our confession, we must begin to recover our practice of worship. One of the sticking points in this discussion is exclusive a capella psalmody. Apart from the RPCNA and a few other like-minded denominations, most of the Reformed world today seems unwilling to commit itself once again to exclusive a capella psalmody. On the other side, exclusive psalmodists are nothing if not committed to the original understanding of the RPW. There are two ways forward. The first is for those who have, as a matter of principle, substantially rejected the RPW to admit as much, so that we can clear the air. It is not helpful when radical revisions of the RPW are presented as mere applications of it. For the rest who profess adherence to the RPW but who are inconsistent with it in practice, it is a matter of time, pastoral care, and patient instruction to help elders and laity to understand the RPW once again. Such instruction will begin to foster the will to adhere to it. There are reasons to think this might happen. As suggested earlier in this work, there is a sort of recovery of Reformed theology, piety, and practice occurring in our time. There is no reason why we cannot include the recovery of the RPW into the agenda along with the law/gospel hermeneutic, historic covenant theology, and the means of grace.

There are those, however, who might wish to recover the ancient Christian practice of a capella worship and the historic understanding of the RPW, but who chafe at being restricted to singing psalms. Some objections that have been voiced, for example, that the Psalter is not christocentric enough, hardly warrant a response. One wonders by which hermeneutic a Reformed reader of the Psalms could conclude they are not christocentric. It is evident that the apostles did not have such scruples as they appealed to the Psalter frequently in their preaching and teaching. The most quoted passage from the Hebrew Scriptures is Psalm 110. Others do not resist exclusive psalmody on the basis that the Psalms are not christocentric, but on the basis that the psalms are typological. They ask a reasonable question: what is there about the RPW that limits Christians to songs from the typological epoch in redemptive history?

It seems unlikely that the exclusive psalmodists will succeed in convincing hymn singers to embrace exclusive psalmody, but perhaps both sides can move and find common ground and peace in the middle in a way that is faithful to the RPW. I propose that those who presently sing uninspired songs should be willing to give them up in favor of inspired, canonical songs only. As is shown below, there is no evidence that the apostolic congregations sang uninspired songs. To those who do not presently restrict themselves to canonical texts it must be asked whether they are willing to give up uninspired songs in favor of New Testament songs. As a matter of principle, it is hard to see how the answer could be no. Where in Scripture are God's people required to sing uninspired songs? We may ask similar questions about the use of instruments in public worship. On what ground do we introduce them into stated services? Where in Scripture are new covenant believers commanded to employ instruments in public worship? It is true that the Psalms and other typological places in Scripture frequently speak of using instruments, for example, Psalm 150:3–5. It is also true, however, that the Psalms contain much language that Christians take upon their lips with more hesitation. Consider the imprecatory language in Psalm 68:21–23:

> But God will strike the heads of his enemies,
>> the hairy crown of him who walks in his guilty ways.
> The Lord said,
>> "I will bring them back from Bashan,
> I will bring them back from the depths of the sea,
> that you may strike your feet in their blood,
>> that the tongues of your dogs may have their portion from the
>> foe." (ESV)

Ordinarily Christians understand such imprecatory language to apply metaphorically, in the new covenant, to sin, the flesh, and the devil. The literal sense of this language was intended for the national covenanted people of God. That covenant is fulfilled and with it the imprecatory language. Christ bore God's wrath against his enemies for all his elect.

It is incoherent to appeal to the literal sense of the language of the Psalter in one case to justify the modern use of one old covenant, typological practice (the use of instruments) and to treat figuratively other practices in the Psalter (e.g., sacrifices and religious war). The tension is obvious. Those who defend instruments in this way are engaging in a highly selective use of the Psalter. All the language of the Psalter belongs to the old covenant; it is all part of the civil and ceremonial codes that have been fulfilled in Christ. A similar hermeneutical problem awaits those who would appeal to the existence of instruments (*kithara*, a harp or lyre) in the Revelation (5:8; 14:2; 15:2; 18:22) as a ground for their use in new covenant worship. First of all, any appeal to the *kithara* of the Apocalypse must presuppose its literal reality. This would entail positing the literal existence of four living beasts, a scroll, the notion that Jesus is literally a lamb, and all these problems would arise from such a hermeneutic applied only to Revelation 5:8. A sound reading of these passages understands them to be highly and intentionally figurative.[157] It also understands that they do not intend to serve as a pattern for public worship during the interadventual period of redemptive history.

Whatever is done in worship must either be an element (Word and prayer) or a circumstance. Since musical instruments are obviously not an element, some conservative Reformed writers have redefined "circumstances" to include them. Edmund Clowney, speaking for many conservative Reformed folk who have revised the historic understanding of the RPW, suggested that musical instruments be regarded as a circumstance and therefore as permissible.[158] One difficulty with such an approach is that, once this box has been opened, it will not be able to contain all the things one might want to put in it. For example, if instruments are circumstances, then why are not sacrifices also circumstances? If so, then circumstances can be fulfilled, since no one who argues that instruments are circumstantial also argues that the typological sacrifices should be reinstituted. In that case, moving musical instruments into the category of circumstances does not really advance the case for their reinstitution in

---

157. G. K. Beale, *The Book of Revelation: A Commentary on the Greek Text*, The New International Greek Testament Commentary (Grand Rapids: Eerdmans, 1999), 358. See also ibid., 37–69; Dennis E. Johnson, *Triumph of the Lamb: A Commentary on Revelation* (Phillipsburg, NJ: P&R, 2001), 6–23.

158. E. P. Clowney, "Distinctive Emphases in Presbyterian Church Polity," in *Pressing toward the Mark: Essays Commemorating Fifty Years of the Orthodox Presbyterian Church*, ed. Charles G. Dennison and Richard C. Gamble (Philadelphia: Committee for the Historian of the Orthodox Presbyterian Church, 1986), 101.

the new covenant, since one would have to argue that though the sacrifices have been fulfilled in Christ, musical instruments have not been fulfilled. It is hard to see how such an argument cannot be special pleading.[159]

The typological, Israelite cultus is totalitarian. It is impossible to observe part of it literally and part of it figuratively. The musical instruments of Psalm 81:2–3 (vv. 3–4 in the MT) are situated in the context of the theocratic ("old covenant") "new moon" and "feast day." In the light of Colossians 2:16 where the Mosaic cultic calendar is explicitly canceled, how can one keep the instruments of Psalm 81 but not the calendar to which they are connected? That is why the older Reformed practice was to assign the whole Israelite cultus to metaphorical observance in the new covenant. For example, Cotton assigned the use of instruments to the ceremonial aspect of the typo-logical period but the singing of psalms to the moral aspect.[160] This seems to be the apostolic mode. Paul exhorts us to be "living sacrifices" (Rom. 12:1). We are not literal sacrifices, laid on an altar, killed, and burned. We are figurative sacrifices. The gift that the Philippians sent to Paul was this sort of sacrifice (Phil. 4:18). Meeting the material needs of the congregation is a metaphorical sacrifice (Heb. 13:16). The church is Christ's temple, and we are also priests offering "spiri-tual sacrifices" (1 Peter 2:5). The older Reformed approach to this problem recognized the proper way of making use of imagery and language from the typological period, at least with respect to worship. For these reasons, it is not satisfactory to import instruments into the category "circumstance."

The question remains, what biblical, confessional, and principled rationale is there for the use of musical instruments? It seems clear from the history of the Reformed churches since the eighteenth century that the chief rationale for the introduction of uninspired praise and musical instruments has been pragmatic. We introduced them on the premise that they would improve the quality of religious experience (QIRE). It seems nearly impossible to see how one can say that Scripture requires the use of uninspired praise and instruments in Christian worship. The introduc-

159. *Pace* Thomas, "The Regulative Principle," 92.
160. Cotton, *The Singing of the Psalmes*, 5–7.

tion of musical instruments into Reformed worship marks a retreat from our confession on grounds that are less than compelling.

An unstated assumption behind the argument from quality seems to be that somehow the God whom we worship values the quality of our singing (as enhanced by instruments). This is a strange assumption. Repeatedly Scripture commands us to "praise Yahweh" (e.g., Pss. 104:35; 105:45; 106:1). References to the quality of the singing of God's people, however, are utterly lacking. The argument from quality seems to rely more upon middle-class Western values than upon biblical or Reformed principle. As a historical matter, the historical evidence from the synagogue is that singing was done without the aid of instruments. The historical evidence from the early postapostolic church is that worship was conducted without instruments. Many, if not most, of the congregants in Reformed churches in the sixteenth century would have been illiterate, and yet none of them used instruments.[161] If it was possible for musically illiterate folk to worship a capella in those periods, it is possible today.

Finally, under this topic, it might be argued that if we are to abandon musical instruments in worship, then we should also abandon modern technologies such as microphones. It is true that both the instrument and the microphone are media, but it is not obvious that musical instruments are just like microphones in every respect. Microphones are used to amplify sound. It is not obvious that amplification fundamentally changes what the minister says or the way he says it. It does not seem that there is anything religious or irreligious about the use of a microphone, but the same is not true of musical instruments. By its nature music is affective. That is its intent. The instrument changes the nature of the affect of a given piece of music. For example, Richard Wagner's *Ring Cycle* (1848–74) is perhaps one of the most affective pieces of music I have experienced. To change the instrumentation of those operas would fundamentally alter them. Similarly, adding musical instruments to congregational singing, in the nature of things, changes the act of singing. The congregation is now singing *with* the instrument. The instrument necessarily colors and leads

---

161. In 1586, the Reformed congregation at Ridderkirk, the Netherlands, had to abandon their attempt to sing metrical psalms because of illiteracy. See Alastair Duke, *Reformation and Revolt in the Low Countries* (London: Hambledon, 1990), 262.

the singing. By definition, an element of worship (Word, sacrament, and prayer) is revealed in scripture (*sola scriptura*). A circumstance, however, is not. A circumstance is where we worship and when, but not how we worship.

To determine whether something is really only a circumstance, let us conduct a thought experiment. What would happen in most congregations were we, without explanation, to take away the minister's microphone? Most likely, those farthest from the pulpit or hardest of hearing would complain but there would be no uprising. Were we to do the same with musical instruments, the results would be rather different. Why? Because musical instruments do not merely amplify sound, in the nature of things, they affect God's people and effect a change in an element of worship in a way that mere circumstances (time, place, posture) do not. They become elemental to worship because of the nature of the created relations between humans, sound, emotion, and religion.[162]

Next, just as conservative Reformed folk should revise their practice to bring it in line with the RPW, those who currently sing only psalms should be willing to enlarge their songbook, not to include uninspired songs, but to include inspired canonical songs. It is at this point that the defense of exclusive psalmody seems weakest. The church may not require of a Christian that he should sing uninspired songs as this constitutes a breach of the RPW and the implied contract between the congregant and the church to protect the liberty of conscience of the Christian. Exclusive psalmodists should be willing to include or at least tolerate the singing of inspired canonical songs since every canonical text is the inspired Word of God. This proposal has the obvious benefit of answering the objection that singing only psalms relegates the church to singing only matter from the typological epoch of redemption. It also has the benefit of demonstrating that D. A. Carson's characterization of the RPW as a form of traditionalism parallel to devotion to the Book of Common

---

162. Researchers such as Mark Jude Tramo, investigating the connection between neurophysiology and music, are concluding that the human brain is "hardwired" so that there may be a "universal set of rules that governs how a limited number of sounds can be combined in an infinite number of ways." William J. Cromie, "Music on the Brain: Researchers Explore the Biology of Music," *Harvard University Gazette* (March 22, 2001); http://www.news.harvard.edu/gazette/2001/03.22/04-music.html (accessed 26 September 2007).

Prayer is incorrect.[163] We are not, or ought not be, "traditionalists" in the sense Carson uses the word. We have a grand tradition, but we must act on principle. If a contemporary setting of a psalm (or other portion of Scripture) is faithful to God's Word and appropriate for corporate worship, we should use it.

Toward advancing this case I offer three arguments. First, though there can be little doubt that the psalms should have "the principal place in the singing of the churches," it is not absolutely certain that the first-century church sang only psalms.[164] Matthew 26:30 says that Jesus and the disciples, "having sung a hymn" (*hymneō*), went out to the Mount of Olives. It is certain that the "hymn" they sang was not an uninspired song, but the *Hallel*, that is Psalms 113–118.[165] As part of his reformation of the church at Corinth, Paul says that, whenever they gather together, "each has a psalm, each has a teaching, each has a revelation" (1 Cor. 14:26). Given the charismatic context, it is possible that Paul uses *psalmos* generically to refer to a song of praise, but it is gratuitous to ignore the possibility that *psalmos* actually refers to a canonical psalm.[166] It is true that Acts 16:25 says that Paul and Silas were singing (*hymneō*) while they were imprisoned. Given, however, that the verb "to sing" does not necessarily denote the singing of an uninspired text, the verb here does not offer proof of the use of such by the apostle. The writer of Hebrews uses *hymneō* in 2:12, quoting the LXX text of Psalm 22:22. In the context of Psalm 22, what is being sung in the "midst of the congregation" is certainly a psalm, and there is no reason to think that the writer to the Hebrews is working with any other assumption. If we keep in mind the principle that we may do only what we must do in public worship, then the argument for the use of uninspired songs cannot be said to have met that burden of proof.

Second, it has seemed to scholars of the New Testament that there are a number of songs in the New Testament. Among these are usually included the Magnificat (Luke 1:46–55), the Benedictus (Luke 1:68–79), and the Nunc Dimittis (Luke 2:29–32). Beyond the traditional songs of

---

163. D. A. Carson, ed., *Worship by the Book* (Grand Rapids: Zondervan, 2002), 54–55.

164. Church Order of the United Reformed Churches, Article 39.

165. W. F. Albright and C. S. Mann, *Matthew*, Anchor Bible 26 (Garden City, NY: Doubleday, 1971), 326.

166. E.g., the NIV and the ESV both translate this noun as "hymn."

the Gospels, scholars have identified the Carmen Christi (Phil. 2:5–11), Colossians 1:15–20, as well as several brief songs in the Apocalypse (Rev. 4:8, 11; 5:9–10, 12–13; 7:10; 15:3–4).[167] Though some of these songs have distinctively explicit christological language, several of them are indistinguishable from the sort of things found in the Psalter.

Third, there is a genuine difference between new and old covenant worship, a difference that is revealed in a striking way in the story of the encounter of Jesus with the Samaritan woman (John 4:5–29). Where the woman at the well was concerned about the circumstances or accidents (i.e., that which can change) of worship, our Lord was concerned about the substance (i.e., that which makes something what it is) of worship. In John 4:23–24 Jesus says: "But the hour is coming, and is now here, when the true worshipers will worship the Father in spirit and truth, for the Father is seeking such people to worship him. God is spirit, and those who worship him must worship in spirit and truth" (ESV). Following Calvin, most Reformed interpreters have understood Jesus' words "worship in spirit and in truth" to mean that we must worship the true God in the correct way.[168] Though it is doubtless true that we must worship the true God truly, is it possible that this text says something more pointed?

Robert Rayburn and Robert Letham have both suggested a different way of reading this text that I believe is more faithful to the context of Jesus' remarks to the woman at the well and that becomes instructive in the current discussions.[169] Rather than understanding "spirit" to mean "that

167. E.g., Ralph P. Martin, *Worship in the Early Church* (Grand Rapids: Eerdmans, 1964; reprint, 1974), 46–52. In contrast, exclusive psalmodists typically deny that there are such things as NT hymns. It is true that it is a question whether Colossians 1:15–20 should be regarded as a hymn. See Steven M. Baugh, "The Poetic Form of Col 1:15–20," *WTJ* 47 (1985): 227–44.

168. See e.g., John Calvin, *Calvin's New Testament Commentaries*, trans. John W. Fraser et al. (Grand Rapids: Eerdmans, 1960), 4:101; Terry Johnson, "The Regulative Principle," 11–12. Leon Morris, *The Gospel according to John* (Grand Rapids: Eerdmans, 1971), 270, rejects the identification of "spirit" here with the person of the Holy Spirit. He takes it to refer to the human attitude toward God. Together with "truth," the expression means "complete sincerity and complete reality in our approach to God." Ernst Haenchen, *A Commentary on the Gospel of John*, trans. Robert Funk, 2 vols. Hermeneia (Philadelphia: Fortress, 1984), 1:223, takes a more radically subjective interpretation of "spirit and truth" by referring it to our experience, God by the gift of the Spirit enabling us to know the revelation.

169. Rayburn, *O Come, Let Us Worship*, 104–16. See also Robert Letham, *The Holy Trinity* (Phillipsburg, NJ: P&R, 2004), 415–17.

which is immaterial," and "truth" to refer primarily to "propositions that accord with reality and the revelation of God" (as distinct from those which do not), we should capitalize Spirit and understand it to refer primarily to the person of the Holy Spirit. In the same way, we should capitalize Truth and see it as a reference to the Second Person of the Trinity, who was addressing the woman at the well.

There are several reasons why we should interpret this text this way. First, it is difficult to imagine that, given the richness of the apostle John's theology, and given the way he often loads key terms with double meaning (e.g., "above/again" in John 3:3), John intended us to read this discourse as flatly as the traditional reading suggests. "Spirit" in the Gospel of John does not mean chiefly "immaterial." John uses the word in both senses perhaps in John 3:6, but in John 3:8 the reference is personal and Trinitarian, and he follows this pattern in John 3:34 and in John 6:63; 7:39; 14:17. John 14:26 makes this association explicit.[170]

Let us follow the narrative in John 4 to substantiate these claims. In John 4:10 Jesus says, "If you knew the gift of God and who is speaking to you . . ." In the traditional interpretation, this line is not very significant. In the proposed trinitarian interpretation, however, it is weighted more heavily.[171] In the trinitarian interpretation "gift" here stands for the Holy Spirit and Jesus' reference to himself stands in the same place here as "Truth" does in verse 24. The trinitarian reading is the strongest way to understand Jesus' subsequent reference to "living water." The "water" (v. 14) that Jesus gives is eschatological (i.e., from heaven and ultimate as opposed to earthly and provisional). In response to Jesus' ethical challenge (vv. 16–19), however, the woman wants to talk again about circumstance (v. 20), but Jesus (v. 21) wants to speak about himself and the Spirit, and he does so in eschatological terms. The force of the expression "the hour

170. See also the close connection between the "spirit" and "truth" in John 15:26 and 16:13. This understanding of John's use of "Spirit" is analogous to Geerhardus Vos's interpretation of "true" and "truth" in the Johannine corpus. Geerhardus Vos, "True and Truth in the Johannine Writings," in Richard B. Gaffin Jr., ed., *Redemptive History and Biblical Interpretation: The Shorter Writings of Geerhardus Vos* (Phillipsburg, NJ: P&R, 1980), 343–51.

171. The reading proposed here is the antithesis of that offered in John Henry Bernard, *A Critical and Exegetical Commentary on the Gospel according to St. John*, 2 vols., International Critical Commentary (Edinburgh: T&T Clark, 1928), 1:144–45, which concludes that we should not derive from this text thoughts that are "peculiar to Christian doctrine."

comes and now is" in verses 21 and 23 is unmistakable. In subsequent occurrences (John 5:25, 28; 16:2, 25, 32), it is clear that "the hour" refers to the final (eschatological) age. Jesus characterizes worship in the new covenant, the age that anticipates the return of Christ and the consummation of all things, as eschatological. Contrary to some interpretations, worship "in the Spirit" is not primarily a reference to the age commenced by Pentecost (which does commence "the last days"; Acts 2:17; Heb. 1:2; James 5:3; 2 Peter 3:3), but to the person of the Holy Spirit poured out in "the last days."[172]

Worship of the true God in the Spirit and in Christ does entail thinking rightly about God. Jesus observes (v. 22) that the Samaritan woman was ignorant, but in this context, to understand "spirit" and "truth" in the traditional way is anticlimactic. She is a Samaritan not a pagan. She knows that God is immaterial. The traditional reading is correct, there is an implied rebuke to her, but in distinction from the traditional reading, there is also an implied answer to her question. The traditional reading has it that Jesus refuses to answer her question and instead points her to the divine attribute of spirituality. A better way of reading this text, however, is to understand Jesus to answer the question by pointing her to the true locus of worship, "in the Spirit and in the Truth," that is, the Father is to be worshiped in the Second and Third Persons of the Trinity.

This reading also makes better sense of the woman's response to Jesus. On the traditional reading, this response seems somewhat random and defensive. Remembering that all of John's narratives are structured to direct us to faith in Christ (John 20:31), it is significant that he moves the narrative from the question of the locus of worship to the question of the Messiah (v. 25), a point of controversy between Jews and Samaritans. Jesus again points to himself, this time becoming completely explicit: "I am he, the one speaking to you," invoking the "I am" formula of Genesis 17:1, and especially Exodus 3:6 and 3:14 as found in the LXX.[173] Rather than simply identifying himself as Messiah, Jesus reiterates the truth that he is *the* truth, he is the true object of worship. The one speaking to the

---

172. See G. R. Beasley-Murray, *John*, 2 vols., Word Biblical Commentary 36 (Waco, TX: Word Books, 1999), 2:62, who takes *pneuma* as a reference to the coming age of the Spirit.

173. See John 6:20, 35, 41, 48, 51; 8:12, 18, 24, 28, and esp. 8:58.

woman, defining the nature of true worship, is the God of the covenant and the maker of the canon of worship. Finally, there is a way in which the traditional spatial understanding of John 4:24 is correct. Though the woman was thinking of the circumstances of worship, Jesus did answer her question about location, but he did not answer it in the way she expected. The location of true worship is "in the Spirit" and "in the truth."

Raymond Brown argues against the interpretation of this passage offered here on the ground that the nouns "spirit" (*pneuma*) and "truth" (*alētheia*) are anarthrous, that is, they do not have definite articles. In that case, Brown concludes, "spirit" is at best an indirect reference to the Holy Spirit.[174] The answer is that the preposition "in" (*en*) controls both the nouns "spirit" and "truth" and has the effect of making them definite, that is, "in *the* Spirit and the Truth." Though it is true that in John *pneuma* can be ambiguous, it frequently refers to the person of the Holy Spirit, and at least sometimes it does so either in a prepositional phrase as in John 3:5, "of water and spirit" (*ex hydatos kai pneumatos*), or without an article or preposition as in John 20:22. There are other examples in John of anarthrous nouns having a definite meaning. For example, *en archē* in John 1:1 is rightly translated "in the beginning," not "in a beginning," despite the absence of the definite article. The expression, in John 1:33, *en pneumati hagiō* ("in the Holy Spirit") is anarthrous in form and definite in meaning. So too in John 5:16, *en sabbatō* does not mean "on a Sabbath," but "on the Sabbath." In each of these cases the definite article is implied.[175] Revelation 1:10 would seem to be conclusive for this understanding of the prepositional phrase in John 4:23–24. It is well and widely recognized that the apostle John was "in the Spirit" (*en pneumati*) on the Lord's Day.[176]

This reading of this passage has significance for our understanding of and adherence to the RPW in the new covenant. First, this passage intentionally distinguishes worship in the new covenant from worship

174. Raymond E. Brown, *The Gospel according to John*, 2 vols., Anchor Bible 29 and 29A (Garden City, NY: Doubleday, 1966), 1:172.

175. I am grateful to my colleague Steve Baugh for his help in understanding the grammar of this passage.

176. The alternative "in spirit" or "in a spirit" make rather less sense in the context of the Apocalypse, where John functions like an Old Testament prophet speaking in the Spirit of Yahweh.

under Moses (John 1:17). Worship "in the Holy Spirit and in Christ" is a way of saying that the old tensions between the Jews and the Samaritans are irrelevant in the hour that "comes and now is." Yes, the Jews knew whom they worshiped (John 4:22) and the Samaritan woman was relatively ignorant, but "in the Spirit and in the Truth" that ignorance will be removed. Salvation is "of the Jews," and Jesus is that salvation (v. 23), but now salvation is for everyone who believes. This is the Johannine way of saying that the dividing wall has been broken down (Eph. 2:14). The "true worshipers" worship the Father "in the Holy Spirit and in Christ." Surely the members of the covenant of grace, who were looking forward to this age by faith, knew this proleptically, and yet not living in the new covenant, they could not know fully what those know who worship "in the Holy Spirit and in Christ," at least not in the same way. We are they upon whom the end of the ages has come (1 Cor. 10:11). This redemptive-historical difference between the shadows and the reality, this entrance into semieschatological worship in the hour that now is, means that it is a mistake to attempt to go backward, to reinstitute the Mosaic ceremonies. It also answers Hughes's concern about the RPW, that it is an inherently Judaizing anchor weighing down Reformed worship.

This reading of the encounter with the Samaritan woman reinforces the canonical principle of worship. It is not that we may do whatever is not forbidden, or that we may do whatever is consistent with the Scriptures, but that we must do whatever is "in the Holy Spirit and in the Truth." In other words, the same Spirit who led the national covenanted people of God out of Egypt (Ex. 13:21) in the pillars of cloud and fire, is the Spirit in whom we worship in the new covenant. The glory of this covenant, however, is unfading (2 Cor. 3:12–18), because, in the new covenant, the final age has been inaugurated and in worship we participate in that blessing. The same Mediator who came to Adam in the garden (Gen. 3:8) and who thundered from Sinai and who revealed himself as the angel of the Lord (Gen. 16), who is *the way, the truth, and the life* (John 14:6), is the same Truth in whom we worship now.[177] We are to worship God with reverence and fear because of the heightened presence of the Lord

177. This argument is elaborated in R. Scott Clark, "What the Bible Is All About," *Modern Reformation* 16 (March/April 2007): 20–24.

of the covenant with his people. The canon, however, has not changed: we may worship the triune God only in the way that he has revealed. The question we ask has not changed: "what must we do?" The locus of our worship, however, in the progress of redemption is relatively different. We are not anticipating the age of the Spirit and the reality of the fulfilment of the promises; we live in that age now and our worship should be characterized by those facts.

Finally, we come to Paul's exhortation in Colossians 3:16: "Let the word of Christ dwell in you richly as you teach and admonish one another with all wisdom, and as you sing psalms, hymns and spiritual songs with gratitude in your hearts to God." And Ephesians 5:19: "addressing one another in psalms and hymns and spiritual songs, singing and making melody to the Lord with all your heart." It is not at all clear that, in these contexts, Paul is actually giving instructions about corporate worship, as the intent seems to be to describe congregational fellowship and mutual edification. Nevertheless, these texts have become loci of discussion in the controversy over the RPW. Exclusive psalmodists argue that "hymns and spiritual songs" are synonyms for psalms.[178] There is prima facie evidence for this claim in the LXX (the Septuagint), which was quoted frequently by NT writers.[179] Nevertheless, Calvin did not read this expression this way, even though he certainly held the RPW most firmly.[180] On the other

178. E.g., Reformed Presbyterian Church of North America, *The Testimony of the Reformed Presbyterian Church of North America*, in The Constitution of the Reformed Presbyterian Church of North America (Pittsburgh: Reformed Presbyterian Church of North America, 1989), 21.5; Brian Schwertley, "The Biblical Case for Exclusive Psalmody," in *The Worship of God* (Ross-shire, UK: Christian Focus, 2005), 197–201.

179. Pss. 6:1; 39:3; 53:1. Ps. 66:1 in the LXX uses the words *hymnos, psalmos*, and *ōdē*, the same terms that Paul uses in Colossians. Cotton, *The Singing of Psalmes*, 2–4, is typical of the seventeenth-century Reformed view.

180. In his commentary on Col. 3:16 Calvin did not treat these terms this way. See John Calvin, *Calvin's New Testament Commentaries*, trans. John W. Fraser et al. (Grand Rapids: Eerdmans, 1960), 11:353. Virtually none of the modern commentaries take these nouns to refer entirely to the Psalter. It is usually conceded that "psalms" probably refers to the Psalter, but it is virtually agreed among commentators that "hymns" are songs about Christ and "spiritual songs" are Holy Spirit–inspired songs of an indeterminate sort. See E. K. Simpson and F. F. Bruce, *Commentary on the Epistles to the Ephesians and the Colossians*, New International Commentary on the New Testament (Grand Rapids: Eerdmans, 1957), 284–85. Bruce suggests possible parallels with Odes of Solomon and the "Song of the Star" in Ignatius's letter to the Ephesians. See also Eduard Lohse, *A Commentary on the Epistles to the Colossians and*

side of this debate, among evangelicals and Reformed revisionists, these texts are often taken as giving warrant for congregations to sing uninspired texts.[181] After all, Paul does say "hymns, and spiritual songs." This conclusion, however, does not follow. It seems clear to most commentators who have no interest in defending exclusive psalmody that, whatever the exact reference of these terms, it is almost impossible to distinguish them sharply.[182] Thus, they must be taken as a whole.

There is an alternative to both the exclusive psalmody interpretation and the interpretation that takes these passages to include uninspired songs. Even if "psalms, hymns, and spiritual songs" do not refer to the Psalter, it is sheer assumption to conclude that these nouns refer to uninspired songs. As B. B. Warfield (1851–1921) observed, "*pneumatikos*" with only one possible exception in the New Testament means "Spirit-given," or "Spirit-led" or "Spirit-determined."[183] The argument that "psalms, hymns, and Spiritual songs" can only refer to canonical psalms is not entirely convincing, however. John McNaugher considered and rejected for several reasons the possibility that Paul was thinking of Spirit-inspired songs.[184] In each case, however, McNaugher begged the question. For example, he argued that Paul forbids what is not edifying. Non-psalm songs would not be edifying; therefore, they were forbidden. McNaugher also argued from silence, for example, there is no explicit command to the apostles to compose songs. It seems evident that God the Spirit gave immediate revelation to those in the apostolic company (1 Cor. 14:30). There is no a priori reason that these revelations might not have included Spirit-inspired

to *Philemon*, Hermeneia (Philadelphia: Fortress, 1971), 151; Markus Barth and Helmut Blanke, *Colossians*, trans. Astrid P. Beck, Anchor Bible (Garden City, NY: Doubleday, 1994). It is widely held that it is not possible to distinguish sharply between the three kinds of songs. William Hendricksen, *Exposition of Colossians and Philemon*, New Testament Commentary (Grand Rapids: Baker, 1964), 162; Peter T. O'Brien, *Colossians and Philemon*, Word Biblical Commentary 44 (Waco, TX: Word, 1982), 208–10.

181. E.g., R. B. Kuiper et al., *Report on the Hymn Question and the Text of Approved Hymns to Be Presented to the Synod of 1939 of the Christian Reformed Church* (Grand Rapids: Synod of the Christian Reformed Church, 1930), 16–19.

182. Lohse, *A Commentary on the Epistles to the Colossians and to Philemon*, 151.

183. B. B. Warfield, "*Pneumatikos* and Its Opposites in the Greek of the New Testament," *The Presbyterian Review* 1 (1880): 561.

184. John McNaugher, "A Special Exegesis of Col. III.16 and Eph. V.19," in *The Psalms in Worship*, ed. John McNaugher (Pittsburgh: United Presbyterian Board of Publication, 1907), 135–37.

hymns and odes. McNaugher's objections are forceful only if one accepts his view from the outset, even for one who is predisposed toward and quite willing to embrace exclusive psalmody.

If "pneumatic" means "Spiritual" and if we read these passages in the light of the proposed exegesis of John 4, perhaps the best way to understand these passages is to refer them to Spirit-inspired songs that include the canonical psalms and more. In his minority report to the Fourteenth General Assembly of the OPC (1947), John Murray seems to have reached a similar conclusion, that no "evidence whatsoever can be adduced" that leads to the conclusion that the psalms, hymns, and spiritual songs to which Paul refers were uninspired.[185] He concluded that there "is warrant for concluding that 'psalms, hymns, and Spiritual songs' refer to inspired compositions. These texts provide us, therefore, with warrant for the singing of inspired songs in the worship of God." He continued that the biblical Psalter "provides us with inspired songs" of the sort described in Ephesians 5:19 and Colossians 3:16.[186] Since we are restricted by God's Word to the use of inspired songs in public worship, and since we acknowledge the "expansion of revelation" if we synthesize these truths, he conceded the possibility of "the use of New Testament songs or New Testament materials adapted to singing."[187]

Murray's argument was not without precedent. The singing of the Decalogue was part of Calvin's 1542 Genevan liturgy.[188] The English Calvinists in Geneva sang the Nunc Dimittis (Luke 2:29–32) and the Lord's Prayer.[189] In the Scottish Reformed Church, from 1562, the congregations sang the Nunc Dimittis and the Magnificat (Luke 1:46–55).[190] It appears that several synods in the Dutch Reformed Church in the

---

185. John Murray, "Song in Public Worship," in *Worship in the Presence of God*, ed. Lachman and Smith, 185. His minority report is also available online at http://opc.org/GA/song.html#Minority (accessed 24 September 2007).

186. Ibid., 190.

187. Ibid., 91.

188. See below.

189. Nick Needham, "Westminster and Worship: Psalms, Hymns? And Musical Instruments?" in *The Westminster Confession into the 21st Century*, ed. J. Ligon Duncan III (Ross-shire, UK: Mentor, 2003), 261.

190. Gordon Donaldson, *The Scottish Reformation* (Cambridge: Cambridge University Press, 1960), 180. Donaldson also mentions the use of the Apostles' Creed and the doxology in worship but does not delineate whether the congregation or the minister recited the creed. Ian B. Cowan

sixteenth century operated on the principle that congregations may sing only inspired songs, and it seems clear from the Church Order adopted at the Great Synod of Dort in 1619 that at least the songs of Mary, Zacharias, and Simeon were to be sung. Thus, the Reformed churches were both inclusive and exclusive in their use of songs. They included songs beyond those in the Psalter but they excluded uninspired songs.

Further, this was not only a Continental theory. The early English Presbyterian Thomas Cartwright (1535–1603) and Paul Baynes (d. 1617) understood Colossians 3:16 and Ephesians 5:19 to teach that Christians should sing more than the psalms.[191] At least one general assembly in the Scottish Presbyterian Church in the seventeenth century imagined the possibility of singing canonical inspired songs beyond the psalms. In a little-known move, the General Assembly of the Scottish Kirk commissioned Zachary Boyd (c. 1590–1653), a preacher in France and Scotland and rector of the University of Glasgow, to prepare a Psalter as part of committee work in considering the Rous Psalter, sent to them by the Westminster Assembly in 1647. He was also commissioned in this period to prepare a translation and collection of New Testament songs which he submitted to the assembly in 1648. In the end, his work was not adopted, but the fact that it was commissioned at least suggests that such a project was not regarded as morally impossible a priori. John Cotton argued that not only the "Psalms of David" but "any other Spiritual songs recorded in Scripture may be lawfully sung in Christian churches such as the song of Moses, and Asaph, Heman and Ethan, Solomon and Hezekiah, Habakkuk and Zechariah, Hannah and Deborah, Mary and Elizabeth, and the like."[192] Is now perhaps, then, the right time to reconsider the theory and practice of the Dutch Reformed churches from 1574 to 1807, the proposal floated among the Scottish Presbyterians from the period of the Westminster Assembly, and the arguments of John Cotton and John Murray?

Finally, there are two other steps that confessional Reformed churches should take toward recovering Reformed worship: 1) recovery

---

mentions only the use of metrical psalms; see *The Scottish Reformation: Church and Society in Sixteenth-Century Scotland* (London: Weinfeld and Nicolson, 1982), 141.

191. Needham, "Westminster and Worship," 263–64.

192. Cotton, *Singing of Psalmes*, 15 (spelling modified).

of Reformed liturgics; 2) a new Psalter. Judging by much contemporary practice, one might gain the impression that Reformed churches have never given much thought to liturgy, but such an impression would be quite false. Each of the Reformed churches in England, Scotland, France, Geneva, Heidelberg, and the Netherlands developed liturgies reflecting the shared understanding of the RPW that was common to all of them.[193]

Consider just three of the major Reformed liturgies from the sixteenth and seventeenth centuries, Geneva, Heidelberg, and the pattern provided by the DPW. Let us begin with Calvin's 1542 Genevan and 1545 Strasbourg liturgies.[194] Given the principle that only that may be done that is required by Scripture, the services are simple and marked by a dialogical or call and response pattern (Ex. 19:7–8).[195] This pattern is also evident in the Scottish orders of worship of 1564, 1641, and in the DPW (1645).[196] Throughout the service the Lord speaks to his people through the office of the minister, and the people respond to the Lord with his Word. The liturgy separated the functions of minister and congregation into reading and singing. As Baird noted, the "Psalms are the responsive part of Calvin's liturgy."[197]

This call and response structure to Calvin's liturgy answers one of the often-repeated objections to the RPW as historically understood, that if the minister can do *x* (quote a hymn, give an extemporaneous prayer, read an uninspired text of any sort), therefore the congregation may do so also.[198] This objection ignores what should be obvious to Reformed folk, that the minister holds a special office in Christ's church and the people hold a distinct general office of believer (Eph. 4:11; 1 Tim. 3:1–11; Titus

---

193. Charles W. Baird, *The Presbyterian Liturgies: Historical Sketches* (Grand Rapids: Baker, 1960). The material of this volume was published originally as part of Charles W. Baird, *Eutaxia* (New York: M. W. Dodd, 1855). It has recently been republished by Wipf & Stock (2006). See also Bard Thompson, ed., *Liturgies of the Western Church* (Philadelphia: Fortress, reprint, 1980).

194. Thompson, *Liturgies*, 197–208.

195. E. Clark Copeland, "The Dialogical Nature of Worship in the Old Testament," in *Worship in the Presence of God*, ed. Lachman and Smith, 35–60.

196. Ward, "Elements and Practice," 116.

197. Baird, *The Presbyterian Liturgies*, 28–29.

198. Kuiper, *As to Being Reformed*, 196.

1:5–9; Heb. 13:17).[199] In the conduct of public worship, not everyone is called to do everything (1 Cor. 14:26).[200]

Here is Calvin's liturgy:

INVOCATION
Our help is in the name of the Lord, who made heaven and earth. Amen.

CONFESSION
My brethren, let each of you present himself before the face of the Lord, and confess his faults and sins, following my words in his heart.

O Lord God, eternal and almighty Father, we confess and acknowledge unfeignedly before thy holy majesty that we are poor sinners, conceived and born in iniquity and corruption, prone to do evil, incapable of any good, and that in our depravity we transgress thy holy commandment without end or ceasing. . . .[201]

[ABSOLUTION]
Let each of you truly acknowledge that he is a sinner, humbling himself before God, and believe that the heavenly Father wills to be gracious unto him in Jesus Christ. To all those who repent in this wise, and look to Jesus Christ for their salvation, I declare that the absolution of sins is effected, in the name of the Father, and of the Son, and of the Holy Spirit. Amen.[202]

CONGREGATIONAL RESPONSE
(The congregation sings the first table of the law.)

MINISTER PRAYS
The Lord be with us. Let us pray to the Lord.

---

199. On the three offices instituted by Christ see Derke P. Bergsma, "Prophets, Priests, and Kings: Biblical Offices" in John Armstrong, ed., *The Compromised Church* (Wheaton, IL: Crossway, 1998), 117–31.

200. Hart, *Recovering Mother Kirk*, 107–16.

201. Thompson, *Liturgies*, 197.

202. Calvin was not permitted to include the absolution in the Genevan liturgy from 1542, but it was used in the liturgy he wrote for Strasbourg and in Heidelberg.

Heavenly Father, full of goodness and grace, as thou art pleased to declare thy holy will unto thy poor servants, and to instruct them in the righteousness of the law. . . .[203]

Congregation Responds with a Psalm[204]

Minister Prays for Illumination

Most gracious God, our heavenly Father! In whom alone dwelleth all the fullness of light and wisdom: Illuminate our minds, we beseech thee, by thine Holy Spirit, in the true understanding of thy word.[205]

Scripture Reading

Sermon

Pastoral (Great) Prayer

Almighty God, heavenly Father, thou hast promised to grant our requests which we make unto thee in the name of thy well-beloved Son Jesus Christ our Lord: by whose teaching and that of his apostles we have been taught to gather together in His name, with the promise that He will be in the midst of us, and will be our intercessor with thee, to obtain all those things which we agree to ask on earth. . . .

[Administration of the Supper as Permitted][206]

203. The full text of examples of Calvin's prayers is published in Thompson, *Liturgies*. An English translation of his Form of Prayers is also published in Henry Beveridge and Jules Bonnet, eds., *Selected Works of John Calvin*, 7 vols. (Grand Rapids: Baker, reprint 1983), 2:100–12.

204. Howard G. Hageman indicates that, in the Strasbourg liturgy, the second table of the Decalogue was sung here. See Howard G. Hageman, *Pulpit and Table: Some Chapters in the History of Worship in the Reformed Churches* (Richmond: John Knox, 1962), 28.

205. Baird, *The Presbyterian Liturgies*, 37.

206. Calvin wished to administer the Supper weekly in Geneva but was prohibited by the city council (*petit conseil*). It is passing strange that four hundred fifty years after Calvin's death most Reformed congregations still act as if they were bound to the decisions of the Genevan city council. In 1561, Calvin confessed that he was "truly pleased with a monthly celebration of the supper (Iam vero singulis mensibus coenam celebrari maximo nobis placeret)" but he added, "Nevertheless I undertook to have recorded in the public acts that our custom is corrupt, in order that correction might be easier and more free for future generations (Curavi tamen referri in acta publica vitiosum esse morem nostrum,

Thanksgiving

Congregation Responds with a Psalm

Benediction

The Heidelberg Liturgy of 1563 followed this pattern with a couple of minor variations, for example, the reading of Psalm 95 followed the invocation. The major difference was that the reading of the law came after the sermon, and it was followed not only by an absolution but also a declaration of judgment (commination) upon the impenitent.

> But as there may be some among you, who continue to find pleasure in your sin and shame, or who persist in sin against their conscience, I declare to such, by the command of God, that the wrath and judgment of God abides upon them, and that all their sins are retained in heaven, and finally that they can never be delivered from eternal damnation, unless they repent.[207]

The declaration of pardon (absolution) and judgment may be unfamiliar to many readers. It should be observed that in both instances the minister is speaking ministerially, not sacerdotally, that is, he is recognizing and declaring what is true of those who believe and those who do not. These declarations do not make things so.

"At the beginning of [the] post-Reformation era all of the Reformed churches had a firm and fixed liturgical life. Scotland, or Switzerland, Heidelberg or the Hague all reveal the same thing—a fixed Reformed liturgy used without variation or exception not only for the celebration of

---

ut posteris facilior esset ac liberior correctio)"; CR, 38:213; Mary Beaty and Benjamin W. Farley, eds., *Calvin's Ecclesiastical Advice* (Edinburgh: T&T Clark, 1991), 96. See also Calvin, *Institutes* 4.17.46, where he argues explicitly for the weekly administration of the Supper: "Longe aliter factum oportuit: singulis ad minimum hebdomadibus proponenda erat Christianorum coetui mensa Domini"; OS, 5:412.18–19; R. Scott Clark, "The Evangelical Fall from the Means of Grace," in *The Compromised Church*, ed. John Armstrong (Wheaton, IL: Crossway, 1998), 133–47.

207. Baird, *Presbyterian Liturgies*, 229.

the sacraments but for ordinary Sunday worship as well."[208] It is against this background of near universal acceptance of the RPW and universal application of it that we must read the DPW. It has been described as a "series of rubrics," which seems accurate enough.[209] Even such a hostile witness as Howard Hageman concedes that "the indications of the *Directory* were generally excellent, scrupulously faithful to the Calvinist structure of worship."[210] The DPW does not provide a detailed order of service, but assumes the basic pattern of Reformed worship, which was a century old by 1644. Following the adoption of the DPW, the liturgy of the Scottish Presbyterian Church was simplified. The call and response structure remained but prayers replaced the votum and call to worship. The confession of sin and acknowledgment of pardon now occur in prayer. The prayer after the sermon is followed by the administration of the sacraments (as appropriate), and the congregation is dismissed "with a solemn blessing."[211] According to Nichols, "in most cases the legatees of the Westminster Assembly Puritans did not care to maintain the full prescriptions of the Directory. The anti-liturgical current moved them farther to the left" so that, by the eighteenth century, a Scottish Presbyterian minister "could get into trouble for following the instructions of the Directory as to reading Scripture and using the Lord's Prayer."[212]

In the seventeenth and early eighteenth centuries, in the Netherlands the commitment of the Reformed churches to the means of grace was challenged by the rise of pietism (e.g., Labadists) and the radicalizing of the Remonstrant movement as it merged with the biblicism of the

---

208. Hageman, *Pulpit and Table*, 37. Hageman's deeply prejudiced account of the theological and spiritual life of Reformed orthodoxy is quite dated and should be read as reflecting the general opinion of orthodoxy before the contemporary study of orthodoxy reflected in the work of Richard Muller, Carl Trueman, Willem van Asselt, and others.

209. Walter Lowrie, *Action in the Liturgy, Essential and Unessential* (New York: Philosophical Library, 1953), 220. J. H. Nichols notes that Lowrie writes of "Calvin's prayer book" but evidently means the DPW. See J. H. Nichols, *Corporate Worship in the Reformed Tradition* (Philadelphia: Westminster, 1968), 180 n. 55.

210. Ibid.

211. *A Directory for Publique Worship of God* (London, 1644), 19. Nichols is surely right when he says that the DPW was written as it was to allow for the various traditions represented at Westminster to reorder the material according to their needs. See Nichols, *Corporate Worship*, 100.

212. Nichols, *Corporate Worship*, 107–8.

285

Socinians.[213] In France and Geneva, the Reformed churches continued to follow the pattern of Calvin's liturgy until the nineteenth century.[214] Of course, the revocation of the Edict of Nantes (1685) drove the French Reformed churches underground until 1787. As they had been before the edict, they were once again *ecclesiae sub cruce* (churches under the cross) or "in the desert."[215] The Genevan liturgy was revised at the same time its theology was revised in a rationalizing direction by the son of Francis Turretin, Jean-Alphonse Turretin (1671–1737), vitiating much of the theology that lay behind the liturgy.[216] These cases illustrate the medieval axiom, *lex orandi, lex credendi* (the law of praying is the law of believing). There is an integral reciprocal relation between what is done in public worship and what a church comes to confess theologically.

Among the American Reformed churches, those denominations with roots in the Scottish Covenanter tradition (e.g., the Reformed Presbyterian Church in North America) have continued to practice the RPW as understood and confessed in the Reformed churches, but they have not been alone. As late as 1928, the synod of the Christian Reformed Church adopted an order of morning worship that preserved the pattern and features of the classical Reformed liturgies, including the use of psalms as congregational response to the Word and the assurance of pardon (absolution).[217] From a historical perspective, American Presbyterians, as we have already seen, may have the greatest distance to go to recover the RPW, but among the confessional Dutch Reformed churches,

213. Hageman, *Pulpit and Table*, 44–47. The Labadists were named for Jean de Labadie (1610–74), a Jesuit convert to Protestantism who held not only to an inspired Bible but inspired interpretation of the Bible. His movement had little interest in the sacraments. This movement, which died fifty years after Labadie's death, is a classic example of the QIRE. On the relations between the Remonstrants and the Socinians in the Netherlands in the seventeenth century see John E. Platt, *Reformed Thought and Scholasticism: The Arguments for the Existence of God in Dutch Theology, 1575–1650*, Studies in the History of Christian Thought 29 (Leiden: E. J. Brill, 1982), 218–38.

214. Hageman, *Pulpit and Table*, 50.

215. Ibid., 51.

216. Ibid., 52–54. See also Martin I. Klauber, "Theological Transition in Geneva from Jean-Alphonse Turretin to Jacob Vernet," in *Protestant Scholasticism: Essays in Reassessment*, ed. Carl R. Trueman and R. Scott Clark (Carlisle, UK: Paternoster, 1999), 256–70.

217. W. Heyns et al., *The Order of Morning Worship on the Lord's Day Adopted by the Synod of the Christian Reformed Church* (Grand Rapids: Christian Reformed Church, 1928).

the liturgical experiments of the last eighty years might be considered a parenthesis between the historic practice and the future reformation of worship. Just as the Reformed churches in the sixteenth and seventeenth centuries and again in the early nineteenth century determined to reform worship according to Scripture as understood by the Reformed churches, so we may do so again. *Ecclesia reformata, semper reformanda.*

Finally, even if the confessional Reformed churches were to accept entirely the arguments offered in this chapter and wanted to begin singing principally the Psalter and secondarily other inspired materials (e.g., the songs of Moses and Miriam in Ex. 15), it would not be easy. Though Terry Johnson is correct to say "the metrical versions of the psalter that are available" today are better than nothing, there is probably no single Psalter that one could recommend without hesitation to a congregation that wanted to reform its worship to sing principally from the Psalter.[218]

Given the history of Reformed worship in the sixteenth and seventeenth centuries, this is a remarkable state of affairs. One of the first things Calvin did in Geneva and Strasbourg was to work toward the formation of a Psalter for Reformed worship. The first collection of seventeen psalms was published in 1539. In Strasbourg he found psalms set to meter by Clement Marot. Calvin himself set five psalms to meter and published a Psalter with a form of prayers in 1541.[219] After Calvin returned to Geneva, Marot continued to work on a more complete Psalter, publishing fifty psalms in 1543. A complete Psalter first appeared for use in Reformed churches in 1562 after Theodore Beza arrived in Geneva to finish the task. This edition essentially remained the Psalter of the French Reformed Church for the next four hundred years.[220] J. H. Nichols says, "[m]usically ... the work of Louis Bourgeois was rivaled by no late workman."[221] He adds, the "Huguenots quite caught Calvin's concept of congregational psalmody. It became their hallmark, in homes, in corporate worship, or

218. Terry L. Johnson, "Restoring Psalm Singing to Our Worship," in *Give Praise to God: A Vision for Reforming Worship*, ed. Philip G. Ryken et al. (Phillipsburg, NJ: P&R, 2003), 279–80.

219. J. H. Nichols, *Corporate Worship*, 57.

220. Ibid., 58.

221. Ibid.

on the battlefield. The French Discipline required all to own their own and bring their liturgical psalters, and to share in the singing."[222]

It is not as if no one knows there is a problem. R. B. Kuiper admitted in 1926 that the Psalter then in use by the CRC was a "rather free rendering of the Psalms as they are found in the Bible."[223] In the intervening eighty years things have not improved greatly. The 1959 Psalter Hymnal continued to employ free renderings of the psalms and added more hymns. The 1986 revision of the Psalter Hymnal did return "to the longstanding Reformed tradition of presenting one complete versification of each psalm set to a single melody," adding to the psalms eighty-six "Bible songs" and four hundred five hymns, but it is unclear whether these developments have helped or hindered a return to psalmody.[224]

The Trinity Hymnal, first published in 1961 by the OPC, evidently ignoring John Murray's minority report to the fourteenth general assembly, scattered the psalms throughout the collection, forcing would-be psalm singers to play hide-and-seek with the psalms.[225] The 1990 revision of the Trinity Hymnal did nothing to change this fundamental problem. The 1994 publication of the Trinity Psalter was a positive development, but the omission of musical notation is a serious defect that necessarily limits its utility.

The other major ecclesiastically sanctioned Psalters in general usage are the Book of Psalms for Singing published by the Reformed Presbyterian Church in North America (1973), and the Book of Praise used by the Canadian Reformed Churches (1995).[226] The latter preserves the old Genevan tunes, but the unfamiliarity and difficulty of some of these tunes

222. Ibid., 58–59. Nichols says that Beza introduced some hymns and that these were approved at Montbéliard in 1598 but adds that "little but psalms were sung in the sixteenth- and seventeenth-century French Reformed Church." He does not say of what sort these hymns were or for what use.

223. Kuiper, As to Being Reformed, 195.

224. Christian Reformed Church, Psalter Hymnal (Grand Rapids: CRC Publications, 1987), 8.

225. Committee on Christian Education, Trinity Hymnal (Philadelphia: Orthodox Presbyterian Church, 1961).

226. Reformed Presbyterian Church of North America, The Book of Psalms for Singing (Pittsburgh: The Board of Education of the Reformed Presbyterian Church of North America, 1973); Canadian Reformed Churches, The Book of Praise (Winnipeg: Standing Committee for the Publication of the Book of Praise of the Canadian Reformed Churches, 1984).

limit its utility. The Book of Psalms for Singing is a carefully produced product of painstaking research. Like the Book of Praise it uses many archaic or unfamiliar tunes. Terry Johnson is right when he says that, in order to restore psalm singing to our worship, we need tunes appropriate to congregational singing. Though there is subjectivity involved in any such judgment, it is not impossible. Such judgments fall under the heading of wisdom. Johnson notes Calvin's distinction between tunes that are "light and frivolous and those that have majesty."[227] He offers five characteristics that make tunes appropriate for use in public worship. Given that we have faithful English language translations of the psalms for singing (i.e., The Book of Psalms for Singing, The Book of Praise, and the Trinity Psalter) our chief need would seem to be better tunes.[228] If the same creativity and skill that are presently devoted to composing hymn tunes and Scripture songs were given to composing new, appropriate psalm tunes, the contemporary reformation of worship would be advanced rapidly.

As in the case of the recovery of the Reformed confession by recovering the practice of confessing, there is no good reason why the Reformed churches that continue to confess the RPW could not reform their practice. There is no reason why the churches could not commission composers to write contemporary tunes appropriate for corporate worship to replace those older tunes that have become shopworn or simply outdated. There is also no good reason why the confessional Reformed churches could not learn to sing God's Word to the best old and new tunes without instruments. After all, congregants regularly learn to master complicated new technologies. If a congregation sang two familiar psalm tunes and learned one new psalm tune each month, within a year's time the congregation would have enlarged its repertoire considerably. Further, it is not difficult to assign the same psalm or other inspired text to a familiar tune with the same meter.

Conclusions

The contemporary Reformed theology and practice of worship is in trouble. The reason for this crisis is that by and large most of us no longer

227. Johnson, "Restoring Psalm Singing to Our Worship," 277–78.
228. Ibid.

think biblically or confessionally about worship. To the degree these characterizations are true, it should not surprise us that our services do not look much today like what they did during the Reformation. It is not simply that the circumstances (time, place, language, and posture) have changed, but rather we no longer organize our services on the basis of the Reformed principle of worship. We no longer ask the Reformed question: what does God require of us? If we are not asking the correct question, there is little possibility of arriving at the correct answer.

Having surveyed the contours of the current discussion concerning the RPW, this chapter has offered paths toward recovering the Reformed theology and practice of worship. Beginning with a brief survey of the history of worship, there is little doubt about Reformed practice in the sixteenth and seventeenth centuries. In the eighteenth and nineteenth centuries, however, Reformed adherence to the RPW wavered and Reformed practice changed considerably. Since the mid-nineteenth century, the original understanding of the RPW has become the minority theology and practice in the Reformed churches. The principal reason for these revisions, however, was not theological or exegetical but pragmatic. The driving force behind the revision of Reformed worship was a desire to accommodate the revivals of the eighteenth century. When the conservative wing of the Dutch Reformed Church (the CRCNA) officially embraced the use of uninspired songs in public worship in the early twentieth century, it seems to have done so without the hindrance of serious historical or even confessional investigation.

Since, in no case, have the Reformed churches repudiated our confessed principle of worship, there is no principled reason why we cannot recover the principle and practice of Reformed worship. This chapter has offered a way forward by restating the RPW and reconsidering it in light of the history of redemption and the biblical instruction about worship. In this survey, we saw that though the ceremonies of the Mosaic epoch have been fulfilled, the substance of worship remains constant. We saw that the RPW was the consensus confession of the Reformed churches in Europe, Britain, and North America in the sixteenth, seventeenth, and early eighteenth centuries. The result of the modern Reformed lapse from the historic understanding and use of the RPW has been to create at least three distinct approaches to worship: those that continue the historic theology and practice, those that share the theology of worship but have a modified or inconsistent practice of the RPW, and finally those progressive Reformed folk who have offered radical theoretical and practical revisions of the RPW. This chapter has offered a way forward to those who still confess the RPW by calling for movement by both sides through a reconsideration of two New Testament passages central to the discussion.

It is one thing to recover the confessional Reformed theology and practice of worship, but what if we reformed our worship and no one came? It is to this question that this work turns in the next and final chapter.

The whole day is to be celebrated as holy to the Lord, both in public and private, as being the Christian sabbath. To which end, it is requisite, that there be a holy cessation or resting all that day from all unnecessary labours; and an abstaining, not only from all sports and pastimes, but also from all worldly words and thoughts.

. . . That what time is vacant, between or after the solemn meetings of the congregation in public, be spent in reading, meditation, repetition of sermons; especially by calling their families to an account of what they have heard, and catechising of them, holy conferences, prayer for a blessing upon the public ordinances, singing of psalms, visiting the sick, relieving the poor, and such like duties of piety, charity, and mercy, accounting the sabbath a delight.

—THE WESTMINSTER DIRECTORY FOR PUBLIC WORSHIP

CHAPTER
8

Whatever Happened to
the Second Service?

I n the 1996 film "The Big Night," two brothers with a family-owned
restaurant found themselves in competition with a large chain restaurant down the street. These two brothers faced a choice: they
could continue to operate the small family restaurant where the food was
prepared with care and attention to quality, or they could try to compete
with the restaurant down the street by cutting costs and quality. As sideline
churches we face the same dilemma. Shall we continue to pay attention
to quality, or shall we try to compete with the religious equivalent of the
so-called box stores? Put another way, the question is whether we shall
become what we confess or something else. One of the pressure points in
our struggle to become and remain Reformed is the second service.

The Contemporary Loss of the Second Service

Classical Reformed practice was to hold two worship services on
the Lord's Day. In recent years, however, the second service or vespers
has fallen on hard times. It is becoming more difficult to find a second
service. Judging by anecdotal evidence, a significant number of Reformed
congregations have eliminated the second service. As a Calvinist, however, I take perverse comfort in knowing that some modern evils are not

really peculiar to our age. The Netherlands (French and Dutch) and German church orders prescribed two services, morning and afternoon. In the morning service there was an exposition of the Scripture (often from the New Testament), and the afternoon sermon was to exposit the Heidelberg Catechism (which was regarded as the ecclesiastically sanctioned summary of the Reformed understanding of the Word) or the Scripture, using the Heidelberg Catechism as a guide. In this way God's people would get a balanced spiritual diet. From the beginning of the Reformed Reformation, however, attendance at the second service was a problem. According to Idzerd Van Dellen and Martin Monsma, "at first people did not take to catechism preaching," and things did not go well because not everyone cared to "go to Church twice a day" on the Sabbath.[1]

The second service was established in the earliest stages of the Reformation in the 1520s and 1530s.[2] The Reformed adopted the second service as a way of instructing God's people in the basics of the faith. Nevertheless, the evening service continued to trouble the Reformed churches at the Synod of Dort (1618–19) where complaints were brought that some ministers (including Remonstrants who opposed the substance and form of catechism preaching) failed to hold the afternoon service and some congregants preferred to work or play.[3] Synod responded by insisting on the second service, imposing censure on disobedient ministers, and instructing ministers to preach brief and understandable sermons. Ministers were encouraged not to neglect the second service on account of small attendance, even though "only the minister's own family should be in attendance."[4] The second service did not become a uniform practice among the Reformed churches in the Netherlands until the middle of the seventeenth century, more than a century after the practice was first instituted.[5]

1. Idzerd Van Dellen and Martin Monsma, *The Church Order Commentary, Being a Brief Explanation of the Church Order of the Christian Reformed Church* (Grand Rapids: Zondervan, 1941), 278.
2. Donald W. Sinnema, "The Second Service in the Early Dutch Reformed Tradition," *CTJ* 32 (1997): 298–333.
3. Ibid., 278–79.
4. Ibid., 279.
5. Ibid., 331.

Poor attendance at the second service is one thing, but it is quite another to cancel the second service altogether, and that is what appears to be happening in our time. For example, much attention has been paid to the decision of the synod of the Christian Reformed Churches in North America in 1995 to permit the ordination of females to the offices of minister and elder.[6] Rather less attention, however, has been given to the decision of that same synod to allow congregations not to hold the second service.[7] Both were monumental decisions. One says something about the authority of Scripture in the church, but the other says something about the relative importance of the means of grace in the life of the church. This chapter argues that the disappearance of the evening service from Reformed churches suggests that the Reformed churches need to recover two confessional doctrines: the means of grace and the Sabbath.

The Necessary Condition: The Sabbath

There are two conditions to recovering the second service. The first and necessary condition is to recover the confessional doctrine of the Christian Sabbath. The second and sufficient condition is our doctrine of the Word and sacraments as the divinely appointed means of grace. This chapter considers these two conditions in order.

Without the doctrine of the Christian Sabbath it will be impossible to restore the evening service to its rightful place in the life of Reformed churches, because it is only when Christians are convinced that there is one day in seven that belongs to the Lord of the Sabbath (Matt. 12:8) in a peculiar way that they will be prepared to reconsider how they spend that day. The doctrine of the Christian Sabbath, however, is necessary in another sense as well. It is necessary because it is a revealed doctrine. Of course there are difficulties in making this claim. J. Douma outlines four obstacles to holding to the traditional Reformed theology and practice

6. Synod of the Christian Reformed Church, *Acts of Synod* (Grand Rapids: Christian Reformed Church in North America, 1995), 726–36.
    7. Ibid., 753–55.

of the Sabbath.[8] First, the Sabbath occurs explicitly for the first time in Scripture in Exodus 16. If it is a creation ordinance, why does it appear formally so late in the biblical revelation? Second, is the creation narrative descriptive or prescriptive? Third, there is no explicit command in the New Testament to observe the Sabbath. Fourth, the historical evidence concerning postapostolic practice from the close of the canon until Constantine is unclear.

There are other difficulties as well. Some regard the law delivered at Sinai as so bound up with the temporary national covenant with Israel that they reject any attempt to salvage anything from the Decalogue for new covenant ethics. Others, such as six-day sabbatarians, reject confessional Reformed theology and practice as contrary to God's Word. Then there is the strong Reformation rhetoric against the Sabbatarians, and there are places in the writings of John Calvin and Zacharias Ursinus that seem to suggest that the day of worship is theoretically a matter of indifference, that the Sunday Sabbath is more a convention than a practice grounded in the nature of the created order.

On top of these exegetical, historical, and theological challenges, advocates of the confessional and traditional Reformed approach to the Christian Sabbath face a mountain of practical questions fostered by cultural pressures that work against Sabbath observance such that Christian employees increasingly must choose between employment and obedience to the Sabbath. These pressures raise questions about what can be done on the Sabbath, by whom, and under what circumstances. In the light of these difficulties, many seem ready to abandon altogether the theology and practice of the Christian Sabbath. Nevertheless, despite the exegetical, historical, and ethical difficulties, the confessional Reformed doctrine of the Christian Sabbath remains the most satisfactory account when all the biblical, historical, and theological data are considered.

The first reason why we ought to hold the confessional doctrine of the Sabbath is that it is biblical. Perhaps because many Reformed folk today read Genesis 1 solely with an eye to the length and nature of the creation days, they overlook what is arguably a more central theme in the revelation

8. J. Douma, *The Ten Commandments: Manual for the Christian Life*, trans. Nelson D. Kloosterman (Phillipsburg, NJ: P&R, 1996), 110–12.

concerning creation: the Sabbath. The seventh day is the culmination of all that has gone before. In Genesis 2:1–3 Scripture says: "Thus the heavens and the earth were finished, and all the host of them. And on the seventh day Elohim finished his work that he had done, and he rested on the seventh day from all his work that he had done. So Elohim blessed the seventh day and made it holy, because on it Elohim rested from all his work that he had done in creation" (Gen. 2:1–3).[9]

From the beginning of chapter 1 until this point, Elohim has been performing mighty creative acts by fiat, by speaking them into existence. Without doubt we are meant to understand that, had he willed, he could have accomplished all the creation in an instant, but the narrative carries us through a sequence establishing a pattern, beginning with verse 5: "And there was evening and there was morning, the first day." This pattern is repeated five more times with each of the creation days bounded by morning and evening. Further, the boundaries of the first day are said to exist even before there are proper astronomical correlates, that is, day and night are said to exist before their ordinary markers (the sun and moon) are said to exist. This anomaly should be noted, and it should cause the reader (or in the case of the original setting, the hearer) to question the reason for the structure of the narrative. Given that God might have arranged his revelation differently from how he did (he might have revealed himself as creating in one day or in eight), we should pay particular attention to the way he is said to have done things.[10] It seems likely that, in the flow of the narrative, where days with boundaries are established before the sun and moon by which day and night are ordinarily marked, we are to note the relative importance of these bounded days. Because the narrative structures each day by "evening and morning," we cannot help but observe at least some continuity with days as we experience them. In its original context, the narrative of the creation days communicated to the Israelites, who had been delivered out of Egypt, that the same Yahweh Elohim who saved them also created them and all that is. In other words, their covenant God was not only the God of grace and salvation, but also the God of

9. Translation modified slightly from the ESV.
10. John Murray, *The Collected Writings of John Murray*, 4 vols. (Edinburgh: Banner of Truth Trust, 1976), 1:206–7.

nature and creation. The narrative has the effect of saying that time and the calendar as we experience them are not mere conventions, but rather they are grounded in the creative will of God.

The creation narrative begins to come to its climax in Genesis 1:31. Elohim is said to see, as it were, all that he had made, and he declared that it was "good." On the seventh day (Gen. 2:2) Elohim is said to have "finished his work that he had done" and "rested the seventh day from all his work that he had done" (ESV). When we consider this language for a moment, we quickly realize that, of course, all this language is thoroughly anthropomorphic, that is, Scripture predicates human attributes to God and his acts in order for us to have some understanding of what happened. We understand that, in the ordinary providence of God, after physical exertion we are fatigued. We need to rest, to recover our strength. If we read this narrative in the light of the rest of Scripture, we quickly realize that the God who spoke creation into existence from nothing (*ex nihilo*) has no need of rest. To suggest that the God of the Bible needs literal rest is the most crass sort of Greco-Roman paganism or Mormonism. In the first instance, God did not literally exert himself to create the cosmos. The biblical language of exertion and rest is solely for our benefit, so that we have some way to think about God and ourselves. Remember that just a few verses earlier (Gen. 1:27) humanity is said to have been created in the image of the Creator God, that is, as finite analogues of the infinite God. For the purposes of this chapter, it does not matter exactly how humans are analogues of God, but chiefly that they are. The stylized anthropomorphic creation narrative, taken in conjunction with the status of the first humans as analogues of the Creator, makes the next verse in the narrative even more significant. In Genesis 2:3 Scripture says, "So God blessed the seventh day and made it holy, because on it God rested from all his work that he had done in creation" (ESV). We ordinarily think of sanctity relative to its opposite, impurity or sin. We should remember, however, that the institution and sanctification of the seventh day occurred before the fall, so that its sanctification cannot be understood relative to uncleanness. The answer to the problem lies in the next clause, "because on it God rested." The sanctity or uniqueness of the seventh day is grounded in God's resting, that is, his "stopping" and his entering into his Sabbath rest. The entering into rest by Elohim is regarded by the text as a deliberate, message-laden act. It sends an implicit message to his analogues: "You are my image-bearers. I 'worked' for six days and rested the seventh. You do the same."

If we consider that God established a pattern of work and rest prior to the entrance of sin (unrest) and death into history, we realize that the work/rest pattern is integral to the way human beings are to relate to time, to one another, and to God their Creator. Further, embedded in the very notion of rest in the prelapsarian state must be an implicit signal about life beyond Adam's probation.[11] That this is so is indicated by the presence of the "tree of life" (Gen. 2:9). Adam was permitted to eat of all the trees in the garden save that one which we might call the tree of death ("the day you eat thereof, you shall surely die"; Gen. 2:17). Each day as he fulfilled his duty as image-bearer, those two trees confronted him, testifying to the blessed state awaiting the fulfilment of the probation or the cursedness awaiting his failure. Each week was marked with a resting from his duties as vicegerent.[12] That rest day was also a message from his Creator about the state of glory to be enjoyed after the probation.

This analogical relation between God as King and humans as vicegerents following the pattern established by the sovereign is reinforced by the very structure of the creation narrative. Since the thirteenth century at least, Christians have recognized a certain parallelism in the creation narrative.[13] In recent discussions that parallelism has been described in terms of "rulers" and "realms." The lights rule the heavens, and God's image-bearers rule the earth. All of them, however, are ruled by God, and his royal dominion is on full display in Genesis 2:2. God has, as it were, worked for six days (i.e., six mornings and evenings). On the seventh, he is pictured as assuming his rightful place as King over creation. Thus, the seventh day, God's rest day and ours, is at the apex of the story of creation. It is not too much to say that it, rather than the length of the days, is the point of the creation narrative. After all, the Sabbath regulation in the Mosaic civil code (e.g., Ex. 31:13–15) made Sabbath breaking a capital

---

11. Nicholas Bownd, *The Doctrine of the Sabbath* (London, 1595), 11–16.

12. This is a traditional Christian designation for Adam. See John Murray, *Collected Writings of John Murray*, 2:41.

13. *ST* 1a.74.1.

crime. We can be confident that we are not reading the centrality of the Sabbath into the creation narrative, since this is exactly how it is inter-preted in Exodus 20:11: "For in six days Yahweh made heaven and earth, the sea, and all that is in them, and rested the seventh day. Therefore Yahweh blessed the Sabbath day and made it holy."

The Sabbath is grounded not only in creation, but it is also grounded in re-creation. As part of the restatement of the Decalogue, in preparation for going into the land, the ground of the Sabbath was restated in Deuter-onomy 5:14–15. Here we are commanded to set aside the seventh day in order that servants may rest (v. 14) as we do. Both masters and servants must rest because we are redeemed slaves delivered "with a mighty hand and an outstretched arm" (v. 15 ESV). So the one in seven pattern of work and rest, of common life and uncommon life, is grounded also in redemption or re-creation. Grace renews nature. The Sabbath, instituted in creation as a picture of our consummate existence with God upon fulfilment of the covenant of works, is now reinstituted as a typological and shadowy pointer to the eternal Sabbath rest earned by the last Adam (1 Cor. 15:45) and the true Israel, Jesus (Matt. 2:15; Gal. 3:16), for all those who believe (Heb. 4 [all]).[14] We whom Yahweh redeemed from slavery (Rom. 6:20–23) are to set aside one day in seven in imitation of the pattern of work and rest established in creation.

The Sabbath was not a minor feature of Israelite life. The Sabbath structured the entire Israelite calendar. As we have seen in the Decalogue,

14. I do not appeal to Hebrews 4 directly as NT proof of the Christian Sabbath, since its interpretation is highly disputed. Geerhardus Vos is correct to say that Hebrews 4:9 teaches that Christianity itself is "a *sabbath-keeping,* an actual realization of that which the sabbath signified at the creation. We are now living in the age of consummation and attainment"; Geerhardus Vos, *The Teaching of the Epistle to the Hebrews* (Phillipsburg, NJ: Presbyterian and Reformed, 1956), 55. See also Andrew T. Lincoln, "Sabbath, Rest, and Eschatology in the New Testament," in *From Sabbath to Lord's Day: A Biblical, Historical, and Theological Investigation,* ed. D. A. Carson (Grand Rapids: Zondervan, 1982), 205–14. Despite the dif-ficulties, it does seem fair to conclude from Hebrews 4 that the writer continues to connect the weekly Sabbath with rest, worship, and consummation so that it supports the major Sab-bath themes pursued in this chapter. For defenses of the appeal to Hebrews 4 as proof of the weekly Christian Sabbath see Joseph A. Pipa Jr., *The Lord's Day* (Ross-shire, UK: Christian Focus, 1997), 114–19; see also Murray, *Collected Writings of John Murray,* 1:223–24; Iain D. Campbell, *On the First Day of the Week: God, the Christian and the Sabbath* (Leominster, UK: Day One, 2005), 151–53.

the Sabbath punctuated each week in the Israelite calendar. The Sabbath was apparently in force, even before they arrived at Sinai. According to Exodus 16:22–30 the Israelites were to gather a double portion of manna. They had six days to gather and on the seventh they were not to gather. Verse 23 says, "Tomorrow is a day of solemn rest, a holy Sabbath to Yahweh." The Sabbath injunction is repeated in verses 26–30. The weekly Sabbath was a reminder of Yahweh's gracious salvation and provision in the desert. There was also a Sabbath instituted for the land every seventh year (Ex. 23:10–12). In an urban society it is perhaps difficult to imagine what it must have meant not to plant or harvest for a year, allowing others to harvest the crops, but imagine not going to work for a year and allowing others to collect your benefits for a year. And every fifty years God's people were to observe the jubilee Sabbath (Lev. 25:8–10), which was to be announced on the day of atonement. These Sabbaths were pointers back to the creation pattern and to redemption, and forward to the fulfilment of the Sabbath and to the eternal rest.

At Sinai, Yahweh entered into a temporary, typological, national covenant with the Israelites. As we have seen, Israel's salvation was purely gracious. Their status as a national people, however, was formally stipulated on their obedience to the 613 commandments of the Torah.[15] The Sabbath was so integral to their status as the national people of God that it was even described as a covenant between Yahweh and his people. Exodus 31:13 says: "You are to speak to the people of Israel and say, 'Above all you shall keep my Sabbaths, for this is a sign between me and you throughout your generations, that you may know that I, Yahweh, sanctify you.'"[16]

Of course, Israel did not fulfil this or any law, and the Lord sent his prophets as covenant lawyers to prosecute the rebellion of his son Israel. We could fill an entire book cataloguing the Lord's complaint against his people throughout hundreds of years of redemptive history, but Isaiah 58:13 is typical of the prophetic prosecution of Israel's unbelief and disobedience. Their disregard for the Sabbath was symbolic of their disregard for both their status as creatures and as redeemed persons. When they

15. The rabbis calculated that there were 613 commandments (*mitzvoth*) in the first five books of the Hebrew Scriptures. See George Foot Moore, *Judaism*, 3 vols. (Cambridge, MA: Harvard University Press, 1958), 2:28, 83.

16. Revised from the ESV.

repented of their Sabbath-breaking ways, from pursuing their own plea-sure instead of the Lord's pleasure, then it would be clear that they were truly believing and penitent. As we have seen, however, the Sabbath was also gospel. Isaiah made that abundantly clear: the Sabbath was about more than our "doing" or "not doing." Yahweh reminded his people that his throne is heaven and "the earth is my footstool" and "the place of my rest" (Isa. 66:1). Yahweh did not enter into a covenant with Israel because of her sanctity, but he describes the consummate state, drawing upon imagery from the typology. The promise of the new heavens and earth is cast in terms of the Israelite Sabbath ("From new moon to new moon, and from Sabbath to Sabbath"), but the promise is universalized: "all flesh" shall worship Yahweh (Isa. 66:23). The prophet Zechariah depicts the consummate state as an eternal day, a "unique day" (ESV) in which the creational pattern of morning and evening is transcended by unending light mirroring the unending seventh day of creation (Zech. 14:7).

There can be little doubt of the importance of the Sabbath in the history of Israel. It has not, however, always seemed obvious to all Chris-tians in all times what to make of the Sabbath in the new covenant. In fulfilment of the old (Mosaic) covenant our Lord himself kept Sabbath perfectly, if not always to the satisfaction of the scribes and Pharisees who accused him of breaking the Sabbath. "One Sabbath he was going through the grainfields, and as they made their way, his disciples began to pluck heads of grain" (Mark 2:23 ESV), for which the Pharisees accused him of breaking the Sabbath (2:24). In response (2:26), Jesus appealed to the example of David (1 Sam. 21:1–7). If King David, who was not a priest and (by implication) was lesser, can eat from the bread of the presence, how much more can King Jesus do so, who is a priest (according to the order of Melchizedek, Ps. 110:4; Heb. 5:6) and greater? He rebuked them for turning the Sabbath on its head: "The Sabbath was made for man, not man for the Sabbath" (Mark 2:27 ESV). The Pharisees had made the Sabbath a burden—and had arranged it so it did not really limit them but they could use it as a tool to control others—when in fact the creational and redemptive purpose of the Sabbath was for joy and renewal. In his acts and speech, God the Son incarnate demonstrated to all with eyes that he is Lord of the Sabbath (Luke 6:5).

Jesus also demonstrated the true nature of the Sabbath by acts of restoration and renewal such as his healing of the man with the withered hand (Mark 3:1–6). On the Sabbath he entered the synagogue, according to custom. Knowing that his enemies were watching to see whether he would, in their view, break the law, Jesus provoked their ire by calling to himself a man with a withered hand. Knowing that the rabbis and Pharisees had long ago established their own legal code in addition to the 613 commandments of the Torah, which they called a "fence around the law," he issued a challenge: "Is it lawful on the Sabbath to do good or to do harm, to save life or to kill?" They were not able to reply because, as the Second Person of the Trinity, he had revealed the Sabbath in creation. Jesus went to the heart of the design and message of the Sabbath: renewal, rest, and realization of the consummation. He healed the man, delivering him from a profound effect of the fall. The contrast between Jesus and the Pharisees could not be sharper.[17] He heals and the Pharisees meet with their worst enemies to plot his murder.

Our Lord not only taught the permanence of the creational (i.e., moral) law (Matt. 5:17–19) and never repealed the creational pattern (which he himself instituted) of setting aside one day in seven,[18] but he also kept Sabbath perfectly every day, having loved his Father and his neighbor (Rom. 5:19). Our Lord was crucified on (Good) Friday, and spent the old Sabbath in the tomb, in another sort of rest. He was raised, however, "on the first day of the week" (Matt. 28:1; Mark 16:2; Luke 24:1; John 20:1). According to the apostle Paul, Jesus' resurrection means his vindication and our justification (Rom. 4:25). The resurrection also has cosmic implications; it means the transformation of the religious calendar for his people.[19] This follows the pattern of redemptive history. The old covenant festival calendar was determined principally by redemption, so it is fitting that the new covenant calendar would be determined by the first act of the new creation (2 Cor. 5:17; Gal. 6:15; Col. 1:15). So, the assignment of the re-creational new covenant Sabbath to the first day of the week is

17. "Those who set themselves up as defenders of the Sabbath were the very ones who were preventing people from knowing the blessing of the God whose day it was." See Campbell, *On the First Day*, 111.
18. Pipa, *The Lord's Day*, 55–56, 73–74.
19. Murray, *The Collected Writings of John Murray*, 1:221–22.

no more arbitrary than the assignment of the creational and typological Sabbath to the last day of the week was arbitrary.

Further, there was an ancient pattern of meeting in holy convocation "on the first day" (e.g., Ex. 12:16; 40:2; Lev. 23:7; Num. 28:18). We have positive evidence from the New Testament that the apostolic church met on the first day of the week. They were meeting together in hiding (John 20:19) when our Lord appeared among them and showed them his wounds. After the ascension, Luke records that the church met together in Ephesus "on the first of the Sabbaths" (Acts 20:7). It is interesting that Luke uses this idiomatic expression, which expression reflects continuity with the earlier Jewish conception and practice of setting aside one day a week for rest and renewal.[20] In 1 Corinthians 16:2, Paul uses a similar expression, speaking of the congregation meeting "on the first of the Sabbath" (*kata mian sabbatou*). Certainly, the apostolic company attended the synagogue in order to preach Christ, but the "seventh day Sabbath was not their preferred day of meeting."[21] Paul assumes that the Christians met on Sunday in observation of the resurrection of Jesus, and his mention of two liturgical acts in his great resurrection discourse seems to connect his doctrine of the resurrection to public worship (1 Cor. 15:1, 29). One of the most intriguing, if perhaps opaque, references to the first day of the week as the Christian Sabbath occurs in the Apocalypse when the apostle John describes himself as having been "in the Spirit" on "the Lord's Day" (Rev. 1:10). The apostle was "in the Spirit." By analogy, he was so "in the day belonging to the Lord." Given its context (and the long history of Christian interpretation), this seems to be the most likely meaning.[22]

In short, the Christian Sabbath is not chiefly grounded in the (old) Mosaic covenant but rather in creation and redemption, both of which transcend that temporary typological covenant. As we will see, this

20. Luke's usage in Acts 20:7 and Paul's usage in 1 Cor. 16:2 reflect the LXX where Ex. 20:8 commands believers literally to "remember the day of the Sabbaths." A similar expression occurs in Ex. 35:3, "on the day of the Sabbaths." Lev. 16:31 says "This Sabbath of Sabbaths shall be a rest to you."

21. Campbell, *On the First Day*, 143.

22. For an alternate interpretation see Meredith G. Kline, *God, Heaven and Har Magedon: A Covenantal Tale of Cosmos and Telos* (Eugene, OR: Wipf & Stock, 2006), 191–93. In general, as fascinating as Kline's suggestions are, in his view of the Sabbath (187–98) it seems that eschatology swallows up rather than renews creation.

understanding is not novel. It has roots in Calvin and the Reformed tradition. According to Patrick Collinson, the Puritan understanding of the Sabbath was based "on the doctrinal assertion that the fourth commandment is not an obsolete ceremonial law of the Jews but a perpetual, moral law, binding on Christians."[23] In the words of Nicholas Bownd (d. 1613), "as it came in with the first Man, so it must not go out but with the last man."[24]

The Historic Christian Pattern

R. J. Bauckham says that before the end of the apostolic period, the early Christian practice was to meet on Sunday (morning and evening). He takes Revelation 1:10 as a temporal referent, that John "receives his visions on the day when the churches meet for corporate worship and on the same day his prophecy will be read aloud (1:3) in the church meeting."[25] He argues that the predominant theme of the Revelation is Christ's lordship and concludes that as the visions were read in the churches, Christians were to understand that, despite their current circumstances, the Christ who had conquered and revealed himself to John, was laying claim to the first day of the week over against the imperial cult and the monthly "Emperor's Day" (*Sebaste*).[26]

The Didache (c. 75–110) used the expression "Lord's Day." The significance of this usage is disputed, but since it repeats the language of Revelation 1:10, if the expression "Lord's Day" in Revelation 1:10 means something like "day of Christian worship," then it likely means the same

23. Patrick Collinson, "The Beginnings of English Sabbatarianism," *Studies in Church History* 1 (1964): 207, as quoted in Bryan W. Ball, *The Seventh-Day Men: Sabbatarians and Sabbatarianism in England and Wales 1600–1800* (Oxford: Oxford University Press, 1994), 43.

24. Bownd, *The Doctrine of the Sabbath*, 6. See also ibid., 21. Most Reformed folk did not agree with Bownd's assertion, however, that there are no ceremonial elements in the Decalogue.

25. R. J. Bauckham, "The Lord's Day," in *From Sabbath to Lord's Day: A Biblical, Historical, and Theological Investigation*, ed. D. A. Carson (Grand Rapids: Zondervan, 1982), 240–41. See also G. K. Beale, *The Book of Revelation: A Commentary on the Greek Text*, The New International Greek Testament Commentary (Grand Rapids: Eerdmans, 1999), 203.

26. Ibid., 244–45.

here.[27] Further, according to C. W. Dugmore, this expression was used the same way in some of the early Christian apocryphal writings.[28] "The Lord's Day, then, very early achieved a position among Christians equal to that of the Sabbath among the Jews."[29] Though there were Saturday Sabbatarians in the early church, the general practice of the orthodox in the postapostolic church seems to have been to keep a Sunday Sabbath. Their practice was in contrast with at least three groups who denied the Sunday Sabbath in favor of a "seventh-day" Sabbath: the Ebionites, the Apollinarians, and the Manicheans.[30]

The pseudepigraphal Epistle of Barnabas (70–150) mainly considered the Sabbath as a foretaste of the consummation, in contrast to the old Jewish Sabbath. He contrasted the Jewish Sabbath with the Christian Sunday in passing.[31] Others of the fathers (e.g., Irenaeus and Tertullian) took the Sabbath command metaphorically, interpreting it to teach a daily resting from sin. It seems evident that much of the early Christian approach to the Sabbath was colored by their response to Jewish critics who accused them of antinomianism.[32]

There were other practical difficulties. As Bauckham observes, there "is no second-century evidence that Sunday was regarded as a day of rest." It is unclear "how much of the day was taken up by Christian corporate activities, but both persecution and economic circumstances must often have kept many Christians at work during the working hours of the day." Nevertheless, Bauckham notes that Sunday was regarded as "the Christian festival."[33] Barnabas (15:9) speaks of celebrating with rejoicing "the eighth day." According to the ancient Christian historian Eusebius, Dionysius of Corinth reported, "Today we have celebrated the Lord's holy day." Peter

---

27. Michael William Holmes, *The Apostolic Fathers: Greek Texts and English Translations*, 3rd ed. (Grand Rapids: Baker, 2006), 170.

28. C. W. Dugmore, *The Influence of the Synagogue upon the Divine Office* (London: Oxford University Press, 1944), 26–27.

29. Ibid., 27.

30. So Francis Turretin, *Institutes of Elenctic Theology*, trans. George Musgrave Giger, 3 vols. (Phillipsburg, NJ: P&R, 1992), 11.13.19. See also R. J. Bauckham, "Sabbath and Sunday in the Post-Apostolic Church," in *From Sabbath to Lord's Day*, ed. Carson, 255–62.

31. Bauckham, "Sabbath and Sunday in the Post-Apostolic Church," 262–64.

32. Ibid., 266–69, 274.

33. Emphasis original.

of Alexandria spoke of "celebrating" the Lord's Day as a "day of rejoicing because of his rising on it." He concludes that it is clear that in the early church "the Lord's Day was a day of festal rejoicing in the Lord's resurrection and the salvation it brings." The evidence that it was fully a day of rest is unclear, but Bauckham concedes that "the conception of Sunday as the Christian festival might lead to a desire for it to be a work-free day, as the Jewish and pagan religious festivals were."[34]

The persistent claims of Saturday Sabbatarians notwithstanding, the evidence that the early Christians regarded the first day of the week as the day of Christian worship and anticipation of the consummation seems clear. Sunday did not become an officially recognized day of rest until Emperor Constantine, in 321, declared a law requiring "total, public rest from work, 'on the most honourable day of the Sun.'"[35] About nine years later, Eusebius of Caesarea made the first formal Christian defense of Sunday as the Christian Sabbath.[36] The regional Synod of Laodicea (Turkey), held in the mid-fourth century, decreed in canon 29 that "Christians must not judaize by resting on the [Saturday] Sabbath, but must work that day, rather honoring the Lord's Day [*Kyriakē*]; and, if they can, resting then as Christians. But if any shall be found to be judaizers, let them be anathema."[37] The twelfth century Greek canonist, Theodore Basalmon (c. 1140–c. 1195), understood this canon to require the cessation of work on Sunday, except on account of "necessity."[38]

Bauckham is certainly correct that Augustine was both the "pinnacle of Western theology in the patristic age" and the "fountainhead of medieval theology in the West."[39] He defended the Decalogue as the moral law against the Manichean dualists. Global claims about what Augustine taught are usually hard to sustain since his theology developed over a long period of time and in response to many different external and internal stimuli. Thus, Bauckham's claim that Augustine "never based

34. Ibid., 275.

35. Ibid., 280.

36. Ibid., 282.

37. Philip Schaff and Henry Wace, eds., *The Seven Ecumenical Councils*, Nicene and Post-Nicene Fathers, Second Series 14 (Grand Rapids: Eerdmans, 1983), 148.

38. Ibid., 149.

39. R. J. Bauckham, "Sabbath and Sunday in the Medieval Church in the West," in *From Sabbath to Lord's Day*, ed. Carson, 300.

the Christian observance of Sunday on the Sabbath commandment" is the sort of claim that must be tested by the sort of detailed research that cannot be attempted in the space of this chapter.[40] Nevertheless, we may be rather more cautious than Bauckham here.

It is more certain that the early and high medieval theologians did take over the idea that, theologically considered, the Sabbath teaches us about the consummation and morally it teaches us our need to rest from sin. Bauckham characterizes, somewhat arbitrarily and unfairly, as "Sabbatarian" various conciliar decisions (e.g., Orléans, 538; Mâcon, 585; Rouen, c. 650) wrestling with the problem of labor on Sundays. As the early church had worked through essential christological and theological questions by developing more sophisticated formulae, so now, as the chaos created and signaled by the collapse of Rome was easing, the early medieval church was able to begin to work through theological and moral questions raised by the application of the moral law to the church and civil society. The various conciliar decisions reflect that growing sophistication. Thus, the church came to distinguish between necessary work and servile labor as it began to reckon Sunday, in the words of the Council of Mâcon, as the "perpetual day of rest foreshadowed in the seventh day and made known to us in the Law and the Prophets."[41]

Synthesizing the main lines of medieval theology, Thomas Aquinas distinguished between civil, ceremonial, and moral laws.[42] In his exposition of what the medieval church regarded as the third commandment (which we call the fourth), Thomas argued for a view of the Christian Sabbath that most confessional Reformed folk would recognize.[43] He argued that Christians ought to regard the Sabbath as a day of rest and worship. There were also discontinuities with the Reformed approach to the Sabbath. In reply to the objection that there is a fundamental discrepancy between the old Sabbath and the new, he argued that the Lord's Day replaced the

40. Ibid., 301.
41. Ibid., 303. Bauckham suggests that the developing doctrine of the Sabbath in the early medieval church was chiefly the product of Christendom. Doubtless the changing social situation of the church was an essential part of all medieval theology and ethics, but his argument that it was not also a biblical or theological conclusion seems arbitrary.
42. *ST* 1a2ae.100.3.
43. Ibid., 2a2ae.122.4.

Jewish Sabbath not by virtue of precept (divine institution) but "by the institution of the church and the custom of Christian people." According to Thomas, the new covenant Sabbath is easier and less regulated than the old.[44] Thomas's interpretation of the fourth commandment has become the magisterial doctrine of the Roman communion.[45]

In the period of the Reformation, there were multiple approaches to the Sabbath. Among the radicals, some of the Anabaptists carried on the Saturday Sabbath praxis of some of the dissenters in the patristic period. There were others who kept a Saturday Sabbath in the sixteenth century, such as the Seventh-Day Baptists. The rationale for the Saturday Sabbath was regarded by the confessional Protestants as legalistic because it failed to recognize the progress of revelation and redemption, and as biblicist because of its naïve, unhistorical hermeneutic. By the middle of the sixteenth century, the same sort of biblicism and moralism that produced the earlier Seventh-Day movements also stimulated the Socinian adoption of the Saturday Sabbath. From the late 1550s there was also a Seventh-Day Baptist movement in England and the Netherlands. Thus, it is important to bear in mind that when Luther and Calvin are found to inveigh against the Sabbatarians, it is these groups they have in their sights, not the mainstream Christian practice of the Sabbath. For example, this is the context for Luther's 1538 treatise, *Against the Sabbatarians*,[46] and his later criticism of certain Austrian Sabbatarians in his lectures on Genesis.[47] One would be hard pressed to distinguish Luther's exposition of the fourth commandment (which he numbered as the third) from that of many Reformed folk.

The other significant background to early Protestant rhetoric concerning the Sabbath was the fairly oppressive ecclesiastical calendar of the

---

44. This way of speaking follows from the medieval "old law/new law" hermeneutic. On this see R. Scott Clark, "Letter and Spirit: Law and Gospel in Reformed Preaching," in *Covenant, Justification, and Pastoral Ministry: Essays by the Faculty of Westminster Seminary California*, ed. R. Scott Clark (Phillipsburg, NJ: P&R, 2006), 331–63. On the force of "custom" in Thomas's ethics see David VanDrunen, *Law & Custom: The Thought of Thomas Aquinas and the Future of the Common Law* (New York: Peter Lang, 2003).

45. *Catechism of the Catholic Church*, 2d ed. (Vatican City: Libreria editrice, 1997), para. 2193.

46. *LW*, 47:57–98.

47. Ibid., 2:362; 7:152.

Roman church which featured many "days of obligation," "holy days" in addition to the Sabbath, so that the Lord's Day became just one among many days. In reaction to the moralism of the medieval church, the early church emphasized Christian liberty from human inventions.

In his Large Catechism (1529), Luther acknowledged the Seventh-Day Sabbath as peculiarly Jewish, but also that the Sabbath was for rest and worship.[48] Inasmuch as the Sabbath command was Jewish, it does not obligate Christians. The "Christian interpretation" of the Sabbath is that we keep holy days "first because our bodies need them." The Sabbath provides rest for working folk. "Second, and most important, we observe them so that people will have time and opportunity of such days of rest, which otherwise would not be available, to attend worship services, that is so that they may assemble to hear and discuss God's Word and then to offer praise, song, and prayer to God."[49]

This moral aspect of the Sabbath "is not restricted, as it was among the Jews, to a particular time."[50] It is a universal obligation for Christians. Contra the Roman church calendar, in principle, no day is better than another, but as a matter of practice there must be at least one day in the week set apart.[51] Whenever "God's Word is taught, preached, heard, read or pondered, there the person, the day, and the work is hallowed."[52] Worship services have been "appointed in order that God's Word may exert its power publicly."[53] Nevertheless, Luther was polemical against Sabbath-breaking. Because the ministry of the Word of God is so important, "God wants this commandment to be kept strictly and will punish all who despise his Word and refuse to hear and learn it, especially at the times appointed." Those who "grossly misuse and desecrate the holy day" through "greed or frivolity" violate the commandment.[54] According to Luther, it is obviously sin to absent one's self from public worship (in

48. Timothy Wengert and Charles Arand et al., eds., *The Book of Concord* (Minneapolis: Fortress, 2000), 397.
49. Ibid.
50. Ibid., 398.
51. Ibid., 399.
52. Ibid.
53. Ibid.
54. Ibid.

favor of spending that time in taverns or getting drunk).[55] Less obviously but as importantly he preached to "that other crowd, who listen to God's Word as they would to any other entertainment, who only from force of habit go to hear the sermon, and leave again, with as little knowledge at the end of the year as at the beginning."[56] The next year, the Augsburg Confession (Art. 28) offered an answer to Thomas and the Roman view that the Christian Lord's Day was instituted by ecclesiastical authority: "The sabbath, which—contrary to the Decalogue, it seems—was changed to Sunday is also cited. No example is brought up more often than this change of the sabbath. Great, they contend, is the power of the church, that it dispensed with a commandment of the Decalogue!"[57]

As Luther's student, Calvin agreed that the Seventh-Day Sabbath was "abolished with the other types on the advent of Christ."[58] The typological Sabbath accomplished three purposes: First, "to furnish the people of Israel with a type of the spiritual rest by which believers were to cease from their own works, and allow God to work in them."[59] Second, that there should be a stated day for public worship, and third, that the working classes might have a "day of rest . . . and thus have some intermission from labor."[60] As a creational institution, eschatology was embedded in the Sabbath. The implicit message of the "succession of day and night" leading up to the Lord's rest day signaled that "the Sabbath never should be completed before the arrival of the last day."[61] With the advent of Christ, the "ceremonial part of the commandment was abolished."[62] Nevertheless, there remains "room among us" under Christ to gather for public services, "for the hearing of the Word, the breaking of the mystical bread, and public prayer," and to give rest to servants. Indeed, if it were possible, it would be

55. Ibid.

56. Ibid.

57. Ibid., 95, 97. (NB: The English translation of the Latin text of the Augsburg Confession is on alternating pages.)

58. John Calvin, *Institutes of the Christian Religion*, trans. H. Beveridge, 2 vols. (Grand Rapids: Eerdmans, 1957), 2.8.28.

59. We will see that the HC took over this language verbatim in Q. 103.

60. Calvin, *Institutes* 2.8.28. See also John Calvin, *John Calvin's Sermons on the Ten Commandments*, trans. Benjamin W. Farley (Grand Rapids: Baker, 1980), 115–32.

61. *Institutes* 2.8.30.

62. Ibid. See also John Calvin, *Commentaries on the Last Four Books of Moses*, trans. Charles William Bingham, 4 vols. (Grand Rapids: Eerdmans, 1950), 2:435–37.

desirable to meet daily, but given our weakness, we should "adopt the rule which the will of God has obviously imposed upon us."[63]

Against his libertine critics, who complained that his observance of the Lord's Day was Judaizing, Calvin argued that "we are not celebrating it as a ceremony with the most rigid scrupulousness supposing a spiritual mystery to be figured thereby. Rather, we are using it as a remedy needed to keep order in the church."[64] As he continued, he made clear that his intent was not to weaken the notion and practice of the Christian Sabbath, but, with Paul, to reject superstition. In the same section he reminds his critics that, according to the apostle Paul, "the Sabbath was retained."[65] In his lecture on Exodus 31:13 he argued for a substantial continuity between the Mosaic covenant and the new covenant but a change in circumstances or accidents. The eternality of the covenant Yahweh made with Israel in the Sabbath has reference to "the new state of things that came to pass at the coming of Christ."[66] The eternality of the law does not transcend its fulfilment in Christ, when "God's covenant assumed a different form."[67]

In his last section on the fourth commandment (in the *Institutes*), Calvin made use of some language to which those who set Calvin against the Reformed confessions appeal. He said that it was "not without reason that the early Christians substituted what we call the Lord's Day for the Sabbath." He continued by criticizing those who treat the Christian Sabbath as if the only difference from the old covenant Sabbath is the change of day.[68] Those who would set Calvin against the later British and European Reformed practice or even against the Westminster Standards on the Sabbath must reckon with the context in which Calvin wrote this section of the *Institutes*, chiefly the reformation of the Roman ecclesiasti-

---

63. *Institutes* 2.8.32. He followed this same pattern in his second catechism. See Henry Beveridge and Jule Bonnet, eds., *Selected Works of John Calvin*, 7 vols. (Grand Rapids: Baker, reprint, 1983), 2:62–63.

64. *Institutes* 2.8.33.

65. Ibid.

66. Calvin, *Commentaries on the Last Four Books of Moses*, 2:443.

67. Ibid.

68. *Institutes* 2.8.34. Some even appeal to the apocryphal story of Calvin "bowling" on the Sabbath. There is no contemporaneous historical evidence for this tale. Given that Calvin usually preached twice and taught catechism in between services and was often in ill health, it is hard to imagine when he would have had time for it.

cal calendar, how he practiced the Sabbath in Geneva, and perhaps most importantly how he preached on the fourth commandment.[69] To give but one example of the pastoral tightrope he had to walk, he defended himself in a 1551 letter to a Reformed pastor in Bern against the charge that he was personally responsible for abolishing the feast days in Geneva, and thus, implicitly, for sponsoring antinomianism. He reminded his correspondent that, in fact, the Genevans had begun observing only the Lord's Day before he arrived.[70] It remained a matter of controversy for several years, since he had to defend himself to the Bernese authorities on these same matters again in 1555.[71]

In his 1555 sermons on Deuteronomy 5:12–14 and 5:13–15 Calvin clearly retained the "shadow vs. substance" hermeneutic for understanding our relations to the typological Sabbath under Moses.[72] That the shadows have been fulfilled, however, does not exhaust Calvin's application of the substance of the Sabbath command to new covenant believers. One element of Calvin's theology and exposition of the Sabbath for which few interpreters account, and which we can consider only inchoately, is that he considered the Sabbath on multiple levels simultaneously. The theological significance of the Sabbath is that believers have been redeemed from sin, but for Calvin, the theological sense of the Sabbath did not exhaust its meaning. The moral sense or the implications of the Sabbath remained in force in every epoch of revelation and redemption.[73] The fourth commandment is not "superfluous to us." That is why Hebrews 4 speaks about

69. See e.g., John H. Primus, "Calvin and the Puritan Sabbath: A Comparative Study," in *Exploring the Heritage of John Calvin*, ed. David A. Holwerda (Grand Rapids: Baker, 1976), 40–75. See also Richard B. Gaffin Jr., *Calvin and the Sabbath* (Ross-shire, UK: Mentor, 1998), chapter 5; idem, "Westminster and the Sabbath," in *The Westminster Confession into the 21ˢᵗ Century: Essays in Remembrance of the 350th Anniversary of the Westminster Assembly*, ed. J. Ligon Duncan III (Ross-shire, UK: Christian Focus, 2004), 123–44.

70. Beveridge and Bonnet, eds., *Selected Works of John Calvin*, 5:287–88. The editors note that Calvin was also charged with abolishing the Sabbath itself, a charge which he refuted in his correspondence.

71. Ibid., 6:163.

72. Calvin, *John Calvin's Sermons on the Ten Commandments*, 98–99. For the early English translation of this sermon see John Calvin, *The Sermons of M. John Calvin upon the Fifth Booke of Moses Called Deuteronomie* (London, 1583; Edinburgh: Banner of Truth Trust, reprint, 1987), 200–205.

73. Calvin, *John Calvin's Sermons on the Ten Commandments*, 102.

the Sabbath. Its true meaning is that we must die to ourselves and learn to be governed by the Holy Spirit.[74] The Sabbath requires us to rest because "we are unable to have a true union and sanctity with him unless we rest from our work. If we continue to hurry about and insist on being busybodies, engaging in what seems best to us, we shall certainly sever the tie between God and ourselves." It is because the Christian Sabbath is the fulfilment rather than the shadow that it is "rebellion" to treat it as an opportunity for license.[75]

> If we turn Sunday into a day for living it up, for our sport and pleasure, indeed, how will God be honored in that? Is it not a mockery and even a profanation of his name? But when shops are closed on Sunday, when people do not travel in the usual way, its purpose is to provide more leisure and liberty for attending to what God commands us that we might be taught by his Word, that we might convene together in order to confess our faith, to invoke his name, [and] to participate in the use of the sacraments.[76]

Calvin was impatient with those who "call themselves Christians" who "think that Sunday exists for the purpose of enabling them to attend to their own affairs and who reserve this day for [that] purpose as if there were no others throughout the week deliberating their business." No better are they who stay indoors to prevent detection, who "do not dare display a manifest scorn on the streets" but who nevertheless treat Sunday as a "retreat for them in which they stand aloof from the church of God."[77]

In fact, on the Sabbath in Geneva there was little time for anything else but worship, rest, and works of mercy. After Calvin's return to Geneva in 1541 the *petit conseil* approved his Ecclesiastical Ordinances that stipulated that there was to be a morning sermon (at daybreak) in each of the city churches. At midday there was catechism instruction in the churches followed by a three o'clock service.[78] Whatever one makes of the details

74. Ibid., 103.
75. Ibid., 105.
76. Ibid., 109.
77. Ibid.
78. Sinnema, "The Second Service in the Early Dutch Reformed Tradition," 300–301. See also Hughes Oliphant Old, *The Shaping of the Reformed Baptismal Rite in the Sixteenth*

of Calvin's theology of the Sabbath, his rhetoric and practice of the Sabbath were virtually indistinguishable from his successors at Westminster Abbey, Edinburgh, and Leiden.

Zacharias Ursinus (1534–83), the principal author of the Heidelberg Catechism and its principal expositor, argued (on the basis of Ex. 16) that there was a Sabbath prior to the formal institution of the Sabbath at Sinai, that, strictly speaking, the New Testament teaches not a "Sabbath," but the Lord's Day. As with Calvin, he was zealous to stress the distinction between the Mosaic observance of the Seventh-Day Sabbath and the Christian Lord's Day. Thus, he argued that when Paul speaks of "new moons and Sabbaths" (Col. 2:16), he was echoing the language of Isaiah 66:23, but he did not make a sharp distinction, as many have since, between the minor new moons and Sabbaths of the Jewish calendar and the weekly Sabbath. Nevertheless, he recognized that the pattern of setting aside one day in seven is grounded not in Mosaic theocratic law, but in creation, which transcends the various epochs of revelation.[79] As with Calvin, the impression is left that Ursinus would not be a Sabbatarian, but he gave these lectures at a time when attendance to Lord's Day worship was a matter of civil law. On the Lord's Day, walking in parks, or lane, or to the local tavern was forbidden. Mockery of those going to church was punishable by a fine.[80] There were two services at Holy Spirit Church each Sabbath, a morning service and an afternoon catechism service at three o'clock.[81]

Dort-era Old Testament scholar and theologian Johannes Wollebius (1586–1629) argued for the existence of a pre-Sinaitic Sabbath on the basis that the Israelites were commanded to "remember" the Sabbath. If they were to remember the Sabbath, it must have existed before Sinai.[82]

Century (Grand Rapids: Eerdmans, 1992), 196–97.

79. Zacharias Ursinus, *Commentary on the Heidelberg Catechism*, trans. George W. Williard (Phillipsburg, NJ: Presbyterian and Reformed, 1985), 562.

80. R. Scott Clark, *Caspar Olevian and the Substance of the Covenant: The Double Benefit of Christ*, Rutherford Studies in Historical Theology (Edinburgh: Rutherford House, 2005), 27.

81. Sinnema, "The Second Service in the Early Dutch Reformed Tradition," 303–4.

82. Johannes Wollebius, *Compendium Theologiae Christianae*, in *Reformed Dogmatics*, ed. John W. Beardslee III, Library of Protestant Thought (New York: Oxford University Press, 1965), 220–21. See also Calvin, *Commentaries on the Last Four Books of Moses*, 2:439–40.

Indeed, as with Calvin and Ursinus, he regarded it is a creational institution.[83] To sanctify the Sabbath means to set it aside for its intended purpose: rest and worship. This is the pattern of the Mosaic Sabbath observance, the "equity" of which continues to bind Christians.[84] Nevertheless, the Mosaic Sabbath was typological.[85] For Wollebius, as for Calvin and Ursinus, to sanctify the Sabbath means to cease from daily labor, but the Sabbath is also intended for worship, the celebration of the sacraments, for meditation on the Word, and for works of charity.[86] Wollebius's most interesting argument was that there are, in the history of redemption, three Sabbaths: the typological (Mosaic) Sabbath, that was fulfilled in Christ; the spiritual Sabbath that we keep by faith in and obedience to Christ; and the eternal Sabbath which is begun in this life and consummated at the last day.[87] The Sabbath is neglected when we fail to rest by doing secular or servile work and when we fail to observe the means of grace.[88]

Toward the end of the seventeenth century, writing from Geneva, Francis Turretin (1623–87) followed Wollebius's argument about the three kinds of Sabbaths in Scripture.[89] He argued for the existence of a pre-Sinaitic Sabbath on the basis of the divine blessing and sanctifying of the Sabbath in the creation narrative.[90] He rejected the notion that Moses was speaking retrospectively in Genesis 1, that he read the Sinaitic revelation back into the creation account. He agreed with Wollebius that the verb "to remember" (Ex. 20:8) indicates the preexistence of the Sabbath before Sinai.[91] The creational Sabbath looked forward to the eschatological state.[92] As a moral creational law the fourth commandment requires the appointment of public assemblies for worship on a fixed day, the sanctification of the Sabbath by cessation from servile works, and physical

83. Wollebius, *Compendium Theologiae Christianae*, 221.
84. Ibid.
85. Ibid., 222.
86. Ibid.
87. Ibid., 223.
88. Ibid., 223–24.
89. Francis Turretin, *Institutes of Elenctic Theology*, trans. George Musgrave Giger, 3 vols. (Phillipsburg, NJ: P&R, 1992), 11.13.3.
90. Ibid.
91. Ibid., 11.13.10.
92. Ibid., 11.13.17.

relief for image-bearers and other creatures.[93] According to Turretin, the transition from Saturday to Sunday is a matter of Christian liberty, but the transition was not arbitrary. The change was grounded in redemptive history. The Christian Sabbath is grounded in apostolic (not postcanonical) authority.[94] When the apostle Paul spoke of "Sabbaths" (Rom. 14:5; Gal. 4:10; Col. 2:16), he did not speak of the weekly Sabbath, but of the ceremonial Sabbaths.[95] Turretin also appealed to the Post-Acta of the Synod of Dort, to which we will turn below.[96]

Wilhelmus à Brakel (1635–1711) is an excellent example of the theology and piety of the *Nadere Reformatie*, a technical Dutch expression that is perhaps best translated as "Dutch Puritanism." Where the other writers in the Reformed tradition surveyed thus far began with the difficulties surrounding the progressive revelation of the Sabbath, Brakel moved quickly to the practice of the Sabbath.[97] He offered a word study of the verb *shabbat* focusing on the root sense "to stop, to cease."[98] His focus, however, was on the praxis and piety of the Christian Sabbath. Where, for Wollebius and Turretin, the Sabbath was equally about rest and worship, Brakel's discussion focused on rest.[99] He enjoined seven virtues in connection with the Sabbath, most of which have to do with right practice. Precisionism is certainly evident in some of the discussion, but one also senses the care of a pastor for sheep who needed practical advice.[100]

Having established the practice, he considered theological questions at some length, remonstrating with the Socinians, Anabaptists, and other antinomians who had only nine commandments.[101] He rejected any typology of Christ in the fourth commandment. Like the rest of the tradition, he grounded the Sabbath in creation, arguing that, because it is creational,

93. Ibid., 11.13.33.
94. Ibid., 11.14.5–7.
95. Ibid., 11.14.16.
96. Ibid., 11.14.28.
97. Wilhelmus à Brakel, *The Christian's Reasonable Service*, trans. Bartel Elshout, 4 vols. (Ligonier, PA: Soli Deo Gloria, 1992), 3:139.
98. Ibid., 3:140.
99. He did discuss the necessity of public worship. See ibid., 3:142.
100. Ibid., 3:143–48.
101. Ibid., 4:149–51; 3:159.

it transcends the typological epoch and continues to obligate Christians. His emphasis on the continuity between Moses and Christ caused him to downplay the ceremonial aspects of Sabbath under Moses (which he conceded reluctantly), which made it more difficult for him to argue for the change from the last day to the first day of the week.[102] Despite some of his emphases, Brakel's treatment of the Sabbath follows the mainstream of the classical Reformed theology of the fourth commandment.

In the nineteenth century, Charles Hodge (1797–1878) followed this same basic outline of the traditional Reformed arguments, grounding the Sabbath in creation even more ardently than some. For Hodge, the original intent of the prelapsarian Sabbath was to celebrate the week of creation.[103] It was also intended to preserve the knowledge of the Creator among his creatures, to point to the spiritual amidst the ordinary, to set aside time for Christian instruction, to provide rest for the weary, and to provide time for spiritual intercourse with God.[104] He argued that the Decalogue is moral (not positive) law, grounded in creation.[105] He appealed to the hebdomadal organization of the week as grounded in the creation fiat, traces of which pattern are witnessed throughout redemptive history (e.g., Gen. 8:10, 12).[106] The change from Saturday to Sunday was a result of the fulfilment of the typological epoch in Christ. The first-day Sabbath is not arbitrary because it is grounded in Christ's resurrection and instituted by the "competent authority" of the apostles.[107]

Though there is some diversity in the ways in which the Sabbath has been understood in the confessional Reformed churches, there has been a significant degree of agreement on the main points. The Christian Sabbath has always been regarded as grounded in creation and in the re-creation of redemption, and instituted for rest, worship, acts of charity, and as a structural pointer to the consummate existence.

102. Ibid., 3:152–58.
103. Charles Hodge, *Systematic Theology*, 3 vols. (New York: Scribner, Armstrong, 1873), 3:321.
104. Ibid., 3:322.
105. Ibid., 3:323–24.
106. Ibid., 3:327–28.
107. Ibid., 3:330–32.

The Confessional Pattern

Though often set against each other on this question, when read carefully with their different contexts in mind, the Reformed confessions are best understood as having substantially the same doctrine of the Christian Sabbath. Before turning to those confessional documents which continue to have ecclesiastical sanction in the Reformed churches today, it is helpful to consider the Second Helvetic Confession written in 1561 by Heinrich Bullinger (1504–75) at the behest of the Palatinate elector Frederick III, and published in 1566. Though much neglected today, the Second Helvetic was highly regarded in the sixteenth century and widely used on the Continent and in Britain and adopted by the Scottish kirk.

In chapter 24 Bullinger argued that "in the ancient churches" there were not only hours set aside in the week for meetings, but also the Lord's Day was set aside by the apostles for a "holy rest, a practice now rightly preserved by our Churches for the sake of worship and love." Identifying the legalism of the Roman church and the Saturday Sabbatarians with Judaizing legalists of Paul's day, Bullinger confessed that "we give no place unto the Jewish observation of the day, or to any superstitions." For those reasons he distinguished between the Christian Lord's Day and the Jewish Sabbath. He had no qualms with voluntary celebrations of "the Lord's Nativity, Circumcision, Passion, Resurrection, and of his Ascension . . . and the sending of the Holy Spirit . . . according to Christian liberty."[108]

The teaching of the HC is often set against the teaching of the Westminster Standards quite unnecessarily and without reference to the two contexts in which the two standards were drafted and adopted.[109] Richard Gaffin is surely right when he says, "The difference between the Puritan Sabbath and Continental Sunday should not be exaggerated, especially so far as the actual practices of churches in the Reformed tradition are in view. . . . Here we may speak of a Reformed consensus

---

108. *Creeds*, 3:899.
109. This is true of the treatment offered in Fred H. Klooster, *Our Only Comfort: A Comprehensive Commentary on the Heidelberg Catechism*, 2 vols. (Grand Rapids: CRC Publications, 2001), 2:978–79.

or, as it may also be put, a consensus of generic Calvinism."[110] The HC was composed to teach the Reformed faith to Germans who had only a few years earlier been Roman Catholic, then suddenly Lutheran, and now, just as suddenly, Reformed. The oppressive legalism and moralism of the Roman theology, piety, and practice were all around them. The Roman critics attacked the Reformed as promoting immorality. Further, the confessional Lutherans were highly critical of the German Reformed as secret moralists. In this chaotic and confused situation, the pastors of the Reformed congregations of the Palatinate set out to teach the people a simple theology and practice of the Sabbath. The Westminster Standards were drafted and adopted about eighty years later in an equally chaotic situation (the English Civil War) but with Roman moralism more a distant memory than a vital threat. Rather than moralism, the Westminster Assembly faced the crisis of wartime antinomianism (as well as highly developed Arminianism, Socinianism, and other challenges). The Anglicans, Independents, and Presbyterians were working out a modus vivendi in what seemed to be a postmonarchical, politico-ecclesiastical situation. Given the different settings and times in which the two documents were composed, the degree to which they agree is remarkable.

In 1563, HC Q. 103 asked, "What does God require in the fourth Commandment?"

> In the first place, God wills that the ministry of the Gospel and schools be maintained; and that I, especially on the day of rest, diligently attend church, to learn the Word of God, to use the Holy Sacraments, to call publicly upon the Lord, and to give Christian alms. In the second place, that all the days of my life I rest from my evil works, allow the Lord to work in me by His Spirit, and thus begin in this life the everlasting Sabbath.[111]

110. Gaffin, "Westminster and the Sabbath," 123–24. On the English Puritan doctrine of the Sabbath see James T. Dennison Jr., *The Market Day of the Soul: The Puritan Doctrine of the Sabbath in England, 1532–1700* (Lanham, MD: University Press of America, 1983); Campbell, *On the First Day*, 158–79.

111. Creeds, 3:345.

The three main themes of the catechism's treatment of the Lord's Day are those we have observed in the main lines of Reformed teaching from Calvin to Hodge: rest, worship, and anticipating eternity. The German text of the catechism says, "God wills firstly (*Gott will erstlich*) the ministry of the Word and schooling (*Predigtamt und Schulen erhalten werden*)." This is, as Fred Klooster says, a reference to the two services required by the 1563 church order. The morning sermon was to be an exposition of Scripture directly, and the afternoon sermon was to be an exposition of Scripture using the catechism.[112]

The catechism uses two nouns as synonyms to describe the Lord's Day, *Feiertag* and *Sabbath*. The traditional English translation of the first noun is "day of rest." Klooster emphasized it as a "day of celebration."[113] The use of Sabbath as a synonym helps us understand the teaching of the catechism. Christians can "begin in this life the eternal Sabbath" only because the Christian Sabbath participates in and reflects the final Sabbath.[114]

The second half of the exposition of the commandment focuses on the spiritual implications of the fourth commandment. In its fullest sense the Sabbath command, just as the first three commands, demands constant devotion to Christ every day not only on the Sabbath. Thus the catechism interprets the Sabbath to teach us to rest from our sins daily (see HC QQ. 88–90). Spiritually, the Sabbath also teaches us to "allow the Lord to work in me by the Spirit." In this way we enter proleptically into the final Sabbath in this life.

There can be no doubt that the authors understood the Lord's Day to be a Christian Sabbath. The German and Dutch Reformed churches certainly adopted it with the understanding that it required Reformed Christians to set aside one day in seven for rest, worship, and anticipation of the consummation. Before they left, the international delegates to the Synod of Dort each gave advice to the Dutch Reformed churches on how catechism services ought to be held.[115] All of them assumed that Sunday

---

112. Klooster, *Our Only Comfort*, 2:981.

113. Ibid., 2:980. The Latin text has "festis diebus." See Niemeyer, 455.

114. Doubtless this is why the Dutch Reformed churches inserted the expression "the Sabbath, that is" after "day of rest." See Gaffin, "Westminster and the Sabbath," 124 n. 2.

115. N. H. Gootjes, "Catechism Preaching," in *Proceedings of the International Conference of Reformed Churches, September 1–9, 1993* (Neerlandia, AB: Inheritance, 1993), 149–51.

was a day of rest to be set aside for worship, rest, and Christian instruction. As part of those deliberations, on 17 May 1619 Synod adopted six rules "on the observation of the Sabbath, or the Lord's Day."[116] Synod recognized that the fourth commandment is partly ceremonial and partly moral. The "rest of the seventh day after creation was ceremonial and its rigid observation peculiarly prescribed to the Jewish people." The moral aspect of the Sabbath transcends the typological, Mosaic administration. A "fixed and enduring day of the worship of God is appointed, for as much rest as is necessary for the worship of God and holy meditation of him." With the Seventh-Day Sabbatarians and Roman legalism in the background, Synod followed Calvin and Bullinger in juxtaposing the abrogated "Sabbath of the Jews" with the "solemnly sanctified" Lord's Day for Christians. This was the apostolic and Christian practice. The Christian Sabbath is "consecrated for divine worship" in order that "one might rest from all servile works" and "from those recreations which impede the worship of God." Synod made the same exceptions that the Westminster Assembly would less than thirty years later, "works of charity and pressing necessity."

Despite the diversity of the Westminster Assembly there was a remarkable consensus on the theology and ethics of the Christian Sabbath. In WCF 21.7 we confess that the Sabbath is first of all "of the law of nature," so that a "due proportion of time be set apart for the worship of God." Because the Sabbath is grounded in creation, it binds "all men in all ages." The Sabbath command is also revealed in Scripture as a "positive, moral, and perpetual commandment" by which God "appointed one day in seven for a Sabbath, to be kept holy unto him . . . from the beginning of the world to the resurrection of Christ." The change from the last day of the week to the first day, that is, the Lord's Day, is grounded in the resurrection of Christ and "is to be continued to the end of the world as the Christian Sabbath."

In WCF 21.8 the divines offered specific guidance on how the Sabbath is to be observed beginning with "a due preparing of their hearts" and "ordering . . . common affairs beforehand."[117] This was the common

---

116. H. H. Kuyper, ed., *De Post Acta of Nahandelingen van de Nationale Synode van Dordrecht in 1618 en 1619 Gehouden* (Amsterdam: Höveker & Wormser, 1899), 184–86.

117. The DPW says that there ought to be "private preparation of every person or family by prayer for themselves, and for God's assistance of the Minister, and for a blessing upon

received wisdom of the Reformed churches and pastors for about a century by the time of the Assembly.[118] If seventeenth-century folk needed
to prepare for the Sabbath, how much more do overstimulated twenty
first—century folk? As a practical matter, unless certain preparations are
made, the Sabbath will be swallowed up in the crush of weekly business.
To take but one practical matter, if families do not prepare a meal for
Sunday or if the big meal for the week is on Sunday, how is the Lord's
Day not more rather than less stressful?

To intensify our difficulties, because of the relatively small number of
Reformed congregations in North America, they tend to be geographi-
cally distant from their congregants. Thus, outside of a few centers of
Reformed churches in the USA, the pews in many Reformed congregations are filled with those who commute to worship. This fact presents
significant challenges to Sabbath keeping in the late modern world.
Nevertheless (to borrow from Hebrews 4:9) there remains a need for
a Sabbath rest for the people of God. Given that the time and place of
meeting for worship is a matter of prudence, some congregations are
experimenting with meeting for catechism and morning worship, a common lunch, and then a brief second service. This not only eliminates
the commute to the second service, but it mitigates the problem of
food preparation on the Lord's Day by spreading the burden. It has the
added benefit of creating significant opportunities for congregational
fellowship.

The goal of Sabbath keeping is to "observe an holy rest all the day from
their own works, words, and thoughts about their worldly employments
and recreations." To the objection that withdrawal from the world is not
possible, I reply by agreeing with Marva Dawn that it is not only pos-

---

his Ministry [sic] and by other such holy exercises, as may further dispose them to a more
comfortable communion with God in his Publique Ordinances." See *A Directory for Publique
Prayer, Reading the Holy Scriptures, Singing of Psalmes, Preaching of the Word, Administration
of the Sacraments, and Other Parts of the Publique Worship of God, Ordinary and Extraordinary*
in *The Humble Advice of the Assembly of Divines Now by Authority of Parliament Sitting at
Westminster* (Audubon, NJ: Old Paths, reprint, 1997), 27.

118. The DPW says, "The Lord's day ought to be so remembered before-hand, as that
all worldly business of our ordinary callings may be so ordered, and so timely and season-
ably laid aside, as there may not be impediments to the due sanctifying of the day when it
comes." Ibid., 26.

sible, it is necessary.[119] One of the great messages of the Sabbath is that there are limits to our "options" (to use De Zengotita's term).[120] Contemporary technology gives us the illusion that we can transcend space and time. The Sabbath is a reminder of our humanity (i.e., our image-bearer status), our finitude, and our frailty. The truth is that the triune God is "everywhere present" (HC 27) and we are not. Remember that the basic notion of the noun *shabbat* is "to stop," and stopping is the prerequisite for the proper use of the first day of the week: spending "the whole time in the public and private exercises of his worship, and in the duties of necessity and mercy."

The Reformed confession of the Sabbath is eminently practical. The divines were writing against the background of James I's "Book of Sports" (1618), which made Sabbath-breaking obligatory and a matter of patriotism.[121] The divines were reasserting, in the language of the Scottish Covenanters, "the crown rights of King Jesus" over against the pretensions of the overreaching English monarchy. In our time, even if we do not face civil imperialism, we face commercial, cultural, and professional imperialism. Sunday is the second busiest shopping day in America, and on the Lord's Day many restaurants are packed with Christians.[122] When Exodus 20:10 speaks of "your male servant or your female servant," does that not include restaurant and shop workers?[123] Many of us have employers that demand more than James I ever asked of his subjects.

All of these instructions are hard-won pastoral wisdom about the challenges of setting aside the first day of the week for worship, rest, and anticipation of the consummation. This is clear in the DPW when it instructs "all the people" to "meet timely for public worship," to be "present at the beginning" and to remain until "after the blessing." These are the words of pastors who have struggled to call a congregation to worship, watching members straggle in late and leave in the midst of the service.

119. Marva J. Dawn, *Keeping the Sabbath Wholly: Ceasing, Resting, Embracing, Feasting* (Grand Rapids: Eerdmans, 1989).

120. See chapter 2 of this work for a discussion of De Zengotita's use of this term.

121. William Maxwell Hetherington, *History of the Westminster Assembly of Divines*, 4th ed. (Edinburgh: James Gemmell, 1878), 57–60.

122. Having worked in the restaurant business in the early 1970s, I well recall the "Sunday rush."

123. *A Directory for Publique Prayer*, 27.

The practical effect of the Sabbath doctrine of the Reformed churches is to say: You have six days to be successful, but the Lord's Day belongs to our Creator and Savior, and it is to be spent in his interests and in the interests of his people.

Before we turn to the next section of this chapter, a brief summary of the first section is in order. When we bear in mind the whole of Scripture as well as the progress of revelation and redemption, we find abundant evidence that the Sabbath that was instituted in creation and restated in typological terms during the temporary Israelite national covenant, was transformed by the resurrection of the Lord of the Sabbath for Christians. However, the essential function of the Sabbath has always been the same: to look forward to the consummation, to rest from daily work, and to worship in public assembly. Whatever variety there has been in Reformed teaching on the Sabbath, there has been a strong consensus on these points, and it is these points that all the Reformed churches confess.

The exegetical and theological difficulties of the Sabbath, however, are not the primary problem today. Let us assume that most Reformed folk do not attend a second service and that perhaps attendance at the morning service is sporadic. Let us further assume that most Reformed Christians today no longer regard the Sabbath as a peculiar day set apart for the three purposes outlined here. Anecdotal evidence suggests that it is not because they have theological or exegetical problems with the Sabbath. Doubtless there is a considerable degree of ignorance in our congregations about the Reformed confession of the Christian Sabbath, but almost certainly the chief difficulty is practical. Our own failure to observe the Sabbath, to interrupt the pressing demands of the culture on our attention, to break away from work, pleasure, the unending stimuli (the Internet, television, and the cell phone), is caused by our failure to reckon ourselves consistently as finite, as bound to creational and revealed patterns. The Sabbath is the antithesis of our hyperstimulated culture. The Sabbath also reminds us that we are a redeemed people who have been "bought with a price," who must therefore honor God with our bodies (1 Cor. 6:20). To the degree these characterizations are true of us, to the same degree we do not long for the consummate existence. Perhaps we are satisfied with our high-tech Nirvana? Whatever the reasons for the contemporary failure to honor the

Lord's resurrection, the consequences for the second service are obvious. Corporate worship requires time and space. We will set aside that time only when our values are rightly ordered and the virtues of rest, worship, and the consummation are meaningful again.

The Sufficient Condition: The Due Use of the Ordinary Means

At least one of the reasons that folk no longer attend the second service is that they do not see the point of it. Most forms of mysticism tell us that God works immediately, that is, without means, agents, or instruments. Pietism tells us that he works primarily through private prayer and devotions.[124] The logic of mysticism and pietism is relentless. If God is thought to work primarily in private ways, apart from the ministry of Word and sacrament in the congregation, why attend any service at all? If God's people have come to think this way, then a proper estimation of the Sabbath alone is not enough to restore the second service. The sufficient condition for restoring the evening service is the recovery of the biblical and confessional doctrine of the means of grace. We need to regain our conviction and confidence that not only *can* God work through means but that he has promised to do so and even that we should not expect him to work apart from those ordained means.[125]

124. For example see Richard J. Foster, *Celebration of Discipline: The Path to Spiritual Growth*, rev. ed. (San Francisco: Harper and Row, 1988); Donald S. Whitney, *Spiritual Disciplines for the Christian Life* (Colorado Springs: NavPress, 1991). At least Whitney mentions public worship, but in neither of these works does one find any consideration of the sacraments or any idea of the means of grace.

125. In reaction to the Socinian reduction of the power of the Word to mere persuasion, Charles Hodge wrote that the Sprit operates "anterior" to the Word. See Charles Hodge, *Systematic Theology*, 3 vols. (New York: Scribner, Armstrong, 1873), 3:474–76. On this see Michael S. Horton, *Covenant and Salvation: Union with Christ* (Nashville: Westminster John Knox, 2007), 226–42; idem, *God of Promise: Introducing Covenant Theology* (Grand Rapids: Baker, 2006), 137–71; idem, *A Better Way: Rediscovering the Drama of God-Centered Worship* (Grand Rapids: Baker, 2002), 93–140; D. G. Hart and John R. Muether, *With Reverence and Awe: Returning to the Basics of Reformed Worship* (Phillipsburg, NJ: P&R, 2002), 133–44; Edmund P. Clowney, "Corporate Worship: A Means of Grace," in *Give Praise to God: A Vision for Reforming Worship*, ed. Philip G.

The biblical writers regard the idea of God's accomplishing his purposes through means or instruments as a given, as completely compatible with the biblical doctrine of divine sovereignty. Consider John 1:3. In verse 1, John teaches the eternality and consubstantiality of God the Son, the Word or Revelation of God. Verse 3 says, "Everything occurred *through him* (*di' autou*), and nothing that happened occurred without him." The grammar of the passage clearly signals that God the Son played an essential and instrumental role in creation. Verse 10 confirms that God created the world through the agency of the Son.

Just as God the Son is the agent of creation, he is also the agent of recreation and redemption. In verse 17 John declares, concerning the progress of redemption and revelation, "the law was given *through* Moses, grace and truth came *through* Jesus Christ." John contrasts two different agents of revelation and salvation. Through Moses, Yahweh revealed types and shadows. In God the Son incarnate, however, he revealed the reality and fulfilment of those types and shadows. John 3:17 says that it is God's will to save the world (for the purposes of this discussion it does not matter how we understand "world") *through* his Son. Just as it was God's will to create and redeem the world through the Son, it is also his will to save his people through the instrument of his gospel preached and administered in his church. In his high-priestly prayer (John 17), our Lord prayed for those whom the Father would bring to faith *through* the preaching of the apostles (John 17:20). The apostle Peter says that the Holy Spirit spoke "*through* the mouth of David" (Acts 1:16). At Pentecost he says that God spoke "*through* the prophet Joel" (Acts 2:16).

The apostle Paul taught the same view of the relation between the work of the Spirit and the use of agents and instruments in Romans 10:14–17:

> But how are they to call on him in whom they have not believed? And how are they to believe in him of whom they have never heard? And how are they to hear without someone preaching? And how are they to preach unless they are sent? As it is written, "How beautiful are the

Ryken et al. (Phillipsburg, NJ: P&R, 2003), 94–105; R. Scott Clark, "The Evangelical Fall from the Means of Grace," in *The Compromised Church*, ed. John Armstrong (Wheaton, IL: Crossway, 1998), 133–47.

feet of those who preach the good news!" But they have not all obeyed the gospel. For Isaiah says, "Lord, who has believed what he has heard from us?" So faith comes from hearing, and hearing through the word of Christ. (ESV)

The logic of Paul's argument is compelling, but it all hinges on the assumption that God has ordained to accomplish his purposes in the world through the use of means, instruments, and agents. Paul has already established (Rom. 4:3–8; 5:1–2; 8:1–8; 9 [all]) that only and all the elect shall be saved by grace alone, through faith alone, in Christ alone. God's people come into possession of righteousness before God only through faith in Christ, but how do they come to faith? Through hearing (*akoē*) the gospel preached. It is certain that the "hearing" of which Paul speaks is not a mystical, immediate revelation because Paul speaks of this hearing in the context of the external preaching of the gospel.

Just as God the Spirit uses the preached gospel to create true faith within his elect, so too he also uses that which Augustine and Calvin called the "visible word" (*verbum visibile*) of the gospel, the sacraments to signify the promise and to seal or certify it.[126] As a sign, the sacrament illustrates visibly the same thing the gospel promises; it declares to our eyes what that gospel promises to all who believe. As a seal it declares that what the gospel promises generally is true in particular to this or that believer.

This is how Paul understand the function of the typological sacrament of circumcision in Romans 4:5–12. Justification does not come to the one who works, but to the one who trusts. It is the nature of the gospel message to direct our attention away from one's self and toward Christ and his finished work for sinners. Faith apprehends Christ and his righteousness. Justification is not predicated upon the intrinsic sanctity of the justified, but upon the imputation of Christ's perfect righteousness to the believer. To try to leverage circumcision (or baptism) into a ground or instrument of justification is extremely perverse. Abraham was justified *sola fide* before he received the sign and seal of covenant initiation, and he was justified *sola fide* after he was initiated. Paul says, Abraham "received the sign of

---

126. Calvin, *Institutes* 4.14.6; OS, 5:263.13–14. The textual apparatus of the Battles edition provides several references to Augustine's usage of the expression.

circumcision as a *seal* (*sphragis*) of the righteousness that he had by faith while he was still uncircumcised." The seal confirmed and certified to Abraham and to all believers that all that Christ promises is true. Hence HC Q. 69 says of baptism, "as certainly as I am washed outwardly with water," and Q. 75 of the Supper, "as certainly as I receive from the hand of the minister, and taste with my mouth, the bread and cup of the *Lord*, which are given me as certain tokens of the body and blood of Christ."[127] As the Reformed churches understand Scripture, God promised to justify and sanctify his people through the means he established to do so and to which he has attached the promises of the gospel.

It is the contention of this book that the antidote for the QIRE is to restore the means of grace to their proper place. As Louis Berkhof reminded us seventy years ago, in the proper sense of the term, "means of grace" (*media gratiae*) refers to "objective channels which Christ has instituted in the Church, and to which he ordinarily binds Himself in the communication of his grace."[128] In Reformed doctrine, "faith, conversion, and prayer are first of all fruits of the grace of God, although they may in turn become instrumental in strengthening the spiritual life. They are not objective ordinances, but subjective conditions for the possession and enjoyment of the blessings of the covenant."[129]

Though this is fundamentally true, it should be remembered that the WSC Q. 88 says that the "outward means" by which Christ communicates to us "the benefits of redemption" are "the word, sacraments, and prayer." Though it seems safe to assume that Berkhof understood his view to be at variance with the Westminster Standards, it is possible to reconcile them. Remember that when the divines spoke of "word, sacraments, and prayer," these three are considered in the context of the public worship service. Further, it is certain that the divines assumed that just as the minister administered the sermon and the sacraments, so also he administered prayer on behalf of the congregation. These prayers were not, then, chiefly subjective, private exercises, but they were virtual expositions of Scripture on behalf of the congregation. Instead

---

127. *Creeds*, 3:329, 332. Italics original.
128. Louis Berkhof, *Systematic Theology* (Grand Rapids: Eerdmans, 1941), 604–5.
129. Ibid., 604.

of being directed at the congregation, they were directed toward the Lord. In other words, they were not entirely subjective exercises; they had an objective character to them.[130]

Nevertheless, Berkhof's distinction between the objective and the subjective is important and needs to be recovered if we are to recover the Reformed confession. Since the eighteenth century the emphasis in American Christianity, including the Reformed churches, has certainly been on the subjective aspects of piety. Berkhof's discussion of the means of grace is outstanding partly because it is unusual.[131] Whether in literature or in the pulpit, contemporary Reformed piety often seems to have more to do with Jonathan Edwards than with Louis Berkhof. We are much more likely to hear sermons and talks about private piety and the immediate experience of God than about the divinely ordained publicly administered means of grace. If Berkhof is correct, however, perhaps attendance to the second service is actually a better indicator of spiritual maturity than are the calluses on our knees or the wear on our Bibles.

When considering the cultivation of true piety and spiritual growth, the Reformed churches confess just this priority of the public over the private. In the middle of the sixteenth century the religious situation in the Netherlands was unsettled to say the least. Europe in general and the Netherlands in particular were littered with spiritualist and radical (i.e., Anabaptist) sects of every conceivable variety. Of course the Roman critics

130. Ed Clowney argued that the Larger Catechism includes prayer as a means of grace because it is a part of public worship, which itself is a means of grace. See Edmund P. Clowney, "Corporate Worship: A Means of Grace," 100.

131. Religious subjectivism in American Reformed Christianity has provoked at least two reactions. First in the nineteenth century the Mercersburg Movement reacted to what John Williamson Nevin usually called "Puritanism," which he used quite imprecisely to describe Reformed subjectivism. The Mercersburg Movement was a contemporaneous parallel to but apparently independent from the Oxford Movement in England. Both movements wished to recover elements of patristic and medieval theology, piety, and practice and were to a large degree either ambivalent or hostile to the Reformation doctrines of justification and worship. The contemporary Federal Vision Movement, which seeks to establish a purely objective covenant theology, also testifies that it is reacting to revivalist subjectivism. Like the Mercersburg Movement, it seeks to synthesize elements of patristic and medieval theology with Reformed theology, and it is ambivalent or hostile toward the Reformed doctrine of justification. One of the burdens of this volume, however, is to demonstrate that it is possible to reject undue religious subjectivism without rejecting classical confessional Reformed theology, piety, and practice.

of the Reformation blamed the unleashing of this chaos on the Protestants, conveniently ignoring the fact that the confessional Protestants disavowed the sectarians as vehemently as Rome did.

Not only did this chaos create apologetic problems for the Reformed churches, it created pastoral problems with which we are intimately familiar today. Guy de Brès (1522–67), a Reformed pastor and the chief author and editor of the Belgic Confession, offered some strong criticisms of the Anabaptists in his 1565 treatise *The Rise, Spring, and Foundation of the Anabaptists*, which offered a fairly sophisticated analysis of a complex movement. Unlike the Lutheran critics who usually dismissed the Anabaptists as Schwenkfelders or *Schwärmerei* (i.e., fanatics) as a group, de Brès categorized fourteen distinct groups within the movement. This is not to say he was less critical of the Anabaptists than the Lutherans were, but just more precise.

Like most confessional Protestants, he recounted some of the outrageous episodes of the early Anabaptist movement, focusing on their subversion of the established civil and ecclesiastical order.[132] He was just as troubled, however, by their religious subjectivism as evidenced by their appeals to private, ongoing special revelation.[133] He engaged the arguments of Thomas Müntzer (c. 1490–1525), directly focusing on the claim of the latter that the confessional Protestant ministers were not sent from God but were "ministers of the dead letter."[134] De Brès complained that the Anabaptists "pretend unto revelations of the Spirit; and despising all reading, they mock at the simplicity of those, which yet follow the dead and killing letter (as they call it)." The Anabaptists claim that "the writing of the Old Testament, and preaching of the eternal word, was not the word of God, but was only the testimony thereof; and that we must search for the word in the internal part, i.e., in our hearts, where God hath put it, that we need not go far to seek it from without us."[135] In contrast to the

---

132. Guy de Brès, *The Rise and Foundation of the Anabaptists or Rebaptized of Our Time*, trans. Joshua Scottow (Cambridge, 1668). This is a partial English translation of Guy de Brès, *La Racine, Source et Fondement des Anabaptistes* (Rouen, 1565). Since this is not primarily a historical work, and since archaic spelling may be a distraction, I have modernized the spelling in these quotations and used modern substitutes for archaic words.

133. De Brès, *The Rise and Foundation of the Anabaptists*, 1–33.

134. Ibid., 38.

135. Ibid., 34.

Anabaptists, de Brès argued that Timothy was not instructed to receive new revelations, but rather to be studious in the Scriptures. The post-canonical office of the Holy Spirit is not to produce "new and unknown revelations" or new doctrine, but it is the office of the Spirit to "confirm in us that which he has already spoken in Scripture."

De Brès was openly contemptuous of those who have "daily some new command from God," who

> are rapt into an ecstasy, and have their visage and countenance changed, lying upon the ground certain hours. Some tremble and quake for two or three hours together; after that, when they are come unto themselves, they prophesy and speak strange things, as if they had been in another world, or as if they had fallen from out of heaven: and they account to have that in common with the Apostle, when he was taken up into the third heaven.[136]

In response to the "dead letter" argument, de Brès argued that, despite the Anabaptist criticism of the confessional Protestants as ministers of the dead letter, the Lord has struck them with "the spirit of giddiness, for having despised the true and only means of coming unto God, which is the Scripture and the Word of God." Müntzer and the other Anabaptists misunderstand 2 Corinthians 3:6. When Paul says that "the letter kills and the Spirit makes alive," Paul is defending himself against false apostles who preach "the law without Christ," thereby causing the people "to recoil from salvation purchased by Christ, and the grace of the new covenant." In that case, the law can only bring death "to those who are under it . . . until by faith we are sent from it under Christ. . . . Thus must we understand how it is said, 'the letter kills': *Paul* called the law, the killing letter, and says, the Spirit quickens, i.e., the ministry of the gospel, which he opposes to the naked law; and he himself calls his preaching the ministry of the Spirit."[137] In other words, 2 Corinthians 3:6 does not

---

136. Ibid., 56.

137. Ibid., 40–41. In fact, the Anabaptists universally rejected the Protestant doctrine of justification *sola gratia, sola fide* on the ground that it promoted immorality. De Brès responded by restating the Protestant doctrine. See ibid., 47–48. Against Müntzer's moralism, he affirmed the logical, moral necessity of good works as the evidence of justification but denied them as the ground or instrument of justification.

juxtapose dead orthodoxy and living faith but law and gospel. According to de Brès, Müntzer was not only an enthusiast, he was a false prophet no better than Muhammad.[138] Against Müntzer's subjectivism, he appealed to the objectivity of the Scripture as the norm against which to judge the claims to new revelation.

Thus, when BC 33 speaks of the sacraments as the "means by which God works in us through the power of the Holy Spirit," it is part of a well-established pattern of thought with roots in Calvin's theology, indeed in the whole Reformation notion of *sola scriptura*.[139] The HC is even more explicit about the centrality of the divinely instituted instruments through which God has promised and even ordained to work by his Spirit. The catechism asks: "Since then, we are made partakers of Christ and all his benefits by faith only, whence comes this faith?" The answer is pointed: "The Holy Spirit works faith in our hearts through the preaching of the holy gospel and confirms it through the use of the holy sacraments."[140]

If there is any difference between the Westminster Standards and the earlier Reformed confessions, it is that the Standards are even more insistent on the means of grace. By the middle of the seventeenth century, the effects of radical religious individualism (e.g., the Brownists and even more radical sectarians) were obvious and the damage it caused a matter of concern. Thus, the divines moved to the doctrine of the means of grace in the first chapter. In WCF 1.7 we confess that despite the truth that "all things" in Scripture are not equally clear or easy to understand, nevertheless, everything "necessary to be known, believed, and observed for salvation" is clearly revealed in Scripture; and "in a due use of the ordinary means, [we] may attain unto a sufficient understanding of them." The phrase "due use of the ordinary means" is at the heart of our piety. The Standards return repeatedly to the notion that it is God's will to use means to accomplish his will (e.g., WCF 3.6; 5.3; 17.3; 18.3; WSC 88). WLC 154 says: "The outward and ordinary means whereby Christ communicates to his church the benefits of his mediation, are all his ordinances; especially the Word, sacraments, and prayer; all which are made

138. Ibid., 47.
139. *Creeds*, 3:424.
140. Ibid., 3:328.

effectual to the elect for their salvation." No tradition has written more deeply or more carefully about the intimate personal relations between the Savior and his saved, but, unlike Meister Eckhart, Catherine of Siena, or Thomas Müntzer, we have located our rather modest mysticism in Word and sacrament. The Spirit works a mystical union through the preaching of the gospel by which he creates faith. He strengthens that union through Word and sacrament.

Consider how William Perkins (1558–1602), the father of English Puritanism, described the Christian life. In his 1558 catechism, *The Foundation of the Christian Religion Gathered into Six Principles*, he made it clear that conversion is not ordinarily a momentary or epochal experience and certainly not chiefly a private religious experience, but rather and ordinarily the result of the prevenient grace of justifying faith which comes through the hearing of the preached gospel and the consequent grace of sanctification received in the means of grace administered in the church.[141] In the first part of the *Foundation*, Perkins summarizes briefly the six principles. Under the fifth principle he asks,

> Q. What are the ordinary or usual means for obtaining of faith?
> A. Faith cometh only by the preaching of the Word and increaseth daily by it: as also by the administration of the sacraments and prayer.[142]

This is virtually identical to the language of HC Q. 65. The only difference between the HC and Perkins is that the latter added prayer as a means of grace, a position later taken up by the Westminster divines in the WCF 14.1.[143]

Many years later, in his 1586 *A Treatise Tending unto a Declaration*, Perkins addressed the question of how sinners, who are part of Christ's visible church, which is composed of believers and unbelievers, can know

141. William Perkins, *The Whole Works of That Famous and Worthy Minister of Christ in the University of Cambridge, M. William Perkins*, 3 vols. (London, 1631), 3:318.

142. Ibid., 148.

143. "The grace of faith, whereby the elect are enabled to believe to the saving of their souls, is the work of the Spirit of Christ in their hearts, and is ordinarily wrought by the ministry of the Word, by which also, and by the administration of the sacraments, and prayer, it is increased and strengthened."

that they are in fact Christians, that is, "in a state of grace."[144] There can be no question whether Perkins was zealous that Christians have a deep and healthy experience of communion with Christ through his Spirit. Nevertheless, the place where Christians find their assurance in the gospel is in the hearing of it preached and in the administration of the sacraments.[145] Perkins wrote at length about the inward work of the Spirit in convicting sinners of their need for a Savior and the "benefits of Christ" that accrue to believers, but he always connected these operations of the Spirit to the preaching of the Word and the administration of the sacraments. The empirical evidence to which Perkins appealed was not a peculiar emotional or heightened state of religious experience, but a joyful reception of God's Word preached, regular attendance to the means of grace, and condemnation of those who do not attend to the means of grace.[146]

John Owen (1616–83), arguably the greatest British theologian of the classical period of Reformed theology, provides another apt contrast to the Edwardsean piety, since both men are described without controversy as Puritans, and, like the Heidelberg Catechism, the warmth of Owen's piety is beyond question. After all, Owen wrote an entire volume devoted to intimate fellowship between God and the Christian: *Of Communion with the God the Father, Son, and Holy Ghost* (1657). In this treatise, in which Owen meditated on the nature of the Christian's fellowship with each of the trinitarian persons, and which gave considerable attention to the subjective religious experience of the Christian, he did not reckon that such occurs outside the divinely ordained objective means of grace. Quite appropriately, under the heading of the Holy Spirit, Owen turned to the "ordinance of the Word." He argued that Stephen accused the Jews of resisting the Holy Spirit because by following the example of Israel in opposing "the prophets in preaching the gospel," they were "resisting the Holy Ghost."[147] The Holy Spirit himself has established the "ministerial dispensation" of "the word of the gospel, the authority, wisdom, and

144. Perkins, *Works*, 1:357.
145. Ibid., 1:364, 373–74.
146. Ibid., 1:359. He repeated and elaborated the same approach in his 1597 treatise, *A Grain of Mustard Seed*. See also ch. 3 of this work.
147. John Owen, *The Works of John Owen*, trans. William H. Goold, 16 vols. (New York: Robert Carter and Brothers, 1851), 2:267.

goodness of the Holy Ghost in furnishing men with gifts for that end and purpose[;] and his presence with them, as to the virtue thereof, is to be eyed, and subjective unto it on that account."[148]

In short, Owen always considered that the subjective enjoyment of blessed communion with God is, by divine ordination, bound up with the external, official administration of the means of grace. Though he certainly distinguished the substance of the benefits of Christ from their outward administration, he never set them against each other. When Owen described the work of God's Spirit, like the HC, Perkins, and the Westminster Standards, he associated it closely with Word and sacrament. In his *Greater Catechism* (1645) 13.3, explaining Christ's prophetic office, Owen said:

> Q. 3. By what means does he perform all this?
> A. In diverse ways; as, first, internally and of humiliation or abasement; secondly, of exaltation or glory, writing his law in our hearts; thirdly, outwardly and instrumentally, by the Word preached.[149]

And when, in chapter 18, he came to describing the internal call of the Holy Spirit in regeneration, he again turned to preaching as the instrument through which the Holy Spirit works:

> Q. 2. What is our vocation, or this calling of God?
> A. The free, gracious act of Almighty God, whereby in Jesus Christ he calls and translates us from the state of nature, sin, wrath, and corruption, into the state of grace and union with Christ, by the mighty, effectual working of his preaching of the Word.[150]

In response to Martyn Lloyd-Jones, one might suggest that the Reformed confessions, William Perkins, and John Owen are all guilty of quenching the Spirit, but in that case, the entire Reformed theology, piety, and practice are guilty of Spirit-quenching. If we are not willing to

148. Ibid., 2:268.
149. Ibid., 1:483. In this quotation and the next I have modified some archaic language and spellings for the sake of readability.
150. Ibid., 1:486.

condemn the entire Reformed tradition, then tying the secret work of the Spirit to the public means of grace cannot be said to be quenching the Spirit.

In response to the Federal Visionists (and some elements of the Mercersburg Movement in the nineteenth century) the Reformed confession is equally opposed to attempts to make the sacraments work *ex opere*, to deny the freedom of the Spirit to operate when and how he will through the ordained means, or to downplay the reality of divine decree behind the administration of the covenant of grace.[151] The Reformed churches confess that God the Spirit has pledged to operate through the preaching of the Word and the use of the sacraments, but in order for God's people to benefit from these means there must be time and space in which to use them. So, we turn now to the case for the second service.

The Second Service

This chapter began by considering the biblical revelation of the patterns of limits built into the creation, built into the nature of things. The creational days were marked out by morning and evening (Gen. 1:5). In the same way, the days of redemption, after the fall, were also marked by a "morning and evening" pattern. As part of the consecration of the Aaronic priesthood, there were to be a morning and evening sacrifice (Ex. 29:38–43). Ezra 3:3 says that, at the rebuilding of the altar in Jerusalem according to the Torah, the priests offered sacrifices morning and evening. There were a morning and evening sacrifice every day (1 Chron. 16:40). The superscription of Psalm 92 is the only one that mentions the Sabbath. Whatever the force of the superscription, it at least tells us how the psalm was traditionally understood. Verses 1–2 say, "It is good to give thanks to Yahweh, to sing praises to your name, O Most High; to declare your steadfast love in the morning, and your faithfulness by night." Psalm

---

151. On the relation of the decree to the external administration of the covenant of grace see R. Scott Clark, "Baptism and the Benefits of Christ: The Double Mode of Communion in the Covenant of Grace," *The Confessional Presbyterian* 2 (2006): 3–19. See also Michael S. Horton, *God of Promise: Introducing Covenant Theology* (Grand Rapids: Baker, 2006), 237–71.

141:2 is attributed to King David, and he speaks of "lifting up" his hands "as the evening sacrifice." Of course these passages were given during the church's typological period so they apply to us only figuratively. Christ is our sacrifice, our priest, and our temple. Nevertheless, they do give evidence that the "morning and evening" pattern of creation has some continuing place in our re-creation.

The evidence for the particular practices of the apostolic church is scanty, and we must be restrained in our use of it. Acts 3:3 suggests, however, that the apostles continued to observe regular hours of prayer in the temple. Acts 5:21 records that the apostles were teaching in the temple in the morning. This indicates attendance to set hours of prayer. It is certain that the apostles attended synagogue services when they were permitted (e.g., Acts 13:14; 14:1; 17:1–4; 18:4, 26). Indeed, the Christians remained connected to the synagogue as late as A.D. 135, though with the adoption of an anti-Christian "blessing" circa 80–90, Christians doubtless felt less welcome from that point forward.[152] The synagogue held two services each (Saturday) Sabbath. This same pattern of two services each (Sunday) Sabbath continued among the early Christians. In his letter to the emperor Trajan (c. 112), Pliny the Younger reported that the Christians met on Sunday before daybreak (*ante lucem*) and then again later in the day.[153] The practice of morning and evening services (matins and vespers) continued through the medieval church and into the Reformation.[154] The Reformed church orders, including Heidelberg (1563), Dort (1619), and the DPW (1644), all called for two services each Sabbath.[155] The entire Christian tradition, East and West, ancient and medieval, Roman and

152. C. W. Dugmore, *The Influence of the Synagogue upon the Divine Office* (London: Oxford University Press, 1944), 2–4.

153. Constantine E. Pritchard and Edward R. Bernard, eds., *Selected Letters of Pliny the Younger* (Oxford: Clarendon, 1896), 124. See also Dugmore, *The Influence of the Synagogue*, 9.

154. C. W. Dugmore, s.v., "Canonical Hours," in *New Westminster Dictionary of Liturgy*, ed. J. G. Davies (Philadelphia: Westminster, 1986).

155. The Heidelberg Church Order is in Wilhelm Niesel, ed., *Bekenntnisschriften und Kirchenordnungen der nach Gottes Wort reformierten Kirche* (Zürich: Evangelischer Verlag A. G. Zollikon, 1938), 136–48. The decree of the Synod of Dort (1619), which was drafted with advice from British and European Reformed churches, is translated and published in Sinnema, "The Second Service," 320–21.

Protestant, has recognized the fundamental creational and re-creational pattern of morning and evening services.

Conclusions

For decades after World War II it was widely accepted that about 40 percent of Americans attend religious services every week. Recent research, however, has called that axiom into question.[156] The results of this research should not surprise confessional Reformed folk. It turns out that decent North Americans lie routinely to pollsters. They tend to overreport their church attendance. They tend to count attendance at weddings and funerals as church attendance. Respondents generally overreport behaviors that will cast themselves in a good light and underreport those behaviors that might bring scorn. They tend to answer according to the way that they identify themselves, not according to what they actually do or do not do. Of course, church attendance varies from region to region, but the overall percentage of weekly church attendance seems to be declining and may hover in the range of 20 to 30 percent. This percentage, however, reflects only attendance at morning services. We can assume that attendance at the second service, when one can be found, is substantially lower. Anecdotal reporting from pastors suggests that of those who attend the morning service, less than 50 percent attend the second service.

As we have seen, attendance at the second service was a problem that plagued Reformed churches for much of the sixteenth and seventeenth centuries. According to Roger Finke and Rodney Stark, church attendance (and membership) and piety was also a problem in eighteenth-century New England, in the wake of the First Great Awakening. They argue that in the second half of the eighteenth century about one-third of all births

156. E.g., see C. Kirk Hadaway and P. L. Marler, "Did You Really Go to Church This Week? Behind the Poll Data," *The Christian Century* 115 (1998): 472–75. This research sparked considerable debate among sociologists. See, e.g., Andrew Walsh, "Church, Lies, and Polling Data," *Religion in the News* 1.2 (1998); http://www.trincoll.edu/depts/csrpl/RIN%20Vol.1No.2/Church_lies_polling.htm (accessed 3 March 2007). The Barna Group reports, however, based on a 1995 survey, overall national church attendance in the USA at 47 percent; http://www.barna.org/FlexPage.aspx?Page=Topic&TopicID=10 (accessed 3 March 2007).

were the result of sexual immorality.[157] In 1776 "only about one out of five New Englanders had a religious affiliation." This does not mean that four-fifths of New Englanders were utterly irreligious, but it does mean that "their faith lacked public expression and organized influence."[158] The Reformed churches, however, confess that Christians ought not only know and believe Christ but that, as we have seen, they should do so in the context of visible congregational attending to the means of grace.[159]

These numbers and percentages may be surprising to some. Finke and Stark are correct that the reason for this surprise is that we are more nostalgic than historical about colonial America. Historians have also sometimes been misled by claims made in the eighteenth century about the numbers of people who were actually members of congregations.[160] Since the middle of the twentieth century, however, historians have known that actual church attendance in the colonial period was around 10–20 percent of the population.[161]

In our setting, as in times past, the second service is a countercultural act of defiance against the antinomian spirit of the age. It is also a statement about the centrality of Word and sacrament to the Christian life. It is a testimony that Christ's people have been redeemed in a community and to a community. It is a confession of faith that God the Spirit uses divinely ordained means to save and sanctify (WCF 14). As history and experience show us, it is not easy, and it is not popular, but it is Reformed, it is worth the effort, and it is the way of the Christian life.

Therefore, in order for us to recover the Reformed theology, piety, and practice of the second service, we must be realistic about the challenges we face, and we must be committed to the Sabbath and to the means of grace as matters of principle. Further, we cannot wait for another revival for attendance to improve, because there is no evidence that the earlier American revivals produced the sort of reformation that our churches want so desperately. Rather than looking to the romance of revival, we

157. Roger Finke and Rodney Stark, *The Churching of America: Winners and Losers in Our Religious Economy* (New Brunswick, NJ: Rutgers University Press, 1997), 22.
158. Ibid., 22–23.
159. Ibid., 22.
160. Ibid., 23–24.
161. Ibid., 24. See also 51–53.

ought to be looking to the realism of the Reformation as the pattern for our future. Just as the Reformed churches gradually inculcated the Reformed theology, piety, and practice over the course of a century after the first stage of the Reformation (the matter of the second service came repeatedly to ecclesiastical assemblies between the mid-sixteenth century and the mid-seventeenth century), so must we be prepared to recover gradually, through instruction, prayer, and discipline, to lead our congregations toward reformation.

This chapter has argued that the necessary condition for recovering the Reformed practice of two services is the recovery of the Reformed confession and practice of the Sabbath. The point is not just that "this is the way we have always done it," but that if only one-half of the faults of the Reformed churches chronicled in this book are true, then the Reformed churches are not actually very Reformed. Assuming for a moment that the second major argument of this book is correct, that being Reformed is a good thing and that the Reformed confession (considered both narrowly and broadly) is the measure of what it is to be Reformed, then we must recover Reformed theology, piety, and practice. Historically, the second service was a primary instrument to achieve that goal. It does not seem coincidental that, at the same time the second service began to disappear, we were also beset by the two basic problems of the QIRC and the QIRE. For the purposes of this argument, it does not matter what the causal relation is between the two events. If there are ants in the kitchen eating sugar, it is probably the case that the sugar drew the ants, but in order to fix the problem, the ants must be destroyed and the sugar removed. Both must be done at about the same time. So it is in this case.

In order to begin moving our congregations in a Reformed direction we must begin reinstituting Reformed practice, since it is axiomatic, as we saw in chapter 7, that it is partly through this practice that our theology and piety are transmitted. If we wait until everyone is theoretically Reformed before they are practically Reformed, the praxis will likely never arrive, and without Reformed praxis the theology and piety will likely never develop. This is why the Synod of Dort instructed ministers to conduct services,

> even if the pastors should be forced at first to preach before a very small audience, to the point of preaching to no one but their own families. If

the pastors give an example with their own families, and consistently encourage others to do likewise, in particular those committed to the Reformed faith, there can be no doubt that, in the course of time, man will end up coming to these sermons regularly.[162]

As our churches realized in the sixteenth and seventeenth centuries, so too we must again realize that the Reformed theology, piety, and practice must be intentionally, conscientiously, patiently, and thoroughly taught to our congregations, to families, to children, to singles, to newcomers, and to those who have been Reformed for generations, or our theology, piety, and practice will be quickly lost and assimilated into the American mainstream religious admixture of pietism and fundamentalism.

As our churches have realized from the beginning, without a theology, piety, and practice of the Sabbath, there will be no time for worship, rest, and renewal. Thus, the first condition of recovering the second service is to take up again the notion that it is God's revealed will in creation and redemption that there ought to be set aside one day in seven for worship, rest, and renewal. The second condition for the recovery of the second service is the Reformed theology of the means of grace. We have seen that this doctrine is a corollary of our doctrine of divine sovereignty. The same God who has elected his people from all eternity, unconditionally, in Christ, has also ordained to use external means to bring his elect to faith and to edify them in that faith.

---

162. Session 14 of the *Acta Synodi Nationalis* . . . *Dordrechti habitae Anno MDCXVIII et MDCXIX*, 27–28, as translated and quoted in Sinnema, "The Second Service," 321. Synod was not using hyperbole. On the challenges faced by Reformed pastors in the Netherlands in attracting congregants to worship see Richard Fitzsimmons, "Building a Reformed Ministry in Holland, 1572–85," in *The Reformation of the Parishes: The Ministry and the Reformation in Town and Country*, ed. Andrew Pettegree (Manchester: Manchester University Press, 1993), 186–91.

Epilogue: Predestination Is Not Enough

This essay has been somewhat retrospective and, accordingly, it is bound to seem conservative and, to some, perhaps even regressive. The argument of this book, however, is not "conservative," at least not as that adjective is usually employed. I have little interest in preserving the status quo in the conservative Reformed churches, if only because we are often conserving the wrong things. The argument of this book is not conservative but radical inasmuch as it is a call for Reformed Christians to return to their confessional roots.

This call to radicalism is liberating in the way that recovering and acting upon principle is always liberating. Since the sixteenth century we have learned some important things. As we have observed already, we learned that Christendom was a mistake and we modified our confession appropriately. We also learned that using the Bible as a textbook for politics or the natural sciences is a mistake. In these examples we have a pattern that suggests that the Reformed theology, piety, and practice are not inherently reactionary. In these examples we have a pattern for facing future challenges on principle.

Just as being confessional enables us to criticize elements of our past, it also places us at odds with some aspects of contemporary Reformed theology, piety, and practice. One place where Reformed confessionalism will place us in conflict with some segments of contemporary Reformed Christianity is in the way the word "Reformed" is defined and used. In a *Christianity Today* article Colin Hanson chronicled the rise of "Young, Restless, and Reformed" leaders in evangelicalism.[1] The essay describes

1. Collin Hansen, "Young, Restless, and Reformed: Calvinism Is Making a Comeback— and Shaking Up the Church," *Christianity Today* 50.9 (2006): 32–38. See also idem,

343

the popularity of and reaction generated by several evangelical leaders, none of whom is identified with a historic Reformed denomination or confession. For the purposes of this argument, however, what interests me about the article and the subsequent discussion is the way the adjective "Reformed" is used. It is clear from the article that what is meant by the adjective "Reformed" is "predestinarian." It never seems to occur to anyone in the discussion to correlate the adjective "Reformed" to the historic Reformed churches and confessions.

Imagine, however, if we were to transport the current discussion to the early seventeenth century, when the Reformed churches were defining themselves in the forge of controversy with Rome, the Arminians, and the rationalists of their day. Imagine that these "young, restless, and Reformed" leaders traveled to the Synod of Dort and presented themselves to the Reformed churches of Europe and England as "Reformed Christians." Would they be accepted as such? Of course, the first questions would be "What do you mean by Reformed?" "Do you confess the BC and the HC?" At that point the discussion would soon fall apart because, though these visitors to the synod would have much in common with the synod on soteriology, they would have rather less in common with them on the doctrines of the church and the sacraments and on the hermeneutics of covenant theology. One cannot doubt that our time travelers would return home disappointed to be rejected by the Synod of Dort, but were they to try again at the Westminster Assembly, they would find a similarly chilly reception.

If our young, restless, and Reformed theologians could not find hospitality at Dort or Westminster, we may fairly ask whether the adjective "Reformed" is properly used of them. If, as this volume has argued, the Reformed confessions are the measure of what it means to be Reformed, then it cannot include those, however earnest, who deny doctrines that are of the essence of the Reformed theology, piety, and practice.

Perhaps even more interesting than our time travel experiment is the question how it came to be that evangelicalism has come to use the word "Reformed" of virtually anyone who holds the doctrine of predestination,

---

Young, Restless, Reformed: A Journalist's Journey with the New Calvinists (Wheaton, IL: Crossway, 2008).

regardless of whatever else one may confess. The first part of the answer is that it is false to assume that predestination is our distinguishing belief from which our whole theology is derived. The second part of the answer, however, is less obvious: it is that we have come to speak of and define *ourselves* by this single doctrine. When broader evangelicalism uses the words "Reformed" and "predestinarian" as synonyms, they are only imitating what they hear and read us saying about ourselves.

As I write, there is yet another widely read and discussed Internet conversation of the so-called Federal Vision. During the discussion, one of the promulgators of the Federal Vision confessed that, thirty-five years ago, the thing that interested him about the Reformed faith was its emphasis on the Bible. He confessed that he regards questions about the RPW or the covenant of works as so much arcana. What attracted him to the Reformed faith, as he understands it, is its world-and-life view, which I take to mean its utility for his program of cultural transformation. He laments that, when he became Reformed, in contrast to the present moment, all that was required was that one be conservative and predestinarian. I take him to be saying that much of what the Reformed churches actually confess does not interest him.

It probably is the case that, in the mid-1970s, the confessions had a lower profile in the NAPARC churches than they do now. As a consequence of the fundamentalist-modernist controversy that had raged for decades, the confessions were, to some degree, marginalized in favor of a broad conservative coalition against theological liberalism. Whatever its virtues, that coalition cannot and should not hold. Through the course of this book we have seen that the offspring of this union do not bear much resemblance to the Reformed faith as summarized in our confessions and as understood by the tradition. As a matter of principle (*ecclesia reformata, semper reformanda*) the pillars of conservatism and predestination are not enough to sustain the churches and Christians that would be Reformed. The choice is squarely before us: we can settle for a lowest common denominator theology, piety, and practice that are different from the prevailing evangelicalism and fundamentalism only in degrees, or we can, with heart and mind, recover the Reformed confession.

Index

347

as historical witnesses, 164, 167, 170
and preservation and transmission of faith, 158
R. B. Kuiper on, 180–81
revisions to, 181–82
Conforti, Joseph A., 86n53
congruent merit, 139
Constantine, 307
contemporary worship, 6
"continued creation" (Edwards), 85
conventicles, 76, 77
conversion, 100
Copernicus, Nicholas, 53–61
Cotton, John, 242, 268, 280
Council of Mâcon, 308
Council of Orléans, 308
Council of Rouen, 308
Council of Trent, 8, 23, 67, 68, 208
covenant, 155–58, 200
covenant community, 120
covenant of grace, 64n82, 200–201, 260
covenant of works, 64, 200–201
covenant theology, 29, 101–2, 265
Cowan, Ian B., 279n190
creation
days of, 4, 41, 44, 47–52, 140
ex nihilo, 298
and Sabbath, 296–98, 318
Creator/creature distinction, 12, 34, 59, 112, 127, 128, 132–34, 145, 150
Criswell, Wally Amos, 46
Cross, Richard, 137
Crouch, Andy, 194
cult and culture, 237
cultural transformation, 345
Cunningham, William, 147

Dabney, Robert Louis, 35–36
Daneau, Lambert, 54–55, 58–59
Danhof-Hoeksema case (Christian Reformed Church), 178

Davies, Brian, 136, 221
Davies, Horton, 228, 236n45
Dawn, Marva, 323
Dayton, Donald, 213–14
dead heterodoxy, 212
dead orthodoxy, 98, 211–12
death of God, 182
de Brès, Guido, 103, 183–84, 185, 331–33
Decalogue, 159, 279
decretive will, 30, 109, 125, 139
Denck, Hans, 76
de potentia Dei absoluta, 102
de potentia Dei ordinata, 102
Descartes, René, 33, 56–57, 58, 86, 182
Deus erga nos, 102, 129–31, 138
Deus in se, 102, 128–31, 138, 142
De Zengotita, Thomas, 51, 324
dialogical pattern in worship, 281
Dickinson, Jonathan, 163
Didache, 246, 305
Dionysius of Corinth, 306
Directory for Public Worship, 233, 239, 249–52, 263, 264, 281, 285, 338
divine sovereignty, 96, 219–20
and human responsibility, 202
and means of grace, 327, 342
divinization, 75
Donaldson, Gordon, 279n190
Donatism, 98
donum superadditum, 223n110
Dordrecht Confession, 76
Douma, J., 295–96
Dowey, Edward A., 187–88
drama, in worship, 235
Dugmore, C. W., 245, 306
Dutch Reformed churches, on worship, 252–57

Eastern Orthodoxy, 193–94
Ebionites, 306

R. Scott Clark (M.Div., Westminster Seminary California; D.Phil., University of Oxford) is professor of church history and historical theology at Westminster Seminary California and associate pastor of the Oceanside United Reformed Church. He has also taught at Wheaton College, Reformed Theological Seminary, Jackson, and Concordia University, Irvine.

Among his publications are *Caspar Olevian and the Substance of the Covenant: The Double Benefit of Christ*; *Protestant Scholasticism: Essays in Reassessment* (editor and contributor); and *Covenant, Justification, and Pastoral Ministry: Essays by the Faculty of Westminster Seminary California* (editor and contributor). A fuller list of his published works appears on page ii of this volume.